# The
# Universal
# Torah

## *Growth & Struggle in the Five Books of Moses*

GENESIS I

DR. PINCHAS POLONSKY

# The Universal Torah

## Growth & Struggle in the Five Books of Moses

### GENESIS I

Originally published as
*Bible Dynamics: Contemporary Torah Commentary*

Following the teaching of
Rabbi Yehuda Leon Ashkenazi (Manitou)
and Rabbi Ouri Cherki

Translated from the Russian
by Betzalel (Todd) Shandelman

5785 / 2025
Israel365

*The Universal Torah: Growth & Struggle in the Five Books of Moses*
*Genesis I*
Copyright © 2025 by Israel365 and P. Polonsky • ppolonsky@gmail.com

English translation of the Torah by the Jewish Publication Society,
New JPS Translation, copyright © 1985. With sincere gratitude for the
permission to use.

ISBN 978-1-957109-91-6

For sales inquiries, contact: store@israel365.com

For feedback and questions, contact the author at ppolonsky@gmail.com

Translation from Russian: Betzalel (Todd) Shandelman
Proofreading: Vassili Schedrin
Cover and interior design by the Virtual Paintbrush

*The Universal Torah: Growth & Struggle in the Five Books of Moses*
is a holy book that contains the name of God and should be treated
with respect.

First Edition 2025

www.Israel365.com

# Contents

Preface to the English Edition................................. XIX
Acknowledgments..............................................XXVII
Introduction...................................................XXIX
General Overview of Genesis and Its Opening Chapters.... XXXIII

**WEEKLY PORTION BERESHIT**

**Chapter 1: The Creation of the Universe in Seven Days ...........3**

1.1. Creation as an Ethical Principal (1:1) .......................... 3
1.2. The First Day: God Creates Light (1:2-3).......................5
1.3 God Reviews, Assesses, and Names (1:4-5) ...................7
1.4. The Second Day: The Separation of the Waters (1:6-8) ....... 9
1.5. The Third Day: The Creation of Dry Land, and Plants, Trees,
and Fruits (1:9-13) ............................................. 10
1.6. The Fourth Day: The Sun, the Moon, and the Stars (1:14-19) . .14
1.7. The Fifth Day: Sea Creatures and Birds (1:20-23) ............17
1.8. The Sixth Day: Animals of the Dry Land, and Human Beings
(1:24-30) ......................................................18
1.9. God Finds the End Result of the Creation "Very Good" (1:31) 23
1.10. The Seventh day: The Sabbath (2:1-3) ......................24

**Chapter 2: Adam and Eve in the Garden of Eden** ...............**27**

2.1. The Creation of the Heavens, the Earth, and Plants (2:4-6). . 27
2.2. God Creates Man (2:7) .....................................31
2.3. The Lord Plants a Garden (2:8-9) .......................... 32
2.4. The Rivers that Issue from Eden (2:10-14). . . . . . . . . . . . . . . 34
2.5. Adam and the Fruits of the Garden (2:15-17) ............... 37
2.6. The Creation of Woman (2:18-25) .........................41

**Chapter 3: The Episode of the Tree of Knowledge of
Good and Evil** .................................................... **50**

3.1. The Fall of Man: His First Sin (3:1-8) .........................50
3.2. The Trial, the Verdict, and the Sentence (3:9-21) ........... 63
3.3. Adam and Eve Are Banished from the Garden (3:22-24) .... 74
3.4. The Sixth, Seventh, and Eighth Days of Creation .......... 77

**Chapter 4: The Two Types of Man** ..............................**80**

4.1. Two Projections that Must be Reconciled..................80
4.2. Dominant Man, Cognitive Man ...........................81
4.3. "Homo" as Genus and "Homo" as Individual ............... 84
4.4. The Difference between Elohim, "God," and Adonai,
"the Lord" ..................................................... 85
The name Elohim, "God" ..................................... 86
Adonai (Y-H-W-H, the Tetragrammaton), "Lord" .............. 87
4.5. The Trees of Knowledge and of Life as Relevant Only
to Adam of the Second Story ................................. 89
4.6. A Systematic Summary of the Differences between
the Two Stories ..............................................91

**Chapter 5: The Creation of the Universe and the Structure
of the Sefirot** ...................................................**94**

5.1. The Concept of the Ten Sefirot............................ 94

5.2. The Sefirot System......................................... 97

5.3. The Cognition Process: Chochmah, Binah, and Da'at........ 99

5.4. Man and Woman as Chochmah and Binah (2:21-23) .........101

**Chapter 6: Understanding the Episode of the Tree of Knowledge of Good and Bad Based on Principles of the Kabbalah.........105**

6.1. Problems in the Episode of the Tree of Knowledge........ 105

6.2. What did Adam gain by eating the fruit of the tree of knowledge?..................................................106

6.3. The Meaning of the Attribute of Da`at, "Knowledge".....108

6.4. Was God Planning to Allow Man to Eat the Fruit of the Tree of Knowledge?........................................ 111

6.5. Prohibition at the Conscious and Unconscious Levels.....113

6.6. The Need for Self-Restraint in Cognition...................116

6.7. The Improper Road to Perfection: A Guaranteed Collision Course.................................................118

**Chapter 7: Cain and Abel ....................................... 120**

7.1. The Birth of Cain (4:1) ...................................... 120

7.2. The Birth of Abel (4:2) ...................................... 122

7.3. The Conflict of the Farmer and the Herdsman.............. 125

7.4. Cain and Abel Bring Their Offerings (4:3-5) ................ 128

7.5. Become Better and You Will Be Forgiven (4:5-7)...........131

7.6. The Murder of Abel (4:8)..................................... 132

7.7. Cain Stands Accused (4:9-12) .............................. 134

7.8. The Mark of Cain (4:13-15) ................................. 136

**Chapter 8: From Adam to Noah ...............................139**

8.1. Cain's Descendants (4:16-24)............................... 139

8.2. The Birth of Seth (4:25-26) ............................... 143

8.3. "This is the Record of Adam's Line" (5:1-32)............... 145

8.4. The Crisis of Humanity Leading up to the Flood (6:1-8) .... 151

**WEEKLY PORTION NOAH**

**Chapter 9: A General Overview of the Story of the Flood ....... 158**

9.1. Noah's Ark (6:9-22) ........................................ 158

9.2. The Flood Begins (7:1-24) .................................. 162

9.3. The End of the Flood (8:1-22) ..............................167

9.4. The Rainbow as a Sign of God's Covenant (9:1-17)........... 171

9.5. Noah and His Sons in the Aftermath of the Flood (9:18-29). .173

**Chapter 10: The Meaning of the Flood ........................... 177**

10.1. Defining the Problem: Did God Act Properly? .............177

10.2. What did the flood accomplish, given that the human
inclination to evil remained unchanged?.......................178

10.3. Did God actually regret having created man? .............179

10.4. The Meaning of the Name "Noah" ........................179

10.5. The Curse of the Earth ................................... 180

10.6. "Noah" as "Undoing the Curse" ..........................181

10.7. Reconciliation with man ................................. 183

10.8. "Divine repentance" and the Internal Contradiction
of Theology................................................... 184

10.9. Correction by Flood ..................................... 186

10.10. The Distortion of Justice and the Death of Society (6:11-13). .186

10.11. Noah and Abraham: Two Kinds of Righteousness (6:9) ... 189

10.12. Building the Ark as an Attempt to Influence Humanity ...191

10.13. Why did the Flood last an entire year? (7:23-24) ......... 193

10.14. Suspension of Life in the Ark and the Reeducation
of Noah....................................................... 194

10.15. After the Flood (8:20-21) ................................. 197
10.16. The Meaning of the Word mabbul, "Flood" (6:17) ........ 198
10.17. The Rainbow in the Cloud (9:13-17). ..................... 200
10.18. Noah and His Sons in the New World (9:20-23).......... 202
10.19. The Flood and the Land of Israel ....................... 204

**Chapter 11: Descendants of Noah's Sons ...................... 205**

11.1. The Descendants of Japheth (10:1-5). ..................... 205
11.2. The Descendants of Ham (10:6-20) ....................... 206
11.3. Shem's Descendants (10:21-32) ........................... 208

**Chapter 12: The Generations of the Tower of Babel ............ 211**

12.1. The Building of the Tower of Babel (11:1-4) ................ 211
12.2. The Destruction of the Tower of Babel (11:5-9) ........... 214
12.3. The Genealogy of Shem, Through Abraham (11:10-27)...... 217
12.4. The History of the Family of Abraham (11:28-32) ......... 220

**WEEKLY PORTION LECH LECHA**

**Chapter 13: Chosenness, Faith, and Monotheism ............. 224**

13.1. Chosenness for a Purpose (12:1-3) ........................ 224
13.2. Existence Determined by the Future .................... 225
13.3. Faith as the Sense of Purpose and Meaning in
the Creation ............................................... 226
13.4. Abraham as Chesed, and the Spreading of Monotheism.. 229
13.5. The Essence of Monotheism as Dialogue with God ...... 230

**Chapter 14: The Dynamics of the Patriarchs as Corrections
to the Sefirot ................................................... 233**

14.1. The Lives of the Patriarchs as the Process of Faceting
the Sefirot .................................................... 233
14.2. The Patriarchs and the Sefirot Tree ...................... 235
14.3. The Trials of the Patriarchs .............................. 237

**Chapter 15: Introductory Remarks on God's Choosing
Abraham ...................................................... 239**

15.1. Midrash: Stories of Abraham's childhood ................. 239
(a) The story of the vanquishing of the sun and moon ......... 239
(b) Abraham smashes the idols................................ 240
(c) The story of the fiery furnace ............................ 240
15.2. Hebrews, Israel, and Jews: The Names of the Nation
and its Land ................................................. 242
15.3. Abraham and Eber's Legacy .............................. 244
15.4. The Covenant of the Patriarchs........................... 245

**Chapter 16: The Beginning of Abraham's Journey ............. 247**

16.1. God Chooses Abraham (12:1-3)............................ 247
16.2. God's Plan and Abraham's Plan (12:4-5) .................. 249
16.3. The Transition from Cosmopolitanism to "Political
Universalism" ................................................ 252
16.4. Abraham's First Test: The Departure from Charan ....... 253
16.5. Changing the World Requires a Nation, and not Merely
Disciples..................................................... 255
16.6. The Lech Lecha Portion as Abraham's Transition to
God's Plan ................................................... 256
16.7. The Founding of the City of Shechem (12:6-7) ........... 257
16.8. Babylon and Egypt........................................ 259
16.9. Abraham Between the Sun and the Moon................. 261
16.10. The Three Jewish Capitals: Shechem, Hebron,
and Jerusalem................................................ 263

16.11. Abraham Proceeds to Egypt (12:8-10) . . . . . . . . . . . . . . . . . . . .264
16.12. Abraham and Sarah in Egypt (12:11-13). . . . . . . . . . . . . . . . . . .266
16.13. Abraham and Pharaoh (12:14-20). . . . . . . . . . . . . . . . . . . . . . . .269

## Chapter 17: Parting of the Ways with Lot and the War with the Kings. . . . . . . . . . . . . . . . . . . . . . . . . . . . . . . . . . . . . . . 272

17.1. Abraham and Lot Part Ways (13:1-13) . . . . . . . . . . . . . . . . . . . . . 272
17.2. Lot: Superfluous Chesed and the House of David . . . . . . . .278
17.3. The Confirmation of God's Covenant – After Lot's
Departure (13:14-16) . . . . . . . . . . . . . . . . . . . . . . . . . . . . . . . . . . . . . 281
17.4. God's Covenant with Abraham: About the Nation and
the Land, but not the Commandments . . . . . . . . . . . . . . . . . . . . . . .283
17.5. Abraham Relocates to Hebron (13:17-18). . . . . . . . . . . . . . . . .284
17.6. The War of the Kings (14:1-16). . . . . . . . . . . . . . . . . . . . . . . . . . . .285
17.7. Abraham and the King of Sodom (14:17-24). . . . . . . . . . . . . . .290

## Chapter 18: The "Covenant Between the Severed Members" . 295

18.1 "Fear not Abraham": The Problem of Killing on the
Battlefield (15:1) . . . . . . . . . . . . . . . . . . . . . . . . . . . . . . . . . . . . . . . . . . .295
18.2. The Problem of Abraham's Posterity (15:2-3). . . . . . . . . . . . . .298
18.3. Abraham Above the Stars (15:4-5). . . . . . . . . . . . . . . . . . . . . . . .299
18.4. "Because he put his trust in the Lord, He reckoned it to
his merit" (15:6). . . . . . . . . . . . . . . . . . . . . . . . . . . . . . . . . . . . . . . . . . . . . 301
18.5. Abraham's Lack of Trust (15:7-8). . . . . . . . . . . . . . . . . . . . . . . . . .303
18.6. The Making of a Covenant: The Course of History and
the Land of the Ten Nations (15:9-21) . . . . . . . . . . . . . . . . . . . . . . . .306

## Chapter 19: Sarah and Hagar. . . . . . . . . . . . . . . . . . . . . . . . . . . . . . .313

19.1. The Discrepancy Between God's Promise and the
Reality (15:18 – 16:1) . . . . . . . . . . . . . . . . . . . . . . . . . . . . . . . . . . . . . . . 313

19.2. Hagar, Sarah's Maidservant (16:1) ...........................315
19.3. Sarah Gives Hagar to Abraham (16:2-3).................... 316
19.4. Abraham and Sarah's Childlessness ...................... 318
19.5. The Legal Status of a Child Born of a Maidservant ........ 319
19.6. Hammurabi's Code: Morality Must Precede Sanctity .....320
19.7. Judaism and Polygamy.................................... 321
19.8. Hagar as Abraham's Preferred Alternative.................322
19.9. The Conflict Between Sarah and Hagar, and Abraham's
Role (16:3-6)................................................... 323
19.10. God's Question to Hagar (16:7-8) ........................325
19.11. The Problem of "Wilderness Religion" ................... 327
19.12. Hagar and Ishmael's Status, and their Roles (16:9-16) .....328

**Chapter 20: The Covenant of Circumcision ................... 333**

20.1. "Walk in My Ways" (17:1-2) ................................333
20.2. "But your name shall be Abraham" (17:3-8)............... 335
20.3. Circumcision as a Sign of the Covenant (17:9-14) ........338
20.4. "For Sarah is Her Name" (17:15-16) .......................340
20.5. Proper Nationalism as the Foundation of Universalism .. 341
20.6. Division of the Inheritance Between Isaac and
Ishmael (17:17-22)..............................................342
20.7. The Circumcision of Abraham's Household (17:23-27)....345

**WEEKLY PORTION VAYERA**

**Chapter 21: The Visit of the Three Angels and Abraham
Challenging God About Sodom ............................... 348**

21.1. The Relationship of the Weekly Portions Lech Lecha
and Vayera....................................................348
21.2. Revelation in the Afternoon: First Steps Toward the
Attribute of Gevurah (18:1) ...................................350

21.3. The Three "Men" as the Unification of Abraham, Isaac, and Jacob (18:2-5) ............................................. 352

21.4. Overcoming Fanaticism .................................... 354

21.5. The "Unclean" Chesed of Ishmael ........................ 356

21.6. The Nature and Roles of Angels ........................... 358

21.7. Abraham's Hospitality as a Religious Value (18:6-8) ....... 359

21.8. The Cave of Machpelah: Jewish Tradition Begins with Adam ..................................................... 360

21.9. Ishmael's Adulthood and His Test (18:7) ................... 361

21.10. Sarah's Laughter: Not Lack of Faith, but Overcoming Gevurah (18:9-15) ............................................. 363

21.11. The Role of Laughter Within a Religious Worldview ...... 367

21.12. God Supports Sarah in Her Laughter ..................... 369

21.13. Abraham Escorts the Angels (18:16) ...................... 370

21.14. God Invites Abraham to the Trial of Sodom (18:17-19) .....371

21.15. Chosenness for a Purpose: The Covenant with Abraham as "the Way of the Lord" ...................................... 372

21.16. The Jewish Ideal: Integration of Mercy and Justice ....... 374

21.17. Sodom's Perverted Justice ................................ 374

21.18. The Trials of Sodom, Lot, and Abraham (18:20-22) ....... 377

21.19. The Destruction of Sodom and Purification of the Gevurah Attribute .............................................. 379

21.20. Abraham Argues with God (18:23-25) .................... 381

21.21. The Divinity Within Us as Justification for Arguing with God ..................................................... 385

21.22. Abraham's Chesed and the Salvation of the Wicked ....386

21.23. Sodom as Abraham's Spiritual Failure .................... 388

21.24. The Responsibility of the Righteous for the Misfortunes of Their Generation ........................................... 389

21.25. A Righteous Individual Within the city (18:26) ........... 390

21.26. Reducing the Required Minimum of Righteous (18:27-33) .................................................... 392

**Chapter 22: The Destruction of Sodom and the Incident of Lot's Daughters** .............................................. **395**

22.1. Lot as Judge of Sodom (19:1)............................... 395
22.2. Conscience and Legislation (19:2-3) ..................... 397
22.3. Lot – Righteous by Sodom Standards ................... 399
22.4. The Inhabitants of Sodom Against Lot (19:4-11) ......... 400
22.5. The Origins of Mashiach in the Depths of Sodom........403
22.6. The Angels Lead Lot Out of Sodom (19:12-16) ...........406
22.7. Do not Look Behind You (19:17-26) ...................... 410
22.8. Abraham Gazes at the Destruction of Sodom (19:27-29) . 413
22.9. Lot's Daughters Resolve to Bear Children from Him (19:30-31)................................................ 415
22.10. Lot is Made Drunk with Wine (19:32-35) ................ 418
22.11. Moab and Ammon, the Sons of Lot's Daughters (19:36-38) ....................................................420
22.12. Moabites and Ammonites: Nations Who Lack Chesed. .422

**Chapter 23: Abraham and Abimelech in Gerar.................. 425**

23.1. Abraham in Gerar (20:1) ...................................425
23.2. Abraham Again Calls Sarah His Sister (20:2) ............. 427
23.3. Abimelech's Guilt (20:3-6) ...............................428
23.4. The Intrinsic Relationship Between Prophecy and Prayer (20:7) .................................................430
23.5. Prayer and Sacrifice – Their Similarities and Differences . 433
23.6. The End of the Conflict over Sarah (20:8-18) ............434

**Chapter 24: The Birth of Isaac and the Expulsion of Ishmael . 440**

24.1. The birth of Isaac (21:1-5) ................................ 440
24.2. The Laughter Concerning Isaac (21:6-8)................... 441
24.3. Ishmael's Mocking Laughter (21:9-10)...................443

24.4. Development Within the Hierarchy ...................... 445

24.5. Why Ishmael Had to Be Born Before Isaac ............... 447

24.6. Sarah Corrects Abraham (21:11-13) ....................... 448

24.7. Hagar and Ishmael in the Desert (21:14-21) ............... 449

## Chapter 25: Abraham and Abimelech in Beersheba ........... 454

25.1. Abimelech Visits Abraham (21:22-23) ..................... 454

25.2. Judaism as the Synthesis of Abraham, Isaac and Jacob ... 456

25.3. The Alliance Between Abraham and Abimelech
(21:24-28) ................................................ 457

25.4. The Essence of Beersheba (21:29-34) ..................... 458

## Chapter 26: Akedat Yitzchak, "The Sacrifice of Isaac" .......... 461

26.1. Lessons from the "Binding of Isaac" ....................... 461

26.2. "God Put Abraham to the Test" (22:1) ..................... 462

26.3. "Take Your Son" (22: 2) .................................... 466

26.4. From Back-to-Back Connection to Face-to-Face
Connection .............................................. 467

26.5. "And Offer Him There as a Burnt Offering" (22:2) ......... 469

26.6. Three Potential Heirs (22:3) ............................. 471

26.7. Three Days on the Road: Abraham's Awareness of
His Actions (22:4) ....................................... 473

26.8. Abraham Chooses Isaac (22:5) ........................... 474

26.9. "We Will Worship and We Will Return to You" ............ 476

26.10. "And the Two Walked Off Together" (22:6) .............. 479

26.11. Gevurah as Subordinate to Hesed (22:7) ................ 480

26.12. "God Will See" (22:7-8) ................................... 482

26.13. The Akedah, the Binding of Isaac (22:9) ................ 484

26.14. Abraham's Double Name: "Abraham! Abraham!"
(22:10-11) ............................................... 485

26.15. Binding, but Not Sacrifice (22:12) ....................... 489

26.16. "On the Mount of the Lord There is Vision" (22:12-14) . . .490
26.17. A Blessing to the Nations (22:15-18). . . . . . . . . . . . . . . . . . . . . . .492
26.18. Abraham's Return (22:19). . . . . . . . . . . . . . . . . . . . . . . . . . . . . . .494

**Chapter 27: The Birth of Rebekah** . . . . . . . . . . . . . . . . . . . . . . . . . . . . . **496**

27.1. The Birth of Rebekah (22:20-24). . . . . . . . . . . . . . . . . . . . . . . .496
27.2. Nahor's Family in Relation to the Family of Abraham . . . . . 497
27.3. Twelve Sons and a Daughter . . . . . . . . . . . . . . . . . . . . . . . . . . . . .499

**WEEKLY PORTION CHAYEI SARAH**

**Chapter 28: Hebron and the Machpelah Cave** . . . . . . . . . . . . . . . . . **502**

28.1. Sarah's Life and Her Three Victories . . . . . . . . . . . . . . . . . . . . . .502
28.2. Hebron as a National Political Center (23:1-2) . . . . . . . . . . .504
28.3. Sarah Redirects Abraham to Hebron (23:2-3) . . . . . . . . . . .506
28.4. Abraham's Dual Status (23:3-4) . . . . . . . . . . . . . . . . . . . . . . . . .507
28.5. "Bury your dead in the choicest of our burial places"
(23:5-6) . . . . . . . . . . . . . . . . . . . . . . . . . . . . . . . . . . . . . . . . . . . . . . . . .508
28.6. The Purchase of the Machpelah Cave (23:7-9). . . . . . . . . . . 510
28.7. A Funerary Cave as a Foothold for the Jewish Nation . . . . . . 511
28.8. The Machpelah Cave and the Universalism of Jewish
Tradition. . . . . . . . . . . . . . . . . . . . . . . . . . . . . . . . . . . . . . . . . . . . . . . . . . 512
28.9. Ephron the Son of Zohar: "Ash on Radiance". . . . . . . . . . . . .513
28.10. Purchasing the Field, and Abraham's Status (23:10-11) . . . .515
28.11. Abraham Bows Twice to the Hittites (23:12) . . . . . . . . . . . . .516
28.12. Drawing Up the Contract (23:13-16) . . . . . . . . . . . . . . . . . . . . .517
28.13. "The field with its cave ... passed to Abraham as his
possession" (23:17-20) . . . . . . . . . . . . . . . . . . . . . . . . . . . . . . . . . . . .519

**Chapter 29: The Marriage of Isaac and Rebekah.** . . . . . . . . . . . . . . .521

29.1. The Command to Marry Isaac to Kindred Family (24:1-4) . 521

29.2. The Importance of Living in the Holy Land (24:5-9) . . . . . . 524

29.3. The Well as a Place of Matchmaking (24:10-11). . . . . . . . . . . 527

29.4. Everyday Stories about the Patriarchs' Slaves . . . . . . . . . . . 528

29.5. Above-Normal Hesed (24:12-14). . . . . . . . . . . . . . . . . . . . . . . . . . 529

29.6. Rebekah's Conduct at the Well (24:15-20) . . . . . . . . . . . . . . . .531

29.7. Rebekah and the Hospitality of the Nahor Family

(24:21-27) . . . . . . . . . . . . . . . . . . . . . . . . . . . . . . . . . . . . . . . . . . . . . . 533

29.8. Eliezer Meets Rebekah's Family (24:28-33). . . . . . . . . . . . . . 536

29.9. Changes of Emphasis in Eliezer's Retelling of His

Assigned Task (24:34-38). . . . . . . . . . . . . . . . . . . . . . . . . . . . . . . . . 537

29.10. Eliezer's Personal Issues with Finding a Wife for Isaac

(24:39) . . . . . . . . . . . . . . . . . . . . . . . . . . . . . . . . . . . . . . . . . . . . . . . . . . 539

29.11. Eliezer's "Cursedness". . . . . . . . . . . . . . . . . . . . . . . . . . . . . . . . .540

29.12. Eliezer's Correction. . . . . . . . . . . . . . . . . . . . . . . . . . . . . . . . . . . 541

29.13. Eliezer's Methods of Persuading Rebekah's Family

(24:40-61). . . . . . . . . . . . . . . . . . . . . . . . . . . . . . . . . . . . . . . . . . . . . . . 543

29.14. The Prohibition of Parents Using Coercion in the

Matter of a Child's Marriage. . . . . . . . . . . . . . . . . . . . . . . . . . . . .549

29.15. Isaac in God's Field (24:62-63) . . . . . . . . . . . . . . . . . . . . . . . .550

29.16. Rebekah Meets Isaac (24:64-67) . . . . . . . . . . . . . . . . . . . . . .551

29.17. Isaac's "Lack of Initiative" as the Attribute of Gevurah . . . 554


**Chapter 30: Abraham's Other Children** . . . . . . . . . . . . . . . . . . . . . . . **556**


30.1. Keturah and Her Children (25:1-4) . . . . . . . . . . . . . . . . . . . . . . 556

30.2 Passing on the Heritage to Isaac (25: 5-6) . . . . . . . . . . . . . . . . 558

30.3. The Fullness of the Realization of Abraham . . . . . . . . . . . . . . 559

30.4. Abraham's Death and Burial (25:7-11) . . . . . . . . . . . . . . . . . . . 561

30.5. Ishmael's Descendants (25:12-18) . . . . . . . . . . . . . . . . . . . . . . . 563

# Preface to the English Edition

THE MIDRASH NOTES that "every generation has its expounders," and new commentaries to the Torah are needed in every generation. Our own times likewise call for new approaches to understanding the Torah. The *Bible Dynamics* commentary, based on the kabbalistic ideas of Rabbi Y. L. Ashkenazi (Manitou), seeks to provide such a new understanding.

The need for new commentaries arises as cultures and societies constantly change and evolve, and are forced to confront new problems. Naturally, the previous commentaries retain their importance, but they are no longer sufficient. New approaches are paramount for preserving the relevance of the Torah for successive generations.

Our own generation is undergoing especially rapid and radical changes in all areas of Jewish life. The following deserve special mention.

- The creation of the State of Israel and the return of the Jewish people to their land have occasioned a dramatic shift in the Jewish worldview. Life in exile demanded from the Jewish people, and from Judaism, an approach that focused on self-preservation, and consistently strived for isolation and conservation. But contemporary Israeli life, in an independent state on equal footing with other nations, places different demands on the Jewish people, and orients them instead toward extroversion: development and advancement, universalism, shared human values, and a need and desire to influence world history and global culture.

- The interest of the peoples of the world in Judaism has increased tremendously in our time. While the Jews were in exile and subjected to persecution, other nations showed little interest in Jewish culture and tradition, because "a poor man's wisdom is scorned" (Ecclesiastes 9:16). The larger world's ever increasing interest in Judaism today is due in large measure to Israel's significant successes and achievements. These changing circumstances require a completely new approach to interpreting the Torah.

- Jewish psychological and cultural integration into the Western world has brought the secular Jewish reader and the non-Jewish reader closer together than ever before. A significant segment of the Jewish people is already so far removed from tradition that it views it from the outside looking in. While those Jews still feel a sentimental attachment to Judaism, overwhelmingly they are already a part of the non-Jewish world, culturally speaking, and can move closer to Judaism only as a part of that larger world.

All these changes create new questions, and new aspects and meanings in the Torah are thus revealed.

The contemporary reader might be a free-thinking

traditional Jew or a Jew entirely removed from tradition, or he might be not even Jewish at all, but undertakes reading the Torah simply because it is an important component of humanity's rich spiritual heritage. The key features and needs of contemporary readers can be summarized as follows:

1. The Torah commentators of the past addressed themselves primarily to observant Jews who lived within the tradition. Contemporary readers are different, and they view the Torah text differently. Most readers today live in a far more open world, which gives them an "external" perspective, in the psychological or even the physical sense. Their view of the Torah too is thus a view "from the outside."

2. The traditional Jewish reader of the past was mainly interested in observing the commandments. It was important for him to understand precisely how the commandments and their details, with which he was already largely familiar, related to the Torah text. A contemporary student of the Torah, on the other hand, is very likely more interested in ideas that will promote his personal development. Rather than viewing the Torah primarily as a source of commandments and laws, the contemporary reader will more typically be seeking values and ideals.

3. For the traditional Jewish reader the Torah was the ultimate legacy. There was never any question of which tradition he should choose; it was only a matter of deepening his knowledge of a text that he took for granted as his very own. For the modern reader, however, the Torah is only one of many spiritual sources with which it must compete. Any Torah commentary today must take this competitive challenge into account.

4. It seems most relevant today to read the Torah as an engaging narrative of uniquely human characters and personalities, each with his or her own challenges and doubts, and having many aspects of greatness to be sure, but shortcomings and flaws as well. Any meaningful reading of the Torah must thus include the dynamics of development – the evolution of people, ideas, and concepts. Commentators of previous ages saw the leading characters of the Torah as a source of lessons and teachings exclusively, and not as personalities per se. In passing from one book of the Torah to the next, those commentators also typically disregarded any transition in the development of ideas and concepts, perceiving the entire Torah instead as a single monolithic, instantaneous event.

\* \* \*

The modern reader's needs are rather difficult to address. One notable attempt toward developing a new understanding of the Torah was made in the mid-twentieth century by Yehuda Leon Ashkenazi (Manitou), a prominent rabbi and Kabbalist, who through his innovative ideas and concepts formulated a new approach to understanding the text of the Torah and its narratives.

Yehuda Leon was born in Algeria in 1922. His father David was the last chief rabbi of Algiers, and the family had its own kabbalistic tradition. He received an education that was both deeply religious and broadly secular.

During the Second World War Ashkenazi fought in the French resistance. He moved to France after the war, and became a key figure in the post-war revival of French Jewry. (By this time, he was known by his cognomen "Manitou.") After the Six-Day War of 1967 he emigrated to Israel, where for three decades he was a dean of the Merkaz Ha-Rav yeshiva of Rabbi Abraham Isaac Kook, and spiritual leader of French Jewry's religious Zionism movement. He died in Jerusalem in 1996.

Teaching mainly in French throughout his life, Ashkenazi exerted a far-reaching influence on French-speaking Jewry. He wrote very little, focusing mostly on lecturing and teaching, with the result that relatively few of his teachings have appeared in other languages, nor even in Hebrew until only very recently. In the English-speaking world (not to mention other languages) Ashkenazi and his ideas are virtually unknown even to this day.

*The Bible Dynamics* commentary is based primarily on the lectures of Ashkenazi's devoted disciple Rabbi Uri Cherki. (But it also includes a number of the author's original ideas and additions.)

Rabbi Uri Cherki is among the most prominent modern Israeli proponents of the ideas of Rabbi Yehuda Leon Ashkenazi-Manitou. The school that Rabbi Cherki has founded presents Rabbi Ashkenazi's approach in a systematic way, through a series of Torah lectures that have never before been published in written form.

The ideas that Rabbi Ashkenazi reveals allow us to see the Patriarchs as dynamic personalities who evolved and changed throughout their lives. He teaches us to ask questions like the following: How did Abraham and Isaac, Jacob and Moses evolve in the course of the Torah's narratives? How did their views and ideas change over time? How and why do the ideas of Leviticus and Numbers differ from those of Genesis and Exodus? And why are the Torah's commandments, and the development of the Jewish nation, presented differently in the book of Deuteronomy as compared with the earlier books of the Torah?

In former times such questions were deemed unacceptable. Instead, the questions were usually posed along the following lines: What is great about Abraham? What example does he set for us, and what is he trying to teach us? How can we reconcile the apparent contradictions between the book of Deuteronomy and the Torah's previous books?

On the other hand, certain questions were never raised. For example: How did Abraham himself change in the course of his life story, and how did he himself understand it? How are we to understand that Deuteronomy has its own unique approach to presenting the commandments? Such questions, for a very long time considered too privileged for the public consciousness, could be discussed only by a narrow coterie of kabbalistic sages.

Even today the members of certain religious circles, upon hearing that the Patriarchs developed as personalities, or that Moses saw the commandments variously in different periods of his personal development, are moved to protest, because they see this viewpoint as portraying the Patriarchs as imperfect, and not "as they must be." After all, if a person is said to have developed, that can only mean that at first there was something that he failed to understand, and only later came to understand. How can we say such things about the Patriarchs, or about Moses? Who are we to judge them? Against their greatness we are all but insignificant; how dare we evaluate their development? Nor can the eternal commandments, given from Heaven, ever develop or change!

People accustomed to this mode of thinking believe that dynamics and development testify *ipso facto* to imperfection, and they therefore deem it unacceptable to speak of the Patriarchs and the commandments in such terms. Such a view of development, however, is the vestige of a medieval mindset, in which any ideal must be completely static, and all truly great things must remain ever constant and unchanging.

To the new-age thinking, however, the value of dynamics and development is, on the contrary, quite obvious. When a person fails to develop or advance, this is seen today as an essential shortcoming, even if that person is one of the "greats." Under this revised approach, the dynamics and development that a person undergoes speak only in his favor, and make him so much greater in our eyes. We sense not only the pragmatic, but also the spiritual and religious value of such personal dynamics. And as concerns the commandments, it seems reasonable and natural that God would reveal different facets of the commandments to the Jewish people in different periods. The particular emphasis in a given era would depend on the Jewish people's stage of development at that time.

These are just some of the the teachings of the Kabbalah that were once transmitted only to select individuals, but today can finally be made public, to become a part of our general consciousness.

* * *

All of a human life is a dialogue between man and God. The participants in this dialogue are individuals, nations, and humankind as a whole. The Almighty wants every human being, and every society, regardless of size, to become more perfect, and to that end He constantly confronts us with new tasks and new problems.

As we manage to cope with each succeeding task, God gives us yet another and another, thus continually advancing us to successively higher levels. When, as sometimes happens, we are not able to cope with a given task, God gives us an easier one, and after we solve it, He returns us to the original, more difficult problem. As we continue solving each subsequent problem in a long series of tasks, humanity gradually improves, and man advances closer and closer to God.

Our ability to understand the Patriarchs as dynamically developing personalities is an essential element of this process. It is our hope that this book will succeed in serving that purpose.

# Acknowledgments

M
Y VERY SPECIAL expression of gratitude goes first to Rabbi Ouri Cherki, one of modern Israel's most outstanding rabbis and religious philosophers, a disciple of Rabbi Z.Y. Kook and Rabbi Y.L. Ashkenazi (Manitou). The lessons of Rabbi Cherki allowed me to explore the uniquely innovative approach to the Torah on which the *Universal Torah* commentary is based.

Next, I wish to thank everyone who helped in creating this book at all its various stages, and especially Mikhail Fridman, without whose support this English translation could never have come to fruition, and Betzalel (Todd) Shandelman, the translator of the book, for his wonderful work, as well as Vassili Schedrin for attentive and thoughtful proofreading.

I have been privileged to benefit from the invaluable advice and support of all the following individuals: Leonid and Irina Margulis, Alexander and Yulia Shlyankevich, Svetlana Rousakovski, Masha Yaglom, Yuri Livshets, Grigory Yashgur, Galina Zolotusky, Michael Sherman and Yulia Yaglom, Boris and Anna Gulko, Michael Leypounskiy, Olga Emdin, Rivka Rosin, Galina Bleikh, Iris Mersel, Ilya Brodsky, Roman Rytov, Anatoly Gurevich, Marat Ressin, Moshe Yanovsky.

My heartfelt thanks are also due to all those who partic-
ipated with me in my work on the original Russian edition
of this book.

*Pinchas Polonsky*

# Introduction

By Rabbi Tuly Weisz

I N THE MODERN era of Jewish learning, few thinkers have succeeded in bridging the world of traditional Torah scholarship with the intellectual, psychological, and philosophical
frameworks that animate contemporary readers. Among them,
Dr. Pinchas Polonsky stands out as a pioneering educator
and thought leader, particularly in his work with the Russian-speaking Jewish world. His multi-volume project, *The
Universal Torah: Growth & Struggle in the Five Books of Moses*,
is a groundbreaking commentary on the Torah that reflects
not only deep fidelity to classical sources, but also a bold,
integrative vision for the renewal of Jewish thought in the
spirit of Rabbi Abraham Isaac Kook and Religious Zionism.

*The Universal Torah: Growth & Struggle in the Five Books
of Moses* does not aim to offer another line-by-line exegesis
or academic analysis. Rather, it seeks to uncover the inner
psychological, narrative, and spiritual dynamics embedded
within the biblical text—what Polonsky calls its "living layers."
In doing so, he invites the reader into a conversation with the
Torah that is personal, philosophical, and purpose-driven.
Drawing from classic Rabbinic sources along with Jewish
mysticism and especially the writings of Rav Kook, Polonsky

crafts a commentary that speaks to the evolving heart of both Jewish and non-Jewish Torah students.

What makes *The Universal Torah: Growth & Struggle in the Five Books of Moses* unique in the landscape of biblical scholarship is its focus on Torah as a developmental process—not just a static source of commandments and stories, but a divine narrative of human and national maturation. Polonsky views the Torah's complexity—its contradictions, moral tensions, and layered voices—not as problems to solve, but as invitations to grow. This aligns closely with Rav Kook's vision of Torah as a dynamic force unfolding across history and consciousness.

For the Russian-speaking world, Polonsky's work was monumental. In a post-Soviet reality where Jewish knowledge had been suppressed for generations, his writings represent a renaissance: Torah not as nostalgia or ritual, but as a living source of meaning and nation-building. Yet even beyond language or region, Polonsky's commentary offers something vital to all Torah students - especially those seeking to harmonize ancient tradition with modern sensibilities.

At Israel365, our mission is to strengthen the connection between the Land of Israel, the People of Israel, and the Nations of the world. We believe that the Jewish Bible is not just sacred Scripture for the Jewish people—but a universal gift meant to inspire and uplift all who seek truth and righteousness.

That's why Israel365 is honored to partner with Dr. Pinchas Polonsky in introducing *The Universal Torah: Growth & Struggle in the Five Books of Moses* to a non-Jewish, English speaking audience. Polonky's commentary provides a deeply Jewish yet universally resonant approach to the Torah—one that respects its original context while unlocking its moral and spiritual insights for a broader readership.

In an age when many are disillusioned by simplistic readings of the Bible, *The Universal Torah* offers a visionary framework: one where the Torah is not frozen in the past, but actively guiding humanity forward. Dr. Polonsky's emphasis on development, evolution, and moral complexity mirrors Israel365's values of responsible leadership, spiritual clarity, and redemptive hope.

This collaboration is more than a publishing effort—it is a fulfillment of the prophetic call:

> *"For out of Zion shall go forth the Torah, and the word of the Lord from Jerusalem." (Isaiah 2:3)*

By making *The Universal Torah: Growth & Struggle in the Five Books of Moses* accessible to readers of all backgrounds, we are helping bring about the kind of spiritual partnership that the Bible envisions: Jews and non-Jews walking together, shoulder-to-shoulder, in reverence and reconciliation, unity and shared commitment to the unfolding of divine history.

## A Living Torah for a Living World

In sum, *The Universal Torah: Growth & Struggle in the Five Books of Moses* is not only a commentary; it is a manifesto for a renewed encounter with the living Word of God. It reclaims the vibrancy, complexity, and divine daring of the biblical text and reintroduces it to a generation hungry for relevance and rootedness. With this work, Dr. Pinchas Polonsky makes a lasting contribution to Jewish intellectual and spiritual life, one that echoes the voice of Rav Kook while speaking boldly in his own.

And with the support and platform of Israel365, Dr.

Polonsky's voice now reaches new ears, new hearts, and new allies on the great journey toward redemption.

This monumental project would not have been possible without the extraordinary contributions of Alex Shlyankevich. Alex is a close student of Rabbi Pinchas, who translated his Russian writings into Hebrew and then English. Additionally, Rabbi Elie Mischel served as the editor of these volumes and is passionately committed to Polonsky's theme of Universal Religions Zionism. Thanks also to Shira Schechter for her assistance.

Rabbi Tuly Weisz
Beit Shemesh, July 2025 / Av 5785

# General Overview of Genesis and Its Opening Chapters

## The Structure of the Torah, and the Place of the Book of Genesis Within It

The Torah (by which we mean here the Five Books of Moses, also known by its Greek name, the Pentateuch) consists of the following books:

1. Genesis is the book of Creation. It tells the story of the creation of the world, and the birth of mankind and the Jewish people. Genesis is also the book of concealment (the natural world hides God's presence, and the universe obscures God's visibility from man). Everything that has ever been created contains within it the potential for any human being, and for humanity as a whole, to advance toward God. But initially that potential is hidden. In the book of Genesis it remains entirely concealed.

2. Exodus is the book of Disclosure, the book of

Revelation. It tells the story of the Exodus, the birth of the Jewish people (which is also a revelation in its own right), and the Revelation at Mount Sinai, where God made His presence known to the world.

3. Leviticus is the book of Holiness – the path by which a human being can find his connection with God. Holiness also provides tools for expediting that journey. Leviticus speaks of the Temple and, in particular, the laws of holiness that relate to food consumption and many other aspects of everyday conduct.

4. Numbers is the book of the Road – the wilderness wanderings. It recounts the travels of the Jewish people *en route* to the Holy Land, and describes the transformation that they undergo along the way.

5. Deuteronomy is the book of Self-determination. In this book Moses delivers his own instructions to Israel on how they are to live autonomously in the Holy Land. (Moses does so entirely of his own initiative. The contents of the book of Deuteronomy are all his own; none of it was dictated to him by God.)

All of these concepts will be explained in much greater detail in the *Universal Torah* introduction that appears at the beginning of each of the five books of the Torah.

### The Names of the Books of the Torah

Many people mistakenly believe that the European names of the Torah books (Genesis, Exodus, Leviticus, Numbers, and Deuteronomy) are of non-Jewish origin. But this is not the case.

In ancient Jewish tradition each book of the five books of

the Torah has two names – one name indicating the overall topic of the book, and a second name that derives from the book's opening words.

The names that reflect the subject matter of each book were eventually translated into Greek and Latin, and from there to other languages, thus becoming fixed in European culture. The names that derive from the opening words of each book are the ones used in Jewish terminology today.

For example, in ancient times the second of the Torah's five books was known as *Sefer Yetziat Mitzrayim*, "the Book of the Exodus from Egypt." This was later shortened to "Exodus."

The third book of the five was called *Torat Kohanim*, "the Law (or teachings) of the Priests." In the European translation *kohen* was replaced by "Levi" as the more general term, and the name of the book became "Leviticus."

The fourth book was known in ancient times as *Chumash ha-Pekudim*, "the Book of the Census," which in the European tradition became "Numbers."

And the fifth book was called *Mishneh Torah*, "the Repetition of the Torah," which then became "Deuteronomy," from the Greek, meaning "the second law."

The title of the Torah's first book strayed furthest from the original. *Sefer ha-Yesharim*, "the Book of the Upright" (or "the Just," i.e., the Patriarchs), became "Genesis" – also from Greek, meaning "birth" or "creation," i.e., "the Book of the Creation of the World."

The contemporary Hebrew names of the Torah books (*Bereshit, Shemot, Vayikra, Bemidbar*, and *Devarim*) are used today for the books themselves and also for the first weekly portion of each book. We therefore distinguish by referring to the Torah books by their European names, while we reserve the Hebrew terms for those initial weekly portions.

# The Structure of the Book of Genesis

Genesis is divided into twelve weekly portions, grouped into six pairs. Each pair treats a single topic, while presenting two different perspectives on that topic. Thus we have the following arrangement:

## (A) The Creation of Humanity

| | |
|---|---|
| (1) *Bereshit* (1:1-6:8): | Mankind-1 |
| (2) (2) *Noach* (6:9-11:32): | Mankind-2 |

## (B) The Patriarchs of the Jewish People

| | |
|---|---|
| (3) *Lech Lecha* (12:1-17:27): | Abraham-1 |
| (4) *Vayera* (18:1-22:24): | Abraham-2 |
| (5) *Chayei Sarah* (23:1-25:18): | Isaac-1 |
| (6) *Toldot* (25:19-28:9): | Isaac-2 |
| (7) *Vayetze* (28:10-32:3): | Jacob-1 |
| (8) *Vayishlach* (32:4-36:43): | Jacob-2 |

## (C) The Sons of Jacob

| | |
|---|---|
| (9) *Vayeshev* (37:1-40:23): | Jacob's sons as individuals-1 |
| (10) *Miketz* (41:1-44:17): | Jacob's sons as individuals-2 |
| (11) *Vayigash* (44:18-47:27): | Jacob's sons as progenitors of the tribes-1 |
| (12) *Vayechi* (47:28-50:26): | Jacob's sons as progenitors of the tribes-2 |

**Weekly Portions:** *Bereshit* **and** *Noach*

The first two weekly portions of Genesis, *Bereshit* and *Noach*, deal specifically with the creation of the human race.

Within the structure of the book of Genesis, those first two portions serve as a preface to the history of the Jewish people. They also set the framework for the future mission of the Jewish people – to be "a kingdom of priests and a holy nation" (Exod. 19:6), "by which all families of the earth shall bless themselves" (Gen. 12:3, 28:14), "a covenant people, a light of nations" (Isa. 42:6).

Humanity has two successive primogenitors – Adam and Noah:

- *Bereshit* is the Torah portion of Adam, the first primogenitor of mankind. It speaks of the essence of man as an individual personality.
- *Noach*, the portion of the second primogenitor of mankind, Noah, speaks of human society as a single multinational entity.

Accordingly, the Hebrew expression *ben adam*, "son of Adam," denotes a person as an individual. And the expression *ben noach*, "son of Noah," means a person as a part of humanity.

The internal structure of these weekly portions is as follows:

(1) *Bereshit*:
- (1:1-3:50) The creation of the world
- (4:1-4:15) Cain and Abel
- (4:16-6:8) The descendants of Cain and Seth, and the events that led to the Flood

(2) *Noach*:
- (6:9-9:17) Noah and the Flood
- (9:18-10:32) The resettlement of peoples after the Flood
- (11:1-11:9) The Tower of Babel
- (11:10-11:32) Humankind after the Tower of Babel

## The First Weekly Portions as "Mysteries of the Torah"

Opinions vary in Jewish tradition as to whether the stories of the *Bereshit* and *Noach* portions are meant to be taken literally.

The Talmud calls these texts "mysteries (or 'secrets') of the Torah." It is unlikely that a straightforward, literal reading is consistent with such a characterization.

Therefore, in our commentary we will not pursue the questions that arise when reading these portions literally – such as the relationship between religion and science in the story of the creation of the world; the question of the actual age of the world; did a flood covering the entire surface of the earth really occur; did one pair of each animal species actually survive in Noah's Ark? And so on.

The true meaning of the Torah stories does not consist in questions of that type. The Torah is not a textbook on astrophysics or geography; rather, it is designed to reveal to men and to mankind their true path in life – the internal mechanisms of the universe. As we study the Torah, that is where the focus of our attentions must be.

# Weekly Portion
# Bereshit

Chapter 1

# The Creation of the Universe in Seven Days

## 1.1. Creation as an Ethical Principal (1:1)

א בְּרֵאשִׁית בָּרָא אֱלֹהִים אֵת הַשָּׁמַיִם וְאֵת הָאָרֶץ:

*(1:1) When God began to create heaven and earth*

**(1:1) When God began:** There are two versions of the Creation story told here in the opening chapters of Genesis. The first story (Gen. 1) speaks of the seven days of Creation. And the second story (Gen. 2 and 3) – of Adam and Eve's brief stay in the Garden of Eden. We will first consider each of the two stories separately, followed then by a discussion of the relationship between the two.

**When God began to create:** The very first action ascribed to the Almighty in the book of Genesis is the action of creating. God is He Who creates. This is His first characteristic.

**God began to create:** The ethical basis of the Abrahamic (i.e., biblical, monotheistic) religions is the principle of *Imitatio Dei* – emulating God. Beginning from the premise that man is created in the image and likeness of God, that principle further asserts that the true path that man must follow is the path that extends and deepens man's "God-likeness" (which must, however, always remain partial and limited, of course).

The Almighty has no visible image. One aspect of God's invisibility is that His representation in human experience is not through visual appearance, but through actions. It thus follows that a person seeking to come closer to God must try to emulate the Almighty in His actions.

Accordingly, every description in the Torah of God's actions is a lesson to man – how he can "become more like God."

And since God is the Creator, the ideal for man (or, more precisely, one such ideal) is to be a creative, to produce something new, and to be guided by creative work. This means, most importantly, that every human being must be the creator of his or her own life. Creative activity is thus the primary religious value, because it is that which brings a person closer to God.

To this the Kabbalah adds: any action that a person undertakes that makes him "more God-like" by bringing him closer to the Almighty enables him to receive and appreciate a greater volume of Divine light, which he then experiences as personal pleasure and satisfaction. This is the source of the pleasure that a person derives from his own creativity, and from other actions that are comparable to Divine acts (as we shall describe below).

***

We should note in addition that the ideal of creativity, and of *imitatio Dei* in general (like any other principle or ideal) must not be absolutized. Different and even opposing ideals can co-exist, provided they balance each other. Moreover, God's law (i.e., observance of Divine commands and restrictions) is the sacred boundary that must never be crossed even in pursuit of an ideal. Adam and Eve are prime examples of what happens when this rule is violated. When Adam and Eve ate the fruit of the tree of knowledge of good and bad, they embraced the unlawful path of becoming like God (see Gen. 3:5), which led to their expulsion from the garden of Eden.

**Heaven and earth:** God created the heavenly and the spiritual, but also the earthly, material, and ordinary. Both of these realms are ultimately Divine. Any search for God solely in the sphere of spirituality will be incomplete. Man must find God in the realm of the ethereal and heavenly, but also in everything that is material and earthly.

## 1.2. The First Day: God Creates Light (1:2-3)

ב וְהָאָרֶץ הָיְתָה תֹהוּ וָבֹהוּ וְחֹשֶׁךְ עַל־פְּנֵי תְהוֹם וְרוּחַ
אֱלֹהִים מְרַחֶפֶת עַל־פְּנֵי הַמָּיִם: ג וַיֹּאמֶר אֱלֹהִים יְהִי
אוֹר וַיְהִי־אוֹר:

*(2) the earth being unformed and void, with darkness over the surface of the deep and a wind from God sweeping over the water –*
*(3) God said, "Let there be light"; and there was light.*

**(2) The earth being unformed and void:** The Hebrew expression *tohu va-vohu* is very well known from this passage, but is otherwise fairly uncommon. (It appears twice more in Hebrew Scripture: Isa. 34:11 and Jer. 4:23, both of which give a clear impression of echoing this verse itself.)

*Tohu va-vohu* can be translated variously: "The earth was in a state of frantic chaos, confusion, formlessness, muddlement, devastation." But all these variants come to emphasize the same point: that no human mind can comprehend or imagine what that initial stage of Creation was like.

As already noted, Jewish tradition calls these first chapters of Genesis "a Divine mystery" – the text must not be taken literally. It therefore makes no sense to look for contradictions – or, conversely, agreement – between the Torah's account and scientific theories (the Big Bang or evolution by natural selection, for example). The book of Genesis offers a different perspective on the structure of the universe than the one which the natural sciences are committed to discovering. The Torah is not a physics or geology textbook, but a book about the essence of man and his place in the world.

**(3) God said, "Let there be light":** The Midrash adds: the original light was so intensely bright that it would have immediately blinded anyone who saw it. The Almighty therefore hid that light away, to be revealed only to the righteous in the World to Come. Thus:

- The Universe is designed such that God is concealed, for only that way can a man not be blinded by His grandeur, and develop independently. The Midrash therefore connects the Hebrew ʽ *olam*, "universe," with *neʽ elam*, "concealed."
- In the course of history mankind gradually advances toward revealment of the original Divine light. And

in this does the essence and meaning of all of man's spiritual quests consist.

**"Let there be light"; and there was light:** In the language of the Torah, the expressions "Let there be light" and "and there was light" are essentially the same (except for a small prefix *va-* that changes the tense from future to past): *yehi or* and *vayehi or*, respectively.

In this regard the Midrash notes that light was created exactly as God had commanded. But in the subsequent days of Creation there are significant differences between what God ordered and what actually arose. We will analyze this important feature of the Creation of the universe at the relevant points in the text.

## 1.3 God Reviews, Assesses, and Names (1:4-5)

ד וַיַּרְא אֱלֹהִים אֶת־הָאוֹר כִּי־טוֹב וַיַּבְדֵּל אֱלֹהִים בֵּין הָאוֹר וּבֵין הַחֹשֶׁךְ: ה וַיִּקְרָא אֱלֹהִים ׀ לָאוֹר יוֹם וְלַחֹשֶׁךְ קָרָא לָיְלָה וַיְהִי־עֶרֶב וַיְהִי־בֹקֶר יוֹם אֶחָד:

*(4) God saw that the light was good, and God separated the light from the darkness.*
*(5) God called the light Day, and the darkness He called Night. And there was evening and there was morning, a first day.*

**(4) God saw that the light was good, and God separated the light from the darkness**: As explained earlier, according to the principle of *imitatio Dei* all descriptions of God's actions in the Torah are actually lessons meant to teach people how they should behave. Thus, just as God separated the light from the darkness, so likewise should a person practice that kind of separation in the world – separating light from darkness, i.e., evaluating what is good and what is bad, knowing the difference and behaving accordingly.

**And there was evening and there was morning, a first day:** Evening is mentioned first, and then morning. Noting this, Jewish law considers a day of twenty-four hours to always begin and end at sunset (or dusk). All dates in the Jewish calendar are calculated this way. But in particular, the observance of Shabbat (the Sabbath) and Jewish festivals always begins at nightfall and continues through nightfall of the following day.

The Hebrew word *erev*, "evening," is cognate with the word *le-arev*, "to mix." And similarly, *BKR*, the root of the word *boker*, "morning," means to "analyze, distinguish, isolate." Indeed, as the sun sets in the evening the outlines of visible objects mix and blur, and in the morning, with the arrival of daylight, those objects again become separate and distinct.

Thus, the words "And there was evening and there was morning" can be further understood as "God first mixed, and then He distinguished." This description emphasizes the fundamental unity and identicality of all things in their "origin," before their essential differences become ultimately apparent.

In this spirit, Jewish tradition inculcates in us a mystical feeling of the profound unity of everything in the universe, notwithstanding that we must, in practical life, distinguish between good and bad, between what is permitted and what is forbidden.

**A first day:** The days of Creation are of course not ordinary days in the conventional meaning of the term. As a general rule, the Hebrew word *yom* does not always mean "day" in the usual sense. It can also denote an interval or era of a particular length, as in this case.

Those who try to reconcile the Torah's account of the Creation with the cosmological (scientific) history of the universe usually understand the "days" of Creation as periods of aeonian length – each lasting many millions or even billions of years.

But it is more generally useful in studying these passages to abandon issues of chronology, and instead to consider the days of Creation as the elements from which the universe is constructed. In particular, the Kabbalah correlates the days of Creation with the *Sefirot*, which constitute, as it were, a palette of colors that God uses to paint the universe. A bit later we will analyze this approach in considerably greater detail.

## 1.4. The Second Day: The Separation of the Waters (1:6-8)

ו וַיֹּאמֶר אֱלֹהִים יְהִי רָקִיעַ בְּתוֹךְ הַמָּיִם וִיהִי מַבְדִּיל
בֵּין מַיִם לָמָיִם: ז וַיַּעַשׂ אֱלֹהִים אֶת־הָרָקִיעַ וַיַּבְדֵּל
בֵּין הַמַּיִם אֲשֶׁר מִתַּחַת לָרָקִיעַ וּבֵין הַמַּיִם אֲשֶׁר מֵעַל
לָרָקִיעַ וַיְהִי־כֵן: ח וַיִּקְרָא אֱלֹהִים לָרָקִיעַ שָׁמָיִם וַיְהִי־
עֶרֶב וַיְהִי־בֹקֶר יוֹם שֵׁנִי:

*(6) God said, "Let there be an expanse in the midst of the water, that it may separate water from water."*
*(7) God made the expanse, and it separated the*

*water which was below the expanse from the water
which was above the expanse. And it was so.
(8) God called the expanse Sky. And there was
evening and there was morning, a second day.*

**(6) God said, "Let there be an expanse in the midst of the
water, that it may separate water from water"**: Transformations of water are mentioned several times in the Creation story: the separation here of the water below from the water above, the separation of the sea from the dry land (Gen. 1: 9), and so on.

Water in Jewish tradition is a symbol of life, mercy, and Divine grace. This grace is transformed in order that the entire world will not be inundated. It is the only way that the world can exist at all.

In this verse the separation of "the water below" and "the water above" teaches us to seek Divine grace in both realms – the upper and the lower worlds. That is, in both the spiritual and the material.

**(8) God called the expanse Sky**: The concept of heaven (sky) changes in the course of this very story. At first the heavens stand in opposition to the earth, but then they separate the sources of Divine grace, which emanates from both the upper and lower worlds. Soon we will see further examples of how the Creation story incorporates such rethinking of fundamental concepts.

### 1.5. The Third Day: The Creation of Dry Land, and Plants, Trees, and Fruits (1:9-13)

ט וַיֹּאמֶר אֱלֹהִים יִקָּווּ הַמַּיִם מִתַּחַת הַשָּׁמַיִם אֶל־
מָקוֹם אֶחָד וְתֵרָאֶה הַיַּבָּשָׁה וַיְהִי־כֵן: י וַיִּקְרָא
אֱלֹהִים | לַיַּבָּשָׁה אֶרֶץ וּלְמִקְוֵה הַמַּיִם קָרָא יַמִּים וַיַּרְא
אֱלֹהִים כִּי־טוֹב: יא וַיֹּאמֶר אֱלֹהִים תַּדְשֵׁא הָאָרֶץ דֶּשֶׁא
עֵשֶׂב מַזְרִיעַ זֶרַע עֵץ פְּרִי עֹשֶׂה פְּרִי לְמִינוֹ אֲשֶׁר זַרְעוֹ־בוֹ
עַל־הָאָרֶץ וַיְהִי־כֵן: יב וַתּוֹצֵא הָאָרֶץ דֶּשֶׁא עֵשֶׂב מַזְרִיעַ
זֶרַע לְמִינֵהוּ וְעֵץ עֹשֶׂה־פְּרִי אֲשֶׁר זַרְעוֹ־בוֹ לְמִינֵהוּ וַיַּרְא
אֱלֹהִים כִּי־טוֹב: יג וַיְהִי־עֶרֶב וַיְהִי־בֹקֶר יוֹם שְׁלִישִׁי:

*(9) God said, "Let the water below the sky be
gathered into one area, that the dry land may
appear." And it was so.*

*(10) God called the dry land Earth, and the
gathering of waters He called Seas. And God
saw that this was good.*

*(11) And God said, "Let the earth sprout
vegetation: seed-bearing plants, fruit trees of
every kind on earth that bear fruit with the seed
in it." And it was so.*

*(12) The earth brought forth vegetation: seed-
bearing plants of every kind, and trees of every
kind bearing fruit with the seed in it. And God
saw that this was good.*

*(13) And there was evening and there was
morning, a third day.*

**(9) God said, "Let the water below the sky be gathered into
one area, that the dry land may appear":** If the earth had
remained completely flooded with water (and in a symbolic
sense, if mercy and grace were found everywhere without
exception), no one could possible survive in such an environment. A person would remain inactive and unable to

develop at all, drowning in all-consuming mercy.

But people must grow up to be creative and constructive. The water was therefore gathered separately, and dry land appeared on which mercy (water) is less abundant, making it possible for humans to advance independently, and for the world to develop.

**(10) God called the dry land Earth, and the gathering of waters He called Seas:** Here the concept of *eretz*, "earth," is transformed. Above (Gen. 1:1) earth is contrasted with heaven ("When God began to create heaven and earth ..."). But here earth stands in opposition to the seas – a completely different meaning,

Throughout the Creation there is a rethinking of concepts, like vessels that are emptied, then refilled, as it were, with new content. And likewise, human creativity requires that we continuously rethink definitions and concepts, constantly revising our terminology.

**And God saw that this was good:** On each day of Creation the Torah says that God saw that what he had done was good. This is because each day represents a different aspect of the universe, and every aspect has goodness laid in its foundation.

Just as God at every stage saw that what He had done was good, so should we cultivate the ability to see that same goodness in the surrounding world – in each of its components, and in the universe as a whole. This is yet another way that humans can approach God by becoming like Him.

**(11-12) And God said: Let the earth sprout ... fruit trees of every kind on earth that bear fruit ... The earth brought forth ... trees of every kind bearing fruit:** Although we find repeated many times in the Creation story the statement, "and it was so" (Gen. 1:7, 9, 15, 24, 30), the book of Genesis is never satisfied with that alone. Rather, it tells us in specific terms just how things in the world came about, and why they are the way they are.

In all the days of Creation except the first, if we compare what God orders with what actually comes into being at His command, we notice significant discrepancies. In this verse, for example, God commanded that "fruit trees of every kind on earth that bear fruit" should appear. That is, the word "fruit" is applied even to the trees themselves. But the next verse says that "the earth brought forth ... trees of every kind bearing fruit." (Just "trees," not "fruit trees").

To explain this discrepancy the Midrash says as follows. The original Divine plan included that the trees themselves would be "fruit" suitable to be eaten as food, just like the fruit that grows on those trees. But the earth produced only "trees bearing fruit" – the trees themselves were not edible. The earth failed, as it were, to comply with the Divine order!

"Trees" and "fruits" are symbolic of process and result. Trees can be seen as only a conduit, a pathway to the emergence of fruits. The trees themselves are not edible and have no food value. Likewise, many processes in our daily lives have no intrinsic value – we engage in those activities only because they "bear fruit." We perform tedious, monotonous work just to earn a salary, we travel boring roads on our way to interesting places, we endure humdrum technicalities in preparation for engrossing events. But when the process itself is enjoyable, things take on an entirely different and added dimension – when we do our favorite work, or go on a pleasant walk, for example. The Midrash believes that in the World to Come "trees" will fulfill God's original order and will become "edible." That is, all human action, besides "bearing fruit," will have value *per se*. That is, all humans in whatever they do will always enjoy both the process and the result in equal measure.

Thus, the Divine word as spoken at the Creation determines the trajectory of the development of the universe as it is ideally meant to be. But what actually arose at the Creation is only the beginning of that path. Moreover, man is given the opportunity and the ability to improve the world according to the Divine plan, and his own condition as well, by arranging the world such that he can do only what he likes to do and what he enjoys doing.

Thus the world was created imperfect, and yet God confirmed that "it was good." The world was not supposed to be perfect from the outset. But humans were given the opportunity to improve and perfect the world, becoming God's partners, as it were, in the creation of the universe.

## 1.6. The Fourth Day: The Sun, the Moon, and the Stars (1:14-19)

יד וַיֹּאמֶר אֱלֹהִים יְהִי מְאֹרֹת בִּרְקִיעַ הַשָּׁמַיִם לְהַבְדִּיל בֵּין הַיּוֹם וּבֵין הַלָּיְלָה וְהָיוּ לְאֹתֹת וּלְמוֹעֲדִים וּלְיָמִים וְשָׁנִים: טו וְהָיוּ לִמְאוֹרֹת בִּרְקִיעַ הַשָּׁמַיִם לְהָאִיר עַל־הָאָרֶץ וַיְהִי־כֵן: טז וַיַּעַשׂ אֱלֹהִים אֶת־שְׁנֵי הַמְּאֹרֹת הַגְּדֹלִים אֶת־הַמָּאוֹר הַגָּדֹל לְמֶמְשֶׁלֶת הַיּוֹם וְאֶת־הַמָּאוֹר הַקָּטֹן לְמֶמְשֶׁלֶת הַלַּיְלָה וְאֵת הַכּוֹכָבִים: יז וַיִּתֵּן אֹתָם אֱלֹהִים בִּרְקִיעַ הַשָּׁמָיִם לְהָאִיר עַל־הָאָרֶץ: יח וְלִמְשֹׁל בַּיּוֹם וּבַלַּיְלָה וּלְהַבְדִּיל בֵּין הָאוֹר וּבֵין הַחֹשֶׁךְ וַיַּרְא אֱלֹהִים כִּי־טוֹב: יט וַיְהִי־עֶרֶב וַיְהִי־בֹקֶר יוֹם רְבִיעִי:

*(14) God said, "Let there be lights in the expanse of the sky to separate day from night; they shall serve*

*as signs for the set times – the days and the years;*
*(15) and they shall serve as lights in the expanse*
*of the sky to shine upon the earth." And it was so.*
*(16) God made the two great lights, the greater*
*light to dominate the day and the lesser light to*
*dominate the night, and the stars.*
*(17) And God set them in the expanse of the sky*
*to shine upon the earth,*
*(18) to dominate the day and the night, and to*
*separate light from darkness. And God saw that*
*this was good.*
*(19) And there was evening and there was*
*morning, a fourth day.*

**(14) As signs for the set times – the days and the years**: One of the functions of the luminaries is to facilitate organizing human life according to a calendar.

**(15) And they shall serve as lights in the expanse of the sky to shine upon the earth:** The luminaries in the heavens exist not for their own sake, but for the illumination of the earth. And by analogy, all that is heavenly (i.e., all spirituality) exists not for its own sake, but in order to illuminate the lives of the people on this earth.

**(16) God made the two great lights, the greater light to dominate the day and the lesser light to dominate the night**: On its face, this verse is self-contradictory. It begins by saying that "God made two great lights." But the same verse soon informs us that in fact one of them is greater and the other lesser.

The Midrash offers the following explanation. The sun

and the moon were originally both large – they were luminaries of equal size. But the moon was unhappy and came before to the Almighty to complain: "Two kings cannot wear the same crown." That is, only one of the two can be dominant. To this God replied: "That being the case, go then and diminish yourself. Since you insist on a hierarchy, it is you who shall be subordinate."

The result was threefold:

1. The moon became smaller than the sun.
2. The moon emits not its own light, but shines with only reflected light.
3. The size of the visible moon is not constant. It decreases as it approaches its new moon phase, then increases again as it becomes a full moon.

Then the Midrash adds that this condition is only temporary. With the correction of the universe in the World to Come, the moon will again become equal to the sun.

This midrash should not be taken literally, of course. In its typical style, the Midrash clothes a philosophical concept in the garb of a parable. It is saying that ideally the luminaries of the world (and man too is a "luminary") should all be equally prominent. But in any real society there is always a hierarchy, someone who is more important and someone else less so, because "two kings cannot wear the same crown." But even while we recognize the need for hierarchy in practice, we must not idealize it. Man's hierarchical social structure is merely an expedient. Ideally, humanity should be striving, if only gradually, to a state where all luminaries (that is, all people) will be equal in size and importance.

## 1.7. The Fifth Day: Sea Creatures and Birds (1:20-23)

כ וַיֹּאמֶר אֱלֹהִים יִשְׁרְצוּ הַמַּיִם שֶׁרֶץ נֶפֶשׁ חַיָּה
וְעוֹף יְעוֹפֵף עַל־הָאָרֶץ עַל־פְּנֵי רְקִיעַ הַשָּׁמָיִם: כא
וַיִּבְרָא אֱלֹהִים אֶת־הַתַּנִּינִם הַגְּדֹלִים וְאֵת כָּל־נֶפֶשׁ
הַחַיָּה ׀ הָרֹמֶשֶׂת אֲשֶׁר שָׁרְצוּ הַמַּיִם לְמִינֵהֶם וְאֵת כָּל־
עוֹף כָּנָף לְמִינֵהוּ וַיַּרְא אֱלֹהִים כִּי־טוֹב: כב וַיְבָרֶךְ אֹתָם
אֱלֹהִים לֵאמֹר פְּרוּ וּרְבוּ וּמִלְאוּ אֶת־הַמַּיִם בַּיַּמִּים
וְהָעוֹף יִרֶב בָּאָרֶץ: כג וַיְהִי־עֶרֶב וַיְהִי־בֹקֶר יוֹם חֲמִישִׁי:

*(20) God said, "Let the waters bring forth swarms of living creatures, and birds that fly above the earth across the expanse of the sky."*
*(21) God created the great sea monsters, and all the living creatures of every kind that creep, which the waters brought forth in swarms, and all the winged birds of every kind. And God saw that this was good.*
*(22) God blessed them, saying, "Be fertile and increase, fill the waters in the seas, and let the birds increase on the earth."*
*(23) And there was evening and there was morning, a fifth day.*

**(20) God said, "Let the waters bring forth swarms of living creatures, and birds that fly above the earth across the expanse of the sky"**: The creatures of sea and sky were created before the terrestrial ones, which were created only the next (sixth) day. The true essence of life derives from water (Divine grace) and from the heavens (ideals and spirituality). Only after those elements of the universe are firmly in place can life then take root on the land where man dwells.

**(21) God created the great sea monsters:** Water (which represents mercy) is the source of all life, but it is also fraught with danger. The first of the sea creatures mentioned are "the great sea monsters." The archetypal sea monster in Jewish tradition is the Leviathan, associated with the Divine impulse that is embodied in nature, but lurks in the depths of the sea. It is both important and dangerous.

**Of every kind:** A salient feature of Divine creation is the diversity of life forms. And, in particular, the very numerous genera, species, and subspecies of animals.

**(22) God blessed them, saying, "Be fertile and increase, fill the waters in the seas, and let the birds increase on the earth":** The animal world, unlike the plants, received God's special blessing. Plants lack a soul; they live only "biochemically." But animals, on the other hand, need more than just biochemistry to survive – they need mental and emotional fortitude. And that is why they receive an additional blessing.

## 1.8. The Sixth Day: Animals of the Dry Land, and Human Beings (1:24-30)

כד וַיֹּאמֶר אֱלֹהִים תּוֹצֵא הָאָרֶץ נֶפֶשׁ חַיָּה לְמִינָהּ
בְּהֵמָה וָרֶמֶשׂ וְחַיְתוֹ־אֶרֶץ לְמִינָהּ וַיְהִי־כֵן: כה וַיַּעַשׂ
אֱלֹהִים אֶת־חַיַּת הָאָרֶץ לְמִינָהּ וְאֶת־הַבְּהֵמָה לְמִינָהּ
וְאֵת כָּל־רֶמֶשׂ הָאֲדָמָה לְמִינֵהוּ וַיַּרְא אֱלֹהִים כִּי־טוֹב:
כו וַיֹּאמֶר אֱלֹהִים נַעֲשֶׂה אָדָם בְּצַלְמֵנוּ כִּדְמוּתֵנוּ וְיִרְדּוּ
בִדְגַת הַיָּם וּבְעוֹף הַשָּׁמַיִם וּבַבְּהֵמָה וּבְכָל־הָאָרֶץ וּבְכָל־
הָרֶמֶשׂ הָרֹמֵשׂ עַל־הָאָרֶץ: כז וַיִּבְרָא אֱלֹהִים ׀ אֶת־
הָאָדָם בְּצַלְמוֹ בְּצֶלֶם אֱלֹהִים בָּרָא אֹתוֹ זָכָר וּנְקֵבָה בָּרָא
אֹתָם: כח וַיְבָרֶךְ אֹתָם אֱלֹהִים וַיֹּאמֶר לָהֶם אֱלֹהִים

פְּרוּ וּרְבוּ וּמִלְאוּ אֶת־הָאָרֶץ וְכִבְשֻׁהָ וּרְדוּ בִּדְגַת הַיָּם
וּבְעוֹף הַשָּׁמַיִם וּבְכָל־חַיָּה הָרֹמֶשֶׂת עַל־הָאָרֶץ: כט
וַיֹּאמֶר אֱלֹהִים הִנֵּה נָתַתִּי לָכֶם אֶת־כָּל־עֵשֶׂב ׀ זֹרֵעַ זֶרַע
אֲשֶׁר עַל־פְּנֵי כָל־הָאָרֶץ וְאֶת־כָּל־הָעֵץ אֲשֶׁר־בּוֹ פְרִי־עֵץ
זֹרֵעַ זָרַע לָכֶם יִהְיֶה לְאָכְלָה: ל וּלְכָל־חַיַּת הָאָרֶץ וּלְכָל־
עוֹף הַשָּׁמַיִם וּלְכֹל ׀ רוֹמֵשׂ עַל־הָאָרֶץ אֲשֶׁר־בּוֹ נֶפֶשׁ חַיָּה
אֶת־כָּל־יֶרֶק עֵשֶׂב לְאָכְלָה וַיְהִי־כֵן:

(24) God said, "Let the earth bring forth every
kind of living creature: cattle, creeping things,
and wild beasts of every kind." And it was so.
(25) God made wild beasts of every kind and
cattle of every kind, and all kinds of creeping
things of the earth. And God saw that this was
good.
(26) And God said, "Let us make man in our
image, after our likeness. They shall rule the
fish of the sea, the birds of the sky, the cattle,
the whole earth, and all the creeping things that
creep on earth."
(27) And God created man in His image, in the
image of God He created him; male and female
He created them.
(28) God blessed them and God said to them, "Be
fertile and increase, fill the earth and master it;
and rule the fish of the sea, the birds of the sky,
and all the living things that creep on earth."
(29) God said, "See, I give you every seed-bearing
plant that is upon all the earth, and every tree
that has seed-bearing fruit; they shall be yours
for food.
(30) And to all the animals on land, to all the
birds of the sky, and to everything that creeps

*on earth, in which there is the breath of life, [I give] all the green plants for food." And it was so.*

**(26) Let us make man**: The Hebrew is, *na ` aseh adam*. The word *adam* has two related meanings. It is the proper name of the first man in this story of the Creation. But more often *adam* means, simply, "man." Even when used in that second, generic sense, the Hebrew word *adam* has no feminine or plural form. It can mean "man" as an individual human being (a man), and also the human race as a whole (mankind).

Grammatically, the feminine form of *adam*, would be *adamah*, which has a different meaning: "earth, land, soil." Thus, the "wife" of mankind is the very earth from which Adam was created (Gen. 2:7), and which by God's decree he cultivates (Gen. 3:17, 23).

**(26) And God said, "Let us make man ...":** The text does not say "Let me make man," but "Let *us* make man." This is the only instance in the Creation story where God's actions are indicated by a verb in the plural form. In all other Divine acts of the Creation a verb in the singular is used.

Just whom does the Almighty mean here when He says "us"? And why is it phrased that way only for the creation of man, but not the heavens, the earth, plants, or animals? The commentators offer many different answers to these questions, each one choosing the answer that is closest to him - the answer that he feels affords him the fullest understanding of the text, and of life.

Of all those answers, we wish to focus on the following one. Here God is addressing the man himself – Adam, the human about to be created, but also every person in the most general sense. God says to him: "Let us together, you and I, make a man out of you." Together we will make of you a human truly worthy of the name. That is why the plural of the verb "to make" is found only here with respect to humans, but not any other elements of the universe, not even the animals. Man, unlike animals, is not born in a ready-made state. Man's completion awaits *him*. He must work to complete himself. This process of the first man's self-transformation will be described in detail in the second Creation story that follows this one (Gen. 2, 3).

As we shall soon explain in detail, Adam spent only one day in the garden of Eden, the sixth day of Creation, at which time the world was still being created. All the events that took place in the garden still belong to the process of Creation – not to "ordinary" life that began after the Creation became complete with Adam and Eve's expulsion. In the garden, Adam radically altered his own nature and acquired new qualities. He "completed himself" – through his dialogue and interaction with God, and sometimes in disagreement with Him.

After man was expelled from the garden his inclination to self-transformation diminished, but did not entirely disappear. Even today it continues to operate within each individual, and also at the level of humanity as a whole.

**(27) And God created man in His image, in the image of God He created him:** This one verse sums up the entire essence of biblical theology, which consists in the fact that God, the Creator of the universe, created human beings in His Own likeness. It thus follows that God loves man, treats him as His Own son, and helps him to develop. The principle of *imitatio Dei* mentioned earlier, the moral imperative of ethical monotheism, is likewise based on the idea of man's likeness to God.

**Male and female He created them:** "Male" and "female" are terms most often applied to animals, and with respect to humans even sound somewhat crude. But this is an exact translation of the Hebrew *zachar u-nekeivah*, which emphasizes the aspect of biological sex. The second Creation story (Gen. 2:23) uses a different terminology – *ish* and *isha* – "man" and "woman." These are words that can be used only with reference to humans.

Thus, in the first Creation story man and woman are created immediately as a couple, like all the other animals of the natural world. This contrasts with the second chapter of Genesis, where we read that Adam was created alone – which runs contrary to nature.

We will explore the differences between the first and second Creation stories in much more detail below.

**(28) God blessed them and God said to them, "Be fertile and increase, fill the earth and master it":** This is God's very first commandment to man. It consists not only in biological reproduction, but also in dominating the world and transforming it.

In essence, God is commanding man to build a civilization. Civilization is "man's power over nature." Thus, the Torah considers civilization, including scientific and technological progress, not merely a "convenience" for mankind, but a true spiritual and religious value – the fulfillment of a Divine commandment. To oppose scientific and technological progress is to oppose spiritual development, and is therefore morally wrong.

The Divine imperative to build a civilization is given to humanity as a whole, seeing that it can be accomplished only by all of humanity collectively, not by any individual person or even a single nation that chooses to act in isolation from all other nations.

**(29-30) God said, "See, I give you every seed-bearing plant ... they shall be yours for food. And to all the animals on land ... [I give] all the green plants for food":** In the garden of Eden, all animals, and Adam and his wife too, were vegetarians.

Rabbi Abraham Isaac Kook (the founder of religious Zionism and the movement for Orthodox modernization of Judaism) maintained that vegetarianism is in fact the ideal in Judaism. But he also stressed that this ideal must not be propagandized, because humanity must come to it naturally and of its own accord.

Other Divine ideals must likewise be adopted by the world only gradually, in the natural course of societal development. (Universal peace is another such ideal.) Any attempt at premature realization of these ideals can only prove disastrous.

## 1.9. God Finds the End Result of the Creation "Very Good" (1:31)

**לא** וַיַּרְא אֱלֹהִים אֶת־כָּל־אֲשֶׁר עָשָׂה וְהִנֵּה־טוֹב מְאֹד
וַיְהִי־עֶרֶב וַיְהִי־בֹקֶר יוֹם הַשִּׁשִּׁי׃

*(31) And God saw all that He had made, and found it very good. And there was evening and there was morning, the sixth day.*

**(31) And God saw all that He had made, and found it very good:** We noted previously that God found every part of the universe good after he had created it. But here the Torah tells us that "God saw all that He had made, and found it very good." This "very good" means that in addition to the high quality of each individual element in the system, all the components taken together were well balanced and consistent with one another.

The Midrash offers us a different understanding of this verse, namely: "God saw all that He had made, and found it very good" means that the world generally inclines toward goodness. But paradoxically, "very good" means that the structure of the world also includes a potential for evil.

In other words, the evil that exists in the world exists precisely for the sake of the good. Absolute goodness cannot exist only as a ready-made gift from God. Rather, it must arise as the result of man's continuing independent development, as he strives to overcome evil. Therefore, because the Almighty wished to give mankind such goodness that is genuine and complete, and not merely a token level of goodness, He also had to lay the potential for evil in the very foundation of the universe, and then to give man the ability to overcome it by his actions. Evil is a necessary element of the universe, and not merely a concession to the world's imperfections.

## 1.10. The Seventh day: The Sabbath (2:1-3)

א וַיְכֻלּוּ הַשָּׁמַיִם וְהָאָרֶץ וְכָל־צְבָאָם: ב וַיְכַל אֱלֹהִים
בַּיּוֹם הַשְּׁבִיעִי מְלַאכְתּוֹ אֲשֶׁר עָשָׂה וַיִּשְׁבֹּת בַּיּוֹם הַשְּׁבִיעִי
מִכָּל־מְלַאכְתּוֹ אֲשֶׁר עָשָׂה: ג וַיְבָרֶךְ אֱלֹהִים אֶת־יוֹם
הַשְּׁבִיעִי וַיְקַדֵּשׁ אֹתוֹ כִּי בוֹ שָׁבַת מִכָּל־מְלַאכְתּוֹ אֲשֶׁר־
בָּרָא אֱלֹהִים לַעֲשׂוֹת:

*(2:1) The heaven and the earth were finished, and all their array.*

*(2) On the seventh day God finished the work that He had been doing, and He ceased on the seventh day from all the work that He had done. (3) And God blessed the seventh day and declared it holy, because on it God ceased from all the work of creation that He had done.*

**(2-3) On the seventh day God finished the work that He had been doing:** That is, the seventh day is itself an essential part of the Creation. God completed the work of Creation by creating the seventh day, the Sabbath, which is different, however, from the rest of Creation, because it is not something material, but a special time whose purpose is to bring holiness into the world.

**And He ceased:** The Hebrew verb *SH-B-T* (whence *Shabbat*, "the Sabbath") has two closely related meanings: to cease, and to rest.

**And He ceased:** I.e., He stopped transforming the universe.

**On the seventh day:** The Torah makes clear that the last day of the week is the seventh day. (It is the day that the world calls "Saturday." In the Christian calendar, the "day of rest" was later moved to Sunday, which in that system also became the "seventh" day of the week.)

**From all the work that He had done**: The word *melachah* is used here, which means "creative work" – work that brings something new into existence. At the Creation of the world only that kind of work was important, and it is precisely the performance of those categories of work that Jewish law prohibits on Shabbat. Writing even a single letter is "creative work," and is therefore forbidden on Shabbat. But transporting even a large and heavy object from place to place within a private domain, although this is obviously work, it is not "creative work," and is therefore not forbidden on Shabbat.

**(3) And God blessed the seventh day:** The essence of a blessing is a positive increase, whether material or spiritual.

**And declared it holy:** Holiness comes about when we use the material elements of the world to improve and reinforce the human connection with God.

**Because on it God ceased from all the work of creation that He had done:** Since the world did not come into existence spontaneously, but was created, it has meaning and purpose. The weekly Shabbat celebrates the creation of the universe – i.e., the meaning and purpose that are embodied within it. The Shabbat therefore brings holiness into the world.

This concludes the first of the two versions of the story of the Creation.

# Chapter 2

# Adam and Eve in the Garden of Eden

## 2.1. The Creation of the Heavens, the Earth, and Plants (2:4-6)

ד אֵלֶּה תוֹלְדוֹת הַשָּׁמַיִם וְהָאָרֶץ בְּהִבָּרְאָם בְּיוֹם עֲשׂוֹת
יְהֹוָה אֱלֹהִים אֶרֶץ וְשָׁמָיִם: ה וְכֹל ׀ שִׂיחַ הַשָּׂדֶה טֶרֶם
יִהְיֶה בָאָרֶץ וְכָל־עֵשֶׂב הַשָּׂדֶה טֶרֶם יִצְמָח כִּי לֹא הִמְטִיר
יְהֹוָה אֱלֹהִים עַל־הָאָרֶץ וְאָדָם אַיִן לַעֲבֹד אֶת־הָאֲדָמָה:
ו וְאֵד יַעֲלֶה מִן־הָאָרֶץ וְהִשְׁקָה אֶת־כָּל־פְּנֵי הָאֲדָמָה:

*(4) Such is the story of heaven and earth when they were created. When the Lord God made earth and heaven –*
*(5) when no shrub of the field was yet on earth and no grasses of the field had yet sprouted, because the Lord God had not sent rain upon the earth and there was no man to till the soil,*
*(6) but a flow would well up from the ground and water the whole surface of the earth –*

**(4) Such is the story of heaven and earth:** Here begins the second of the two versions of the story of the Creation.

**Such is the story of heaven and earth when ... the Lord God made earth and heaven:** This verse serves as a header line for what follows, and shows that the story starts here anew from the very beginning, with the creation of heaven and earth. The story of Adam in the garden of Eden that follows is not an elaboration of the details of the first version of the story, but a new, different version.

The two versions (which we shall call "the first story" and "the second story") recount the same set of events, but describe them differently:

- The first story (Gen. 1:1-2:3) details what happened on each of the seven days of Creation. Each day gets roughly the same amount of coverage, and the story concludes with a description of the Sabbath.
- The second story (Gen. 2:4-3:24) opens with a brief overview of how the heavens, the earth, and plants were created. It then recounts in detail Adam and his wife's stay in the garden of Eden and their expulsion from it, which ends the second Creation story.

The two stories differ in style, emphasize different ideas, and refer to God by different names. Each story has its own perspective on the essence of man, his ideals, and the tasks facing him.

Having already presented above the first Creation story, we now present our reading of the second story, followed by a comparison of the two.

Since the essence of man is portrayed differently in the two stories, we will call those two descriptions "first Adam" and "second Adam." He is of course one and the same person, but considered from two points of view.

**When the Lord God made earth and heaven:** The first story calls the Almighty *Elohim*, translated as "God,", while the second uses the name *Adonai Elohim*, "the Lord God."

The name of an object is not only what people call it, but also an indicator of how they relate to it. For example, the same person can have different names within his family circle, at the workplace, and in official documents. Similarly, each of God's various names highlights a different aspect of Divine manifestation in the world – i.e., a different type of human connection with God. In this respect the first story differs significantly from the second.

**(5) When no shrub of the field was yet on earth ... because the Lord God had not sent rain upon the earth and there was no man:** Here we already have the first contradiction between the two Creation stories. In the first story plants appeared on the third day, even before man, whereas in the second Creation story, so long as Adam had not yet been created neither did any plants grow. And below (Gen. 2:19) we find the same contradiction regarding the animals. In the first story they appear before man, but in the second, man is created first, and only then the animals.

We can try to reconcile such contradictions and to smooth over the difficulties. For example, the Midrash (which we will cite in greater detail below) explains that "vegetation was planted on the third day, but it did not grow until the sixth day, after Adam appeared."

There is, however, another approach, in which, rather than trying to reconcile the contradictions, we perceive them as a different perspectives on the world. In the first Creation story everything that fills the universe – luminaries, plants and animals – are all created before man and independent of him. Man arrives at the very end, when the world is ready and waiting for him. This emphasizes that the world has its own independent value, and is important in its own right, while man is only an appointed official, as it were, of that world – entrusted with governing and managing it.

But in the second story the situation is presented differently – the world makes no sense at all without mankind. Without man nothing in the universe has any value *per se*. He is not only in charge of running the universe, but its very essence.

We will further expand on these two approaches below.

**Because the Lord God had not sent rain upon the earth and there was no man**: The Midrash adds: when Adam was created, he saw that plants already existed, but they were not yet growing. He tried to understand the reason for that. He examined the plants, and determined they lacked water. So Adam prayed for rain, and in response to his prayer rain began to fall, and the garden was able to grow.

This midrash is telling us that Adam ruled the world through knowledge. It was sufficient in the garden just to ponder a problem and devise a solution. The world was immediately transformed simply as the result of that knowledge.

**And there was no man to till the soil:** We noted earlier that grammatically, *adamah*, "earth," is the feminine form of *adam*, "man." The earth and the human race are described here as forming a couple, as it were.

**(5) No man to till the soil:** Thus, in both the first and second stories Adam cultivates the earth and transforms the world. But that cultivation is presented differently.

In the first Creation story, Adam is instructed to rule the

world that was created earlier, but even without him the world is extremely significant as its own independent entity. In the second story, Adam is commanded to eat from the trees of the garden, i.e., metaphorically, to experience the world, which exists only to provide Adam with objects of cognition. This world has no actual value of its own.

**(6) But a flow would well up from the ground and water the whole surface of the earth**: An alternate translation is: "But there went up a mist from the earth, and watered the whole surface of the ground." As long as the earth is waiting for man to appear, there is no rain. The earth's vitality is maintained only through a mist. Before the arrival of man, the vitality of the world is ephemeral at best.

### 2.2. God Creates Man (2:7)

ז וַיִּיצֶר יְהוָה אֱלֹהִים אֶת־הָאָדָם עָפָר מִן־הָאֲדָמָה
וַיִּפַּח בְּאַפָּיו נִשְׁמַת חַיִּים וַיְהִי הָאָדָם לְנֶפֶשׁ חַיָּה:

*(7) the Lord God formed man from the dust of the earth. He blew into his nostrils the breath of life, and man became a living being.*

**(7) ... From the dust of the earth. He blew into his nostrils the breath of life:** The "dust of the earth" - the physical essence of nature - unites with the breath of life that the Lord "blows into his nostrils," i.e., with man's Divine soul. Only then does Adam become a living being.

Both of these components in man are Divine. Therefore, any disregard for material life, any attitude that is concerned "only with the spiritual," cannot lead to a full life for mankind or for any person.

### 2.3. The Lord Plants a Garden (2:8-9)

ח וַיִּטַּע יְהֹוָה אֱלֹהִים גַּן־בְּעֵדֶן מִקֶּדֶם וַיָּשֶׂם שָׁם אֶת־
הָאָדָם אֲשֶׁר יָצָר: ט וַיַּצְמַח יְהֹוָה אֱלֹהִים מִן־הָאֲדָמָה
כָּל־עֵץ נֶחְמָד לְמַרְאֶה וְטוֹב לְמַאֲכָל וְעֵץ הַחַיִּים בְּתוֹךְ
הַגָּן וְעֵץ הַדַּעַת טוֹב וָרָע:

*(8) The Lord God planted a garden in Eden, in the east, and placed there the man whom He had formed.*
*(9) And from the ground the Lord God caused to grow every tree that was pleasing to the sight and good for food, with the tree of life in the middle of the garden, and the tree of knowledge of good and bad.*

**(8) The Lord God planted a garden in Eden**: Eden and the garden of Eden are distinct concepts. In the next verse (Gen. 2:10) the text says, "A river issues from Eden to water the garden." I.e., the garden is located near Eden, adjacent to it.

A garden is a space where trees grow, from which visitors to the garden can derive sustenance. Eden (Hebrew, *eiden*, literally "pleasure, elegance, finesse, consummate perfection") is the source of water and vitality that feeds the garden.

**(8) And placed there the man whom He had formed**: God puts Adam in the Garden, but not in Eden. Thus, Adam was originally placed not in paradise itself, but only on the threshold of paradise.

And now two paths lie before him. Adam can advance to Eden, to a more sublime region of the universe. Or he can be expelled from the garden into the outside world.

Given that human history has taken the second path, the task of humanity is not merely to return to the garden, but to finally reach Eden.

**(9) Every tree that was pleasing to the sight and good for food, with the tree of life in the middle of the garden, and the tree of knowledge of good and bad**: All the trees in the garden were "pleasing to the sight and good for food" – including the tree of life and the tree of knowledge of good and bad.

In later sections we will explain in detail that Adam's problem was not about eating from the tree of knowledge. A thirst for knowledge of good and bad is by no means sinful. On the contrary – it is the realization of the Divine plan.

The problem, however, was that Adam acquired knowledge of good and bad before he was permitted to do so. For all knowledge there is a proper time. It was premature knowledge that led to the breakdown of the system, and to Adam and Eve's expulsion from the garden.

**With the tree of life in the middle of the garden, and the tree of knowledge of good and bad:** These two trees correspond to man's two most driving passions, which were also second Adam's two greatest objects of fear and centers of attraction: the passion for personal immortality, and the passion for essential knowledge (that is, such knowledge of good and bad that had the power to alter and advance Adam as a person).

Both of these passions distinguish him from the first Adam, who had no such aspirations.

The Adam of the first Creation story represents, more likely, not just an individual human being, but an entire race – all of humanity. From the very beginning he is focused on being fertile and increasing, as God had commanded him to do (Gen. 1:28), and thus he views himself and his descendants as an indivisible unit. He therefore has no reason to fear his own personal mortality, because even after his death the race will live on.

Also, Adam of the first story has no passion for essential knowledge. Since he is a ruler and a leader, his only interest is in the technical knowledge that will enable him to successfully rule the kingdom. He is not interested in essential knowledge, which can change him as a person, but has only very limited practical value.

In later sections we will explore the difference between first Adam and second Adam in greater detail.

## 2.4. The Rivers that Issue from Eden (2:10-14)

י וְנָהָר יֹצֵא מֵעֵדֶן לְהַשְׁקוֹת אֶת־הַגָּן וּמִשָּׁם יִפָּרֵד וְהָיָה לְאַרְבָּעָה רָאשִׁים: יא שֵׁם הָאֶחָד פִּישׁוֹן הוּא הַסֹּבֵב אֵת כָּל־אֶרֶץ הַחֲוִילָה אֲשֶׁר־שָׁם הַזָּהָב: יב וּזְהַב הָאָרֶץ הַהִוא טוֹב שָׁם הַבְּדֹלַח וְאֶבֶן הַשֹּׁהַם: יג וְשֵׁם־הַנָּהָר הַשֵּׁנִי גִּיחוֹן הוּא הַסּוֹבֵב אֵת כָּל־אֶרֶץ כּוּשׁ: יד וְשֵׁם הַנָּהָר הַשְּׁלִישִׁי חִדֶּקֶל הוּא הַהֹלֵךְ קִדְמַת אַשּׁוּר וְהַנָּהָר הָרְבִיעִי הוּא פְרָת:

*(10) A river issues from Eden to water the garden, and it then divides and becomes four branches. (11) The name of the first is Pishon, the one that*

*winds through the whole land of Havilah, where the gold is.*

*(12) (The gold of that land is good; bdellium is there, and lapis lazuli.)*

*(13) The name of the second river is Gihon, the one that winds through the whole land of Cush.*

*(14) The name of the third river is Tigris, the one that flows east of Asshur. And the fourth river is the Euphrates.*

**(10) A river issues from Eden:** We might be puzzled to find that here in the midst of the story of Creation, while the universe and man are still being formed, there is an unexpected interpolation of "metaphysical geography" – the mention of the rivers of Egypt and Mesopotamia.

In Jewish tradition the expression "to drink of the river's waters" has also a figurative meaning: to feed on the culture and vitality of a given nation or country. Thus, this verse is teaching us more than geography. It is teaching us that the cultural sources that later appeared in Egypt and Babylonia in fact originated much earlier, in the garden of Eden, during mankind's primordial existence there. Those cultures are offshoots of the "river" that issues from Eden.

In the story of Abraham, later in this book of Genesis, the integration of these fundamental world cultures into Jewish tradition will be considered in greater detail, as a topic in its own right.

(Of course, there is no point in trying to identify the actual location of Eden based on the descriptions here of these rivers. The story of the Creation is not intended as a geography lesson. Rather, it is a description of the internal spiritual structure that underlies the universe and all of human life within it.)

**(10) A river issues from Eden to water the garden:** The source of the water is Eden; the garden only draws nourishment from it. Thus, the garden is not the highest point. Eden is on a higher level than the garden.

**And it then divides and becomes four branches**: Only one river flows out of Eden, and its unity is preserved in the garden. But that unity then terminates, and four main rivers are formed instead – that is, the sources of four different directions taken by human civilization.

**(11-12) The name of the first is Pishon, the one that winds through the whole land of Havilah, where the gold is. (The gold of that land is good; bdellium is there, and lapis lazuli)**: Opinions differ in Jewish tradition concerning the identification of this river, Pishon. Some say it is the White Nile, but according to others (e.g., Josephus Flavius) it is the Indus or the Ganges. If so, Pishon is the source of Indian civilization, in which, as this verse tells us, gold and precious stones play a particularly important role (as compared, say, with Egypt and Mesopotamia).

**(13) The name of the second river is Gihon:** Jewish Tradition identifies Gihon with the Nile. Egypt is thus the second of the fundamental civilizations of mankind.

**The one that winds through the whole land of Cush:** Cush is Ethiopia (or perhaps even the whole of northeast Africa). The sources of the Nile are located there.

**(14) The name of the third river is Tigris, the one that flows east of Asshur:** Asshur is Assyria. This is the third of the four fundamental world civilizations. Along with Babylon, it is mentioned later in the book of Genesis in connection with the resettlement of nations immediately after the Flood (Gen. 10:10-11).

**And the fourth river is the Euphrates:** Babylonian civilization is very closely associated with the Euphrates.

## 2.5. Adam and the Fruits of the Garden (2:15-17)

טו וַיִּקַּח יְהֹוָה אֱלֹהִים אֶת־הָאָדָם וַיַּנִּחֵהוּ בְגַן־עֵדֶן לְעָבְדָהּ וּלְשָׁמְרָהּ: טז וַיְצַו יְהֹוָה אֱלֹהִים עַל־הָאָדָם לֵאמֹר מִכֹּל עֵץ־הַגָּן אָכֹל תֹּאכֵל: יז וּמֵעֵץ הַדַּעַת טוֹב וָרָע לֹא תֹאכַל מִמֶּנּוּ כִּי בְּיוֹם אֲכָלְךָ מִמֶּנּוּ מוֹת תָּמוּת:

*(15) The Lord God took the man and placed him in the garden of Eden, to till it and tend it.*
*(16) And the Lord God commanded the man, saying, "Of every tree of the garden you are free to eat;*
*(17) but as for the tree of knowledge of good and bad, you must not eat of it; for as soon as you eat of it, you shall die."*

**(15) The Lord God took the man and placed him in the garden of Eden, to till it and tend it**: Literally, "to work it and to guard it." Adam does not sit idle in paradise. He tills the garden, tends it and protects it.

And yet, as Adam and Eve are expelled from the garden God tells Adam (Gen. 3:19): "By the sweat of your brow shall you get bread to eat." And then we read, "So the Lord God banished him from the garden of Eden, to till the soil from which he was taken" (Gen. 3:23). This shows that the work that Adam performed in the garden prior to the expulsion was not "by the sweat of his brow" – it was intellectual, not physical work. As already noted, Adam had no need of physical strength to till and tend the garden. He did so through his spiritual and intellectual powers.

But after Adam is expelled from the garden, powers of the mind are not enough. He must then toil physically – "by the sweat of his brow."

**To till it and tend it:** "Tend it" here in the Hebrew is *leshom-rah*, "to guard it." Adam must protect the garden not from the serpent or from the other animals, who pose no actual threat to the garden. The only creature on earth capable of destroying the garden is Adam himself. When he later violates God's instructions, the garden will cease to exist for him. Thus, the greatest potential for destroying it lies with Adam. He must guard and protect the garden, first and foremost, from *himself*.

The commandment to preserve and protect the garden was given not only to Adam at the metaphysical level, but as an instruction to the entire human race. This is the ecological principle of protecting all of the environment from man's destructive influences. We must therefore regard such protection as a religious value and a Divine commandment.

But at the same time, it is essential that we do not absolutize the ecological principle. It must be properly balanced against the opposing point of view by incorporating it into the comprehensive structure of all the values that we uphold. God commands man not only to protect nature (the "garden"), but also to build civilization – to "fill the earth, master it, rule... all the living things that creep on earth" (Gen. 1:28). In other words, to transform the earth. This entails a generally moderate approach to ecology that balances man's technological prowess for transforming the world against the need to protect and preserve the environment. Judaism rejects the kind of environmental extremism that exalts virgin, unspoiled nature to the detriment of technological progress and the advancement of human civilization.

**(16) And the Lord God commanded the man, saying, "Of every tree of the garden you are free to eat:** The Hebrew here for "you are free to eat" is *achol tochel*. Such reduplicated phraseology appears often in the Torah, and is difficult to capture in translation, but following convention, those two words here would be translated as "you shall surely eat." Or, in this case, even more forcefully: "Of every tree of the garden you must eat!" It is not merely permission, but an actual command to eat from every other tree except this one.

The positive command to eat from every tree of the garden (rather than the prohibition of eating from the tree of knowledge of good and bad) is in fact the very first commandment that Adam receives. Here, eating from those trees is meant in a metaphorical sense. Through cognition, study, and assimilation of the full diversity of the external world man is commanded to make it a part of himself. This is the meaning of God's command to Adam to eat the fruits of every tree of the garden.

It was in acquiring this knowledge – "eating of every tree" – that Adam's work in the garden consisted. And since the garden was the place where God's presence was manifest, the connection between the material and the spiritual was likewise manifested there in a very explicit form. Adam's spiritual and intellectual work of comprehending the world was immediately realized also on the material level.

In the popular conception paradise is a place of relaxation. But the Jewish idea is quite different. A person who finds himself in paradise is occupied with work – intellectual work.

Are peace and idleness really the ideal paradise? If they are, one can die there of boredom! Rather, paradise must be a place where one works and creates ("to till and tend the garden"). But it is not physically strenuous work. It is enough there to experience, to devise, to understand, and to invent. The material result, the embodiment of those efforts, is realized spontaneously.

**(17) But as for the tree of knowledge of good and bad, you must not eat of it:** Adam was permitted to partake of almost every branch of knowledge ("every tree"). Only this one tree was forbidden to him. And yet, the meaning of the prohibition is not explained. To Adam, who has set his sights on acquiring knowledge of every kind, it is incomprehensible. The prohibition is therefore a major problem for him.

**For as soon as you eat of it, you shall die":** Literally, "For on the [very] day you eat from it, you shall die." Adam did in fact eat the fruit of that tree, the tree of the knowledge of good and bad, but he did not die that day. We must therefore understand "you shall die" to mean, "you will become mortal" – which did actually happen immediately, as soon as he transgressed the Divine command.

***

Having prohibited Adam from partaking of the tree of knowledge of good and bad, God nonetheless does not at this stage declare the tree of life likewise off-limits to Adam, although this does occur later (Gen. 3:22-24). There are a number of options for understanding this, of which we offer two:

- The two trees are essentially one and the same tree. The aspect of knowledge of good and bad was actually a "portal" to the discovery of its aspect as the tree of life.
- Before Adam's fall, the tree of life was not forbidden to man. That became necessary only because of the distortion of man's nature that arose as the result of his eating prematurely from the tree of knowledge of good and bad.

## 2.6. The Creation of Woman (2:18-25)

יח וַיֹּאמֶר יְהֹוָה אֱלֹהִים לֹא־טוֹב הֱיוֹת הָאָדָם לְבַדּוֹ אֶעֱשֶׂה־לּוֹ עֵזֶר כְּנֶגְדּוֹ: יט וַיִּצֶר יְהֹוָה אֱלֹהִים מִן־ הָאֲדָמָה כָּל־חַיַּת הַשָּׂדֶה וְאֵת כָּל־עוֹף הַשָּׁמַיִם וַיָּבֵא אֶל־הָאָדָם לִרְאוֹת מַה־יִּקְרָא־לוֹ וְכֹל אֲשֶׁר יִקְרָא־לוֹ הָאָדָם נֶפֶשׁ חַיָּה הוּא שְׁמוֹ: כ וַיִּקְרָא הָאָדָם שֵׁמוֹת לְכָל־הַבְּהֵמָה וּלְעוֹף הַשָּׁמַיִם וּלְכֹל חַיַּת הַשָּׂדֶה וּלְאָדָם לֹא־מָצָא עֵזֶר כְּנֶגְדּוֹ: כא וַיַּפֵּל יְהֹוָה אֱלֹהִים | תַּרְדֵּמָה עַל־הָאָדָם וַיִּישָׁן וַיִּקַּח אַחַת מִצַּלְעֹתָיו וַיִּסְגֹּר בָּשָׂר תַּחְתֶּנָּה: כב וַיִּבֶן יְהֹוָה אֱלֹהִים | אֶת־הַצֵּלָע אֲשֶׁר־לָקַח מִן־הָאָדָם לְאִשָּׁה וַיְבִאֶהָ אֶל־הָאָדָם: כג וַיֹּאמֶר הָאָדָם זֹאת הַפַּעַם עֶצֶם מֵעֲצָמַי וּבָשָׂר מִבְּשָׂרִי לְזֹאת יִקָּרֵא אִשָּׁה כִּי מֵאִישׁ לֻקֳחָה־זֹּאת: כד עַל־כֵּן יַעֲזָב־אִישׁ אֶת־ אָבִיו וְאֶת־אִמּוֹ וְדָבַק בְּאִשְׁתּוֹ וְהָיוּ לְבָשָׂר אֶחָד: כה וַיִּהְיוּ שְׁנֵיהֶם עֲרוּמִּים הָאָדָם וְאִשְׁתּוֹ וְלֹא יִתְבֹּשָׁשׁוּ:

*(18) The Lord God said, "It is not good for man
to be alone; I will make a fitting helper for him."
(19) And the Lord God formed out of the earth all
the wild beasts and all the birds of the sky, and
brought them to the man to see what he would
call them; and whatever the man called each
living creature, that would be its name.
(20) And the man gave names to all the cattle
and to the birds of the sky and to all the wild
beasts; but for Adam no fitting helper was found.
(21) So the Lord God cast a deep sleep upon the
man; and, while he slept, He took one of his ribs
and closed up the flesh at that spot.
(22) And the Lord God fashioned the rib that He
had taken from the man into a woman; and He
brought her to the man.
(23) Then the man said, "This one at last
Is bone of my bones
And flesh of my flesh.
This one shall be called Woman,
For from man was she taken."
(24) Hence a man leaves his father and mother
and clings to his wife, so that they become one
flesh.
(25) The two of them were naked, the man and
his wife, yet they felt no shame.*

**(18) The Lord God said, "It is not good for man to be
alone"**: This might be translated very literally as "Being is
not good [when] a person is alone." The problem is not that
loneliness is uncomfortable, or that a person is bored without company, although that too is true. No, the problem is

much deeper. If Adam is alone, it means that all of existence is improperly constructed and arranged.

The Midrash explains: God inhabits the upper worlds alone. Thus, if Adam likewise is to be alone in the lower worlds, he will fancy himself a complete and perfect reflection of God.

Man can properly develop only through plurality and diversity, not through "the one and only correct point of view."

**(18) It is not good for man to be alone:** This is a problem only for Adam of the second Creation story. Adam of the first story is always busy transforming the world around him, and is thus never alone. Moreover, about first Adam we read, "And God created man in His image … male and female He created them" (Gen. 1:27). In the first story, Eve was created immediately, together with Adam. Loneliness is a problem only for second Adam, because he is focused on acquiring knowledge, and on the inner world of his own soul.

Note too that the first Creation story says about every aspect of the universe, "And God saw that this was good." But in the second story we find from the very beginning quite the opposite assessment, "It is not good" for man to be alone.

The world of the first story is positive from the very start, and remains so throughout. Adam lives in harmony with his surroundings and rules over them. Conversely, the world of the second story is problematic from the start. It very soon devolves into conflict, and ends with a tragic exile.

**I will make a fitting helper for him**: The Hebrew is *eizer ke-negdo*. The Hebrew word *neged* can mean "correspondingly, in like manner, to the same extent." Thus the translation given here, "a fitting helper."

But *neged* just as often means "against, in opposition to." According to that sense of the word, the literal meaning of *eizer ke-negdo* is "a helper who opposes him" (or, a "helper-opponent"). Paradoxically, the partners of a couple help each other by virtue of their opposition. The opposition is itself the help.

A counterbalance is needed in any system, whether personal, familial, social, or even mechanical. Without that opposition equilibrium will be lacking – in the system itself, and in the people who depend on it. In order for Adam to develop and advance, a counterbalance is therefore created for him within the family – a "helper-opponent."

(Of course, everything said about Adam in this context applies equally to both men and women, because the word *haadam* means a person, i.e., a human being, whether male or female.)

**(19) And the Lord God formed out of the earth all the wild beasts and all the birds of the sky:** After God has spoken of Adam's need for a helper-opponent, we would have expected to read next about the creation of Eve. But first the Torah tells us about the creation of animals.

**And brought them to the man to see what he would call them:** As already noted, any name reflects not just the object itself, but the manner in which people relate to it. Thus, to name something or someone is to establish the type of connection it will have with other people and things.

**And whatever the man called each living creature, that would be its name:** In the first Creation story, the animal world existed before man and independently of him. But in the second story, the world is constructed such that it centers around mankind. The essence of the animals is therefore determined by the names that Adam gives them, the nature of the animals' connection to man, their function with respect to him.

**(20) And the man gave names to all the cattle and to the birds of the sky and to all the wild beasts:** Because Adam understood the precise relationship of each living creature to man, he was able to give them names.

**But for Adam no fitting helper was found:** Adam had to feel convinced based on his own experience that no animal could be his mate. Only after this experience of communicating with the world did Adam "grow up" – he became capable of having a relationship with a woman. Hence the narrative proceeds from there directly to the creation of Eve.

**(21) So the Lord God cast a deep sleep upon the man:** The operation of creating Eve from a part of Adam happens in a dream. In the course of any development process there are often stages that, although indispensable for achieving the result, are nonetheless difficult for a person to witness directly. If he sees such stages in all their explicit detail, he cannot perceive the results normally later. Therefore, such critical stages of development must occur while hidden from the person's consciousness.

**He took one of his ribs and closed up the flesh at that spot:** Originally, Adam was complete and self-sufficient. But the flip side of self-sufficiency is unwillingness and unreadiness to advance and develop. In order to promote Adam's development, God removed one of his ribs, thus rendering him incomplete, and giving rise to a desire within him to find his missing part – his alter ego.

**(22) And the Lord God fashioned the rib that He had taken from the man into a woman; and He brought her to the man**: "Fashioned" here in the Hebrew is *vayiven* – literally, "built, constructed," from the Hebrew root *B-N-H*, associated also with the concept of *binah*, "intuition, discernment." Thus, in this verse the verb *vayiven* can also mean that by creating Eve and bringing her to Adam, God gave Adam an added dimension of understanding. A little later we will discuss the importance of this concept for understanding the Kabbalah's approach to the relationship between man and woman (see 8.4).

**(23) Then the man said, "This one at last:** With "at last," here Adam himself acknowledges the importance of his previous experiences for appreciating what he is now being given. Now that he is thoroughly convinced that the animals cannot not provide a mate for him, he is able to appreciate the creation of a mate from his very self.

**Is bone of my bones and flesh of my flesh. This one shall be called Woman, for from man was she taken:** It is from this initial unity that future compatibility can be created. If Adam's mate had been taken from a source completely separate and independent of him, that compatibility could not have come about.

**This one shall be called Woman, for from man was she taken":** Only at this moment do the concepts of man and woman appear. These go beyond the mere biological differences between the sexes as emphasized in the first Creation story (see Gen. 1:27).

**Woman:** The Hebrew word *ishah* can mean either "woman" or "wife."

Adam continues to give names to the entities of the surrounding world, and so he names his mate as well. However, it is not a proper name, but a functional one, similar to Adam's earlier assessment of the animals with respect to himself. This approach, which perceives Woman only in terms of her function, shows that Adam does not yet see her as an independent personality. In the near future, this mistake will lead to the problem of the tree of knowledge of good and bad.

Only during the process of his expulsion from the garden will Adam perceive his relationship to his wife in a new light, and he will give her the proper name Eve (*Chavah*).

**(24) And clings to his wife, so that they become one flesh:** Jewish tradition understands this "clinging" to mean intimate relations, and "become one flesh" as meaning birth of a child. I.e., together they create common flesh – a new human being. According to this interpretation, marriage alone is not "clinging" that makes a couple "one flesh," and can be dissolved.

In the Christian view, however, the words "so that they become one flesh" are often understood as referring to marriage, and not only to bearing children. This view therefore deems marriage indissoluble.

**Hence a man leaves his father and mother and clings to his wife, so that they become one flesh**: This verses uses the same terminology as the previous one, "man" and "woman." (As already mentioned, *ishah* can mean either "woman" or "wife.") Thus it continues to express Adam's awareness of the relationship between himself and his wife.

A straightforward reading of the text sees these words not as a continuation of the direct quote from Adam, but an idea articulated by God: "I, the Almighty, have arranged that a man leaves his parental home, unites with his wife, and bears children with her. This assures continuity of the generations within the human race."

The Midrash, however, understands these words as spoken by Adam based on his own experience – that immediately after God brought Woman to Adam (Gen. 1: 22), he "clung" to her, i.e., entered into an intimate relationship with her, and they "became one flesh" – she gave birth to a child (Cain). It was then that Adam understood and acknowledged the fact of procreation as the path of human development, which is what he is describing in this verse.

Note too that since there is no gap between cognition and realization in the garden, there is also no gestation period – the interval between "knowing" a spouse and having children. In subsequent sections we will examine this idea in greater detail.

**(25) The two of them were naked, the man and his wife, yet they felt no shame:** As spouses, they had no reason whatsoever to feel shame at each other's nakedness. Any such shame they might have felt was shame before God. And in fact, after they partake of the fruit of the tree of knowledge of good and bad, "then the eyes of both of them were opened and they perceived that they were naked; and ... hid from the Lord God among the trees of the garden" (Gen. 3:8).

Accordingly, the Midrash understands this absence of shame at being naked as referring not only to their physical nakedness, but also the psychological aspect – a state of "I have nothing to hide." And likewise, their shame and their need to be clothed meant that something new had happened that they did indeed need to hide.

Thus, their need to be clothed arose not as the result of their knowledge of good and bad, but because they had violated God's commandment. So long as they were not guilty of any wrongdoing, they are had no reason to be ashamed and nothing to hide from the world. This was their "nakedness." But after transgressing, they cannot be fully transparent to the outer world. They need clothes.

Chapter 3

# The Episode of the Tree of Knowledge of Good and Evil

## 3.1. The Fall of Man: His First Sin (3:1-8)

א וְהַנָּחָשׁ הָיָה עָרוּם מִכֹּל חַיַּת הַשָּׂדֶה אֲשֶׁר עָשָׂה יְהֹוָה
אֱלֹהִים וַיֹּאמֶר אֶל־הָאִשָּׁה אַף כִּי־אָמַר אֱלֹהִים לֹא
תֹאכְלוּ מִכֹּל עֵץ הַגָּן: ב וַתֹּאמֶר הָאִשָּׁה אֶל־הַנָּחָשׁ מִפְּרִי
עֵץ־הַגָּן נֹאכֵל: ג וּמִפְּרִי הָעֵץ אֲשֶׁר בְּתוֹךְ־הַגָּן אָמַר
אֱלֹהִים לֹא תֹאכְלוּ מִמֶּנּוּ וְלֹא תִגְּעוּ בּוֹ פֶּן־תְּמֻתוּן:
ד וַיֹּאמֶר הַנָּחָשׁ אֶל־הָאִשָּׁה לֹא־מוֹת תְּמֻתוּן: ה כִּי
יֹדֵעַ אֱלֹהִים כִּי בְּיוֹם אֲכָלְכֶם מִמֶּנּוּ וְנִפְקְחוּ עֵינֵיכֶם
וִהְיִיתֶם כֵּאלֹהִים יֹדְעֵי טוֹב וָרָע: ו וַתֵּרֶא הָאִשָּׁה כִּי
טוֹב הָעֵץ לְמַאֲכָל וְכִי תַאֲוָה־הוּא לָעֵינַיִם וְנֶחְמָד הָעֵץ
לְהַשְׂכִּיל וַתִּקַּח מִפִּרְיוֹ וַתֹּאכַל וַתִּתֵּן גַּם־לְאִישָׁהּ עִמָּהּ
וַיֹּאכַל: ז וַתִּפָּקַחְנָה עֵינֵי שְׁנֵיהֶם וַיֵּדְעוּ כִּי עֵירֻמִּם הֵם
וַיִּתְפְּרוּ עֲלֵה תְאֵנָה וַיַּעֲשׂוּ לָהֶם חֲגֹרֹת: ח וַיִּשְׁמְעוּ אֶת־
קוֹל יְהֹוָה אֱלֹהִים מִתְהַלֵּךְ בַּגָּן לְרוּחַ הַיּוֹם וַיִּתְחַבֵּא
הָאָדָם וְאִשְׁתּוֹ מִפְּנֵי יְהֹוָה אֱלֹהִים בְּתוֹךְ עֵץ הַגָּן:

*(3:1) Now the serpent was the shrewdest of all the wild beasts that the Lord God had made. He said*

*to the woman, "Did God really say: You shall not eat of any tree of the garden?"*

*(2) The woman replied to the serpent, "We may eat of the fruit of the other trees of the garden.*

*(3) It is only about fruit of the tree in the middle of the garden that God said: 'You shall not eat of it or touch it, lest you die.'"*

*(4) And the serpent said to the woman, "You are not going to die,*

*(5) but God knows that as soon as you eat of it your eyes will be opened and you will be like divine beings who know good and bad."*

*(6) When the woman saw that the tree was good for eating and a delight to the eyes, and that the tree was desirable as a source of wisdom, she took of its fruit and ate. She also gave some to her husband, and he ate.*

*(7) Then the eyes of both of them were opened and they perceived that they were naked; and they sewed together fig leaves and made themselves loincloths.*

*(8) They heard the sound of the Lord God moving about in the garden at the breezy time of day; and the man and his wife hid from the Lord God among the trees of the garden.*

**(3:1) The serpent:** As already noted, the entire Creation story of Genesis is meant to be understood not literally but allegorically. This applies, in particular, to the episode of the serpent and Adam and his wife's transgression of eating the fruit of the tree of knowledge of good and bad.

One point that is paramount in this regard is that Jewish

tradition considers the serpent not a seducer from the outside, but the personification of the "evil inclination" that lurks within every human being. The conversation in the garden with the "serpent" represents the internal dialogue of every person with his or her own passions.

It is not merely a story of seduction and deception. Rather, the story is emphasizing that God created man as a complex and internally contradictory being, because it is those very traits that give man the capacity to develop. And an essential aspect of that complexity is that man is curious – he craves what is forbidden. He is very good at convincing himself of what he wants to believe, and that he should behave badly. All this is very problematic, of course, but necessary for man's development. And those are the qualities that the serpent personifies – man's "evil inclination."

In the Torah's account of the episode, only the woman speaks directly with the serpent. But, as noted, Adam at this stage still considers his wife an inseparable extension of himself (he does not see her as her own independent person). The world's first couple therefore engages in this dialogue with the serpent together, albeit from the female point of view.

**Now the serpent was the shrewdest:** Except for a slight difference in vocalization, *arum*, the Hebrew word used here for "shrewd," is the same as the word for naked, "*arom.*" In all events, both words are spelled the same, they are homonyms. In this chapter that word is used to describe Adam and his wife's nakedness (Gen. 2:25), and also the serpent's shrewdness (Gen. 3:1, which immediately follows Gen. 2:25). Thus, the Torah is telling us quite clearly that there is a connection between those two meanings of the word.

As already mentioned, Adam's nakedness meant, firstly, psychological nakedness. At that point he still had nothing to hide. Because no one posed any threat to Adam, he had no need to adopt a defensive stance. This was, as it were, the kind of "primitive naivete" that leaves a person unprepared for any deception. And therefore, even the simplest trickery (perpetrated by the person's own inner evil inclination) leads immediately to a negative result – in this case a violation of a Divine command.

Adam and his wife come to understand that such naivete is dangerous ("Then the eyes of both of them were opened and they perceived that they were naked" – Gen. 3:7), because it leaves a person vulnerable to treachery. And so they now understand that they need "clothes."

It is important to note that while Adam was in the garden, the process of his creation was not yet complete. Adam and his wife became ordinary people in the full sense only after their expulsion from the garden. But here man's formation is still a work in progress, and he himself participates actively in that process.

**Now the serpent was the shrewdest of all the wild beasts that the Lord God had made:** He was the shrewdest *of all the wild beasts* – but not more shrewd than human beings. Although the serpent was ultimately able to "outwit" the humans, this was not a part of the plan from the outset. And this means that man is capable of resisting the serpent – he can in fact cope with his "evil inclination."

**He said to the woman:** The serpent addresses himself not to Adam, but to Adam's wife. Or, more precisely, he appeals to the feminine side of the world's first human couple. There are several possible reasons for this:
- The woman is more emotional, and thus easier to persuade.

- Since Adam's wife was created after he had already received the commandment not to eat from the tree of knowledge of good and bad, she knows of this prohibition only from Adam, not directly from God. She is therefore more apt to disregard its importance.

The woman's perception of this commandment is itself the first example in human history of a "religious tradition." It thus incorporates within itself all the attendant shortcomings of tradition, as compared with teachings received directly from God.

**"Did God really say: You shall not eat of any tree of the garden?":** The Torah's presentation here of the serpent's words is a classic example of the techniques of deception (including also self-deception). This method, which has remained substantially unchanged through the ages, has been the method of choice for deceivers and seducers in every era.

Firstly, the serpent does not explicitly encourage the woman to violate the prohibition. He begins with generally amiable conversation, showing interest in people's problems, sympathizing with them and expressing, as it were, a genuine desire to help them. His primary tactic is to exaggerate the prohibition in order to make it seem awkward and unnatural. Before the serpent is finished, God is already a ruthless autocrat who forbids people from partaking of the fruit of any and all trees. But at the same time the serpent never says any of this in so many words; he only creates this mood and this image through his adept use of well-phrased leading questions.

The goal of such a provocative dialogue is to force the human to make excuses. As soon as the woman becomes defensive, she will almost certainly err in some detail. The attack then exploits that small mistake so as to discredit and delegitimize the system in its entirety.

**(2) The woman replied to the serpent, "We may eat of the fruit of the other trees of the garden:** Since the serpent conducts himself like a friend, the woman too responds to him kindly, hesitant to refute his words head-on. She does not say, "All that is a lie," but formulates her response in positive terms: "The situation is not nearly as bad as you say." But this desire on her part to speak gently and avoid conflict itself increases the likelihood that she will commit a serious error.

**(3) It is only about fruit of the tree in the middle of the garden that God said: 'You shall not eat of it or touch it, lest you die' ":** Although she does not identify this tree by name, it is for her "the tree in the middle of the Garden" – at the very center of her attention.

**God said: 'You shall not eat of it or touch it, lest you die':** The fact is that God never forbade touching the tree. The woman is exaggerating the prohibition. Because she is defending herself, she errs and exaggerates.

**(4) And the serpent said to the woman, "You are not going to die:** In order to demolish the prohibition the serpent must first remove any fear of punishment.

The Midrash adds the following. In order to make his refutation of the Divine word more convincing to the woman, the serpent actually pushed her against the tree. When she touched it and nothing untoward happened, the serpent said: "You stated that touching the tree would cause death, but as you can see, no such thing has happened. And that means that everything else that you were saying is also wrong. You can eat the tree's fruit as well with no ill effects." Thus, when the woman added her own strictures to God's words, this only worked against her.

The meaning of this midrash is that a person's "evil inclination" quickly detects even the lesser inaccuracies in his position, and seeks, using those errors as examples, to demonstrate that he is wrong about the overall picture as well.

The Midrash is also teaching us not to confuse the essence of a thing with "additions" grafted on to it for its protection. In Jewish tradition (and, incidentally, in many other religious and social frameworks as well), the principle of "building a fence around the law" is very common. The "fence" is a set of supplemental prohibitions designed to distance a person from the possibility of a yet more serious violation of a core precept. The Midrash is not opposed to the concept itself of building that fence around the law, but it is teaching us the importance of distinguishing between the law itself, and the fence built around the law to protect it.

**(5) But God knows that as soon as you eat of it your eyes will be opened and you will be like divine beings who know good and bad":** After removing all fear of the consequences of a violation, the serpent must now make the violation itself attractive.

In fact, the serpent spoke the truth. But it was only a partial truth. By eating the fruit of the tree of knowledge, Adam did indeed acquire Divine qualities. But Adam and his wife, by "illicitly acquiring" elevated levels of knowledge, destroyed their ability to cope with the special powers that they possessed in the garden, and thus inexorably doomed themselves to expulsion. The serpent, however, said nothing about that aspect.

Thus, the main deception perpetrated by the serpent on Adam and his wife consisted, essentially, of presenting elements of partial truth as the whole truth. (He spoke of the spiritual qualities that they would acquire by eating the fruit, but he did not inform them what the full consequences would be.)

Throughout the future history of mankind, learning how to deal with this form of deception will be essential to correcting Adam's error in the garden. In any situation one must strive to grasp the complete picture, rather than focusing on only its most alluring aspects. We must analyze the full consequence of our actions, and not get carried away by catchy slogans. This is an important element of growth and maturation for every individual, and no less so for humanity as a whole.

**Your eyes will be opened:** This much is undoubtedly true: a person who has experienced good and bad, and knows the difference between them, sees the world in a completely different way.

**And you will be like divine beings:** But this is also true: knowledge of good and bad brings a person closer to God. It is important to note that the desire to be like God is one of man's most compelling desires, and the serpent uses this fact to his advantage.

**(6) When the woman saw:** I.e., she understood and acknowledged the correctness of the serpent's arguments.

**That the tree was good for eating and a delight to the eyes, and that the tree was desirable as a source of wisdom**: Invariably, in any object of desire three characteristics are especially attractive to people: that it is tasty, that it is beautiful, and that it is interesting.

**She took of its fruit and ate:** We might have expected the woman to first discuss the matter with Adam. Such a discussion could have brought to light the very points that the serpent was so careful to hide. But she did not do so.

Engaging in a discussion of relevant issues, even those that at first seem quite "obvious," will very often reveal potential problems, and prevent serious mistakes in judgment.

**She also gave some to her husband, and he ate**: The English translation here has elided one additional word that appears in the Hebrew – *immah*, "with her." Thus, the literal translation is: "She also gave [some] to her husband *with her*, and he ate."

But "with her" seems superfluous here (which is why the translation has chosen to omit it.) However, we accept as a general principle that there is no superfluous word (or even letter) in the Torah. It must be assumed that a word that appears superfluous on its face is in fact imparting some additional level of meaning to the text. And so it is in this case.

The Midrash explains: Adam's wife offered Adam the fruit precisely at the moment when he was "with her" – that is, engaged with her in intimate relations. At such a moment, Adam was incapable of rationally discussing the problem that his wife had raised. (As already noted, Adam and his wife began their sexual relationship immediately, even before they had eaten the fruit of the tree of knowledge of good and bad.)

But there is another possible interpretation of *immah*,

"with her," namely: Adam did not refuse his wife's offer, because he considered the two of them a single, indivisible unit – he was "with her." As noted earlier, Adam at this stage calls her "the woman," i.e., he relates to her and refers to her by function: "Then the man said, 'This one at last is bone of my bones and flesh of my flesh. This one shall be called Woman, for from man was she taken'" (Gen. 2:23). He sees his wife as an extension of himself – flesh of his flesh, like his own hand, say, or leg. They act as a single unit. It she eats the fruit, then he eats "with her," and there is no need for any discussion about it.

According to either of the two interpretations of "with her," the problem is rooted in the fundamental absence of dialogue between Adam and his wife. In terms of modern psychology, Adam and Eve's relationship is based on a "natural" romantic love between "soul mates" who need one another to be complete (as opposed to a conscious love, a relationship that is created in a dialogue – purposefully, decisively, and with intention). Romantic love, or romance, although exalted and extolled by the Romanticism, is by no means seen here as an ideal.

**(7) Then the eyes of both of them were opened and they perceived that they were naked ... and made themselves loincloths**: The serpent had said that their eyes would be opened, and they would be like divine beings who know good and bad. And both of those points were actually realized. But hardly in the manner that the woman was expecting based on the serpent's words. The "opening of the eyes" led to the shame of nakedness, and the unlawful path of becoming like God led to their expulsion from the garden.

As already noted, they have no reason to be ashamed of physical nudity, since they are husband and wife, and there is no one else with them in the garden. Hence, the "perception of nakedness" mentioned here is about spiritual and psychological, not physical, nakedness.

By partaking of the fruit of the tree of knowledge of good and bad, they had "eaten" the understanding of good and evil – it entered into them and became an actual part of them. (A little later, using the terminology of the Kabbalah, we will significantly expand on this idea.) The result was that their "eyes were opened" to the nature of good and bad. They experienced the sensation of good and bad – they were able to feel how good can become bad and vice versa. This is the true "opening of the eyes" – the ability to feel and experience the world's complexity and multi-faceted versatility.

At that point they "perceived that they were naked," i.e., psychologically naked with respect to this mixture of good and bad. Previously they had no need to clothe themselves – they conducted themselves openly and trustingly. But now they understood that in a complex world such openness is far too dangerous.

They need clothes, firstly, as a psychological defense, the kind that allows a person to stand in opposition to (i.e., to remain independent of) the world at large. Clothing validates the inviolability of their personal space, and removes them from the realm of the natural world. They become subjects, as it were, and not merely objects.

This need to clothe their psychological nakedness reflects a new awareness of their situation. They now understand that they were far too gullible with respect to the serpent. All this influences their desire to establish a "psychological defense," as expressed in the loincloths that they have now made for themselves.

Adam and his wife violated God's commandment because of the overwhelming sense of unity between them, which rendered any dialogue between them and any discussion of the problem superfluous and therefore impossible. Dialogue is possible only between two distinct interlocutors who still maintain some distance between themselves.

The purpose of the loincloths was to separate them from each other, to give each of them independence and subjectivity. They therefore covered their intimate organs, which was their point of strongest connection.

**They sewed together fig leaves:** The well-known idiom and image of a fig leaf as a cover of nakedness derives from this verse.

**They sewed together fig leaves and made themselves loincloths**: This is the first recorded action undertaken by man on his own initiative, with the goal of transforming the surrounding world. Before eating the fruit of the tree of knowledge of good and bad, Adam and his wife fit neatly into the situations and tasks that God (or the serpent) had established for them – i.e., the natural world, both external and internal. But now man's conflict with God and with nature has given him the impetus for independent creativity.

**(8) They heard the sound of the Lord God moving about in the garden:** The Hebrew, here translated as "sound," is *kol*, which more often means "voice." It was not God moving about, but His voice.

In other words, it was not God Himself passing through the garden, but the dissemination of the Divine voice, i.e., His message – Revelation. The entire period of Adam's stay in the garden represents the process of human development, an important part of which is dialogue with God.

**And the man and his wife hid:** It is natural for a human being to "hide from God." Dialogue with God is always difficult and painful, because it requires a person to examine and correct his shortcomings.

**And the man and his wife hid from the Lord God**: The verse below (Gen. 3:10) emphasizes that they were hiding because they realized that they were "naked," and were loath to have an encounter with God in such circumstances. Adam and his wife, after being burnt by their failure to live up to the previous Divine instruction, the prohibition of eating from the tree of knowledge of good and bad, are hardly looking for a new Revelation at this time. They are hiding from it.

After "his eyes were opened," man's relationship with God became more complicated. His previous childish attitude was simplistic but understandable: God is the source of everything good and right, and you just have to obey Him. But after a child has gone through a crisis and matured as the result of it, it is no longer easy for him to open up and relate to his parents.

Although Adam and his wife have violated the prohibition, at the same time they feel that they have made spiritual progress – their eyes have been opened. Does this mean that by forbidding them to eat that fruit God has misled them? And if so, how can they now believe in a new Revelation? The complete trust they had put in God seems to them now, in retrospect, very naive. But they have no new and better approach to replace it. The entire episode has thrown them for a loss, and all they can do is hide. A meeting with God is the last thing they want right now.

**Among the trees of the garden:** Actually, the Hebrew is not *be-toch atzei ha-gan*, "among the *trees* of the garden," plural, but be-toch etz ha-gan – literally, "among the *tree* of the garden." It means, of course, the one special tree – the tree whose fruit they had eaten in violation of God's commandment.

Adam and his wife hide from God as they delve ever deeper into the problems of knowing good and bad. That is, they ask and probe impenetrable questions about good and bad.

This is the classic method of hiding from God and avoiding a direct encounter with Him. Instead of engaging in dialogue, the person evades and postpones the inevitable, all the while convincing himself that he is well on the road to solving important metaphysical problems that are in fact inherently unsolvable.

## 3.2. The Trial, the Verdict, and the Sentence (3:9-21)

ט וַיִּקְרָא יְהֹוָה אֱלֹהִים אֶל־הָאָדָם וַיֹּאמֶר לוֹ אַיֶּכָּה:
י וַיֹּאמֶר אֶת־קֹלְךָ שָׁמַעְתִּי בַּגָּן וָאִירָא כִּי־עֵירֹם אָנֹכִי וָאֵחָבֵא: יא וַיֹּאמֶר מִי הִגִּיד לְךָ כִּי עֵירֹם אָתָּה הֲמִן־הָעֵץ אֲשֶׁר צִוִּיתִיךָ לְבִלְתִּי אֲכָל־מִמֶּנּוּ אָכָלְתָּ: יב וַיֹּאמֶר הָאָדָם הָאִשָּׁה אֲשֶׁר נָתַתָּה עִמָּדִי הִוא נָתְנָה־לִּי מִן־הָעֵץ וָאֹכֵל: יג וַיֹּאמֶר יְהֹוָה אֱלֹהִים לָאִשָּׁה מַה־זֹּאת עָשִׂית וַתֹּאמֶר הָאִשָּׁה הַנָּחָשׁ הִשִּׁיאַנִי וָאֹכֵל: יד וַיֹּאמֶר יְהֹוָה אֱלֹהִים | אֶל־הַנָּחָשׁ כִּי עָשִׂיתָ זֹּאת אָרוּר אַתָּה מִכָּל־הַבְּהֵמָה וּמִכֹּל חַיַּת הַשָּׂדֶה עַל־גְּחֹנְךָ תֵלֵךְ וְעָפָר תֹּאכַל כָּל־יְמֵי חַיֶּיךָ: טו וְאֵיבָה | אָשִׁית בֵּינְךָ וּבֵין הָאִשָּׁה וּבֵין זַרְעֲךָ וּבֵין זַרְעָהּ הוּא יְשׁוּפְךָ רֹאשׁ וְאַתָּה תְּשׁוּפֶנּוּ עָקֵב: טז אֶל־הָאִשָּׁה אָמַר הַרְבָּה אַרְבֶּה עִצְּבוֹנֵךְ וְהֵרֹנֵךְ בְּעֶצֶב תֵּלְדִי בָנִים וְאֶל־אִישֵׁךְ תְּשׁוּקָתֵךְ וְהוּא יִמְשָׁל־בָּךְ: יז וּלְאָדָם אָמַר כִּי־שָׁמַעְתָּ לְקוֹל אִשְׁתֶּךָ וַתֹּאכַל מִן־הָעֵץ אֲשֶׁר צִוִּיתִיךָ לֵאמֹר לֹא תֹאכַל מִמֶּנּוּ אֲרוּרָה הָאֲדָמָה

בַּעֲבוּרֶךָ בְּעִצָּבוֹן תֹּאכְלֶנָּה כֹּל יְמֵי חַיֶּיךָ: יח וְקוֹץ וְדַרְדַּר
תַּצְמִיחַ לָךְ וְאָכַלְתָּ אֶת־עֵשֶׂב הַשָּׂדֶה: יט בְּזֵעַת אַפֶּיךָ
תֹּאכַל לֶחֶם עַד שׁוּבְךָ אֶל־הָאֲדָמָה כִּי מִמֶּנָּה לֻקָּחְתָּ כִּי־
עָפָר אַתָּה וְאֶל־עָפָר תָּשׁוּב: כ וַיִּקְרָא הָאָדָם שֵׁם אִשְׁתּוֹ
חַוָּה כִּי הִוא הָיְתָה אֵם כָּל־חָי: כא וַיַּעַשׂ יְהֹוָה אֱלֹהִים
לְאָדָם וּלְאִשְׁתּוֹ כָּתְנוֹת עוֹר וַיַּלְבִּשֵׁם:

*(9) The Lord God called out to the man and said
to him, "Where are you?"*
*(10) He replied, "I heard the sound of You in the
garden, and I was afraid because I was naked,
so I hid."*
*(11) Then He asked, "Who told you that you were
naked? Did you eat of the tree from which I had
forbidden you to eat?"*
*(12) The man said, "The woman You put at my
side – she gave me of the tree, and I ate."*
*(13) And the Lord God said to the woman, "What
is this you have done!" The woman replied, "The
serpent duped me, and I ate."*
*(14) Then the Lord God said to the serpent,
"Because you did this,
More cursed shall you be
Than all cattle
And all the wild beasts:
On your belly shall you crawl
And dirt shall you eat
All the days of your life.*
*(15) I will put enmity
Between you and the woman,
And between your offspring and hers;
They shall strike at your head,
And you shall strike at their heel."*

*(16) And to the woman He said,*
*"I will make most severe*
*Your pangs in childbearing;*
*In pain shall you bear children.*
*Yet your urge shall be for your husband,*
*And he shall rule over you."*
*(17) To Adam He said, "Because you did as your*
*wife said and ate of the tree about which I*
*commanded you, 'You shall not eat of it,'*
*Cursed be the ground because of you;*
*By toil shall you eat of it*
*All the days of your life:*
*(18) Thorns and thistles shall it sprout for you.*
*But your food shall be the grasses of the field;*
*(19) By the sweat of your brow*
*Shall you get bread to eat,*
*Until you return to the ground –*
*For from it you were taken.*
*For dust you are,*
*And to dust you shall return."*
*(20) The man named his wife Eve, because she*
*was the mother of all the living.*
*(21) And the Lord God made garments of skins*
*for Adam and his wife, and clothed them.*

**(9) The Lord God called out to the man and said to him,**
**"Where are you?"**: Literally, the Hebrew *ayekka* means
"where are you?" But God's question to Adam here is not
about location. God means: "What is going on with you?"
He is calling on Adam to analyze his situation.

Because God wants man to develop and advance, He
poses a question that invites and requires introspection. In

fact, all of human life is, essentially, a series of such Divine questions.

**(10) He replied: "I heard the sound of You in the garden, And I was afraid**: Here again the literal translation is, "I heard *Your voice* in the garden, and I was afraid." Adam does not want to hear God's voice, to receive a new Revelation. Psychologically he is not prepared for that.

**Because I was naked, so I hid":** The Hebrew *ki eirom anochi* includes no actual verb, and is better translated in the present tense: "Because I am naked." (Past tense would be, *ki eirom hayiti*, "for I was naked.")

Although Adam and his wife are now wearing loincloths, he continues to consider himself naked. This means that although the loincloths were, psychologically speaking, sufficient clothing in the interior of the garden, they were insufficient for conversing with God.

An encounter with God requires a person to be seriously "clothed," that is, it demands an elevated sense of one's own personality and independence. Adam felt that he was ill-prepared in that respect – that mere "loincloths" were not sufficient clothing for receiving Revelation.

**I was naked, so I hid**: Adam feels that an encounter with God at this time is a real threat to him. If he is not sufficiently clothed – i.e., if he is not protected as a personality – that encounter and that Revelation can destroy him.

This is true in other situations as well. A person who is not prepared to meet God will sooner succumb in that experience than advance.

Likewise, mankind's overall lack of preparedness for such a meeting with the Divine is the reason that God in our world remains hidden, never making His presence overt.

**(11) Then He asked: "Who told you that you were naked?**:
God is asking Adam: "What makes you think that nakedness
is a problem?"

**Did you eat of the tree from which I had forbidden you to
eat?"**: God continues to pose questions that are designed
to help Adam come to an understanding of his situation.

**(12) The man said: "The woman You put at my side—she
gave me of the tree, and I ate"**: Instead of answering God's
question, and thereby taking responsibility for what has
happened, Adam passes the buck, as it were, betraying his
excessive dependence on his wife.

**The woman You put at my side**: This detail is extraneous,
and completely irrelevant for answering the question that
was asked. It demonstrates Adam's lack of gratitude to the
Almighty: a gift graciously bestowed is blamed as the source
of serious problems.

Adam's words also express an idea that is quite prevalent
in our times as an excuse for denying responsibility. Namely:
the criminal is not to blame – he was motivated (even compelled) by his circumstances to commit the crime. The fault
for the crime committed lies not with the criminal himself,
but only with his environment and with society.

**(13) And the Lord God said to the woman: "What is this
you have done!":** By appealing to the woman separately,
God is emphasizing her independence as a personality in
her own right.

**The woman replied: "The serpent duped me, and I ate":** Another possible translation is, "The serpent seduced me, and I ate." The woman is saying: "The serpent made it look so attractive that I could not possibly resist."

The serpent is too important to the woman, almost central to her world. This will require a correction, to be achieved in the process of the expulsion from the garden.

**(14) Then the Lord God said to the serpent:** In the preceding verses God gave Adam and his wife each their turn to speak, and to offer some defense of their actions. But He gives the serpent no such opportunity. The serpent is not a distinct personality; it merely represents man's inner drives and aspirations. God therefore does not question the serpent, but instead proceeds immediately to pronouncing the serpent's verdict and sentence.

**"Because you did this, more cursed shall you be than all cattle and all the wild beasts:** If we understand the serpent not as an ordinary animal, but as a personification of man's evil inclination, then we should understand the expression "more cursed shall you be than all cattle and all the wild beasts" to mean "more cursed than all other human passions." At the very beginning of this story (Gen. 3:1), we were told that the serpent (i.e., the evil inclination) "was the shrewdest of all the wild beasts that the Lord God had made." That is, more cunning than all other passions. And here likewise the evil inclination is "cursed" (i.e., its status is reduced) in comparison with all other passions.

**On your belly shall you crawl and dirt shall you eat all the days of your life:** Since the woman has stated that she was unable to resist the arguments of the serpent, the situation changes such that conversations with the serpent become impossible (or at least much less likely).

Says the Midrash: "Previously the serpent had legs, but now the Almighty has deprived it of those." At the beginning of the story the serpent conversed with the woman; that is, it was on the level with humans. But now the situation is changing. The serpent, and the evil inclination it represents, is at the bottom, in terms of its position ("on belly") and also the food ("dirt") that nourishes it.

**(15) I will put enmity between you and the woman, and between your offspring and hers; they shall strike at your head, and you shall strike at their heel"**: In the garden initially there was a dialogue between man and his evil inclination. But that dialogue failed: human weakness proved decisive, and the struggle ended in man's defeat.

God therefore now transforms the relationship between the man and the serpent into a conflict, because the overall effect of that conflict will be to protect man from the serpent's influence. On the battlefield one tries to kill the enemy, not to enter into dialogue with him.

This is a necessary measure, but also a major loss for all. Instead of entering into dialogue with his evil inclination, man must now fight to suppress it. And of course such a war cannot be won.

In the course of his future development, man, by his own efforts, in order to return to the level he formerly occupied in the garden of Eden, will need to overcome this state of war and learn to engage in constructive dialogue with his "evil inclination." In the modern world, a significant part of psychology and cultural studies is directed toward overcoming just that conflict, and searching for such a dialogue.

**(16) And to the woman He said, "... Yet your urge shall be for your husband, and he shall rule over you":** The woman decided to eat the fruit after conversing with the serpent, without consulting Adam. That is, her connection with the serpent was more meaningful to her than her connection with Adam. Her correction therefore lies in strengthening her psychological dependence on her husband, in order to weaken the dominance of the serpent.

However, this dependence of woman on man is not positive overall. It was established very early in human history as a necessary measure. But in order for humanity to rise again to its former level in the garden of Eden, this dependence must be overcome. That will happen in the long process of the development of civilization, including the development of psychology, and advances in the structure of society.

**(16) And to the woman He said, "I will make most severe your pangs in childbearing:** This too is an aspect of strengthening the connection between women, family, and children. That which is achieved only with great difficulty is incomparably more greatly valued and appreciated.

Likewise, the challenges that will arise after the expulsion from the garden are a necessary measure for the early stages of human history. For humanity to return to the level of the garden of Eden, the difficulties of pregnancy and the pain of childbirth must be overcome. In the process of the development of civilization, this happens gradually through advances in medical science.

**(17) To Adam He said, "Because you did as your wife said ... cursed be the ground because of you; by toil shall you eat of it all the days of your life:** The woman's ordeal entails difficulty in pregnancy and childbirth, but Adam's hardship is connected with feeding himself and his family. In modern terms – earning a livelihood.

By eating the fruit of the tree of the knowledge of good and bad at his wife's urging, Adam demonstrated excessive dependence on her – that his "nourishment" derived, as it were, completely from her. God therefore reorients Adam to being properly sustained by the earth – surmounting agricultural obstacles in order to grow crops. By overcoming these difficulties his position as head of the family is reinforced, and he becomes less dependent on his wife.

**(18) But your food shall be the grasses of the field**: Here man is commanded to remain a vegetarian. But he failed to uphold this principle and took to eating animals. After the Flood, God will endorse that practice (Gen. 9:3).

**(19) By the sweat of your brow shall you get bread to eat:** As already noted, even in the garden Adam was expected to work (see Gen. 2:15). But only after the expulsion did he have to work "by the sweat of his brow." This underscores the essential point that Adam's work in the garden consisted not of physical work, but intellectual endeavors.

In the garden there was sufficient understanding and knowledge such that a command, as soon as it was properly expressed, was in the material world as good as fulfilled. But now man must not only understand what is correct behavior – he must bring it to fruition himself.

However, requiring Adam to engage in physical labor is a compulsory measure enforced by the Almighty. The early history of mankind required it, because only in its confrontation with the material world can spiritual development take place. If, however, man is to rise again to the level of the garden of Eden, he must eventually transcend this need to "work by the sweat of his brow." That is, civilization must ascend to the level of achievement where man can transform the material world through the power of his understanding, without any actual physical effort.

**Until you return to the ground—for from it you were taken. For dust you are, and to dust you shall return":** At the moment of their expulsion from the garden Adam and his wife become mortal. The entire future development of civilization – in science and technology, and also in the humanitarian realm – is targeted at finding a means to overcoming human mortality.

**(20) The man named his wife Eve:** The world knows Adam's wife as Eve, of course. But it is important to note that Adam gave his wife a personal name only at this moment, as they are being expelled from the garden of Eden. Until now she was known only functionally and impersonally as "Adam's wife," or just "the woman."

Only now does Adam begin to perceive his wife as an independent personality. Thus Adam, of his own accord, and without direct instruction from God, is already beginning to correct his mistakes.

**Eve**: In Hebrew, *Chavah* – literally, "giver of life." The essence of this name is that by this time she has already given birth to a child. (For more on this point see the commentary on Gen. 4:1 below.)

**Because she was the mother of all the living:** The straightforward meaning is that Eve is the mother of the entire human race, because all people who have ever lived were and are Eve's descendants.

However, we can also understand this verse as saying that Eve is the mother of every living thing. In this second Creation story the entire world exists only for man and in connection with him. The birth of Adam's descendants is therefore the reason for the existence of every form of life in the world.

**(21) And the Lord God made garments of skins for Adam and his wife:** Adam and his wife had already made loincloths for themselves (Gen. 3:7), which insulated them from the outside world and gave them a sense of psychological security. But those loincloths were not sufficient to enable the couple to engage in dialogue with God.

Moreover, Adam and Eve are now gradually transitioning into a society. Social life in the full sense requires a high degree of separation between individuals, and for that loincloths are not enough.

**Garments of skins:** In the Hebrew, "skins" appears here in the singular – ʿ *or*, "skin, hide, or leather." Opinions vary in Jewish tradition as to the meaning of the word ʿ *or* here – whether these garments were made of a material similar to animal skin, or of a material like that "which grows on animal skin," i.e., God made for them woolen garments. Or, God now gave them skin, that is, their own human skin, meaning that until then Adam and Eve were not corporal beings in the full human sense. In all events, the garments that God made for Adam and Eve were real and substantial.

(However, there is even an opinion that these were "garments made from light." The Hebrew words for "skin" and "light" are very close – ʿ *or* and *or*, respectively – which in European pronunciation of Hebrew are usually not distinguished at all.)

**And clothed them:** Thus, man's efforts to create clothing for himself, which at first he did at his own initiative and as the result of his sin, are now confirmed from Above.

***

Question: are we to believe that Adam and his wife's situation in the garden of Eden, being completely naked as they were, was the ideal?

Answer: no, nothing of the kind. That state was by no means ideal, but only the starting point from which their further development had to proceed. The goal of that development is not to revert to the garden, the starting point, but to return to Eden, which represents a new stage of development that will continue from there. Clothing is one aspect of that development.

### 3.3. Adam and Eve Are Banished from the Garden (3:22-24)

כב וַיֹּאמֶר ׀ יְהֹוָה אֱלֹהִים הֵן הָאָדָם הָיָה כְּאַחַד מִמֶּנּוּ לָדַעַת טוֹב וָרָע וְעַתָּה ׀ פֶּן־יִשְׁלַח יָדוֹ וְלָקַח גַּם מֵעֵץ הַחַיִּים וְאָכַל וָחַי לְעֹלָם: כג וַיְשַׁלְּחֵהוּ יְהֹוָה אֱלֹהִים מִגַּן־עֵדֶן לַעֲבֹד אֶת־הָאֲדָמָה אֲשֶׁר לֻקַּח מִשָּׁם: כד וַיְגָרֶשׁ אֶת־הָאָדָם וַיַּשְׁכֵּן מִקֶּדֶם לְגַן־עֵדֶן אֶת־הַכְּרֻבִים וְאֵת לַהַט הַחֶרֶב הַמִּתְהַפֶּכֶת לִשְׁמֹר אֶת־דֶּרֶךְ עֵץ הַחַיִּים:

*(22) And the Lord God said, "Now that the man has become like one of us, knowing good and bad, what if he should stretch out his hand and*

*take also from the tree of life and eat, and live
forever!"
(23) So the Lord God banished him from the
garden of Eden, to till the soil from which he
was taken.
(24) He drove the man out, and stationed east of
the garden of Eden the cherubim and the fiery
ever-turning sword, to guard the way to the tree
of life.*

**(22) And the Lord God said: "Now that the man has
become like one of us, knowing good and bad:** The "us"
means God and man. The Almighty here confirms the words
of the serpent: "As soon as you eat of it your eyes will be
opened and you will be like divine beings" (Gen. 3:5).

Thus, eating the fruit of the tree of knowledge of good
and bad did actually advance mankind. But that advancement was achieved through improper means, and therefore
now requires correction through Adam and Eve's expulsion
from the garden.

**What if he should stretch out his hand and take also from
the tree of life**: Until now, the tree of life was not forbidden
to man. (Only the tree of knowledge of good and bad was
forbidden. All other trees were permitted.) But now that man
has violated the commandment, it has become necessary
to separate him from the tree of life.

**And eat, and live forever!":** To live forever a person must
eat from the tree of life repeatedly, and not just once. But
because expulsion from the garden blocks all access to
that tree, man now becomes mortal. Although awareness of

his own mortality creates a fundamental existential problem for man, it is this problem that motivates a person to realize and acknowledge his mistakes, and to correct them through repentance.

**(23) So the Lord God banished him from the garden of Eden:** The verb used here is *shallach*, literally "to send forth." The root *SH-L-CH* may have positive connotations – to send a person on a commission for his own benefit. This aspect of meaning suggests that Adam and Eve's expulsion from the garden of Eden was not a punishment, but a means of correction.

**To till the soil:** In the garden, knowledge and understanding were themselves enough to change the world. This afforded man enormous opportunities, but it also alienated him from reality and led to serious errors. In order to be able to correct himself, man is now faced with the reality of having to physically cultivate the land.

**(24) He drove the man out:** Here (compared to Gen. 3:23 above) a different verb is used – *garesh*, "expel, drive out" – which has exclusively negative associations. Adam is being sent away not only for his correction, but in order to deny him access to the garden.

**And stationed east of the garden of Eden the cherubim:** A cherub (plural *keruvim* or cherubim) is a kind of angel that straddles the boundary between different worlds. Here the cherubim separate the garden of Eden from the ordinary world.

In Exodus (25:18, and also elsewhere), the cherubim are described as an essential element in the structure of the

Temple. In that case their purpose is to separate the sacred space of the Temple from the ordinary world. We will discuss the cherubim in more detail in our commentary to the given passages of the book of Exodus.

**The cherubim and the fiery ever-turning sword:** A fiery (luminous) ever-turning sword is a ray – a straight line – that, when spinning, has the appearance of a circle.

In the Kabbalah, a ray (*kav*) is the manifestation of Divine Providence that advances the world toward its goal, while a circle (*iggul*) represents the natural world. Thus, the ray that has the appearance of a circle as described in this verse is the hand of Providence externally disguised as nature – the ordinary course of events.

**To guard the way to the tree of life:** Guarding the way to the tree of life means that Divine providence is not detectable in the material world, because it is disguised as ordinary, natural processes.

Any person who can transcend this safeguard, i.e., who is able to detect "the ray behind the circle" – the guiding ray of Providence behind the mask of the natural course of events – will be able to pass through the barrier separating man from the tree of life. And thus can one overcome death.

## 3.4. The Sixth, Seventh, and Eighth Days of Creation

Adam's exile from the garden meant that he became mortal, i.e., he became human in the conventional sense of the word. Thus, the moment of that expulsion is the completion of the creation of man and of the creation of the world.

When we reconcile the first and second Creation stories,

we understand that Adam's short-lived stay in the garden took place on the sixth of the seven days of Creation. And the expulsion happened at the end of the sixth day, just before the onset of Shabbat, at the moment when God was completing the transformation of the universe.

The first day of the "normal," ordinary functioning of the universe, when the Creation is already complete, is the Shabbat of the first Creation story. Adam and Eve pass this day outside the garden.

As noted earlier, in the first Creation story each of the days ends with the phrase "And there was evening, and there was morning, a [day number]th day." But the description of the seventh day, Shabbat, does not end with any such words. Thus, the seventh day seems to have never reached its completion.

Indeed, the Midrash explains: "God's Sabbath, on which the Almighty rests and refrains from remaking the universe, has not ended. It continues on. It is the very world we are living in.

According to this approach:

- On the sixth day humanity was initially created and assumed its basic form.
- The seventh day, God's Sabbath, represents the entire history of human civilization, which continues even until today. The number seven is associated with the cycle of nature, as we find also in other aspects of the Torah.
- The eighth day is not mentioned in the Creation story, although the concept does appear later in the Torah. It symbolizes a transition to the "supra-natural" level – the level at which man's connection to God becomes overt, and is no longer hidden (as it is for us today in this natural, ordinary world). Tradition associates the

attainment of this level with those commandments in which the "eighth day" is mentioned – for example, circumcision (Gen. 17:12) and the Temple service (Lev. 9:1). The eighth day is understood as representing the World to Come, the world in which man will engage in open dialogue with God. The entire history of mankind, taking place on the "seventh day," is seen as preparation for humanity's transition to that "eighth day."

It is interesting and important to note that Jewish chronology, which reckons its years from the creation of the world (*anno mundi*), begins its count not from the first but from the last day of Creation; i.e., that count does not include the first six days. The decisive initial moment in Jewish chronology is the moment that the creation of man became complete – the moment of his expulsion from the garden.

According to the Jewish calendar, the current year (in which this is being written, 2020 CE) is the 5780th year of man's existence within the interval that is "God's Sabbath."

Chapter 4

# The Two Types of Man

## 4.1. Two Projections that Must be Reconciled

Thus, the book of Genesis opens with two stories about the creation of the universe and of man:

- The first story (Gen. 1:1-2:3) describes in detail the seven days of Creation, giving each day (i.e., each aspect of Creation) approximately equal space, and ending with a description of the Sabbath day.
- The second story (Gen. 2:4-3:24) speaks only briefly of the creation of heaven, earth, and plants. It then goes on to describe in detail the creation of man and the episode of the garden of Eden. The second story ends with man's expulsion from the garden.

These two stories give us two "projections" – two different views of one and the same event. The Adams of the first and second stories represent two sides of man's inner essence. The Torah submits these two views for our analysis, and wants us to understand the conflict between them.

Each of the stories has been analyzed above in isolation. Let's now see whether we can reconcile and unify them.

In our comparative analysis of the two stories of Creation that follows, we largely follow the ideas of Rabbi Joseph Dov Soloveitchik, a foremost Jewish religious philosopher of the second half of the twentieth century, and leader of the American Modern orthodox movement. However, some elements of the analysis are our own original contributions.

## 4.2. Dominant Man, Cognitive Man

One of the first differences between the two Creation stories that command our attention concerns the question of the independent value of the external universe – the world in which God places man.

In the first of the two stories, each day of Creation is given approximately the same space and level of detail. The sixth day, and man's appearance on that day, receive roughly the same amount of coverage as each of the other days, when the dry land and the seas, the heavenly bodies, and the plants and animals appeared. This means that from the first story's point of view the world has independent value. Since it is given a place in the Torah, it is quite reasonable to conclude that the universe is valuable in God's eyes. In this sense, we can say that the first story is cosmocentric.

But in the second story, the situation is different. Only two or three lines describe the creation of the greater world (Gen. 2:4 5). The story consists primarily of details of the creation of man. This means that from the point of view of the second story, only human beings have any real value. As no other part of the universe merited a detailed description, we conclude that those parts have only incidental significance at best, being only a proving ground for perfecting the human soul. The universe apart from man has no inherent value *per se*. In this sense, the second story is anthropocentric.

In the first story, Adam is created "in the image and likeness of God," and is tasked with ruling over nature (Gen. 1:26). Man is king, and all of nature is his kingdom. He realizes his human value and his Divine potential by transforming the world. Creative and active, man builds and promotes civilization. In this respect he is likened to the Almighty, the Creator of the universe. Thus, a person who creates and transforms does so not merely to satisfy his own practical needs, but as the fulfillment of a Divine mandate. It is therefore proper and expected that we experience nothing less than true religious delight when we witness the achievements of science and of human civilization that are transforming the world.

And yet, the foundation of man's greatness is the grandeur of the world itself, and the enormous value embodied within it. Clearly, the true dignity of a king lies not in his own power or wisdom, but in the greatness of the kingdom that flourishes under his rule and because of it.

The second story also emphasizes Adam's own Divine origins. About that the first story says, "The Lord God formed man from the dust of the earth. He blew into his nostrils the breath of life, and man became a living being" (Gen. 2:7). But the second story views the Divine greatness of man differently. Nothing is said here about man's dominion over the natural world. For the second story this is not essential. The second Adam is by no means the king of outer space, which holds no interest for him. He is a world unto himself, and within himself. God commands him "to eat of every tree of the garden" (Gen. 2:16), that is, to incorporate the entire universe into his own being. He is concerned not with dominating the world around him, but with the transformation of his own soul, the knowledge of good and bad.

In contrast to the first story, in which God creates the entire universe before creating man, and that world is therefore independent of him and valuable even in and of itself, the universe of the second Creation story exists only as an adjunct to man. "No shrub of the field was yet on earth and no grasses of the field had yet sprouted, because the Lord God had not sent rain upon the earth and there was no man to till the soil" (Gen. 2:5).

In the first story there is Adam and the world. But in the second story – Adam and the garden. The world exists on its own, independently of man. But the garden exists only for man's sake, so that he may eat its fruits and develop and advance himself.

The universe of the first story is immense. Adam is appointed ruler of the natural world, but achieving true dominance over the continents and the seas, over the sun and stars, will require extensive labor on his part – enormous efforts in the scientific, technical, and social spheres to enable civilization to develop.

Moreover, in the first story God gives Adam no limiting commandments. Adam is limited only by reality itself.

In contrast, the circumstances of the second story are quite different. There is no immense universe for man to dominate – an extremely difficult task at best. In the garden, all trees are accessible; their fruits sit only an arm's length away. But God suddenly commands man to restrain himself in the presence of one of those trees and not dare to taste its fruit. This entails no physical difficulty whatsoever, but it demands supreme moral effort, and in the end that restraint proves no less difficult than the sum total of all the scientific and technical efforts of building civilization, as in the first story.

Thus, the Torah speaks of two types of *Homo divinus*

(Divine man). Those two realize their divinity in completely different directions.

In the first Creation story, man is *adam ha-kovesh*, the dominating "man of power," *Homo dominans*. The Almighty entrusts him with the task of "filling the earth and mastering it" (Gen. 1:28). He therefore looks outward, focusing on his ability to transform the world.

But in the second story, man is *adam ha-ochel*, an "eating, consuming man," who consumes and assimilates into himself all knowledge about the world, a "knowing man," *Homo cognoscens*. He aspires to be an *ochel*, "eater, consumer," because the Almighty has commanded him to know the world by eating the fruits of all the trees of the garden. His entire life is focused on the process of cognition in all its various stages. He seeks to "eat" everything, to absorb and contain the whole world within himself. His attentions are turned inward to his own experiences and sensations.

### 4.3. "Homo" as Genus and "Homo" as Individual

The first Creation story describes Adam as a member of the human race. His female counterpart is created simultaneously with him, and the two of them are instructed to "be fertile and increase, fill the earth and master it" (Gen. 1:28). These processes are interconnected, because "filling the earth" and "mastering" it cannot be achieved by an individual, but only when all of mankind as a unified race embraces that task.

"Man" in the expression "man as master of nature" does not mean an individual human being, but humanity as a whole. Therefore, although Adam of the first Creation story is a self-sufficient personality created in the image and likeness of God, he can fully realize the purpose of his human existence only within the framework of humanity as a unified society.

The second story, on the other hand, describes man as an autonomous individual focused on his sensations and experiences. Adam's wife is not created simultaneously with him; he receives her only after experiencing a certain episode of personal loneliness (Gen. 2:18). More precisely, Adam gets a wife only after a personal crisis, in which he unsuccessfully tries to find a mate among the animals (Gen. 2:20).

Moreover, the second story says nothing explicit about the importance of bearing children, but alludes to it only obliquely within the context of the phases of general human experiences that Adam and his wife also undergo (Gen. 2:24). The names of their offspring and a detailed account of their children's lives appear only later, after the expulsion (Gen. 4:1 ff.).

Adam of the first story was created as one component of a harmonious family unit, as a member of humankind and nature as a whole. He cannot be alone, because being alone is antithetical to his very essence.

But second Adam is presented as inherently lonely and conflicted. Crises of personality are an integral aspect of his humanity.

## 4.4. The Difference between *Elohim*, "God," and *Adonai*, "the Lord"

In the first story the Almighty is always *Elohim*, "God." The second story refers to God as *Adonai Elohim*, "the Lord God".

As already noted, a name is not merely a handle for referring to an object. Just as significant, if not more so, is the use of a name to define the nature of the connection that humans establish with it.

Almost everything in our everyday experience has not just one name, but several, and the names of persons are especially numerous. We variously identify a person by given name, surname, nickname, title, and so on. Different names and types of names thus represent different types of relationships with the objects, persons, or ideas so named.

Likewise, the different names by which we refer to God are indicative not of differences in the essence of God himself, which is immutable and never varies, but of the different types of connection that humans create and maintain with God; i.e., the different ways that the Almighty's presence manifests in our world. When certain verses in the Torah refer to God by names specific to those passages, the Divine names so used indicate the types of relationships between man and God that are operating in those passages.

## The name *Elohim*, "God"

The Divine name *Elohim* encountered in the first story is by no means specific to the Almighty. Just as in the western vocabulary words such as "god," "gods," and "divine," do not necessarily refer to the Almighty – that is, to the One God of the Jewish scriptures – so can the Hebrew word *elohim* refer, more generally, to a variety of "higher powers," including even "other" (i.e., false) gods, and even more generally, to magnitude, power, and judgment. Thus, *elohim* is, as it were, not a proper noun, but a common, descriptive noun.

Grammatically, *Elohim* is a plural noun. But when used to refer to the Almighty, it takes a singular verb, e.g., *bara Elohim* (Gen. 1:1) – literally, "Divine [powers] created." According to Jewish tradition, this grammatical anomaly expresses, as it were, "a plurality of higher forces acting in unison." The harmony of the laws of nature and the beauty of the surrounding world is the manifestation of the Almighty in the attribute of *Elohim* – God as the "soul of the universe," responsible for the natural order.

*Elohim* designates also the God Who manifests in the law – both natural and moral law. Moreover, *Elohim* is the God Who proclaims and exacts judgment, because judgment means, essentially, actualizing the law.

In summation then, Tradition understands the Divine name *Elohim* as "the name of Divinity as manifested in judgment, law, and order." But it also applies to other worldly forces that govern nature, law, and order.

But all these attributes are "cold" and detached with respect to mankind. According to this worldview, a human being is just one component of the universe (who dominates, however, all other creatures and creations), and the same laws that govern the other elements of the universe govern humankind as well. Man does not stand out from the world as something fundamentally different. This man is the Adam of the first Creation story. And that is why God in that story is called *Elohim*.

### *Adonai* (*Y-H-W-H*, the Tetragrammaton), "Lord"

But unlike *Elohim*, God's name *Adonai* (the Tetragrammaton, "the four-letter name," *Y-H-W-H*) refers exclusively to the Almighty. I.e., it is the name of God's that is reserved for Him alone.

According to Jewish tradition, this four-letter name is "ineffable," that is, "unpronounceable." Accordingly, in manuscripts and printed texts of the Torah the letters of this name never have their own vowels. Rather, the four-letter name is always vocalized, if at all, with vowels borrowed from either *Adonai* (most common) or *Elohim* (less common).

Grammatically, the combination of the four Hebrew letters *yod, he, vav, he* (*YHWH*) can be seen as a kind of fusion of the past, present and future tenses of the Hebrew verb *HYH*, "to be" (which is why this name is sometimes translated as "The Eternal"). However, it would be better to consider this name a kind of unique and special "hieroglyph," rather than an ordinary Hebrew word derived through normal grammatical rules.

When addressing the Almighty (in prayer, or when the Torah is read publicly), this name is pronounced as if written *Adonai*, ("[my] Lord"), and from this substitution comes the common translation of this word as "Lord" in English, or its equivalent in European languages.

But when in Hebrew this name is used in the "third person" – i.e., when it is used not to address God directly, or in formal prayer or reading of scripture, but when Jews refer to or speak *about* God, e.g., in discussions of the meaning of the prayers or of general Torah concepts – it is traditionally pronounced *HaShem*, which means, simply, "The Name." (That is, "the name I am not allowed to enunciate here, but surely you know which and Whose name I mean.")

The Tetragrammaton *YHWH* speaks of the Almighty as a "Personality" Who stands above and outside of the natural world of human experience. It is a level of Divinity that exceeds the level of *Elohim*. It is the exaltation of God above nature, law, and order, and the transcendence of these earthly categories. It represents the miraculous and the supernatural, Divine grace, and paradox.

A person's connection with such a level of Divinity is

expressed in the concept of *berit* – "covenant, union, pact." A covenant is a special contract between God and man whose purpose is to transcend and surmount natural elements.

Thus, *Elohim* and the Tetragrammaton *YHWH* represent two "opposite" manifestations of the Almighty.

*Elohim* is the Almighty as the God of Nature, Who works through the natural order of things. In this mode God's connection with man is as with any other part of the world, through nature. It is the name that the Torah uses to refer to God in the first Creation story.

Conversely, the Tetragrammaton refers to the Almighty as the God of the Covenant, Who exceeds the natural, Who transcends nature. This is God's name in the second Creation story.

The combination of both levels of Divinity is expressed in the phrase *Adonai Elohim*, "Lord God." It means: "The Almighty Who engages in personal dialogue with man, but is manifested in the harmonious functioning of the laws of nature and human experience."

## 4.5. The Trees of Knowledge and of Life as Relevant Only to Adam of the Second Story

The tree of knowledge and the tree of life, while centrally important to the second Creation story, are not mentioned at all in the first story. This means that these trees are critical to second Adam, but are of no interest to first Adam.

First Adam, who dominates the world, considers himself firstly an integral part of the human race. He perceives himself as one of the elements of humanity. He is therefore concerned primarily not with personal immortality, but with the immortality of his species – perpetuating himself in his descendants and followers. Personal death for him amounts to nothing more than tearing just one of the millions of threads in a fabric. Although, like any living being (that is, at a purely biological level), he too fears death, the problem of individual immortality is not critical to him.

Accordingly, the tree of life, which confers individual immortality, is not a driving passion for "dominant Adam," and nothing is said about it in the first story.

Nor does Adam of the first story have any passion for knowledge of good and bad. As a ruler, he is quite pragmatic with respect to matters of knowledge: he needs to know only as much as is required to properly manage the world. It is a scientific approach. Knowledge has to be "operational."

But knowledge of good and bad is a completely different kind of knowledge. It is essential knowledge, vital for the development of one's own soul, but by no means of pragmatic importance. It has no "practical application." Therefore, first Adam has no interest in such knowledge.

But for second Adam the situation is quite different. The tree of knowledge and the tree of life are at the very center of the garden – i.e., they are the center of attraction for everything that he is and aspires to.

For second Adam knowledge is important *per se*, irrespective of its application. Cognition is the expansion of his inner world, and this in itself is valuable to him. He is concerned with the development of his inner world exclusively; "pragmatic" knowledge for correcting the outside world is of no interest to him. He is preoccupied with eternal, essential, unsolvable problems, especially the question of knowledge of good and bad.

For *Homo cognoscens*, personal immortality too is critical, because what he values most is his inner world, and upon his death that world will cease to exist. Death for him is not merely the severing of just one of millions of threads in a fabric. Rather, it is nothing less than the collapse and disappearance of the entire universe.

## 4.6. A Systematic Summary of the Differences between the Two Stories

We can thus formulate the following outline of the differences between the two Creation stories:

| Dominant Man<br>*Adam ha-kovesh / Homo dominans* | Cognitive Man<br>*Adam ha-ochel / Homo cognoscens* |
|---|---|
| The first Creation story is cosmocentric. | The second Creation story is anthropocentric. |
| Each of the seven days deals with one aspect of Creation, and equal space is given to all. | The entire story is focused on man. Other aspects of Creation are mentioned only briefly. |
| The world has independent, objective value, irrespective of man. | Man is the only true value. The external world has no independent value; it is only a proving ground for man's internal development. |
| Man dominates the world around him. | Man is "a world unto himself." |
| Man is portrayed as representing the entire human genus, and man and woman are therefore created simultaneously.<br>First, the story speaks of the importance of bearing children ("Be fertile and increase"), and only then about realizing human potential ("fill the earth and master it"). | Man is portrayed as a distinct, individual personality, and Adam is therefore created alone (and lonely). First he is tasked with realizing his human potential ("Of every tree of the garden you must eat" – alternate translation). Only then, after experiencing the crisis of loneliness, is he given a mate. The only mention of childbearing is an oblique allusion. |

| | |
|---|---|
| The male-female relationship is a partnership for creating a family and bearing children, the foundation of human existence and advancement. | The relationship between man and woman is that she is a "a fitting helper" (or "helper-opponent") for him. This facilitates his proper personal development, man's knowledge of himself, and man and woman's knowledge of each other. |
| Because every person considers himself, most importantly, a part of humanity, he is more concerned with the immortality of the entire human race than with his own personal immortality. | Because every person considers himself, most importantly, an individual personality, he is very concerned with his personal immortality. The question of humanity as a whole is not even considered. |
| The path that humanity embraces is what is most important to every human being, because that is the continuation of his own existence. | Every human being's personal world is the most important thing to him. Other people and even all of humanity are not his world, but different worlds beyond his. |
| The emphasis is on pragmatic knowledge, because human realization consists in transforming the world, and pragmatic knowledge is conducive to and necessary for that. | The emphasis is on the non-pragmatic knowledge of good and bad, because human realization consists in advancing and developing one's soul. |
| Man's world is the entire universe. As such, it has no specially designated center. | Man's environment is a garden – a separate, small corner of the universe. And it has a well-defined center – the tree of knowledge of good and bad and the tree of life. |
| Man lives in harmony with his family and with the world. There are no explicit, restrictive commandments that he must observe. | Man is lonely. He lives in an inherently contradictory world, as the most alluring fruit is the very fruit he is forbidden to eat. |

| The Almighty is called *Elohim* – "the God of Nature." Man's encounter with God happens through nature, law, and order. | The Almighty is called *Adonai Elohim* – "the God of the Covenant, as manifested through nature." Man's encounter with God happens *beyond* nature – through the supernatural, Divine grace, and paradox. |
| --- | --- |

It is important to note that both Adams are God-like. Each embodies one of the two aspects of Divinity: man who dominates the world, and man as "an entire world within himself."

To come closer to God, and to become like Him, every person must combine and integrate both of those aspects. We must walk on two legs, so to speak, alternately advancing each leg in turn – domination over the world on the one hand, and inner advancement and enrichment of our souls on the other. In the larger sense, these two aspects correspond to the technical and humanitarian spheres of civilization. Any attempt to advance in only one direction to the detriment of the other, to treat them not as adjuncts but as opposing forces – regardless of which of the two directions is given prominence – will not lead to an acceleration of progress, but will amount to "throwing one leg too far forward." The person will lose his balance and will very soon fall.

And in fact, that is exactly what happened to man in the episode of the tree of knowledge of good and bad, which we will consider in greater detail below.

Chapter 5

# The Creation of the Universe and the Structure of the *Sefirot*

## 5.1. The Concept of the Ten Sefirot

As noted in the preface to this volume, this commentary is heavily influenced by Kabbalistic ideas. Although we have not used the terminology of the Kabbalah in the earlier parts of the commentary, to make further progress in understanding the Creation story we must now do precisely that.

We will introduce Kabbalistic terminology only gradually, as required to shed light on the text of the Torah and its meaning.

\*\*\*

The foundation of the Kabbalah's conceptual apparatus is the ten *Sefirot*. These are ten fundamental parameters into which any integral system can be decomposed, be it the universe (macrocosm), or man (microcosm), or the Jewish people, or any other self-contained, integral system of any size or scale.

Using the language of the *Sefirot* makes it possible to view the world around us differently, to see things that we did not notice before. One goal of this commentary on the book of Genesis is to allow the reader to experience this new perception at a basic level at least.

Needless to say, our presentation of such complex ideas must be imprecise and only approximate. But we hope that it will serve as a worthy introduction – only the first step in the reader's advancement toward a deeper and fuller understanding of this far-reaching area of knowledge.

\*\*\*

Each *Sefirah* (literally "counting," plural *Sefirot*) is "a distinct and bounded aspect of Divine manifestation", which (unlike the Divinity as a whole, which is infinite) can be reckoned and described.

To name only a few examples of such "bounded aspects of Divine manifestation": Will, Illumination, Understanding, Grace, Justice, and Beauty. All of these are Divine and immensely significant, but none of them encompasses the Divine manifestation in its entirety.

We can think of the *Sefirot* as a palette of colors with which God draws the universe and governs it. Each *Sefirah* is one of the colors in the palette.

Just as white light (sunlight) can be decomposed into a full spectrum of distinct and "finite" colors, and a complex picture can then be painted with them, so does each separate and distinct *Sefirah* stand out from the Almighty's infinite light.

The *Sefirot* are the basic elements of the spiritual structure of the universe, parameters of the Divine governance of the world. And man's own internal structure can likewise be seen as consisting of these same *Sefirot*, since man, after all, is created in the image and likeness of God. (Every human being, through introspection, will find each of the ten *Sefirot* within himself.)

Of the ten *Sefirot*:

- The first three *Sefirot* are considered "internal" ("higher, concealed") attributes, describing the design of the universe.
- The remaining seven *Sefirot* are "external" ("lower, manifest") attributes – the realization of the aforementioned design. Therefore, these seven manifest themselves sequentially over the seven days of Creation.

An analogous structure manifests itself as well in any other integral, creational entity – in the formation and structure of the Jewish people, for example.

## 5.2. The *Sefirot* System

Presented graphically, the system of the *Sefirot* usually appears as follows:

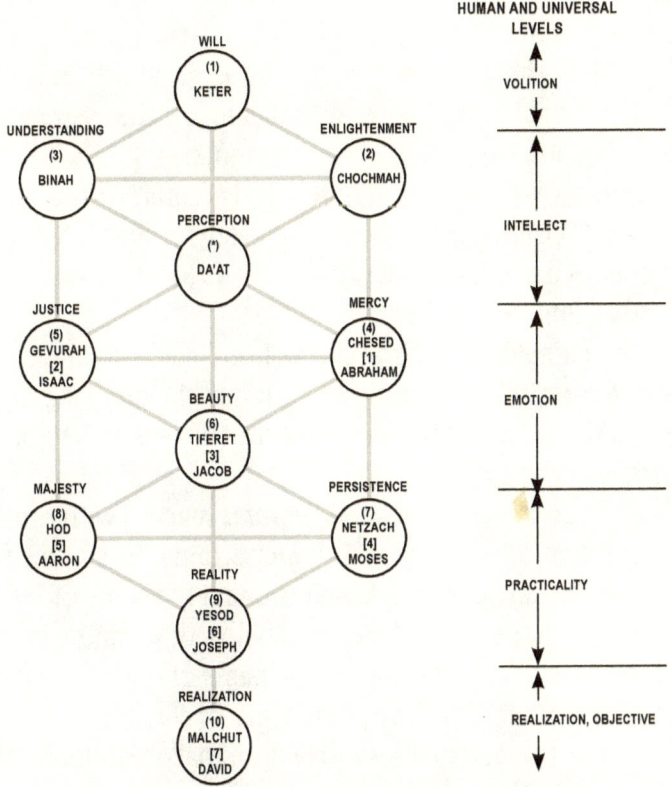

The *Sefirot* system describes the process of descent of the Divine light from the primordial Divine Will (*Keter*, "Crown") that motivates it, unto its concrete realization in our world (*Malchut*, "royalty, kingdom").

In the diagram above, the number corresponding to each *Sefirah* is indicated in parentheses at the top of its circle. But the *Sefirah* of *Da`at* has no number, and is marked instead with an asterisk (*).In the Kabbalah, *Sefirot* could be seen from both "external" and "internal" perspective. From the "external" perspective, *Keter* is a proper Sefirah, while *Da῾at* is not – it is "less" than a proper *Sefirah* and is not quite an independent element. From the "internal" perspective, *Da῾at* is a proper *Sefirah*, while *Keter* is seen as the element "above" the system of *Sefirot* – the primary will of God. Thus, there are ten *Sefirot* in total from both "external" and "internal" perspective, although in fact the system (and the diagram) has a total of eleven elements.

Hebrew is read from right to left. Therefore, for example, *Sefirah* (4), *Chesed*, seen on the right vertical line (*Sefirot* 247), precedes *Sefirah* (5), *Gevurah*, which is located on the left vertical line (*Sefirot* 358).

The name of each *Sefirah* is written inside its circle, and above the circle is an approximation of the meaning of the *Sefirah*. (Those are by no means literal translations of the names of the *Sefirot*!).

Each of the seven "lower" *Sefirot* is marked with the day of creation to which that *Sefirah* pertains. This number (1 through 7) can be seen in brackets under the name of *Sefirah* in each of those seven circles. And below this number in each of those seven *Sefirah* circles, the name of one of the Patriarchs (or other founding personality of the Jewish nation) appears – the personality with whom that attribute is most closely associated.

For example, the *Sefirah* of *Chesed* represents the category of Mercy. It is number 4 of the ten *Sefirot*, and corresponds to the first day of Creation. Among the founding personalities of Jewish history this attribute corresponds to Abraham, the first Patriarch of the Jewish nation, with whom the quality of *Chesed* is most closely associated.

The conceptual meaning of the *Sefirah* of *Gevurah* can be approximated in English as "Justice." (The literal meaning of the Hebrew word *gevura*" is "might, power.") It is the fifth among the ten *Sefirot*, and corresponds to the second day of Creation. Of the leaders of the Jewish people, *Chesed* corresponds to Isaac, the second Patriarch, whose most prominent personal quality was *Gevurah*.

We will not analyze in full detail here the structure of each *Sefirah*, but in the course of the narrative we will elaborate on those elements of the structure that are needed to shed light on the given passages of the Torah.

Here we will consider the application of the three "upper" *Sefirot* to the process of cognition, and later – discussing the stories of the three primary Patriarchs (Abraham, Isaac, and Jacob) – we will explain how the three *Sefirot* of the emotional level can be applied for understanding the Torah.

## 5.3. The Cognition Process: *Chochmah, Binah,* and *Da'at*

The following is an illustration of how the *Sefirot* system can be applied for achieving a deeper understanding of the relationship between Adam and his wife (and, thus, man and woman generally) in the second Creation story.

For this to work we will need to consider the three *Sefirot* related to the process of cognition: *Chochmah, Binah,* and *Da'at.* These three attributes are associated with the events in the garden of Eden, the essence of which was knowledge of the universe (expressed allegorically as "eating the fruits of every kind of tree"), and with the crisis that arose in that connection.

Upon consulting a standard Hebrew dictionary we learn that the word *chochmah* means "wisdom," *binah* means "understanding, intuition," and *da' at* means "knowledge."

However, the Kabbalistic understanding of these terms does not coincide with the literal meanings of those words.

*Chochmah*, the first stage of cognition, is enlightenment, illumination, an initial idea of an object as a whole, the answer to the question: "What?"

*Binah*, the second stage of cognition, is an understanding of the structure of an object, its conceptual makeup and its function, the answer to the question: "How?"

For example, at the level of *Chochmah* a person knows what he wants to say, but does not yet know how to say it. At the *Binah* level he already has the ability to express that thought.

The word *Binah* at its grammatical radix is cognate with the root *BNH*, *boneh*, *livnot*, "to build," *ben*, "son" (i.e., the essential element of building a family or clan), and the Hebrew word *even*, "rock, stone" – which is building material. Here the two-consonant radix *B-N* is common to roots associated with the concept of construction. Thus, *Binah* represents the building of a structure.

Thus, *Chochmah* is an idea that is already understood internally, but not yet formulated. And *Binah* is its formulation – its development into a formalized structure.

In the Kabbalah, when establishing a correspondence between the letters of the Tetragrammaton yod, he, vav, he (YHWH) and the sequence of the Sefirot, Chochmah corresponds to ׳, yod, and Binah corresponds to ה, he. These are the first and second letters of the Divine name, respectively.

*Chochmah,* the fundamental point of cognition, corresponds to *yod*, which graphically is only a point having no internal structure. The letter ׳, *yod*, has no inner space – its "white part" is completely outside of it. Such lack of internal space symbolizes this letter's outward orientation, its extroversion. Thus, *Chochmah*, illumination, is a "point" that seeks to expand and unfold in order to acquire an external form.

(Note that the expression "not one iota" is obviously of Hebrew origin, since the letter *yod*, which in Aramaic and likewise in Greek is called "iota," is the smallest of all the letters of the Hebrew alphabet.)

*Binah* corresponds to the letter ה, *he*, which, on the contrary, has inner space in the fullest sense, almost like a fence built around a perimeter. This is due to the concept of *Binah* as "constructing a building," the essence of which is allocating and organizing internal space. This reflects the introversion of the *Binah* attribute, its inward orientation.

A little later we will consider *Chochmah* and *Binah* as representing the relationship between man and woman, and *Da'at* as their connection with the tree of knowledge of good and bad.

## 5.4. Man and Woman as *Chochmah* and *Binah* (2:21-23)

The process of creating Woman is described in the Torah as follows:

> *(21) So the Lord God cast a deep sleep upon the man; and, while he slept, He took one of his ribs and closed up the flesh at that spot.*
> *(22) And the Lord God fashioned the rib that He had taken from the man into a woman; and He brought her to the man.*
> *(23) Then the man said, "This one at last*
> *Is bone of my bones*
> *And flesh of my flesh.*
> *This one shall be called Woman (ishah),*
> *For from man (ish) was she taken."*

**(23)** This one shall be called Woman (ishah), for from man (ish) was she taken: The Torah here is emphasizing the grammatical connection between the words *ish*, **איש**, and *ishah*, **אשה**. Namely: The letters *aleph*, **א**, and *shin*, **ש**, which taken together spell the word *eish*, **אש**, "fire," are common to both *ish* and *ishah*, "man" and "woman," while only the letters *yod* and *he* distinguish them.

Thus, since *Chochmah*, as just explained, corresponds to the letter *yod*, and *Binah* to the letter *he*, the relationship between man and woman corresponds to the connection between *Chochmah* and *Binah*.

The following diagram illustrates this relationship:

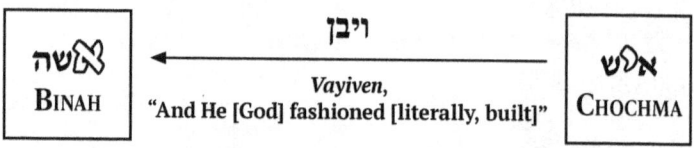

**(22) And the Lord God fashioned (literally, built) the rib that He had taken from the man into a woman:** The process of creating Woman from the rib of Adam (the arrow in the above diagram, representing the progression from *Chochmah* to *Binah*) is described in the Torah with the word *vayiven*, **ויבן**, "fashioned, built, rebuilt."

At the same time, because of the relationship of the roots of the words *boneh, livnot*, "to build," and *Binah*, "understanding," the same verb *vayiven* can be understood not only as "he (re)built," but as "he endowed with the additional attribute of *Binah*." When God took Adam's rib and rebuilt it into Woman, out of *Chochmah* a new attribute appeared: *Binah*. (Apart from its concrete, literal meaning, "rib," the Hebrew word *tzeila`* can also mean "side, edge, aspect.")

The letter *yod*, which represents *Chochmah*, has no inner space and "is all outside," symbolizing male extraversion, a man's outward orientation, his realization outside of himself. The letter *he*, *Binah*, which has space inside, symbolizes female introversion – woman's realization within.

This difference between man's extroverted orientation and woman's introverted orientation manifests itself at several levels:

(i) Anatomical differences.

(ii) Physiological differences: for a man, time flows outside of himself, but for a woman – within her, in the form of menstrual and hormonal cycles.

(iii) Differences in the process of childbirth: a man produces his child outside of himself; a woman builds her child within her own body.

(iii-a) Moreover, in the process of conception and childbirth a man contributes a cell, spermatozoon, in which a potential of a future child already resides, but it has not yet manifested itself externally. This is *Chochmah*, the "idea" of an obejct. But after a man's spermatozoon fertilizes a woman's ovum, a woman during her pregnancy actually builds the child out of that man's one cell. This is *Binah*, "building" or "understanding" of an object.

(iv) Differences in psychology and value orientation: a man normally strives outwardly – for self-realization in the outside world – building his career, for example. But for a woman, the more important value is normally her self-realization in her own inner space, hedged off from the outside world – building her family and her home. (These differences are not absolute, of course. Self-realization in external achievements is important for women as well. And building a family and a home are also important goals for a man. But as a general principle, men and women differ significantly in these aspects.)

(v) Differences in decision-making: men are mostly

occupied with determining what needs to be done, but women – with how to do it.

So we see that the aspects of masculine vs. feminine character correlate according to that same *Chochmah-Binah* scheme. Thus, we have used concepts of the Kabbalah to perceive the structural similarity and connection between aspects of the world's functioning that initially seemed entirely unrelated.

Chapter 6

# Understanding the Episode of the Tree of Knowledge of Good and Bad Based on Principles of the Kabbalah

## 6.1. Problems in the Episode of the Tree of Knowledge

In this section we will try, by applying concepts of the Kabbalah, to answer the following questions:

(i) What benefit did Adam receive from eating the fruit of the tree of knowledge of good and bad, and in what way did it change him? In other words, what does "knowledge of good and bad" actually mean?

(ii) Why did God forbid that tree to man? We take it as a given that the Almighty wants every person to advance by understanding the world more deeply. Wasn't this tree one of the best paths to such advancement?

(iii) Why did God expel Adam from the garden? If the problem was only that Adam had to be prevented from eating the fruit of the tree of life (Gen. 3:22), was it not possible to protect Adam from that in some other way, without expelling him from the garden entirely?

There is no end to these types of questions, of course. We will propose just one of many possible approaches to answering the questions just posed.

In the following discussion, we will proceed from the premise that since God created man in His likeness and image, God treats man as a son. And that God loves mankind and strives for his advancement and success in every way that a human father would. Absenting that premise, which is in fact the very foundation of the Torah's view of the relationship between God and man, no inquiry into the biblical God or reasoning about His relationship to man is possible.

## 6.2. What did Adam gain by eating the fruit of the tree of knowledge?

Let us then begin with the first of the three questions posed earlier. How did eating the fruit of the tree of knowledge of good and bad benefit Adam? How exactly did it change him?

The simple answer will obviously not suffice. It goes something like this: "By eating that fruit, Adam learned what good and bad are. Until then he had no idea what good and bad actually were, or even that there was such a concept of good and bad."

But wasn't God's command, to eat from every other tree but that one, itself a message about what should and should not be done? In other words, that there is right and wrong, good and bad?

Of course, God's commands are only a basic introduction to understanding the concepts of good and bad. But isn't this also the level of a child who has received clear instructions from his parents of what to do and not to do? Although the child does not yet understand the meaning of those instructions, surely we cannot say that he is totally clueless about the concepts themselves.

Moreover, if man had no understanding at all of good and bad, God could not have held him accountable for violating the prohibition, just as we cannot hold a child responsible for improper behavior on issues in which he has no ability whatsoever to distinguish between good and bad.

It thus seems obvious that man must have had at least a basic understanding of the concept of good and bad even before he ate the fruit of the tree of knowledge.

A better answer to that question (what did Adam gain by eating the fruit) might be that he acquired emotions – an actual desire to commit acts of good or bad. This approach would presume that before the incident of the tree of knowledge of good and bad man had no emotional aspirations, that he was essentially just a rational calculating machine. But then, after eating the fruit, he became a "real" human being with all the emotions and passions that that entails.

But this approach too seems incorrect. Let's think about this. If man had no passions, and was only a rational mechanism that always followed instructions to the letter, then he would never have come to violate God's commandment! We must therefore conclude instead that Adam had passions, attractions, and desires even before he ate the fruit of the tree of knowledge.

Nor can we agree with the supposition that the result of eating the fruit of the tree of knowledge was Adam and his wife's sexual relationship, which, according to this version was the direct consequence of "the fall of man." But as already noted, God commanded Adam and his wife from the very beginning to "be fertile and increase" (Gen. 1:28).

Thus, sex and childbearing cannot have come about under the influence of the tree of knowledge, let alone having been the consequence of breaking a commandment.

In summation then: From the very fact that God gave Adam the commandment we must conclude that Adam already had at least a basic grasp of the concept of good and bad. Moreover, his subsequent violation of that commandment shows that he already had passions and aspirations as well. So the original question returns. Given that Adam already had all that, how did he change and what new characteristics did he acquire by eating the fruit of the tree of knowledge of good and bad?

### 6.3. The Meaning of the Attribute of *Da`at*, "Knowledge"

To understand the meaning of the episode, we need to analyze the very concept of *Da`at* (literally, knowledge), which the Torah uses in the expression *etz ha-da`at tov va-ra`*," "the tree of *knowledge* of good and bad."

According to the Kabbalah, the *Sefirot* of the intellect develop sequentially as follows. The first stage is *Chochmah* (the initial understanding of a concept as a single, integral point or idea). *Binah* then extends that understanding (wherein the preliminary idea develops further into a detailed knowledge of the overall structure). Only then can the person proceed to acquire *Da`at*, "knowledge, cognition," which is the process of internalizing and establishing a personal connection with the subject. He must "eat" (assimilate) the concept, as it were.

Let us illustrate this with a concrete example:

(i) When a person knows (in principle) that there is a process that we call "reading," this is the level of *Chochmah*.

(ii) When he knows the meaning of each letter, and how words are formed from them, this is the level of *Binah*.

(iii) When he can finally put all that together and actually read, then he has achieved *Da`at*. This is "eating" – consuming, assimilating, internalizing – i.e., mastering the topic or skill, making it his very own.

Human understanding that has attained the level of *Da`at* goes beyond a mere intellectual action; rather, it reaches to the very foundations of one's personality. The fruit of the tree of knowledge enters into the knower, and changes him. A person who can read is an entirely different person from one who cannot read. This is why the Hebrew term *da`at* is used also to refer to an intimate relationship, as in, "Now the man *knew* his wife Eve, and she conceived and bore Cain" (Gen. 4:1). *Da`at*, means not just obtaining or acquiring knowledge, but the kind of knowledge and cognition that create a solid internal connection.

That is the level that Adam attained with respect to knowledge of good and bad, the level of *Da`at* that he achieved by eating that fruit, and which gave him much more than information about good and bad. Rather, it immersed and engaged him in a profoundly intimate connection with good and bad, by making good and bad integral elements of the human personality.

Until then, man knew that good and bad existed – i.e., he had a concept of them at the level of *Chochmah*. He even knew just what actions he was allowed to undertake and which were forbidden. Thus, he had also attained the level of *Binah* with respect to good and bad.

However, he had not yet had any actual personal experience with them. His knowledge of good and bad remained theoretical. Man had passions and inclinations that fascinated and attracted him (for otherwise he would not and could not have violated the prohibition). However, they were not yet a part of his inner essence, but distinct, as it were, from his personality. Only after eating the fruit did Adam assimilate good and bad within himself – he felt an inextricable connection of his personality with good and bad. In other words, with respect to good and bad he ascended to the level of *Da'at*.

The Midrash says as follows. The serpent in the garden is the *yetzer ha-ra'*, man's "evil inclination" – the personification of the human passion to do bad things. At first the serpent lay outside of man. This was a state of the world in which a person could distinguish the serpent's influence from that which came from within himself. He could distinguish his passions from his personality, just as we can today distinguish and distance our personality from "external information" that we know because we have read it in books, even if we cannot relate to it from within ourselves. But once man had eaten and digested the fruit of the tree of knowledge of good and bad, that separation became impossible, because good and bad were now an integral part of the human personality, a part of man's own "I."

After eating that fruit, Adam acquired not an intellectual ability to distinguish between good and bad, but, on the contrary, a sense of their indistinguishability. It was not two separate trees, a tree of good and a tree of bad, but just one tree. Both attributes were combined in one and the same tree, demonstrating that good and bad had grown together as one, for they have a common root in the Divine universe.

The fruit of this tree unites good and bad within itself, allowing a person to possess knowledge of both attributes in their utter inseparability. This is a crucial point that advances a person spiritually. A person who lacks this perception cannot truly understand good and bad.

A child sees the world in black and white. To him good and bad live on different shores. But as a person matures, his world becomes filled with intermediate hues and shades, a continuous spectrum of transitions that connect the polar opposites.

Thus, by eating the fruit of the tree of knowledge Adam came to understand the impossibility of separating good and bad unambiguously. That understanding is simply a necessary and positive stage in the process of becoming an aware and responsible adult.

But all that happened because Adam had violated a commandment. Adam plucked the fruit of the tree of knowledge prematurely, when that fruit had not yet ripened. Or more precisely, but what is the same thing, Adam himself had not yet ripened to readiness to receive self-knowledge at that level.

Because every type of self-knowledge has its proper time.

## 6.4. Was God Planning to Allow Man to Eat the Fruit of the Tree of Knowledge?

Was the prohibition of eating the fruit of the tree of knowledge of good and bad meant to be absolute and everlasting? Or was that prohibition perhaps only temporary, and God was planning to permit that fruit to Adam at some future time?

The Torah text gives no clear and unambiguous answer to this question. But note that Torah says, "And from the ground the Lord God caused to grow every tree that was pleasing to the sight and good for food, with the tree of life in the middle of the garden, and the tree of knowledge of good and bad" (Gen. 2:9). Thus, both of those trees, along with every other tree in the garden, are described as "pleasing to the sight and good for food."

The Midrash therefore contends that God was indeed planning from the very outset to allow man to eat the fruit of the tree of knowledge. But Adam jumped the gun – as the Midrash says, just three hours before the arrival of Shabbat. (Recall that the entire episode takes place on the sixth day of Creation, what we call Friday. These "three hours" mean that Adam and Eve transgressed well before God's work of the sixth day was complete.)

Had Adam not eaten the fruit and violated the prohibition, the Midrash continues, the Almighty would have allowed him to recite the Sabbath *kiddush* over the juice of the fruit of that tree. (*Kiddush* is a benediction that is recited over wine every Friday night at the onset of Shabbat, and which serves to officially consecrate the holy day.)

Shabbat *kiddush* is normally recited over wine. This midrash alters our understanding of what happened in the garden, by telling us that cognition of good and bad is, as it were, an "intoxicating influence."

Wine deprives a person of rational, clear-headed, "sober" analytical activity. But at the same time, even while obscuring the clarity of details, it sparks the imagination and awakens emotions allowing for an integral, holistic view of the world and what is happening in it. Thus it adds an essential aspect to man's knowledge of the world.

A viewer who closely examines every brushstroke on the canvas of a painting deprives himself of the opportunity to see the whole picture. Likewise, if we examine every phenomenon in the world under the microscope of our minds, we may lose sight of the main point. The expression *in vino veritas*, "there is truth in wine," apart from its conventional, popular meaning, expresses also this same idea. A person who is *too* sober, who subjects everything to cold, rational analysis, in fact fails to see the world as it is, and does not really understand it.

Of course God wanted man to mature, to develop and advance in his knowledge, to feel the very essence of both good and bad within his soul. God therefore intended to eventually allow man to partake of the fruit of the tree of knowledge.

The prohibition was only temporary. And that was Adam's mistake - he understood the ban as permanent and eternal, which led him to believe that unless he violated the prohibition he would never be able to move forward in that aspect.

## 6.5. Prohibition at the Conscious and Unconscious Levels

The reason for forbidding Adam temporarily to eat the fruit of the tree of knowledge was to prepare him to eat that fruit correctly. That is, to eat it such that man, having internalized the connection between good and bad, would avoid any wrongdoing, and would not destroy the world in which he lives.

That preparation was to consist of two parts:

(i) By eating the fruits of every other tree Adam would gradually grow and mature, as he learned about life in all its aspects.

(ii) By refraining from eating the fruit of the tree of knowledge of good and bad, man would eventually internalize within himself the general principle of observing Divine commandments, making it an immanent, essential part of his nature and personality.

Every human being experiences prohibition at various

levels. Some prohibitions exist at a conscious level and under a person's control, but when that control is suddenly removed, a violation will ensue. But other prohibitions migrate to the level of the subconscious, and are thus imprinted on the human mind to such a degree that they (barring extreme circumstances) will not be violated even when conscious control is removed.

Even when inebriated a person will not, by far, violate any and all prohibitions indiscriminately. By restricting control of his consciousness, intoxicating beverages free a person from only those prohibitions that are restrained by the power of the mind. Conversely, alcohol poses no threat to deeply assimilated prohibitions that have already infiltrated the subconscious. A civilized human being will not take to robbing or killing after drinking a small amount of wine. But a savage who has only recently begun to abide by civilized behavioral norms may in fact be induced, under the influence of even slight intoxication, to engage in such criminal behavior.

Had Adam resisted temptation and not eaten the fruit, even without understanding the meaning of the commandment, the Divine prohibition would then, through his own self-restraint, have become an integral element of his personality, a feature of his subconscious. "If I must not, then I must not!" – irrespective of whether or not I understand the reasons.

This would have laid the necessary groundwork for Adam's next stage of cognition – the awareness level of *Da`at* with respect to good and bad. And then Adam, having recited the Sabbath *kiddush* on the juice of the tree of knowledge, could have combined two mutually exclusive elements – acquiring "intoxicating knowledge" even while preserving his complete control over the world. Adam could then have remained in the garden of Eden, and would not have been driven out.

So, here we come to the reason why Adam's eating the fruit of the tree of knowledge resulted in his expulsion from the garden, and protecting the tree of life from him would not have been sufficient.

The garden was a situation of enormous opportunity given to mankind. In the garden, as we discussed earlier, there was no divide between human cognition and realization. As man had unlimited potential to experience and know the world, he was its sovereign master. His knowledge alone was enough to change the universe. Eating the fruit brought in its wake a mixture of good and bad in the human soul: Adam realized within himself the knowledge that good and evil are essentially inseparable, that they derive from a single source.

But such knowledge is not only important; it is downright dangerous. Likening its effect to that of wine is not a mere figure of speech. Having "drunk the wine" of knowledge of good and bad, but at the same time retaining full power over the world (i.e., remaining in the Garden), man could have avoided observing any and all restrictions, and would eventually have destroyed all of Creation.

For the sake of analogy, let us try to imagine that Adam, living in the garden of Eden and enjoying unlimited power there, was, as it were, standing at the "control panel" of the entire universe. Wielding such immense power is the realization of man's Divinity, and is thus a very good thing. But on the other hand, drinking wine is also not bad, and the knowledge of good and bad brings Adam closer to God. The problem is that these two types of "good" are grossly incompatible: there is no place for a habitual drinker at the control panel of a nuclear reactor.

As we deepen our knowledge of good and bad within ourselves, we cannot always manage to remain within the required boundaries; that is, to understand evil but not to perform malevolent acts. When intoxicated we cannot avoid pressing the wrong button or flipping the wrong lever – which in the garden of Eden could easily destroy the world.

In order to prevent any such monumental catastrophe, God expelled man from the garden, thereby limiting the extent of his power over the world.

## 6.6. The Need for Self-Restraint in Cognition

We noted earlier that Adam of the second Creation story, "cognitive man," *Homo cognoscens*, by no means cogitates in order to wield power. His cognition, *Da`at*, is preoccupied not with acquiring practical information, but with forming connections deep inside his soul with the diversity of the universe. *Da`at* must be thought of not as objective, impersonal information, but as knowledge that participates in (or leads to participation in) the object of that knowledge in an empathic relationship with it. In this sense, human cognition is truly "cognition." (From *co*, "with, together," and *gnosis*, "knowledge.")

And since cognition in the garden was inseparable from realization, every act of cognition there led to genuine, tangible changes in the world.

The Midrash cited above speaks further of how Adam gained true knowledge of plants by penetrating into their inner nature with a feeling of such profound empathy that plants became a part of his personality – he attained the level of *Da`at*. But then, when Adam came to understand that rain is a vital necessity, he began to pray for it, whereupon the Almighty sent rain upon the earth, and the plants grew. Thus Adam's knowledge of plants was immediately realized in the flourishing of the garden.

As he sensed that the animals were a part of himself, Adam was able to give them names, i.e., to correlate the animals with himself by structuring the animal world and its relationship to humans. When Adam knew animals at that level, they became a part of his household. He "tamed" them.

Knowing his wife was then Adam's next challenge. The immediate result of that knowledge was the birth of their child. (Cain and Abel, the Midrash makes clear, were both born in the garden.) Since there was never a gap between cognition and realization in the garden, human pregnancy and childbirth became a painful and protracted process only after Adam and Eve's expulsion.

The process of knowing the world was not just permitted to Adam; it was *required* of him by fiat. From the very outset God commanded Adam: "From every tree of the garden you shall surely eat" (Gen. 2:16 – alternate translation).

Adam therefore craves knowledge of good and bad. But he must deal with the Divine prohibition – a veritable wall that blocks his process of cognition. Not only is that prohibition incomprehensible to "cognitive Adam," which is why he feels no motivation whatsoever to observe it. But much more – it is the very contradiction and antithesis of his entire being.

\* \* \*

In satisfying his profound urge for knowledge, *Homo cognoscens* does it not only for his own sake, but as a service to God, his fulfillment of the commandment, "From every tree of the garden you must eat." Performing this service is for him something natural, understandable, and enjoyable.

But man's fulfillment of the second part of that commandment, the prohibition of eating the fruit of the tree of knowledge of good and bad, runs counter to his entire essence as *Homo cognoscens*. To him this prohibition is pointless, and an unbearable challenge.

Observing that prohibition demands from him a different kind of service. It is the service of restricting knowledge, of suspending the process of approaching God. Finding a balance between approaching God and blocking that approach, between the joys of the cognitive process and the need to place boundaries on cognition, is an inordinately difficult and challenging task.

## 6.7. The Improper Road to Perfection: A Guaranteed Collision Course

Did eating the fruit of the tree of knowledge help Adam to advance to a higher stage of development? Did he become more perfect by virtue of that transgression?

On the one hand, it seems intuitively clear to us that a person who has eaten the fruit of the tree of knowledge, and understands that good and bad are inextricably linked, surely understands this world better than someone who has no concept of that connection, and in the utter simplicity of his soul can see the world as only black and white.

But on the other hand, is it possible in principle that violating a Divine instruction – committing a grievous sin – can lead to human advancement? Is it not self-evident that the result of such a sin can only be a fall?

And yet, it seems to us that both of those contradictory statements are true. Having tasted the fruit of the tree of knowledge, Adam indeed ascended to a new level of understanding. But at the same time, the inevitable result of his transgression was that he would fall.

God wished to allow man to attain the heights and the depths of knowledge of good and bad, not from the very outset, but only after learning first to uphold God's commandments, even if he could not initially comprehend their meaning. Unless he first acquired that vital capability, Adam would never be able to cope with his prematurely acquired level of *Da῾at*.

A thirst for knowledge is of course an inseparable part of what it means to be human, and a necessary part of human life. The problem begins only when man's thirst for knowledge overwhelms every other consideration, including his connection with God, ultimately leading to his destruction.

The prohibition of eating the fruit of the tree of knowledge was only a temporary imperative that served to teach man the skill of abiding by restrictions. After all, the ability to restrain oneself and not partake of that which is forbidden is itself a necessary stage of human advancement. The awareness of the limitations of cognition is itself a form of cognition. Only after having achieved that level could Adam have advanced yet further.

Eating the fruit of the tree of knowledge put Adam, as it were, behind the wheel of a vehicle with a vastly more powerful engine. This ultimately moved him further down the road. But because Adam had not yet acquired even the most basic driving skills, the inevitable result had to be a catastrophic wreck.

Chapter 7

# Cain and Abel

## 7.1. The Birth of Cain (4:1)

א וְהָאָדָם יָדַע אֶת־חַוָּה אִשְׁתּוֹ וַתַּהַר וַתֵּלֶד אֶת־קַיִן
וַתֹּאמֶר קָנִיתִי אִישׁ אֶת־יי:

*[1] Now the man knew his wife Eve, and she
conceived and bore Cain, saying, "I have gained
a male child with the help of the Lord."*

**[1] Now the man knew his wife Eve, and she conceived and
bore Cain**. With reference to birth, the words "knew" and
"conceived" are seemingly superfluous, as they add nothing
to the meaning of the story. But this only means that they
must be understood at a deeper level – indicating certain
stages in Adam and Eve's personal development. That is,
these terms indicate that Adam and Eve changed significantly and developed not only through the birth of their
child, but even earlier, at the time of sexual knowledge and
conception. And the same is true of humans in general.

**And bore Cain, saying, "I have gained a male child with the help of the Lord".** The word *kaniti* is more literally translated as "I have acquired." The name Cain is grammatically related to (indeed, it derives from) *kaniti*. Cain's essence is that he is a "person who acquires." He longs to "acquire the world" and transform it, which is why he chooses, as we will soon see, to engage in agriculture. By no means should these longings be seen as something negative; on the contrary, this desire fully corresponds to the Divine command to "fill the earth and master it" (1:28). However, it is also not without its problems, and Cain must subsequently grapple with those.

**"I have gained a male child with the help of the Lord".** The words "the help of" are an interpolation by the translator. They do not appear in the original Hebrew, which translates literally as, "I have gained a male child with the Lord."

Thus, there are two related but different senses to Eve's message. First, as per the English interpolation just noted: "I have gained a male child with (i.e., through) *the help of* the Lord." And second, "I have acquired this male child and, with him, I have acquired the Lord too." That is, she has acquired a new level of Godliness. Besides getting a son with the birth of Cain, Eve had also acquired the status of a parent, that is, a creator.

God is fundamentally both Giver and Creator – He created man and gave him life. Initially, then, a person who receives the gift of life from God has been created and is a receiver, but he not does not yet himself create or give. This chasm that initially separates a person from God is a very significant human problem. But we remedy that situation by creating children in our own image and likeness, just as God does (1:26, 9:3), which provides us with a path for getting closer to God by exercising our ability not only to receive, but also to give. And above all – to give life.

Of course, bearing a child is not the only way to become a creator. One can get closer to God also through other creative acts and positive actions. But giving birth to a child is one of the most important ways of achieving that.

From this perspective, Cain is at the center of the world, because through him Adam and Eve became parents and creators, and drew closer to the Lord. Therefore, the Torah does not say (as it typically would) "she gave birth to a son and called him Cain." Rather, it is written, "she gave birth to Cain"; that is, to "acquisition" – she gave birth to her own new status.

## 7.2. The Birth of Abel (4:2)

ב וַתֹּסֶף לָלֶדֶת אֶת־אָחִיו אֶת־הָבֶל וַיְהִי־הֶבֶל רֹעֵה צֹאן
וְקַיִן הָיָה עֹבֵד אֲדָמָה:

*[2] She then bore his brother Abel. Abel became a keeper of sheep, and Cain became a tiller of the soil.*

**[2] She then bore his brother Abel.** The literal meaning of the Hebrew is, "she continued to give birth – to his brother Abel." The idea of "continued" underscores that this second birth was not completely independent from the first and was on par with it, but only secondary in relation to it. Nor does the Torah state here, as it states previously with Cain, that "Adam knew Eve and she conceived." Those details are not significant for the birth of Abel, because they are not a new stage in the development of Adam and Eve.

**His brother Abel.** If the essence of Cain is to be a son, to "acquire the world" and change Adam and Eve's status by making them parents, then the essence of Abel is to be a brother, that is, an adjunct and complement in some sense to Cain's existence. (There would have been no need to state the obvious, that Abel was Cain's brother, unless the Torah wished to make a particular point about this brotherhood.)

The birth of Abel does not affect Adam and Eve's status, for they are already parents. But it radically changes Cain's status and creates a new reality for him: he ceases to be an only son, and becomes a brother. Abel's assigned task is to correct Cain, to unseat him from his central position, and to create for him and for the world the concept of brotherhood. Thus Cain is transformed from "only son" into "son and brother", who must now take into account the existence of "the other", and the need to share with him.

This "downgrade" is a major problem for every firstborn who must face it. As is well known, if a brother or sister is born in a situation where the first and (until now) only child has already realized his central place in the family – when he is, say, between three and five years old – a serious crisis can ensue. The firstborn, who suddenly discovers that someone else is now laying claim to his place, experiences severe frustration that can engender envy and even hatred. The parents' joyful statement about the imminent appearance in their home of a brother or sister brings about as much joy to the first child as if a husband were to tell his wife, "I love you so very much, my dear! Oh, and by the way, I will soon be marrying a second wife."

Cain failed this test of brotherhood; the consequences of that have remained a heavy burden on the entire subsequent history of mankind, even up until our own days. Conflicts between firstborns and their younger brothers are an oft-recurring theme throughout this entire Book of Genesis, finding their resolution only in the Book of Exodus, in the relationship of Moses and Aaron.

**Abel.** In Hebrew, *hevel*. This is the word used to refer to the warm wisp of vapor that leaves the mouth in the frosty air of winter and then disappears immediately. The same word also symbolizes utter futility and insignificance, as it is written in the famous opening verse of the Book of Ecclesiastes, "Vanity of vanities, all is vanity." Thus, the two brothers are antipodes. If Cain represents acquisition, stability, and solidity, then Abel is airiness, transience, ephemeralness.

However, all this ephemeralness refers only to Abel himself in isolation. In his relationship with Cain, it becomes something completely different. Abel is the "hot steam" that boils, transforms, and corrects. His calling is to correct Cain, to append a cipher ('0') to Cain's unit ('1'). Cain was to become the foundation of civilization's development, and Abel was charged with pointing out Cain's errors, in order to correct and improve him.

The birth of a younger brother performing this role is a terrible ordeal for any firstborn child.

**Abel became a keeper of sheep, and Cain became a tiller of the soil.** When Adam was expelled from the Garden of Eden, he was told that thenceforth, "by the sweat of your brow shall you get bread to eat" (3:19). Cain assumes this task – surely a very noble and worthy act.

However, for all the importance of farming, it also carries the danger that the farmer will become so mired in his own tract of land that he will not even notice the world around him. Notice that *oved adamah* ("tiller of soil") here can also be read as *eved adamah*, "a slave of the land." (This is because the Torah here spells *oved* defectively; that is, without the letter *vav* that would more typically provide the *o* vowel sound.)

No one politely pleads with the earth to yield its bounty; rather, the earth is *ordered*, slave-like, to do so. But it is a truism that when a person keeps slaves, he himself also lives within a paradigm of slavery. The entire life of a farmer who works the earth consists of giving "orders." Thus, a farmer's profession harbors for him the danger that he will himself acquire a slave mentality. Enter Abel, who has been given to Cain for just that purpose – to serve as a counterbalance to Cain's position, by showing him that there are also other possibilities in life.

**Abel became a keeper of sheep.** Abel is the "vapor man", a *luftmensch*. He therefore chooses a profession that will not tie him down to any particular place. A shepherd's work requires constant peregrinations. He is free to observe the world around him and analyze it. He observes nature and the heavens, and is not enslaved by a tract of earth.

Sheep cannot be completely and physically controlled. While a shepherd does give orders to his sheep, he must also cajole and persuade his sheep, in order to nurture the necessary behaviors he wishes to see in them. Abel is thus by nature an educator, called upon to educate Cain as well. This is the primary task of Abel's life, but in pursuing it he will suffer catastrophic failure.

### 7.3. The Conflict of the Farmer and the Herdsman

The confrontation between farmers and herdsmen that was so prevalent in the ancient world was not only economic or military in nature, but also ideological. This confrontation can be seen in many chapters of the Torah – for example, the conflict between Joseph and his brothers (37:5), and the hatred of the Egyptian farmers for the Jewish cattle-men (43:32, 46:34).

The farmer and the herdsman have completely different views of the world. Since farming brings incomparably higher profits, only on the basis of farming are civilizations built – the great ancient civilizations of Egypt and Mesopotamia, for example.

The farmer looks down, for he is absorbed in his plot of land. A man of narrow hereditary space, he is born and dies in the very house in which his ancestors lived. His family has lived in their little village for centuries, and it is all they know.

As was especially true in antiquity, the farmer often needs the significant organizational power of the state. For example, no single village using only its own resources and influence could possibly build the irrigation channels it needs. The agricultural civilizations of antiquity were therefore formed as extensive empires.

But the cattle breeder is a man of freedom and space, which means that he has a different level of consciousness. He is poorer than the farmer, but he is not limited to his tract of land. He gazes at the heavens, and at the world around him. He travels about, meets many different kinds of people, and sees a variety of lifestyles. This way, his horizons are incomparably broader. Because herders are spiritually stronger than farmers, pastoral peoples, as history demonstrates, have captured agricultural societies and ruled them as kings, but not vice versa.

At the same time, his not having his own land obviously indicates that the herdsman lacks rootedness, and that his position is always in flux. In a certain sense, a homeless people that has no land can never be a real nation.

The correction and synthesis of these conflicting priorities can be found in Jewish agriculture in the Land of Israel, which is unique and special because:

1. After settling in the Land of Israel the Jews became farmers. But long before that the Jewish patriarchs were herdsmen. The basis of Jewish religious attitudes in relation to this survives in the ecclesiastical word "pastor." A pastor is a shepherd who leads his flock. This clearly expresses a pastoral rather than an agricultural attitude toward the world.

2. Irrigation in the Land of Israel is not based on a system of diverting water from a river that is already flowing along the ground, but on rainfall. The Torah (Deut. 11:11) very clearly emphasizes this distinction between the Land of Israel and Egypt, where water for irrigation is taken from the Nile. A farmer in the Land of Israel gazes up at the sky and asks, "Will it rain?" He is therefore neither enslaved by the earth nor fixated on it.

3. The Priests and the Levites who performed the service in the Temple did not have their own land. This means that there was always a prominent stratum of the Jewish nation that was not tied to farming and who were always "gazing at the heavens", imparting a definite quality of "airiness" to the Jewish people.

In the Torah's story about Cain and Abel, the problematic nature of farming and rootedness is at the heart of the conflict. Abel was faced with the task of raising Cain to a new level of awareness by teaching him to look up, and not only down.

The relationship of a person to his land should not be one of ownership (even though the essence of "Cain the acquirer" *is* that sense of ownership), but, rather, a relationship of cooperation between man as "tenant farmer" and God, Who is the true owner of the land. Abel's task is to prevent people from becoming ossified in materialism, by imbuing their lives with an element of changeability and movement, and encouraging communication not only with the earth but with the heavens as well.

Because Cain and Abel could not successfully cope with this problem, it fell to all of humanity to seek and find a solution. This process continues up until today.

### 7.4. Cain and Abel Bring Their Offerings (4:3-5)

ג וַיְהִי מִקֵּץ יָמִים וַיָּבֵא קַיִן מִפְּרִי הָאֲדָמָה מִנְחָה לַיי׃
ד וְהֶבֶל הֵבִיא גַם־הוּא מִבְּכֹרוֹת צֹאנוֹ וּמֵחֶלְבֵהֶן וַיִּשַׁע
יי אֶל־הֶבֶל וְאֶל־מִנְחָתוֹ׃ ה וְאֶל־קַיִן וְאֶל־מִנְחָתוֹ לֹא
שָׁעָה...

*[3] In the course of time, Cain brought an offering to the Lord from the fruit of the soil.*
*[4] And Abel, for his part, brought the choicest of the firstlings of his flock. The Lord paid heed to Abel and his offering.*
*[5] But to Cain and his offering He paid no heed...*

**[3] In the course of time.** Literally, "It happened at the end of [a certain number of] days." This indicates the end of a well-defined period in the cycle of life. Mankind (in the person of Cain and Abel), having passed its initial stage of mere physical development, now ponders the spiritual foundations of its existence.

As a rule, in the text of the Torah and Tanakh, the expression "at the end of days" is understood to refer to the onset of the Messianic era (see Rashi, Gen. 49:1). Here, however, it means the end of the agricultural cycle – the harvest period. But for Cain, this time is in fact quite consistent with the concept of the Messianic era, because it is marked by success in the most important activity of his life – possessing and developing the earth.

**Cain brought an offering to the Lord from the fruit of the soil.** Only after his life had been properly organized did Cain bring a gift to the Almighty. He brought not the first fruits but the last, the remainder.

Cain's action *per se* is very significant and entirely positive. After all, an offering to God is the basis for the correct positioning of human life on earth. On the other hand, Cain's offering entails an error that requires correction. One should make an offering to God not from remnants but from the first fruits, as an acknowledgement that the ability to create new life is itself a gift from the Almighty, and that only thanks to Him has the crop grown.

In Jewish tradition, what remains at the end of the harvest also becomes a gift – but to the poor, so that they too can enjoy some of the agricultural wealth that has been attained.

Cain, believing that one should be kind and share with everyone – even with God – thus puts God on equal footing with the poor. And because of this fundamental error, his gift cannot be accepted.

**[4] And Abel, for his part, brought.** The literal translation is, "And Abel – he too brought..." Abel brought his gift only as a supplement to Cain's. Until Cain brought his gift – that is, until humanity realized the need to connect with the

Almighty – it was impossible to begin correction, to improve that connection and correct the details.

**And Abel, for his part, brought the choicest of the first-lings of his flock.** By his example, Abel taught Cain the two requirements for presenting a gift to the Almighty: The gift must be from the first fruits, and it must be from the best.

As the firstborn child, Cain's attitude toward God as "indigent" is rooted in his egocentric ideas, in which the rest of the world is consigned to the periphery.

On the contrary, Abel is fundamentally a "brother"; that is, in his perception of the world there is always *ab initio* someone else who has primacy. It is therefore natural for Abel to place God before himself.

**The Lord paid heed to Abel and his offering.** God confirmed the correctness of Abel's approach, endorsing not only the offering itself, but also its motives.

**[5] But to Cain and his offering He paid no heed.** God told Cain that he must work on himself and learn from Abel. Cain, however, had difficulty learning from his younger brother.

It would be wrong to consider Abel "good" and Cain "bad." Cain is the primary character of the two actors in this drama, because only his descendants will be preserved in mankind. Abel is not a a self-sufficient figure, for nothing will remain of him in the future – he has no heirs. Abel cannot build humanity on his own, but he does have the potential to correct Cain.

## 7.5. Become Better and You Will Be Forgiven (4:5-7)

ה ...וַיִּחַר לְקַיִן מְאֹד וַיִּפְּלוּ פָּנָיו: ו וַיֹּאמֶר יי אֶל־קַיִן
לָמָּה חָרָה לָךְ וְלָמָּה נָפְלוּ פָנֶיךָ: ז הֲלוֹא אִם־תֵּיטִיב
שְׂאֵת וְאִם לֹא תֵיטִיב לַפֶּתַח חַטָּאת רֹבֵץ וְאֵלֶיךָ
תְּשׁוּקָתוֹ וְאַתָּה תִּמְשָׁל־בּוֹ:

*[5] ... Cain was much distressed and his face fell.*
*[6] And the Lord said to Cain, "Why are you*
*distressed, and why is your face fallen?*
*[7] Surely, if you do right, there is uplift. But if*
*you do not do right sin couches at the door; its*
*urge is toward you, yet you can be its master."*

**[5] ... Cain was much distressed and his face fell.** Instead of thinking about the causes of the incident and ways to remedy the situation, Cain is overwhelmed with disappointment and hopelessness.

A person's lot in life is determined, to a very great extent, by maintaining a constructive attitude toward his mistakes, wishing to understand and correct them without blaming others, and not falling into despondency.

**[6] And the Lord said to Cain, "Why are you distressed."** God tells Cain that his reaction is wrong. If he improves, he will be forgiven. But even if he cannot improve, he can still dominate sin rather than succumbing to it. The world is not deterministic; mistakes do not close the path to their correction. God wants Cain to feel confidence in his strengths and capabilities. If Cain improves, he can surpass Abel, and reach an even higher level than him.

## 7.6. The Murder of Abel (4:8)

ח וַיֹּאמֶר קַיִן אֶל־הֶבֶל אָחִיו וַיְהִי בִּהְיוֹתָם בַּשָּׂדֶה
וַיָּקָם קַיִן אֶל־הֶבֶל אָחִיו וַיַּהַרְגֵהוּ:

*[8] Cain said to his brother Abel ... and when they
were in the field, Cain set upon his brother Abel
and killed him.*

**[8] Cain said to his brother Abel.** Cain makes a decisive step
towards correction. He turns to Abel and offers to engage
with him in dialogue. He overcomes his feeling of resent-
ment and attempts constructive communication with Abel.
He wants to improve. God has told Cain that he must change,
and Cain is indeed trying to change! Moreover, Cain turns to
Abel as one does to a brother, acknowledging the brotherhood status that Abel had imposed on him simply by virtue
of his birth, and which itself was the source of many of Cain's
problems. This is a serious spiritual advancement for Cain.

**Cain said to his brother Abel ....** Here, squarely in the middle of a verse, the story breaks off. The cantillation symbols
indicate a strong break, best expressed in translation by an
ellipsis or sometimes a series of dashes. The Torah declines
to reveal what Cain actually said, or Abel's answer.

The Midrash supplements the Torah's narrative with different versions of their dialogue (a quarrel over property,
or the Temple, or a woman). Be that as it may, such a con-
spicuous omission of the content of Cain's words from the
Torah text itself would suggest that the words that were
spoken are not important. What is important is that Cain
appeals to Abel and is willing to bridge their gap through

their brotherhood – to understand and to learn.

Abel does not answer Cain, because he sees in Cain not a person with whom one can engage in dialogue, but someone that he must influence and educate. Abel arrogantly believes that it is enough to show Cain his own example of a proper and successful sacrifice. He will not belittle himself by engaging in "small talk", nor does he try to understand his brother, who wants to discuss his problems with Abel. So Cain kills Abel. If one is called upon to be a teacher and one considers himself a shepherd and a leader, but does not engage in fellowship nor see in his fellow man an actual person, then he is an unworthy shepherd.

**And when they were in the field**. The field is the workplace where both Cain and Abel had to realize themselves. It is precisely Abel's failure to realize his pedagogical potential that leads to tragedy. Abel, whose calling is to be a teacher, refuses to take responsibility for this role, and he therefore dies.

**Cain set upon his brother Abel.** The emphasis here on "his brother" indicates that Abel is rebelling against the whole idea of brotherhood. Cain cannot bear the humiliation of being considered a mere object of education, which is how Abel regards Cain, and this is the reason that Abel will not engage with him dialogue. And so Cain rebels, destroying the very brotherhood with Abel that he had already acknowledged.

**And killed him**. The final break in their brotherly relations is expressed through murder.

Of course, none of the above rationalizations can justify

Cain's actions. He is deemed a criminal and subjected to commensurate punishment. But neither does Cain's crime absolve Abel of *his* guilt. Having resolved to be a teacher, Abel must bear responsibility for the unsuccessful results of his teaching.

## 7.7. Cain Stands Accused (4:9-12)

ט וַיֹּאמֶר יי אֶל־קַיִן אֵי הֶבֶל אָחִיךָ וַיֹּאמֶר לֹא יָדַעְתִּי הֲשֹׁמֵר אָחִי אָנֹכִי: י וַיֹּאמֶר מֶה עָשִׂיתָ קוֹל דְּמֵי אָחִיךָ צֹעֲקִים אֵלַי מִן־הָאֲדָמָה: יא וְעַתָּה אָרוּר אָתָּה מִן־הָאֲדָמָה אֲשֶׁר פָּצְתָה אֶת־פִּיהָ לָקַחַת אֶת־דְּמֵי אָחִיךָ מִיָּדֶךָ: יב כִּי תַעֲבֹד אֶת־הָאֲדָמָה לֹא־תֹסֵף תֵּת־כֹּחָהּ לָךְ נָע וָנָד תִּהְיֶה בָאָרֶץ:

*[9] The Lord said to Cain, "Where is your brother Abel?" And he said, "I do not know. Am I my brother's keeper?"*
*[10] Then He said, "What have you done? Hark, your brother's blood cries out to Me from the ground!*
*[11] Therefore, you shall be more cursed than the ground, which opened its mouth to receive your brother's blood from your hand.*
*[12] If you till the soil, it shall no longer yield its strength to you. You shall become a ceaseless wanderer on earth."*

**[9] Where is your brother Abel?.** More precisely, "What has happened to your brother Abel?" This question is the clear echo of God's question to Adam (3:9): "Where are you?" But whereas there God demands of Adam only to answer for himself, here Cain is being asked to answer for his brother as well. At first a person is responsible only for himself, but as he grows up over time he must bear responsibility for his fellow human beings; that is, for others besides himself.

**And he said, "I do not know."** Cain never tries to deceive God or to cover up the murder. His answer would be better translated as "I do not *want* to know", that is, I want to know neither Abel, nor his brotherhood. Cain's "I do not know" reinforces the connection of this story to the sin of Adam and Eve, who ate from the fruit of the Tree of Knowledge. But if Adam in the Garden of Eden at least wants to know (although he approaches this desire very incorrectly), Cain actually refuses to know. A teacher's failings discourage the student from wanting to participate at all in the process of learning.

**Am I my brother's keeper?**. Cain's answer, "I do not know", would have sufficed to answer God's question. By adding "Am I my brother's keeper?" (addressing a question that God has not even asked), Cain shows that it is the brother-hood relationship that is critical for him. "I turned to Abel as my brother, but he had no interest in responding to me. I see no reason to try to preserve something that Abel him-self rejected."

**[10] Your brother's blood cries out to Me from the ground ... which opened its mouth to receive your brother's blood from your hand.** In deciding to be a farmer, Cain took responsibility for the land, but he did not want to take responsibility for his brother, Abel. Therefore, everything that happened to Abel in his life is now absorbed by the earth.

**[12] It shall no longer yield its strength to you.** It is no longer possible for you to engage in agriculture. You must find yourself a different occupation.

**You shall become a ceaseless wanderer on earth.** Having killed Abel, Cain must now wander, wearing the shoes, so to speak, of his dead brother and gradually adjusting to them, as he recreates within himself the counterbalance of which he has by his own misdeed deprived himself.

### 7.8. The Mark of Cain (4:13-15)

יג וַיֹּאמֶר קַיִן אֶל־יְיָ גָּדוֹל עֲוֹנִי מִנְּשֹׂא: **יד** הֵן גֵּרַשְׁתָּ
אֹתִי הַיּוֹם מֵעַל פְּנֵי הָאֲדָמָה וּמִפָּנֶיךָ אֶסָּתֵר וְהָיִיתִי נָע
וָנָד בָּאָרֶץ וְהָיָה כָל־מֹצְאִי יַהַרְגֵנִי: **טו** וַיֹּאמֶר לוֹ יְיָ לָכֵן
כָּל־הֹרֵג קַיִן שִׁבְעָתַיִם יֻקָּם וַיָּשֶׂם יְיָ לְקַיִן אוֹת לְבִלְתִּי
הַכּוֹת־אֹתוֹ כָּל־מֹצְאוֹ:

*[13] Cain said to the Lord, "My punishment is
too great to bear!
[14] Since You have banished me this day from
the soil, and I must avoid Your presence and
become a restless wanderer on earth – anyone
who meets me may kill me!"
[15] The Lord said to him, "I promise, if anyone
kills Cain, sevenfold vengeance shall be taken
on him." And the Lord put a mark on Cain, lest
anyone who met him should kill him.*

**[13] My punishment is too great to bear!.** We see no remorse yet. Cain seems not the least concerned about having murdered Abel, and does not admit of any wrongdoing. He only complains about the severity of the punishment. "I have been charged with exorbitant guilt (punishment) that is more than I can bear."

**[14] Since You have banished me this day from the soil, and I must avoid Your ... anyone who meets me may kill me!** Cain's orientation is to the land and to ownership of land. In his perception, a person who has no land of his own is insignificant – he is nobody, and has no right to exist. Cain therefore sees exile as a punishment so severe that he cannot bear it.

Cain believes that a vagabond is of no importance to the Almighty, and is invisible in God's presence. Thus, in his own estimation he is outside the law, and anyone can kill him with impunity. Cain's attitude towards Abel is based on the same erroneous view of the "worthlessness of the wanderer." But now that he experiences the fate of a wanderer, he must adjust his outlook.

**[15] And the Lord put a mark on Cain, lest anyone who met him should kill him**. This "mark of Cain" is by no means the mark of a villain, but only a mark of protection. On the contrary, God acknowledges Cain's complaint as well-founded, and gives him a distinguishing, protective symbol.

The word used here for the mark that God gave Cain is *ot*, usually translated as "sign." But everywhere in the Torah that the word *ot* is used, it is not just an ordinary sign, but an indicator of the Divine presence. And in the current context too, God is giving Cain clear evidence that he has a mission, and it is therefore forbidden to kill him. This sign allows Cain (as well as his family and other people closest to him) to understand that being a wanderer who has no land of his own is not the same as being a non-person; on the contrary, such a person can be the carrier of a highly critical mission. The mark Cain receives from God is thus a part of his re-education.

Overall, this re-education was quite successful. An important part of Cain's heritage has been preserved in humankind. Noah's wife was a descendant of Cain, which means that Noah's three sons – and thus all of humanity – carry within them a piece of Cain.

# Chapter 8

# From Adam to Noah

## 8.1. Cain's Descendants (4:16-24)

**טז** וַיֵּצֵא קַיִן מִלִּפְנֵי יי וַיֵּשֶׁב בְּאֶרֶץ־נוֹד קִדְמַת־עֵדֶן: **יז**
וַיֵּדַע קַיִן אֶת־אִשְׁתּוֹ וַתַּהַר וַתֵּלֶד אֶת־חֲנוֹךְ וַיְהִי בֹּנֶה
עִיר וַיִּקְרָא שֵׁם הָעִיר כְּשֵׁם בְּנוֹ חֲנוֹךְ: **יח** וַיִּוָּלֵד לַחֲנוֹךְ
אֶת־עִירָד וְעִירָד יָלַד אֶת־מְחוּיָאֵל וּמְחִיָּיאֵל יָלַד אֶת־
מְתוּשָׁאֵל וּמְתוּשָׁאֵל יָלַד אֶת־לָמֶךְ: **יט** וַיִּקַּח־לוֹ לֶמֶךְ
שְׁתֵּי נָשִׁים שֵׁם הָאַחַת עָדָה וְשֵׁם הַשֵּׁנִית צִלָּה: **כ** וַתֵּלֶד
עָדָה אֶת־יָבָל הוּא הָיָה אֲבִי יֹשֵׁב אֹהֶל וּמִקְנֶה: **כא**
וְשֵׁם אָחִיו יוּבָל הוּא הָיָה אֲבִי כָּל־תֹּפֵשׂ כִּנּוֹר וְעוּגָב:
**כב** וְצִלָּה גַם־הִוא יָלְדָה אֶת־תּוּבַל קַיִן לֹטֵשׁ כָּל־חֹרֵשׁ
נְחֹשֶׁת וּבַרְזֶל וַאֲחוֹת תּוּבַל־קַיִן נַעֲמָה: **כג** וַיֹּאמֶר לֶמֶךְ
לְנָשָׁיו עָדָה וְצִלָּה שְׁמַעַן קוֹלִי נְשֵׁי לֶמֶךְ הַאְזֵנָּה אִמְרָתִי
כִּי אִישׁ הָרַגְתִּי לְפִצְעִי וְיֶלֶד לְחַבֻּרָתִי: **כד** כִּי שִׁבְעָתַיִם
יֻקַּם־קָיִן וְלֶמֶךְ שִׁבְעִים וְשִׁבְעָה:

*[16] Cain left the presence of the Lord and settled
in the land of Nod, east of Eden.*
*[17] Cain knew his wife, and she conceived and
bore Enoch. And he then founded a city, and
named the city after his son Enoch.*

*[18] To Enoch was born Irad, and Irad begot Mehujael, and Mehujael begot Methusael, and Methusael begot Lamech.*

*[19] Lamech took to himself two wives: the name of the one was Adah, and the name of the other was Zillah.*

*[20] Adah bore Jabal; he was the ancestor of those who dwell in tents and amidst herds.*

*[21] And the name of his brother was Jubal; he was the ancestor of all who play the lyre and the pipe.*

*[22] As for Zillah, she bore Tubal-cain, who forged all implements of copper and iron. And the sister of Tubal-cain was Naamah.*

*[23] And Lamech said to his wives, "Adah and Zillah, hear my voice; o wives of Lamech, give ear to my speech. I have slain a man for wounding me, and a lad for bruising me.*

*[24] If Cain is avenged sevenfold, then Lamech seventy-sevenfold."*

**[16] Cain left the presence of the Lord.** He accepted upon himself his Divine punishment, and assumed the fate of the wanderer Abel, the brother whom he had killed.

**And settled in the land of Nod.** Literally "the Land of Wandering," in which it is impossible to become rooted in the ground. Cain therefore proceeds to build the city, but he does not cultivate the land.

**East of Eden.** Despite his exile, Cain does not lose his connection with the Garden of Eden, the ideal of man's existence in this world.

**[17] Cain knew his wife, and she conceived and bore Enoch.** "Knowing" and conceiving, and not only birth, are mentioned here again, because Cain and his family have now moved on to a new stage of how they understand life.

**And bore Enoch.** In Hebrew, "Chanoch" originates from *chinnuch*, which means "education" or "renewal." Although the first educational process under the leadership of Abel proved unsuccessful and led to murder, Cain learns to give life to others by becoming a father. That experience is a part of the process of Cain's correction. Assimilating within himself some of Abel's characteristics, Cain now realizes the importance of education.

**And he then founded a city, and named the city after his son Enoch.** Having forfeited the opportunity to practice agriculture, Cain creates a city - a completely new form of social organization -in which innovation, not land, is the central reality. This corresponds also to the meaning of the term *chinnuch*.

**[18] To Enoch was born Irad ... Mehujael ... Methusael ... Lamech ... [20] Adah bore Jabal; he was the ancestor of those who dwell in tents and amidst herds. ... Jubal; he was the ancestor of all who play the lyre and the pipe. [22] ...Tubal-cain, who forged all implements of copper and iron.** After several generations of city life, the explosive development of the civilization of Cain's descendants begins - in technology, economics, military affairs, and culture.

**[20] ... Jabal; he was the ancestor of those who dwell in tents and amidst herds. [21] ... Jubal; he was the ancestor of all who play the lyre and the pipe.** We see that Cain's descendants bear names phonetically similar to Abel's, and also that they embrace the shepherding professions characteristic of Abel. This demonstrates that the civilization of Cain's descendants was rooted in some of Abel's ideas.

The Torah speaks here not just of simple shepherds, but of "the ancestor of those who dwell in tents and amidst herds." This suggests industrial organization of livestock. Likewise, the Torah speaks here not just of simple musicians, but of "the ancestor of all who play the lyre and the pipe." In other words, this is about the music industry. But at the same time, nothing is said about cultivating the land. This is a purely urban civilization that is wealthy and technologically advanced, and has developed within itself certain features of the murdered Abel.

**[22] And the sister of Tubal-cain was Naamah.**. Literally, "pleasant." It is a very positive name, and highlights the most positive aspects of the civilization of Cain's descendants. The Midrash considers her Noah's wife, which means that humanity will continue to reproduce and develop, synthesizing the descendants of Seth and the descendants of Cain (through Noah and his wife, respectively). This tells us that Cain has found correction and improvement in his descendants.

**[19] Lamech took for himself two wives.** The fact that the Torah even mentions this tells us that Lamech was unusual in this regard. Ever since Adam and Eve, monogamous marriage was the accepted, dominant practice.

**[23] And Lamech said to his wives, "Adah and Zillah, hear my voice; o wives of Lamech, give ear to my speech. I have slain a man for wounding me, and a lad for bruising me.**

**[24] If Cain is avenged sevenfold, then Lamech seventy-sevenfold."** The meaning of this "Song of Lamech" is quite unclear. The Midrash believes that Lamech here boasts of the murders committed by his ancestor Cain and Lamech's son Tubal-cain. The civilization of the descendants of Cain, although it flourishes materially, also has a discernible spiritual crisis.

## 8.2. The Birth of Seth (4:25-26)

כה וַיֵּדַע אָדָם עוֹד אֶת־אִשְׁתּוֹ וַתֵּלֶד בֵּן וַתִּקְרָא אֶת־שְׁמוֹ שֵׁת כִּי שָׁת־לִי אֱלֹהִים זֶרַע אַחֵר תַּחַת הֶבֶל כִּי הֲרָגוֹ קָיִן: כו וּלְשֵׁת גַּם־הוּא יֻלַּד־בֵּן וַיִּקְרָא אֶת־שְׁמוֹ אֱנוֹשׁ אָז הוּחַל לִקְרֹא בְּשֵׁם יי:

*[25] Adam knew his wife again, and she bore a son and named him Seth, which means "God has provided me with another offspring in place of Abel," for Cain had killed him.*
*[26] And to Seth, in turn, a son was born, and he named him Enosh. It was then that men began to invoke the Lord by name.*

**[25] Adam knew his wife again.** The birth of a new son, Seth, requires Adam to know his wife Eve on a new, enhanced level.

**Seth**. Literally, "stability." Another offspring in place of Abel, for Cain had killed him. Seth must perform the function of Abel, which is become a counterweight to Cain, but he must do it correctly. Abel was too ephemeral, too "airy." A more stable Seth must become his replacement.

**She bore a son and named him Seth.** About Cain the Torah (4:1) did not say, "she bore a son and named him Cain," but, more directly, "she gave birth to Cain." In other words, that birth, the very fact of bearing a child for the first time, was itself an "acquisition" for Eve – a change in her status.

And then (4:2) Abel was born, but only as "his brother Abel" – his calling is to serve as opposition to Cain.

Only Seth is born as a son, *ben*, which is closely related to the verb *boneh* (*livnot*, "to build"), for it is on him that the primary construction of further civilization rests.

**[26] And to Seth, in turn, a son was born.** The further construction of civilization proceeds through the birth of sons, through generational change.

**And he named him Enosh.** The name means, literally, "human" – precisely in the sense of human rather than Divine (but also "human" as opposed to animal).

Enosh also means "mortal." Adam sensed that he was above all the creation of the Almighty's hands, while Seth senses that he is the progenitor of the new human race, taking the place of Abel and Cain. Only at the level of Enosh does Seth's awareness of himself as a mortal become a leading factor.

**It was then that men began to invoke the Lord by name.** A person who is keenly aware that he is mortal and finite requires support from God, who is immortal and infinite. He then begins to "invoke the Lord's name" when naming objects that he sees in the world around him. (He identifies those wordly objects with God.)

Although this suggests a deeply religious feeling, it also –
as the Midrash tells us – marks the onset of idolatrous practices among mankind. Spiritual parameters play a central
role in Seth's civilization – unlike Cain's civilization, which
was thoroughly pragmatic.

## 8.3. "This is the Record of Adam's Line" (5:1-32)

א זֶה סֵפֶר תּוֹלְדֹת אָדָם בְּיוֹם בְּרֹא אֱלֹהִים אָדָם בִּדְמוּת
אֱלֹהִים עָשָׂה אֹתוֹ: ב זָכָר וּנְקֵבָה בְּרָאָם וַיְבָרֶךְ אֹתָם
וַיִּקְרָא אֶת־שְׁמָם אָדָם בְּיוֹם הִבָּרְאָם: ג וַיְחִי אָדָם
שְׁלֹשִׁים וּמְאַת שָׁנָה וַיּוֹלֶד בִּדְמוּתוֹ כְּצַלְמוֹ וַיִּקְרָא אֶת־
שְׁמוֹ שֵׁת: ד וַיִּהְיוּ יְמֵי־אָדָם אַחֲרֵי הוֹלִידוֹ אֶת־שֵׁת
שְׁמֹנֶה מֵאֹת שָׁנָה וַיּוֹלֶד בָּנִים וּבָנוֹת: ה וַיִּהְיוּ כָּל־יְמֵי
אָדָם אֲשֶׁר־חַי תְּשַׁע מֵאוֹת שָׁנָה וּשְׁלֹשִׁים שָׁנָה וַיָּמֹת:
ו וַיְחִי־שֵׁת חָמֵשׁ שָׁנִים וּמְאַת שָׁנָה וַיּוֹלֶד אֶת־אֱנוֹשׁ: ז
וַיְחִי־שֵׁת אַחֲרֵי הוֹלִידוֹ אֶת־אֱנוֹשׁ שֶׁבַע שָׁנִים וּשְׁמֹנֶה
מֵאוֹת שָׁנָה וַיּוֹלֶד בָּנִים וּבָנוֹת: ח וַיִּהְיוּ כָּל־יְמֵי־שֵׁת
שְׁתֵּים עֶשְׂרֵה שָׁנָה וּתְשַׁע מֵאוֹת שָׁנָה וַיָּמֹת: ט וַיְחִי
אֱנוֹשׁ תִּשְׁעִים שָׁנָה וַיּוֹלֶד אֶת־קֵינָן: י וַיְחִי אֱנוֹשׁ אַחֲרֵי
הוֹלִידוֹ אֶת־קֵינָן חֲמֵשׁ עֶשְׂרֵה שָׁנָה וּשְׁמֹנֶה מֵאוֹת שָׁנָה
וַיּוֹלֶד בָּנִים וּבָנוֹת: יא וַיִּהְיוּ כָּל־יְמֵי אֱנוֹשׁ חָמֵשׁ שָׁנִים
וּתְשַׁע מֵאוֹת שָׁנָה וַיָּמֹת: יב וַיְחִי קֵינָן שִׁבְעִים שָׁנָה
וַיּוֹלֶד אֶת־מַהֲלַלְאֵל: יג וַיְחִי קֵינָן אַחֲרֵי הוֹלִידוֹ אֶת־
מַהֲלַלְאֵל אַרְבָּעִים שָׁנָה וּשְׁמֹנֶה מֵאוֹת שָׁנָה וַיּוֹלֶד בָּנִים
וּבָנוֹת: יד וַיִּהְיוּ כָּל־יְמֵי קֵינָן עֶשֶׂר שָׁנִים וּתְשַׁע מֵאוֹת
שָׁנָה וַיָּמֹת: טו וַיְחִי מַהֲלַלְאֵל חָמֵשׁ שָׁנִים וְשִׁשִּׁים
שָׁנָה וַיּוֹלֶד אֶת־יָרֶד: טז וַיְחִי מַהֲלַלְאֵל אַחֲרֵי הוֹלִידוֹ
אֶת־יֶרֶד שְׁלֹשִׁים שָׁנָה וּשְׁמֹנֶה מֵאוֹת שָׁנָה וַיּוֹלֶד בָּנִים
וּבָנוֹת: יז וַיִּהְיוּ כָּל־יְמֵי מַהֲלַלְאֵל חָמֵשׁ וְתִשְׁעִים שָׁנָה
וּשְׁמֹנֶה מֵאוֹת שָׁנָה וַיָּמֹת: יח וַיְחִי־יֶרֶד שְׁתַּיִם וְשִׁשִּׁים
שָׁנָה וּמְאַת שָׁנָה וַיּוֹלֶד אֶת־חֲנוֹךְ: יט וַיְחִי־יֶרֶד אַחֲרֵי

הוֹלִידוֹ אֶת־חֲנוֹךְ שְׁמֹנֶה מֵאוֹת שָׁנָה וַיּוֹלֶד בָּנִים וּבָנוֹת: **כ** וַיִּהְיוּ כָּל־יְמֵי־יֶרֶד שְׁתַּיִם וְשִׁשִּׁים שָׁנָה וּתְשַׁע מֵאוֹת שָׁנָה וַיָּמֹת: **כא** וַיְחִי חֲנוֹךְ חָמֵשׁ וְשִׁשִּׁים שָׁנָה וַיּוֹלֶד אֶת־מְתוּשָׁלַח: **כב** וַיִּתְהַלֵּךְ חֲנוֹךְ אֶת־הָאֱלֹהִים אַחֲרֵי הוֹלִידוֹ אֶת־מְתוּשֶׁלַח שְׁלֹשׁ מֵאוֹת שָׁנָה וַיּוֹלֶד בָּנִים וּבָנוֹת: **כג** וַיְהִי כָּל־יְמֵי חֲנוֹךְ חָמֵשׁ וְשִׁשִּׁים שָׁנָה וּשְׁלֹשׁ מֵאוֹת שָׁנָה: **כד** וַיִּתְהַלֵּךְ חֲנוֹךְ אֶת־הָאֱלֹהִים וְאֵינֶנּוּ כִּי־ לָקַח אֹתוֹ אֱלֹהִים: **כה** וַיְחִי מְתוּשֶׁלַח שֶׁבַע וּשְׁמֹנִים שָׁנָה וּמְאַת שָׁנָה וַיּוֹלֶד אֶת־לָמֶךְ: **כו** וַיְחִי מְתוּשֶׁלַח אַחֲרֵי הוֹלִידוֹ אֶת־לֶמֶךְ שְׁתַּיִם וּשְׁמוֹנִים שָׁנָה וּשְׁבַע מֵאוֹת שָׁנָה וַיּוֹלֶד בָּנִים וּבָנוֹת: **כז** וַיִּהְיוּ כָּל־יְמֵי מְתוּשֶׁלַח תֵּשַׁע וְשִׁשִּׁים שָׁנָה וּתְשַׁע מֵאוֹת שָׁנָה וַיָּמֹת: **כח** וַיְחִי־לֶמֶךְ שְׁתַּיִם וּשְׁמֹנִים שָׁנָה וּמְאַת שָׁנָה וַיּוֹלֶד בֵּן: **כט** וַיִּקְרָא אֶת־שְׁמוֹ נֹחַ לֵאמֹר זֶה יְנַחֲמֵנוּ מִמַּעֲשֵׂנוּ וּמֵעִצְּבוֹן יָדֵינוּ מִן־הָאֲדָמָה אֲשֶׁר אֵרְרָהּ יי: **ל** וַיְחִי־לֶמֶךְ אַחֲרֵי הוֹלִידוֹ אֶת־נֹחַ חָמֵשׁ וְתִשְׁעִים שָׁנָה וַחֲמֵשׁ מֵאֹת שָׁנָה וַיּוֹלֶד בָּנִים וּבָנוֹת: **לא** וַיְהִי כָּל־יְמֵי־לֶמֶךְ שֶׁבַע וְשִׁבְעִים שָׁנָה וּשְׁבַע מֵאוֹת שָׁנָה וַיָּמֹת: **לב** וַיְהִי־נֹחַ בֶּן־חֲמֵשׁ מֵאוֹת שָׁנָה וַיּוֹלֶד נֹחַ אֶת־שֵׁם אֶת־חָם וְאֶת־יָפֶת:

[1] This is the record of Adam's line. When God created man, He made him in the likeness of God; [2] Male and female He created them. And when they were created, He blessed them and called them Man.

[3] When Adam had lived 130 years, he begot a son in his likeness after his image, and he named him Seth. [4] After the birth of Seth, Adam lived 800 years and begot sons and daughters. [5] All the days that Adam lived came to 930 years; then he died. [6] When Seth had lived 105 years, he begot Enosh.

*[7] After the birth of Enosh, Seth lived 807 years and begot sons and daughters.*

*[8] All the days of Seth came to 912 years; then he died.*

*[9] When Enosh had lived 90 years, he begot Kenan.*

*[10] After the birth of Kenan, Enosh lived 815 years and begot sons and daughters.*

*[11] All the days of Enosh came to 905 years; then he died.*

*[12] When Kenan had lived 70 years, he begot Mahalalel.*

*[13] After the birth of Mahalalel, Kenan lived 840 years and begot sons and daughters. [14] All the days of Kenan came to 910 years; then he died.*

*[15] When Mahalalel had lived 65 years, he begot Jared.*

*[16] After the birth of Jared, Mahalalel lived 830 years and begot sons and daughters.*

*[17] All the days of Mahalalel came to 895 years; then he died.*

*[18] When Jared had lived 162 years, he begot Enoch.*

*[19] After the birth of Enoch, Jared lived 800 years and begot sons and daughters.*

*[20] All the days of Jared came to 962 years; then he died.*

*[21] When Enoch had lived 65 years, he begot Methuselah.*

*[22] After the birth of Methuselah, Enoch walked with God 300 years; and he begot sons and daughters.*

*[23] All the days of Enoch came to 365 years.*

*[24] Enoch walked with God; then he was no more, for God took him.*

*[25] When Methuselah had lived 187 years, he begot Lamech.*

*[26] After the birth of Lamech, Methuselah lived 782 years and begot sons and daughters.*

*[27] All the days of Methuselah came to 969 years; then he died.*

*[28] When Lamech had lived 182 years, he begot a son.*

*[29] And he named him Noah, saying, "This one will provide us relief from our work and from the toil of our hands, out of the very soil which the Lord placed under a curse."*

*[30] After the birth of Noah, Lamech lived 595 years and begot sons and daughters.*

*[31] All the days of Lamech came to 777 years; then he died.*

*[32] When Noah had lived 500 years, Noah begot Shem, Ham, and Japheth.*

**[1] This is the record of Adam's line.** Literally "This is the book of the generations of Adam." There is an obvious parallel here to the verse, "Such is the story (literally "generations") of heaven and earth when they were created" (2:4), which introduced the history of the development of the world immediately after the Creation. Likewise, here begins a new characterization of the history of mankind.

**Record.** The Hebrew word is *toledot*, "generations", one of the most important concepts in the Torah. It can refer either to a given person's origin (his ancestry) or to his posterity

– his descendants as well as his accomplishments. The concept of *toledot* positions man as a link in the chain of generations, orienting him to be responsible not only for himself, but also for the entire chain –the segment of the chain that he has inherited, and also the part that he has produced (or will produce).

**The record of Adam's line.** Unlike in nature, where the birth of new generations is the central concept, for mankind reflection is equally important – thinking about one's chosen path, and comparing the present to the past as a means of evaluating progress. Therefore, what is most significant for any individual is not just the creation of his line, but the "record" of that line.

The Talmud, in discussing the question of "which is the most important verse in the Torah?", suggests two candidates: "Love your neighbor as yourself: I am the Lord." (Leviticus 19:18), and our verse here, "This is the record of Adam's line." The development of civilization as a result of the change of generations is an essential element of the Torah's Divine teachings, for only through this process can a person advance spiritually and come closer to God.

**[2] Male and female He created them ... He blessed them and called them Man.** "He called *them*"; that is, them both and not just one of them. Only through their union do a man and a woman become fully human.

**[1] This is the record of Adam's line ... He made him in the likeness of God ... Adam begot a son in His likeness after His image, and he named him Seth.** The starting point for Seth's civilization (unlike the descendants of Cain's civilization) is man's likeness to God as an idea to be transmitted to subsequent generations – the idea of perceiving the world as "the record of the birth of mankind, who were created in God's likeness."

**[9] When Enosh had lived 90 years, he begot Kenan.** The name "Kenan" is very similar to "Cain" (in the Hebrew, only the last letter of "Cain" needs to be repeated to form "Kenan"). Namely, Kenan carries some of Cain's features. A convergence is taking place here: Cain's civilization assimilates some of Abel's features, and Seth's civilization incorporates the positive elements of Cain's culture.

**[24] Enoch walked with God; then he was no more, for God took him.** The most essential value of Seth's civilization is its communication with God.

**[28] When Lamech had lived 182 years, he begot a son. [29] And he named him Noah, saying, "This one will provide us relief from our work and from the toil of our hands, out of the very soil which the Lord placed under a curse."** This verse clearly connects the name Noah with the idea of *nachem*, "to comfort." This concept is critical to understanding the entire story of the Flood, which begins very soon.

But the connection between Noah and *nachem* is only partial (only the first two of the three letters of the root *nachem* appear in "Noah"). Had Lamech meant to emphasize this connection, he should probably have named his son "Nechamah" (consolation) or "Menachem" (consoler). But the name "Noah" carries the additional meaning of "lightness" or "simplicity." This idea is crucial for understanding the story of the Flood, and for "providing relief from the toil of our hands upon the soil which the Lord has cursed." We shall discuss this in more detail below.

## 8.4. The Crisis of Humanity Leading up to the Flood (6:1-8)

א וַיְהִי כִּי־הֵחֵל הָאָדָם לָרֹב עַל־פְּנֵי הָאֲדָמָה וּבָנוֹת יֻלְּדוּ לָהֶם: ב וַיִּרְאוּ בְנֵי־הָאֱלֹהִים אֶת־בְּנוֹת הָאָדָם כִּי טֹבֹת הֵנָּה וַיִּקְחוּ לָהֶם נָשִׁים מִכֹּל אֲשֶׁר בָּחָרוּ: ג וַיֹּאמֶר יי לֹא־יָדוֹן רוּחִי בָאָדָם לְעֹלָם בְּשַׁגַּם הוּא בָשָׂר וְהָיוּ יָמָיו מֵאָה וְעֶשְׂרִים שָׁנָה: ד הַנְּפִלִים הָיוּ בָאָרֶץ בַּיָּמִים הָהֵם וְגַם אַחֲרֵי־כֵן אֲשֶׁר יָבֹאוּ בְּנֵי הָאֱלֹהִים אֶל־בְּנוֹת הָאָדָם וְיָלְדוּ לָהֶם הֵמָּה הַגִּבֹּרִים אֲשֶׁר מֵעוֹלָם אַנְשֵׁי הַשֵּׁם: ה וַיַּרְא יי כִּי רַבָּה רָעַת הָאָדָם בָּאָרֶץ וְכָל־יֵצֶר מַחְשְׁבֹת לִבּוֹ רַק רַע כָּל־הַיּוֹם: ו וַיִּנָּחֶם יי כִּי־עָשָׂה אֶת־הָאָדָם בָּאָרֶץ וַיִּתְעַצֵּב אֶל־לִבּוֹ: ז וַיֹּאמֶר יי אֶמְחֶה אֶת־הָאָדָם אֲשֶׁר־בָּרָאתִי מֵעַל פְּנֵי הָאֲדָמָה מֵאָדָם עַד־בְּהֵמָה עַד־רֶמֶשׂ וְעַד־עוֹף הַשָּׁמָיִם כִּי נִחַמְתִּי כִּי עֲשִׂיתִם: ח וְנֹחַ מָצָא חֵן בְּעֵינֵי יי:

*[1] When men began to increase on earth and daughters were born to them,*

*[2] The sons of the powerful saw how beautiful the daughters of men were and took wives from among those that pleased them.*

*[3] The Lord said, "My breath shall not abide in man forever, since he too is flesh; let the days allowed him be one hundred and twenty years."*

*[4] It was then, and later too, that the Nephilim appeared on earth – when the sons of the powerful cohabited with the daughters of men, who bore them offspring. They were the heroes of old, the men of renown.*

*[5] The Lord saw how great man's wickedness was on earth, and how every plan devised by his mind was nothing but evil all the time.*

*[6] And the Lord regretted that He had made*
*man on earth, and His heart was saddened.*
*[7] The Lord said, "I will blot out from the earth*
*the men whom I created – men together with*
*beasts, creeping things, and birds of the sky; for*
*I regret that I made them."*
*[8] But Noah found favor with the Lord.*

**[1] When men began to increase on earth.** As the result of
its numerical increase, mankind is moving away from the
family structure and moving on to organization of society
on a larger scale.

**And daughters were born to them.** Needless to say, daughters had been born all along. What is meant is that some of
those daughters now acquired a new and special social status,
which led also to attendant social conflicts concerning them.

**[2] The sons of the powerful saw how beautiful the daugh-
ters of men were and took wives from among those that
pleased them.** This verse speaks of the moral crisis leading
up to the Flood, but its exact interpretation is unclear, and
there are several ways of understanding it.

In the original Hebrew of the text, "sons of the powerful"
is *benei ha-elohim,* "sons of *Elohim.*" Since the word *elohim*
can refer either to God or to humans of elevated social status
(such as rulers or judges; see Exodus 4:16, 7:1, 21:6), just who
were these "sons of *elohim*"? Whose sons were they, actually?

Several interpretations of the term "sons of *elohim*" have
been suggested, as follows:

I. The *benei ha-elohim* are the "sons of distinguished,

noble people," and the *benot ha-adam*, the "daughters of men" whom they married are girls from the common people. The crime of the sons of the nobility was that they took daughters "from among those that pleased them", that is, by force, without seeking the consent of the girls themselves.

II. These *benei ha-elohim*, "the sons of God," were the descendants of Seth. They are called "the sons of God" because the understanding of the Divine among mankind was preserved in Seth's descendants. In this case the *benot ha-adam*, "daughters of men," are daughters of the descendants of Cain, and the crime of Seth's sons is that they were so attracted to the girls' physical beauty (they "saw how beautiful the daughters of men were") that they allowed their children to intermarry with Cain's descendants. The result was that the children born from these unions adopted Cain's culture, and were educated in improper elements of human behavior. Thus there no longer remained any hope for the salvation of mankind.

III. The Midrash suggests a third interpretation. The "sons of God" are angels who descended to earth as emissaries of the Almighty. But instead of fulfilling the task that God had assigned to them, those angels took to marrying human women. (It is important to understand that such Midrashim are not to be taken literally.)

**[3] The Lord said, "My breath shall not abide in man forever, since he too is flesh; let the days allowed him be one hundred and twenty years."** These words can be understood in two ways: (a) God is setting a limit on human life expectancy. Henceforth no human can live longer than 120 years. Or (b) God is establishing an interval of 120 years for humanity to repent and correct itself. If they fail to do so, they will then be destroyed by the Flood.

**[4] It was then, and later too, that the Nephilim appeared on earth-when the sons of the powerful cohabited with the daughters of men, who bore them offspring. They were the heroes of old, the men of renown.** After God set a limit of 120 years for mankind, the Torah further tells us about the birth of these "giants," but it is not clear from the text whether this was a positive circumstance or a negative one.

Grammatically, the word *Nephilim* can be understood in two ways:

I. As "giants," or "greats," referring to Shem, Ham, and Japheth, the sons of Noah. (Since their mother Naamah came from Cain's descendants, this marriage was also a situation of "the divine beings cohabited with the daughters of men.") Until Noah's three sons grew up and became independent, the Flood could not happen, because there would have been no one from whom to recreate humankind anew. God therefore allocated 120 years for their birth and maturation.

II. As "the fallen" – who themselves fell and also caused the world's downfall, because the world disintegrates when high-ranking officials neglect their duties and oppress ordinary people.

**[5] The Lord saw how great was man's wickedness on earth, and how every plan devised by his mind was nothing but evil all the time. [6] And the Lord regretted that He had made man on earth, and His heart was saddened. [7] The Lord said, "I will blot out from the earth the men whom I created - men together with beasts, creeping things, and birds of the sky; for I regret that I made them."** God has now finally made His decision concerning the Flood.

The word *nachem*, "to regret," used twice in this passage, is the very same word as *nachem*, "to console," used by Lamech above (5:29) in naming his son Noah. We will have more to say about this concept a little later.

**[8] But Noah found favor with the Lord.** "Noah found favor" means that on his actual merits alone Noah did not deserve to be spared in the flood.

# Weekly Portion
# Noah

Chapter 9

# A General Overview of the Story of the Flood

NOAH IS THE second weekly portion of the Torah, and also the second portion having a thoroughly universal (i.e., not specifically Jewish) character. It presents a view of humanity as consisting of nations, and not merely individuals. Although *toledot*, "posterity" (see 5:1), is the first significant word of this portion, the name of the portion is "Noah," not "Toledot." This is because each of the Torah's weekly portions takes its name not from its first word, or even its first significant word, but from one of its first several words that best represents the entire weekly portion.

After providing a general overview of the story of the Flood with only minimal remarks, we will then try to gain a better understanding by delving more deeply into the story.

## 9.1. Noah's Ark (6:9-22)

ט אֵלֶּה תּוֹלְדֹת נֹחַ נֹחַ אִישׁ צַדִּיק תָּמִים הָיָה בְּדֹרֹתָיו
אֶת־הָאֱלֹהִים הִתְהַלֶּךְ־נֹחַ: י וַיּוֹלֶד נֹחַ שְׁלֹשָׁה בָנִים
אֶת־שֵׁם אֶת־חָם וְאֶת־יָפֶת: יא וַתִּשָּׁחֵת הָאָרֶץ לִפְנֵי

הָאֱלֹהִים וַתִּמָּלֵא הָאָרֶץ חָמָס: **יב** וַיַּרְא אֱלֹהִים אֶת־
הָאָרֶץ וְהִנֵּה נִשְׁחָתָה כִּי־הִשְׁחִית כָּל־בָּשָׂר אֶת־דַּרְכּוֹ
עַל־הָאָרֶץ: **יג** וַיֹּאמֶר אֱלֹהִים לְנֹחַ קֵץ כָּל־בָּשָׂר בָּא לְפָנַי
כִּי־מָלְאָה הָאָרֶץ חָמָס מִפְּנֵיהֶם וְהִנְנִי מַשְׁחִיתָם אֶת־
הָאָרֶץ: **יד** עֲשֵׂה לְךָ תֵּבַת עֲצֵי־גֹפֶר קִנִּים תַּעֲשֶׂה אֶת־
הַתֵּבָה וְכָפַרְתָּ אֹתָהּ מִבַּיִת וּמִחוּץ בַּכֹּפֶר: **טו** וְזֶה אֲשֶׁר
תַּעֲשֶׂה אֹתָהּ שְׁלֹשׁ מֵאוֹת אַמָּה אֹרֶךְ הַתֵּבָה חֲמִשִּׁים
אַמָּה רָחְבָּהּ וּשְׁלֹשִׁים אַמָּה קוֹמָתָהּ: **טז** צֹהַר ׀ תַּעֲשֶׂה
לַתֵּבָה וְאֶל־אַמָּה תְּכַלֶּנָּה מִלְמַעְלָה וּפֶתַח הַתֵּבָה בְּצִדָּהּ
תָּשִׂים תַּחְתִּיִּם שְׁנִיִּם וּשְׁלֹשִׁים תַּעֲשֶׂהָ: **יז** וַאֲנִי הִנְנִי
מֵבִיא אֶת־הַמַּבּוּל מַיִם עַל־הָאָרֶץ לְשַׁחֵת כָּל־בָּשָׂר
אֲשֶׁר־בּוֹ רוּחַ חַיִּים מִתַּחַת הַשָּׁמָיִם כֹּל אֲשֶׁר־בָּאָרֶץ
יִגְוָע: **יח** וַהֲקִמֹתִי אֶת־בְּרִיתִי אִתָּךְ וּבָאתָ אֶל־הַתֵּבָה
אַתָּה וּבָנֶיךָ וְאִשְׁתְּךָ וּנְשֵׁי־בָנֶיךָ אִתָּךְ: **יט** וּמִכָּל־הָחַי
מִכָּל־בָּשָׂר שְׁנַיִם מִכֹּל תָּבִיא אֶל־הַתֵּבָה לְהַחֲיֹת אִתָּךְ
זָכָר וּנְקֵבָה יִהְיוּ: **כ** מֵהָעוֹף לְמִינֵהוּ וּמִן־הַבְּהֵמָה
לְמִינָהּ מִכֹּל רֶמֶשׂ הָאֲדָמָה לְמִינֵהוּ שְׁנַיִם מִכֹּל יָבֹאוּ
אֵלֶיךָ לְהַחֲיוֹת: **כא** וְאַתָּה קַח־לְךָ מִכָּל־מַאֲכָל אֲשֶׁר
יֵאָכֵל וְאָסַפְתָּ אֵלֶיךָ וְהָיָה לְךָ וְלָהֶם לְאָכְלָה: **כב** וַיַּעַשׂ
נֹחַ כְּכֹל אֲשֶׁר צִוָּה אֹתוֹ אֱלֹהִים כֵּן עָשָׂה:

[9] **This is the line of Noah. Noah was a righteous man; h**e *was blameless in his age; Noah walked with God.*

[10] *Noah begot three sons: Shem, Ham, and Japheth.*

[11] *The earth became corrupt before God; the earth was filled with lawlessness.*

[12] *When God saw how corrupt the earth was, for all flesh had corrupted its ways on earth,*

[13] *God said to Noah, "I have decided to put an end to all flesh, for the earth is filled with lawlessness because of them: I am about to destroy them with the earth.*

*[14] Make yourself an ark of gopher wood; make it an ark with compartments, and cover it inside and out with pitch.*

*[15] This is how you shall make it: the length of the ark shall be three hundred cubits, its width fifty cubits, and its height thirty cubits.*

*[16] Make an opening for daylight in the ark, and terminate it within a cubit of the top. Put the entrance to the ark in its side; make it with bottom, second, and third decks.*

*[17] "For My part, I am about to bring the Flood-waters upon the earth – to destroy all flesh under the sky in which there is breath of life; everything on earth shall perish.*

*[18] But I will establish My covenant with you, and you shall enter the ark, with your sons, your wife, and your sons' wives.*

*[19] And of all that lives, of all flesh, you shall take two of each into the ark to keep alive with you; they shall be male and female.*

*[20] From birds of every kind, cattle of every kind, every kind of creeping thing on earth, two of each shall come to you to stay alive.*

*[21] For your part, take of everything that is eaten and store it away, to serve as food for you and for them."*

*[22] Noah did so; just as God commanded him, so he did.*

**[9] This is the line of Noah. Noah was a righteous man.**
After the word *toledot,* "offspring," a list of descendants would usually appear. Noah, above all, "gave birth to" his own righteousness. This can be understood both in a positive sense, in that he was "a very righteous person," and as

a criticism: Noah was focused on himself and on his own righteousness. Other people were not important to him.

**He was blameless in his age.** This is a limiting characteristic. Yes, Noah was blameless, but only within his own age.

**Noah walked with God.** This turn of phrase can be understood two ways:

(1) Noah walked with God, but not with people. He cared about his own righteousness, not about his fellow humans.

(2) Noah walked with God – *with* God, rather than *before* God; that is, he did what he was told, but made no effort to "walk *before* (i.e., ahead of) God" as Abraham did (17:1, see commentary there). Abraham takes issue with God and argues with Him about the destruction of the city of Sodom. But Noah, with no complaint whatsoever, simply accepts the news of the destruction of all of humankind without challenging it.

**[10] Noah begot three sons. Shem, Ham, and Japheth**. From the perspective of the Torah three races will be born from those three sons: the Japhetic peoples of the white race inhabiting Europe; the Semites of the yellow race inhabiting Asia; and the Hamites of the black race inhabiting Africa. (Of course, this is only an approximate description.) The Land of Israel is at the junction point of all these three regions, since the Divine light must emanate from Israel to all mankind.

**[11] The earth became corrupt before God; the earth was filled with lawlessness. [12] When God saw how corrupt the earth was, for all flesh had corrupted its ways on earth, [13] God said to Noah, "I have decided to put an end to all flesh, for the earth is filled with lawlessness because**

**of them.."** Here several times the Torah identifies the two primary sins that led to the Flood: corruption ("all flesh had corrupted its ways on earth" in relation to the Almighty) and evildoing (perversion of every man's behavior toward his fellow man). We will examine this issue in greater detail below.

**[17] I am about to bring the Flood - waters upon the earth.** Adding the words "waters upon the earth" is necessary in order to indicate that the essential meaning of the Flood was not in the flood itself, but in "obliterating the final structure." Later we will cover this point in greater detail.

**[18] And you shall enter the ark, with your sons, your wife, and your sons' wives.** The men and the women are mentioned separately. In the ark they remain apart, for intimacy is forbidden to them.

**[22] Noah did so; just as God commanded him, so he did.** Noah executes orders precisely. He asks no questions, and does not object.

### 9.2. The Flood Begins (7:1-24)

א וַיֹּאמֶר יי לְנֹחַ בֹּא־אַתָּה וְכָל־בֵּיתְךָ אֶל־הַתֵּבָה כִּי־ אֹתְךָ רָאִיתִי צַדִּיק לְפָנַי בַּדּוֹר הַזֶּה: ב מִכֹּל | הַבְּהֵמָה הַטְּהוֹרָה תִּקַּח־לְךָ שִׁבְעָה שִׁבְעָה אִישׁ וְאִשְׁתּוֹ וּמִן־ הַבְּהֵמָה אֲשֶׁר לֹא טְהֹרָה הִוא שְׁנַיִם אִישׁ וְאִשְׁתּוֹ: ג גַּם מֵעוֹף הַשָּׁמַיִם שִׁבְעָה שִׁבְעָה זָכָר וּנְקֵבָה לְחַיּוֹת זֶרַע עַל־ פְּנֵי כָל־הָאָרֶץ: ד כִּי לְיָמִים עוֹד שִׁבְעָה אָנֹכִי מַמְטִיר עַל־הָאָרֶץ אַרְבָּעִים יוֹם וְאַרְבָּעִים לָיְלָה וּמָחִיתִי אֶת־ כָּל־הַיְקוּם אֲשֶׁר עָשִׂיתִי מֵעַל פְּנֵי הָאֲדָמָה: ה וַיַּעַשׂ נֹחַ כְּכֹל אֲשֶׁר־צִוָּהוּ יי: ו וְנֹחַ בֶּן־שֵׁשׁ מֵאוֹת שָׁנָה וְהַמַּבּוּל

הָיָה מַיִם עַל־הָאָרֶץ: **ז** וַיָּבֹא נֹחַ וּבָנָיו וְאִשְׁתּוֹ וּנְשֵׁי־
בָנָיו אִתּוֹ אֶל־הַתֵּבָה מִפְּנֵי מֵי הַמַּבּוּל: **ח** מִן־הַבְּהֵמָה
הַטְּהוֹרָה וּמִן־הַבְּהֵמָה אֲשֶׁר אֵינֶנָּה טְהֹרָה וּמִן־הָעוֹף
וְכֹל אֲשֶׁר־רֹמֵשׂ עַל־הָאֲדָמָה: **ט** שְׁנַיִם שְׁנַיִם בָּאוּ אֶל־
נֹחַ אֶל־הַתֵּבָה זָכָר וּנְקֵבָה כַּאֲשֶׁר צִוָּה אֱלֹהִים אֶת־נֹחַ:
**י** וַיְהִי לְשִׁבְעַת הַיָּמִים וּמֵי הַמַּבּוּל הָיוּ עַל־הָאָרֶץ: **יא**
בִּשְׁנַת שֵׁשׁ־מֵאוֹת שָׁנָה לְחַיֵּי־נֹחַ בַּחֹדֶשׁ הַשֵּׁנִי בְּשִׁבְעָה־
עָשָׂר יוֹם לַחֹדֶשׁ בַּיּוֹם הַזֶּה נִבְקְעוּ כָּל־מַעְיְנֹת תְּהוֹם
רַבָּה וַאֲרֻבֹּת הַשָּׁמַיִם נִפְתָּחוּ: **יב** וַיְהִי הַגֶּשֶׁם עַל־הָאָרֶץ
אַרְבָּעִים יוֹם וְאַרְבָּעִים לָיְלָה: **יג** בְּעֶצֶם הַיּוֹם הַזֶּה בָּא
נֹחַ וְשֵׁם־וְחָם וָיֶפֶת בְּנֵי־נֹחַ וְאֵשֶׁת נֹחַ וּשְׁלֹשֶׁת נְשֵׁי־בָנָיו
אִתָּם אֶל־הַתֵּבָה: **יד** הֵמָּה וְכָל־הַחַיָּה לְמִינָהּ וְכָל־
הַבְּהֵמָה לְמִינָהּ וְכָל־הָרֶמֶשׂ הָרֹמֵשׂ עַל־הָאָרֶץ לְמִינֵהוּ
וְכָל־הָעוֹף לְמִינֵהוּ כֹּל צִפּוֹר כָּל־כָּנָף: **טו** וַיָּבֹאוּ אֶל־נֹחַ
אֶל־הַתֵּבָה שְׁנַיִם שְׁנַיִם מִכָּל־הַבָּשָׂר אֲשֶׁר־בּוֹ רוּחַ חַיִּים:
**טז** וְהַבָּאִים זָכָר וּנְקֵבָה מִכָּל־בָּשָׂר בָּאוּ כַּאֲשֶׁר צִוָּה אֹתוֹ
אֱלֹהִים וַיִּסְגֹּר יי בַּעֲדוֹ: **יז** וַיְהִי הַמַּבּוּל אַרְבָּעִים יוֹם
עַל־הָאָרֶץ וַיִּרְבּוּ הַמַּיִם וַיִּשְׂאוּ אֶת־הַתֵּבָה וַתָּרָם מֵעַל
הָאָרֶץ: **יח** וַיִּגְבְּרוּ הַמַּיִם וַיִּרְבּוּ מְאֹד עַל־הָאָרֶץ וַתֵּלֶךְ
הַתֵּבָה עַל־פְּנֵי הַמָּיִם: **יט** וְהַמַּיִם גָּבְרוּ מְאֹד מְאֹד
עַל־הָאָרֶץ וַיְכֻסּוּ כָּל־הֶהָרִים הַגְּבֹהִים אֲשֶׁר־תַּחַת כָּל־
הַשָּׁמָיִם: **כ** חֲמֵשׁ עֶשְׂרֵה אַמָּה מִלְמַעְלָה גָּבְרוּ הַמָּיִם
וַיְכֻסּוּ הֶהָרִים: **כא** וַיִּגְוַע כָּל־בָּשָׂר | הָרֹמֵשׂ עַל־הָאָרֶץ
בָּעוֹף וּבַבְּהֵמָה וּבַחַיָּה וּבְכָל־הַשֶּׁרֶץ הַשֹּׁרֵץ עַל־הָאָרֶץ
וְכֹל הָאָדָם: **כב** כֹּל אֲשֶׁר נִשְׁמַת־רוּחַ חַיִּים בְּאַפָּיו מִכֹּל
אֲשֶׁר בֶּחָרָבָה מֵתוּ: **כג** וַיִּמַח אֶת־כָּל־הַיְקוּם | אֲשֶׁר |
עַל־פְּנֵי הָאֲדָמָה מֵאָדָם עַד־בְּהֵמָה עַד־רֶמֶשׂ וְעַד־עוֹף
הַשָּׁמַיִם וַיִּמָּחוּ מִן־הָאָרֶץ וַיִּשָּׁאֶר אַךְ־נֹחַ וַאֲשֶׁר אִתּוֹ
בַּתֵּבָה: **כד** וַיִּגְבְּרוּ הַמַּיִם עַל־הָאָרֶץ חֲמִשִּׁים וּמְאַת יוֹם:

*[1] Then the Lord said to Noah, "Go into the ark,
with all your household, for you alone have I found
righteous before Me in this generation.*

[2] *Of every clean animal you shall take seven pairs, males and their mates, and of every animal that is not clean, two, a male and its mate;*

[3] *Of the birds of the sky also, seven pairs, male and female, to keep seed alive upon all the earth.*

[4] *For in seven days' time I will make it rain upon the earth, forty days and forty nights, and I will blot out from the earth all existence that I created."*

[5] *And Noah did just as the Lord commanded him.*

[6] *Noah was six hundred years old when the Flood came, waters upon the earth.*

[7] *Noah, with his sons, his wife, and his sons' wives, went into the ark because of the waters of the Flood.*

[8] *Of the clean animals, of the animals that are not clean, of the birds, and of everything that creeps on the ground,*

[9] *Two of each, male and female, came to Noah into the ark, as God had commanded Noah.*

[10] *And on the seventh day the waters of the Flood came upon the earth.*

[11] *In the six hundredth year of Noah's life, in the second month, on the seventeenth day of the month, on that day all the fountains of the great deep burst apart, and the floodgates of the sky broke open.*

[12] *The rain fell on the earth forty days and forty nights.*

[13] *That same day Noah and Noah's sons, Shem, Ham, and Japheth, went into the ark, with Noah's wife and the three wives of his sons.*

[14] *They and all beasts of every kind, all cattle of every kind, all creatures of every kind that creep on the earth, and all birds of every kind, every bird, every winged thing.*

[15] *They came to Noah into the ark, two each of all*

*flesh in which there was breath of life.*

*[16] Thus they that entered comprised male and female of all flesh, as God had commanded him. And the Lord shut him in.*

*[17] The Flood continued forty days on the earth, and the waters increased and raised the ark so that it rose above the earth.*

*[18] The waters swelled and increased greatly upon the earth, and the ark drifted upon the waters.*

*[19] When the waters had swelled much more upon the earth, all the highest mountains everywhere under the sky were covered.*

*[20] Fifteen cubits higher did the waters swell, as the mountains were covered.*

*[21] And all flesh that stirred on earth perished – birds, cattle, beasts, and all the things that swarmed upon the earth, and all mankind.*

*[22] All in whose nostrils was the merest breath of life, all that was on dry land, died.*

*[23] All existence on earth was blotted out – man, cattle, creeping things, and birds of the sky; they were blotted out from the earth. Only Noah was left, and those with him in the ark.*

*[24] And when the waters had swelled on the earth one hundred and fifty days.*

**[2] Of every clean animal you shall take seven pairs ... and of every animal that is not clean, two ... [3] Of the birds of the sky also, seven pairs ... [4] For in seven days' time I will make it rain upon the earth.** Some of the clean cattle will be needed later for making a sacrifice (8:20), which is why Noah must take more than just the two needed for future reproduction.

(The number "seven" is chosen, quite possibly, as realizing the instruction, "For in seven days' time I will make it rain upon the earth." Also, the number seven in Judaism very often represents nature, as opposed to the number eight, which symbolizes that which is beyond nature. The two sevens here could be an allusion to the fact that in the course of the Flood, the world – indeed, nature itself – will undergo a radical change.)

Thus, the concept of clean and unclean animals relates here to the opportunity for the Jewish people – as the priests of mankind (Exod. 19:6) – to bring sacrifices in the future. Exactly the same criteria of "cleanness" determine the fitness of the various categories of animals to be used for food (see Lev. 11:8).

**[5] And Noah did just as the Lord commanded him ... [16] And the Lord shut him in.** Noah follows orders precisely, but he so lacks self-sufficiency, and is so helpless, that he cannot even close the entrance to the Ark when the time comes. God must do it for him.

**[7] Noah, with his sons, his wife, and his sons' wives, went into the ark.** The men separately and the women separately.

**[23] All existence on earth was blotted out ... And when the waters had swelled on the earth one hundred and fifty days ....** Even after all the people and animals outside the ark were already dead, the water continued to rise. Thus, the significance of the Flood was not only in the death of the evildoers.

**Only Noah was left.** The word *ach*, "only," is superfluous, adding nothing to the story. The Midrash understands it as a "reduction" – i.e., a limiting qualifier: "Noah was *just barely alive*," for he, too, almost died. We shall consider this Midrash in more detail below.

## 9.3. The End of the Flood (8:1-22)

אַ וַיִּזְכֹּר אֱלֹהִים אֶת־נֹחַ וְאֵת כָּל־הַחַיָּה וְאֶת־כָּל־
הַבְּהֵמָה אֲשֶׁר אִתּוֹ בַּתֵּבָה וַיַּעֲבֵר אֱלֹהִים רוּחַ עַל־הָאָרֶץ
וַיָּשֹׁכּוּ הַמָּיִם: ב וַיִּסָּכְרוּ מַעְיְנֹת תְּהוֹם וַאֲרֻבֹּת הַשָּׁמַיִם
וַיִּכָּלֵא הַגֶּשֶׁם מִן־הַשָּׁמָיִם: ג וַיָּשֻׁבוּ הַמַּיִם מֵעַל הָאָרֶץ
הָלוֹךְ וָשׁוֹב וַיַּחְסְרוּ הַמַּיִם מִקְצֵה חֲמִשִּׁים וּמְאַת יוֹם:
ד וַתָּנַח הַתֵּבָה בַּחֹדֶשׁ הַשְּׁבִיעִי בְּשִׁבְעָה־עָשָׂר יוֹם לַחֹדֶשׁ
עַל הָרֵי אֲרָרָט: ה וְהַמַּיִם הָיוּ הָלוֹךְ וְחָסוֹר עַד הַחֹדֶשׁ
הָעֲשִׂירִי בָּעֲשִׂירִי בְּאֶחָד לַחֹדֶשׁ נִרְאוּ רָאשֵׁי הֶהָרִים: ו
וַיְהִי מִקֵּץ אַרְבָּעִים יוֹם וַיִּפְתַּח נֹחַ אֶת־חַלּוֹן הַתֵּבָה
אֲשֶׁר עָשָׂה: ז וַיְשַׁלַּח אֶת־הָעֹרֵב וַיֵּצֵא יָצוֹא וָשׁוֹב עַד־
יְבֹשֶׁת הַמַּיִם מֵעַל הָאָרֶץ: ח וַיְשַׁלַּח אֶת־הַיּוֹנָה מֵאִתּוֹ
לִרְאוֹת הֲקַלּוּ הַמַּיִם מֵעַל פְּנֵי הָאֲדָמָה: ט וְלֹא־מָצְאָה
הַיּוֹנָה מָנוֹחַ לְכַף־רַגְלָהּ וַתָּשָׁב אֵלָיו אֶל־הַתֵּבָה כִּי־מַיִם
עַל־פְּנֵי כָל־הָאָרֶץ וַיִּשְׁלַח יָדוֹ וַיִּקָּחֶהָ וַיָּבֵא אֹתָהּ אֵלָיו
אֶל־הַתֵּבָה: י וַיָּחֶל עוֹד שִׁבְעַת יָמִים אֲחֵרִים וַיֹּסֶף שַׁלַּח
אֶת־הַיּוֹנָה מִן־הַתֵּבָה: יא וַתָּבֹא אֵלָיו הַיּוֹנָה לְעֵת עֶרֶב
וְהִנֵּה עֲלֵה־זַיִת טָרָף בְּפִיהָ וַיֵּדַע נֹחַ כִּי־קַלּוּ הַמַּיִם מֵעַל
הָאָרֶץ: יב וַיִּיָּחֶל עוֹד שִׁבְעַת יָמִים אֲחֵרִים וַיְשַׁלַּח אֶת־
הַיּוֹנָה וְלֹא־יָסְפָה שׁוּב־אֵלָיו עוֹד: יג וַיְהִי בְּאַחַת וְשֵׁשׁ־
מֵאוֹת שָׁנָה בָּרִאשׁוֹן בְּאֶחָד לַחֹדֶשׁ חָרְבוּ הַמַּיִם מֵעַל
הָאָרֶץ וַיָּסַר נֹחַ אֶת־מִכְסֵה הַתֵּבָה וַיַּרְא וְהִנֵּה חָרְבוּ פְּנֵי
הָאֲדָמָה: יד וּבַחֹדֶשׁ הַשֵּׁנִי בְּשִׁבְעָה וְעֶשְׂרִים יוֹם לַחֹדֶשׁ
יָבְשָׁה הָאָרֶץ: טו וַיְדַבֵּר אֱלֹהִים אֶל־נֹחַ לֵאמֹר: טז צֵא
מִן־הַתֵּבָה אַתָּה וְאִשְׁתְּךָ וּבָנֶיךָ וּנְשֵׁי־בָנֶיךָ אִתָּךְ: יז
כָּל־הַחַיָּה אֲשֶׁר־אִתְּךָ מִכָּל־בָּשָׂר בָּעוֹף וּבַבְּהֵמָה וּבְכָל־

הָרֶמֶשׂ הָרֹמֵשׂ עַל־הָאָרֶץ הוֹצֵא (הַיְצֵא) אִתָּךְ וְשָׁרְצוּ
בָאָרֶץ וּפָרוּ וְרָבוּ עַל־הָאָרֶץ: **יח** וַיֵּצֵא־נֹחַ וּבָנָיו וְאִשְׁתּוֹ
וּנְשֵׁי־בָנָיו אִתּוֹ: **יט** כָּל־הַחַיָּה כָּל־הָרֶמֶשׂ וְכָל־הָעוֹף
כֹּל רוֹמֵשׂ עַל־הָאָרֶץ לְמִשְׁפְּחֹתֵיהֶם יָצְאוּ מִן־הַתֵּבָה: **כ**
וַיִּבֶן נֹחַ מִזְבֵּחַ לַיי וַיִּקַּח מִכֹּל ׀ הַבְּהֵמָה הַטְּהֹרָה וּמִכֹּל
הָעוֹף הַטָּהוֹר וַיַּעַל עֹלֹת בַּמִּזְבֵּחַ: **כא** וַיָּרַח יי אֶת־רֵיחַ
הַנִּיחֹחַ וַיֹּאמֶר יי אֶל־לִבּוֹ לֹא־אֹסִף לְקַלֵּל עוֹד אֶת־
הָאֲדָמָה בַּעֲבוּר הָאָדָם כִּי יֵצֶר לֵב הָאָדָם רַע מִנְּעֻרָיו
וְלֹא־אֹסִף עוֹד לְהַכּוֹת אֶת־כָּל־חַי כַּאֲשֶׁר עָשִׂיתִי: **כב** עֹד
כָּל־יְמֵי הָאָרֶץ זֶרַע וְקָצִיר וְקֹר וָחֹם וְקַיִץ וָחֹרֶף וְיוֹם
וָלַיְלָה לֹא יִשְׁבֹּתוּ:

[1] God remembered Noah and all the beasts and all
the cattle that were with him in the ark, and God
caused a wind to blow across the earth, and the
waters subsided.

[2] The fountains of the deep and the floodgates of
the sky were stopped up, and the rain from the sky
was held back;

[3] The waters then receded steadily from the earth.
At the end of one hundred and fifty days the waters
diminished,

[4] So that in the seventh month, on the seventeenth
day of the month, the ark came to rest on the
mountains of Ararat.

[5] The waters went on diminishing until the tenth
month; in the tenth month, on the first of the month,
the tops of the mountains became visible.

[6] At the end of forty days, Noah opened the window
of the ark that he had made

[7] And sent out the raven; it went to and fro until the
waters had dried up from the earth.

[8] Then he sent out the dove to see whether the waters

*had decreased from the surface of the ground.*

*[9] But the dove could not find a resting place for its foot, and returned to him to the ark, for there was water over all the earth. So putting out his hand, he took it into the ark with him.*

*[10] He waited another seven days, and again sent out the dove from the ark.*

*[11] The dove came back to him toward evening, and there in its bill was a plucked-off olive leaf! Then Noah knew that the waters had decreased on the earth.*

*[12] He waited still another seven days and sent the dove forth; and it did not return to him any more.*

*[13] In the six hundred and first year, in the first month, on the first of the month, the waters began to dry from the earth; and when Noah removed the covering of the ark, he saw that the surface of the ground was drying.*

*[14] And in the second month, on the twenty-seventh day of the month, the earth was dry.*

*[15] God spoke to Noah, saying,*

*[16] "Come out of the ark, together with your wife, your sons, and your sons' wives.*

*[17] Bring out with you every living thing of all flesh that is with you: birds, animals, and everything that creeps on earth; and let them swarm on the earth and be fertile and increase on earth."*

*[18] So Noah came out, together with his sons, his wife, and his sons' wives.*

*[19] Every animal, every creeping thing, and every bird, everything that stirs on earth came out of the ark by families.*

*[20] Then Noah built an altar to the Lord and, taking*

*of every clean animal and of every clean bird, he offered burnt offerings on the altar.*

*[21] The Lord smelled the pleasing odor, and the Lord said to Himself: "Never again will I doom the earth because of man, since the devisings of man's mind are evil from his youth; nor will I ever again destroy every living being, as I have done.*

*[22] So long as the earth endures, seedtime and harvest, cold and heat, summer and winter, day and night shall not cease."*

**[6] At the end of forty days, Noah opened the window of the ark that he had made.** Noah himself opens the window; he does not wait for God to do it for him. After spending months in the ark, Noah gradually becomes self-sufficient.

**[15] God spoke to Noah, saying, [16] "Come out of the ark, together with your wife, your sons, and your sons' wives.** Husbands and wives leave the ark together. That is, intimacy and childbearing are now again permitted.

**[18] So Noah came out, together with his sons, his wife, and his sons' wives.** But even so, Noah and his family at first do not accept that permission. The men and the women leave the ark separately.

**[21] And the Lord said to Himself: "Never again will I doom the earth because of man, since the devisings of man's mind are evil from his youth.** At the beginning of the Flood story, this tendency of man to evil (6:5) is the basis for his destruction. But here, on the contrary, it serves as the basis for forgiveness. Later we will discuss this issue in more detail.

## 9.4. The Rainbow as a Sign of God's Covenant (9:1-17)

**א** וַיְבָרֶךְ אֱלֹהִים אֶת־נֹחַ וְאֶת־בָּנָיו וַיֹּאמֶר לָהֶם פְּרוּ
וּרְבוּ וּמִלְאוּ אֶת־הָאָרֶץ: **ב** וּמוֹרַאֲכֶם וְחִתְּכֶם יִהְיֶה עַל
כָּל־חַיַּת הָאָרֶץ וְעַל כָּל־עוֹף הַשָּׁמָיִם בְּכֹל אֲשֶׁר תִּרְמֹשׂ
הָאֲדָמָה וּבְכָל־דְּגֵי הַיָּם בְּיֶדְכֶם נִתָּנוּ: **ג** כָּל־רֶמֶשׂ אֲשֶׁר
הוּא־חַי לָכֶם יִהְיֶה לְאָכְלָה כְּיֶרֶק עֵשֶׂב נָתַתִּי לָכֶם אֶת־
כֹּל: **ד** אַךְ־בָּשָׂר בְּנַפְשׁוֹ דָמוֹ לֹא תֹאכֵלוּ: **ה** וְאַךְ אֶת־
דִּמְכֶם לְנַפְשֹׁתֵיכֶם אֶדְרֹשׁ מִיַּד כָּל־חַיָּה אֶדְרְשֶׁנּוּ וּמִיַּד
הָאָדָם מִיַּד אִישׁ אָחִיו אֶדְרֹשׁ אֶת־נֶפֶשׁ הָאָדָם: **ו** שֹׁפֵךְ
דַּם הָאָדָם בָּאָדָם דָּמוֹ יִשָּׁפֵךְ כִּי בְּצֶלֶם אֱלֹהִים עָשָׂה
אֶת־הָאָדָם: **ז** וְאַתֶּם פְּרוּ וּרְבוּ שִׁרְצוּ בָאָרֶץ וּרְבוּ־בָהּ:
**ח** וַיֹּאמֶר אֱלֹהִים אֶל־נֹחַ וְאֶל־בָּנָיו אִתּוֹ לֵאמֹר: **ט** וַאֲנִי
הִנְנִי מֵקִים אֶת־בְּרִיתִי אִתְּכֶם וְאֶת־זַרְעֲכֶם אַחֲרֵיכֶם:
**י** וְאֵת כָּל־נֶפֶשׁ הַחַיָּה אֲשֶׁר אִתְּכֶם בָּעוֹף בַּבְּהֵמָה וּבְכָל־
חַיַּת הָאָרֶץ אִתְּכֶם מִכֹּל יֹצְאֵי הַתֵּבָה לְכֹל חַיַּת הָאָרֶץ:
**יא** וַהֲקִמֹתִי אֶת־בְּרִיתִי אִתְּכֶם וְלֹא־יִכָּרֵת כָּל־בָּשָׂר עוֹד
מִמֵּי הַמַּבּוּל וְלֹא־יִהְיֶה עוֹד מַבּוּל לְשַׁחֵת הָאָרֶץ: **יב**
וַיֹּאמֶר אֱלֹהִים זֹאת אוֹת־הַבְּרִית אֲשֶׁר־אֲנִי נֹתֵן בֵּינִי
וּבֵינֵיכֶם וּבֵין כָּל־נֶפֶשׁ חַיָּה אֲשֶׁר אִתְּכֶם לְדֹרֹת עוֹלָם:
**יג** אֶת־קַשְׁתִּי נָתַתִּי בֶּעָנָן וְהָיְתָה לְאוֹת בְּרִית בֵּינִי וּבֵין
הָאָרֶץ: **יד** וְהָיָה בְּעַנְנִי עָנָן עַל־הָאָרֶץ וְנִרְאֲתָה הַקֶּשֶׁת
בֶּעָנָן: **טו** וְזָכַרְתִּי אֶת־בְּרִיתִי אֲשֶׁר בֵּינִי וּבֵינֵיכֶם וּבֵין
כָּל־נֶפֶשׁ חַיָּה בְּכָל־בָּשָׂר וְלֹא־יִהְיֶה עוֹד הַמַּיִם לְמַבּוּל
לְשַׁחֵת כָּל־בָּשָׂר: **טז** וְהָיְתָה הַקֶּשֶׁת בֶּעָנָן וּרְאִיתִיהָ
לִזְכֹּר בְּרִית עוֹלָם בֵּין אֱלֹהִים וּבֵין כָּל־נֶפֶשׁ חַיָּה בְּכָל־
בָּשָׂר אֲשֶׁר עַל־הָאָרֶץ: **יז** וַיֹּאמֶר אֱלֹהִים אֶל־נֹחַ זֹאת
אוֹת־הַבְּרִית אֲשֶׁר הֲקִמֹתִי בֵּינִי וּבֵין כָּל־בָּשָׂר אֲשֶׁר עַל־
הָאָרֶץ:

*[1] God blessed Noah and his sons, and said to them,*
*"Be fertile and increase, and fill the earth.*
*[2] The fear and the dread of you shall be upon all the*

*beasts of the earth and upon all the birds of the sky –*
*everything with which the earth is astir – and upon*
*all the fish of the sea; they are given into your hand.*
*[3] Every creature that lives shall be yours to eat; as*
*with the green grasses, I give you all these.*
*[4] You must not, however, eat flesh with its life-blood*
*in it.*
*[5] But for your own life-blood I will require a*
*reckoning: I will require it of every beast; of man,*
*too, will I require a reckoning for human life, of every*
*man for that of his fellow man!*
*[6] Whoever sheds the blood of man, by man shall his*
*blood be shed; for in His image did God make man.*
*[7] Be fertile, then, and increase; abound on the earth*
*and increase on it."*
*[8] And God said to Noah and to his sons with him,*
*[9] "I now establish My covenant with you and your*
*offspring to come,*
*[10] And with every living thing that is with you –*
*birds, cattle, and every wild beast as well – all that*
*have come out of the ark, every living thing on earth.*
*[11] I will maintain My covenant with you: never again*
*shall all flesh be cut off by the waters of a flood, and*
*never again shall there be a flood to destroy the*
*earth."*
*[12] God further said, "This is the sign that I set for*
*the covenant between Me and you, and every living*
*creature with you, for all ages to come.*
*[13] I have set My bow in the clouds, and it shall serve*
*as a sign of the covenant between Me and the earth.*
*[14] When I bring clouds over the earth, and the bow*
*appears in the clouds,*
*[15] I will remember My covenant between Me and*

*you and every living creature among all flesh, so*
*that the waters shall never again become a flood to*
*destroy all flesh.*
[16] *When the bow is in the clouds, I will see it and*
*remember the everlasting covenant between God*
*and all living creatures, all flesh that is on earth."*
[17] *"That," God said to Noah, "shall be the sign of the*
*covenant that I have established between Me and all*
*flesh that is on earth."*

**[1] God blessed Noah and his sons, and said to them, "Be**
**fertile and increase, and fill the earth.** After the Flood,
Noah and his family are afraid to have children. God therefore
repeats His command to "be fruitful and multiply" (see 1:28).

**[3] Every creature that lives shall be yours to eat; as with**
**the green grasses, I give you all these.** Prior to the Flood
humans were allowed to eat only plants. Now they are
allowed to eat animals as well, but there are some limitations.

**[4] You must not, however, eat flesh with its life-blood in**
**it.** The prohibition of eating any part of an animal that is still
alive is universal, and applies to all of humanity. (In this verse
and the next, the word "blood" means "life.")

## 9.5. Noah and His Sons in the Aftermath of the Flood (9:18-29)

**יח** וַיִּהְיוּ בְנֵי־נֹחַ הַיֹּצְאִים מִן־הַתֵּבָה שֵׁם וְחָם וָיָפֶת
וְחָם הוּא אֲבִי כְנָעַן: **יט** שְׁלֹשָׁה אֵלֶּה בְּנֵי־נֹחַ וּמֵאֵלֶּה
נָפְצָה כָל־הָאָרֶץ: **כ** וַיָּחֶל נֹחַ אִישׁ הָאֲדָמָה וַיִּטַּע כָּרֶם:
**כא** וַיֵּשְׁתְּ מִן־הַיַּיִן וַיִּשְׁכָּר וַיִּתְגַּל בְּתוֹךְ אָהֳלֹה: **כב**

וַיַּרְא חָם אֲבִי כְנַעַן אֵת עֶרְוַת אָבִיו וַיַּגֵּד לִשְׁנֵי־אֶחָיו
בַּחוּץ: **כג** וַיִּקַּח שֵׁם וָיֶפֶת אֶת־הַשִּׂמְלָה וַיָּשִׂימוּ עַל־
שְׁכֶם שְׁנֵיהֶם וַיֵּלְכוּ אֲחֹרַנִּית וַיְכַסּוּ אֵת עֶרְוַת אֲבִיהֶם
וּפְנֵיהֶם אֲחֹרַנִּית וְעֶרְוַת אֲבִיהֶם לֹא רָאוּ: **כד** וַיִּיקֶץ נֹחַ
מִיֵּינוֹ וַיֵּדַע אֵת אֲשֶׁר־עָשָׂה לוֹ בְּנוֹ הַקָּטָן: כה וַיֹּאמֶר
אָרוּר כְּנָעַן עֶבֶד עֲבָדִים יִהְיֶה לְאֶחָיו: **כו** וַיֹּאמֶר בָּרוּךְ
יי אֱלֹהֵי שֵׁם וִיהִי כְנַעַן עֶבֶד לָמוֹ: **כז** יַפְתְּ אֱלֹהִים לְיֶפֶת
וְיִשְׁכֹּן בְּאָהֳלֵי־שֵׁם וִיהִי כְנַעַן עֶבֶד לָמוֹ: **כח** וַיְחִי־נֹחַ
אַחַר הַמַּבּוּל שְׁלֹשׁ מֵאוֹת שָׁנָה וַחֲמִשִּׁים שָׁנָה: **כט** וַיִּהְיוּ
כָּל־יְמֵי־נֹחַ תְּשַׁע מֵאוֹת שָׁנָה וַחֲמִשִּׁים שָׁנָה וַיָּמֹת:

[18] *The sons of Noah who came out of the ark were Shem, Ham, and Japheth – Ham being the father of Canaan.*

[19] *These three were the sons of Noah, and from these the whole world branched out.*

[20] *Noah, the tiller of the soil, was the first to plant a vineyard.*

[21] *He drank of the wine and became drunk, and he uncovered himself within his tent.*

[22] *Ham, the father of Canaan, saw his father's nakedness and told his two brothers outside.*

[23] *But Shem and Japheth took a cloth, placed it against both their backs and, walking backward, they covered their father's nakedness; their faces were turned the other way, so that they did not see their father's nakedness.*

[24] *When Noah woke up from his wine and learned what his youngest son had done to him,*

[25] *He said, "Cursed be Canaan; the lowest of slaves shall he be to his brothers."*

[26] *And he said, "Blessed be the Lord, the God of Shem; let Canaan be a slave to them.*

*[27] May God enlarge Japheth, and let him dwell in the tents of Shem; and let Canaan be a slave to them."*
*[28] Noah lived after the Flood 350 years.*
*[29] And all the days of Noah came to 950 years; then he died.*

**[20] Noah, the tiller of the soil, was the first to plant a vineyard.** Literally, "Noah, the man of the earth, began." After the Flood, Noah restores man's collaboration with the earth. He becomes the "man of the earth" who deals with the real problems of the world around him.

**Noah ... was the first to plant a vineyard.** Not only a vineyard is meant. Noah essentially restores agriculture in its entirety. The emphasis on grapes (wine) here indicates that Noah is not prepared to be satisfied with only the minimum requirements of life. His attitude is one of taking joy in life. And this is a positive thing.

**[21] He ... became drunk, and he uncovered himself within his tent.** However, too quick a transition to the positive can have exactly the opposite effect. The transition from detachment from the outside world (typical of Noah before the Flood) to engagement with the world (Noah after the Flood) happens too quickly, without proper preparation on Noah's part, and this brings Noah to crisis and collapse. Noah himself can no longer rectify the situation – only his children can accomplish that.

**[22] Ham, the father of Canaan, saw his father's nakedness and told his two brothers outside. ... [24] When Noah woke up from his wine and learned what his youngest son had done to him, [25] He said, "Cursed be Canaan;**

**the lowest of slaves shall he be to his brothers."** Although Ham committed the act (a simple reading of the text would indicate that he is guilty of publicizing his father's disgrace) it is Ham's son Canaan who is cursed. Apparently, Canaan was the initiator of Ham's actions.

**[26] And he said, "Blessed be the Lord, the God of Shem; let Canaan be a slave to them. [27] May God enlarge Japheth, and let him dwell in the tents of Shem.** The civilization of the Semitic peoples is based on two things: The concept of a "tent" (the ordering of proper relations among people, and especially closely related people; that is, ethics) and an in-depth understanding of Divinity, i.e., the fact that "the Lord is the God of Shem."

The basis of the civilization of the Japhetic peoples is the concept of "expansiveness" – the expansion of territory and space, science and art, and aesthetics.

Among the descendants of Japheth, the above blessings manifest most prominently in the Greeks, and among the descendants of Shem – in the people of Israel. Today, thousands of years after Noah, we see the realization of these blessings. As concerns "conquering space" – in all senses of the term – and aesthetics, the Japhetic (European) nations are the leaders of humanity. But those same nations have adopted from the Jews everything that relates to the essential questions of ethics and religion. Indeed, in this sense "Japheth dwells in the tents of Shem."

Chapter 10

# The Meaning of the Flood

## 10.1. Defining the Problem: Did God Act Properly?

What is the meaning of the Flood? Why did it happen? And how did the world change as a result of the Flood?

The simple explanation – that people began to behave badly and God decided to punish and destroy them – is clearly not sufficient. Evil itself was not destroyed; even after the Flood the world is full of evil. Moreover, if it was simply a matter of God punishing the evildoers, then what He did was just too cruel – destroying all of mankind, the good and the bad, without distinction. Moreover, isn't it God Himself Who creates people such as they are – good or bad? Where is Divine justice and mercy?

Note that from a religious point of view, we should not ignore our intuitive human sense of justice, to instead take the position that whatever God has decided is *ipso facto* just – by definition. On the contrary, Judaism views the intuitive human sense of justice as one of the manifestations of the image of God in man. Our need to seek and find justice in historical processes – that is, in God's actions – is a fundamental religious sense. It is wrong to suppress that feeling.

Very often the source of the conflict between our conscience and the sacred texts is not that our moral sense is leading us astray (although that does in fact happen quite often). Rather, the source of the conflict is that we misunderstand the Torah. In order to advance in our understanding, we must not be afraid to pose difficult questions, and to delve into the themes of the Torah in search of the answers to those questions.

## 10.2. What did the flood accomplish, given that the human inclination to evil remained unchanged?

After the Flood, the evil inclination in man did not disappear, nor did it seem to have even changed at all.

The causes of the Flood are described in the Torah as follows: "The Lord saw how great was man's wickedness on earth, and how every plan devised by his mind was nothing but evil all the time. And the Lord regretted that He had made man on earth, and His heart was saddened. The Lord said, 'I will blot out from the earth the men whom I created – men together with beasts, creeping things, and birds of the sky; for I regret that I made them.' But Noah found favor with the Lord" (6:5-8).

The above passage serves as a preface to the story of the Flood. People are mired in evil, and the thoughts entertained by the human heart are categorically "evil all the time." Humanity must therefore be destroyed.

But even after the Flood the situation has still not changed much: "The Lord smelled the pleasing odor, and the Lord said to Himself: 'Never again will I doom the earth because of man, since the devisings of man's mind are evil from his youth; nor will I ever again destroy every living being, as I have done. So long as the earth endures, seed-time and harvest, cold and heat, summer and winter, day and night shall not cease'" (8:21-22).

Thus, from the same premise – man's inclination to evil – opposite conclusions are drawn. Before the Flood, man's inclination to evil requires that he be destroyed. But after the Flood a completely different conclusion is drawn, namely, that because man is prone to evil, he must be allowed to live. How can we explain this 180-degree about-face? And was man after the Flood really the same as he had been before?

## 10.3. Did God actually regret having created man?

The Torah uses a rather strange expression to describe God's decision to bring the Flood: "And the Lord regretted that he had made man on earth" (6:6). Do these words mean that God was disappointed in the human race, and He therefore decided to destroy them? Did God not know from the outset that things would turn out that way, or at least that they might? Applying to God the concept of regret seems strange to begin with. Nonetheless, the given passage ("The Lord regretted that he had made man") is a key to understanding the causes of the Flood.

## 10.4. The Meaning of the Name "Noah"

Noah is the main character in the story of the Flood. The prophet Isaiah (54:9) calls the Flood the "waters of Noah," which emphasizes his central role, and even his personal responsibility for what happened in the Flood.

Who was Noah?

The name "Noah" literally translates as "easy," or "convenient." But the Torah explains the name somewhat differently. "When Lamech had lived 182 years, he begot a son. And he named him Noah, saying, 'This one will console us (*yenahamenu*) from our work and from the toil of our hands, out of the very soil which the Lord placed under a curse'" (5:28-29). Thus, Lamech derived the name "Noah" from the Hebrew root *nachem*, translated here as "(to) console." Accordingly, Noah's task is to "console humankind that suffers from their toil upon the earth that the Lord has cursed." And that consolation was in fact realized when after the Flood God said: "Never again will I doom the earth because of man" (8:21).

Why did God curse the earth, and what was the nature of that curse?

## 10.5. The Curse of the Earth

Adam in the Garden of Eden was at such a level that with his knowledge and will he could directly control the Universe. After being expelled, he lost that initial level, but not entirely: his spiritual parameters remained directly connected to the outside world. Humans could no longer directly control the Universe with their spirituality, but the influence of that spirituality on the earth's produce remained. And since humanity did not behave adequately, this influence was expressed not in a blessing, but in a curse.

As God expelled Adam and Eve from the Garden of Eden, He said the following words: "Cursed be the ground because of you" (3:17). When you work the land hoping to reap its produce, it will sprout for you only thorns and thistles.

Then, after Cain killed his brother Abel, the curse of the land further intensified: "Therefore, you shall be more cursed than the ground, which opened its mouth to receive your brother's blood from your hand. If you till the soil, it shall no longer yield its strength to you. You shall become a ceaseless wanderer on earth" (4:11-12).

But humanity continued to behave badly, with tensions in the relationship between man and the earth becoming critical.

The curse, then, is found in the ability of the land to punish a person for his crimes by producing "thistles and thorns" instead of a bountiful harvest. In other words, the earth then was morally sensitive, reacting to the moral level in man. A farmer in that era, to be successful, needed not only to understand the principles of agronomy – above all, he had to be a worthy human being.

That the earth would react so acutely to the level of human righteousness was not *per se* a bad thing. On the contrary, there was an increased level of opportunity – but that meant equally the ability to achieve blessings and the possibility of losing benefits. And since human behavior continued to spiral downward, those possibilities went in the direction of a "curse upon the earth."

## 10.6. "Noah" as "Undoing the Curse"

The whole story about the Flood is built around the concept of *nechamah*, "consolation," but the meaning of this concept requires further clarification. The expression *nichum avelim*, "consoling the mourners," can serve as one example of the use of this concept. When a person's close relative dies, friends and relatives come to comfort him. The purpose of this consolation is not to help the mourner to avoid confronting the reality of death, to distract him from his grief, or to make him forget about the dead. On the contrary, according to Jewish tradition, consoling a mourner means, above all, just to sit with the mourner in silence. Because for a mourner, being consoled means being reconciled to the reality of death. Consoling a mourner reconciles him with reality. And *nechamah*, as a general term, means being reconciled to some difficult reality.

Now we can better understand what Lamech meant when he spoke of consolation "from our work and from the toil of our hands, out of the very soil which the Lord placed under a curse" (5:29). "Consolation", as we have just said, means to be reconciled with reality. Lamech is hoping that Noah will be able to reconcile God with the low moral level of man. By effecting this reconciliation, Noah will make our work easier, and will make life on earth easier, that is, it will make our lives more *noach*. "We are imperfect, so do not demand too much from us. Let the power of our influence on the earth be limited – otherwise the curse will only increase, and it will soon become impossible for anyone to live."

In other words, had the Almighty not intervened, had He not sent the Flood to change the world, then this world would have collapsed on its own. The Flood was therefore not just an act of punishment, but an act of mercy. This is emphasized in the verse: "The Lord saw how great was man's wickedness on earth... And the Lord said, "I will blot out from the earth the men whom I created" (6:5). Here "the Lord" is expressed in Hebrew using God's four-letter name, the Tetragrammaton. The entire Flood story refers to God only as the "Lord"; that is, the Tetragrammaton is used throughout – which, as we have mentioned previously, is the Divine Name of mercy rather than of judgment. Divine Mercy intervened in the Flood story for the preservation of the Universe, so that man would not be allowed to destroy it.

## 10.7. Reconciliation with man

We can now better understand the verse which speaks of the causes of the Flood: "And the Lord regretted that He had made man on earth, and His heart was saddened." (6:6). Since *vayinnachem*, "regretted," derives from the same Hebrew root as *nechamah*, "consolation," we can translate this verse as, "And the Lord was consoled, being reconciled with the fact that He made man on earth."

God was reconciled to the fact that man could not cope with the immense power given to him, and that it is impossible to demand of him an immediately high level of morality. The situation therefore required God's intervention and correction: weakening man's connection with the earth, and reducing his level of influence on the world. God needed to be reconciled to the fact that man exists *on earth* such as he is. And therefore *His heart was saddened*.

The reason for that grief is not only that God had to destroy a whole generation of people, but – first and foremost – that it was necessary to reduce man's level by depriving him of the ability to exert direct spiritual influence on the world around him, and by making the earth immune to the level of human righteousness. This restriction becomes yet another concealment of the Divine Countenance, and yet another level of exile that would follow immediately after Adam's expulsion from the Garden. Ground level gets lower, and the Divine Presence (Shechinah) is further removed from our lower world and ascends to higher worlds.

When Adam was still in the Garden of Eden, the Divine Presence was "below," i.e., it was obvious. With the expulsion from the Garden, the Divine Presence "rose upward." And with the Flood, it rose yet higher, becoming even less tangible in the lower world. God became even more hidden from the world, and it was difficult for God, as it were, to make peace with that concealment. And exactly the same way, in the verse, "The Lord said, 'I will blot out from the earth the men whom I created ... for I regret that I made them'" (6:7), the word *nichamti*, "regretted," "repented," which one? has the meaning, "I am consoled and have made peace with their being that way, because I created them."

God regretted and repented – in the sense that He reconciled with man's weaknesses.

### 10.8. "Divine repentance" and the Internal Contradiction of Theology

Let us stop to examine once more the problem of saying that God repents, or changes His mind.

On the one hand, we find in Scripture (I Sam. 15:29) a statement that seems diametrically opposed to any such idea. "The Glory of Israel does not deceive or change His mind (repent), for He is not human that He should change His mind." Theologically, the application of this concept to the Omniscient God, who knows the future in advance, is indeed problematic. But on the other hand, the Torah says of God many times that He changed His mind (i.e., His decision. Note in passing, that God's repentance is explicitly discussed in the Book of Samuel (I Sam. 15:11), immediately before Samuel says of God that He does *not* repent. Thus, underscoring that "God does not repent" is a problem belonging to Samuel himself, and not regarding how we understand God).

How are we to reconcile this apparent contradiction? The answer, it seems, is that the Divine does not neatly fit into the formal structure of Boolean logic. Moreover, in our perception of God there inevitably are aspects that are logically incompatible. For the Divine is infinite, while our understanding – our every thought and concept – is finite and limited. No intellectual system is capable of embracing Divinity in its entirety; there will always be details that do not fit into any given scheme, and even logically contradict it.

Theology may try to resolve this contradiction by saying that God does not actually change His mind; it only appears so to us. In the story of the Golden Calf, for example (Exodus 32:14), after Moses prays for Israel, the Torah says "And the Lord renounced the punishment He had planned to bring upon His people" (but a word of the same root, *hinachem*, is used; literally, "and the Lord changed His mind"). As concerns the punishment of the Jewish people, theology might very well say that God was planning all along to forgive the Jews, and was only testing Moses, but the Torah uses the word *vayinachem* ("changed his mind") because it is the way of the Torah to express ideas in conventional human terms.

The same explanation could probably be applied to virtually every instance where the Torah says that "God changed His mind." However, theology's smoothing over of the rough edges in this manner does not solve the original problem, because the question of why the Torah would say here that "God changed His mind" nonetheless remains, in spite of all the difficulties that such a statement entails.

The most plausible answer is that the Torah is written to serve, first and foremost, not as a philosophical treatise about God, but as a set of lessons for teaching us proper behavior in life. When the Torah says that "God changed His mind," it wants to teach us that in orienting our thinking to man's likeness to God, we can change our point of view in the course of life, just as God does. We should not consider our own change of position as a weakness, because, on the contrary, it indicates flexibility and a willingness to change. Since the world that God created is dynamic and always changing, any approach to the world would be inadequate if it did not give us the option to "change one's mind."

### 10.9. Correction by Flood

Thus, the Flood changed the system of relations between man and the world, and corrected and facilitated the future life of mankind. But that generation of people had to be destroyed, because they were incorrigible. God chose Noah to create a new line of humans, who would have limited possibilities to influence the world, but also would not have sufficient power to destroy the Universe.

In the generations from Adam to Noah, the world had collapsed and gone to ruin because the earth was responding to man's spiritual level. The Flood was the only way to reverse this trend.

### 10.10. The Distortion of Justice and the Death of Society (6:11-13)

יא וַתִּשָּׁחֵת הָאָרֶץ לִפְנֵי הָאֱלֹהִים וַתִּמָּלֵא הָאָרֶץ חָמָס׃
יב וַיַּרְא אֱלֹהִים אֶת־הָאָרֶץ וְהִנֵּה נִשְׁחָתָה כִּי־הִשְׁחִית
כָּל־בָּשָׂר אֶת־דַּרְכּוֹ עַל־הָאָרֶץ׃ יג וַיֹּאמֶר אֱלֹהִים לְנֹחַ
קֵץ כָּל־בָּשָׂר בָּא לְפָנַי כִּי־מָלְאָה הָאָרֶץ חָמָס מִפְּנֵיהֶם
וְהִנְנִי מַשְׁחִיתָם אֶת־הָאָרֶץ׃

*[11] The earth became corrupt before God; the earth was filled with lawlessness.*

*[12] When God saw how corrupt the earth was, for all flesh had corrupted its ways on earth,*
*[13] God said to Noah, "I have decided to put an end to all flesh, for the earth is filled with lawlessness because of them: I am about to destroy them with the earth.*

The whole passage is built around two key words: *shachat* – "depravity" or "perversion," and *chamas* – "robbery" or "evildoing." These words are repeated here in various derivative grammatical forms, forming the axis of the story.

*Shachat* is a crime against the Almighty: idolatry, sexual perversion, murder, and the like. *Shachat* (like *chamas*) means, first and foremost, such crimes that are considered the norm in a given society. The Midrash says: "Where there is *shachat*, all – both the ungodly and the righteous – are subject to destruction." As a reaction to humans "corrupting their ways," the punishment itself likewise "corrupts its ways," that is, confusion comes to the world and punishment no longer distinguishes between the righteous and the ungodly. All are destroyed.

The reason that the righteous are punished along with the wicked in this way is that as a general rule, the righteous are judged not merely by their own by personal righteousness, but by the degree of their influence on society. Unlike the evildoer, who is required by God, to correct himself before anything else, a righteous person is expected to correct the world around him. The righteous are given greater spiritual powers, and are therefore responsible for others in their circle. In this sense, Noah was hardly a person of exalted stature.

*Chamas*, "evildoing," means "crimes that are not viewed as crimes"; that is, situations of human behavior that is obviously criminal, and yet the given society does not perceive such actions as crimes. The Midrash cites various examples. These include continuously robbing people of small sums that the court will not deal with, and thus no one is ever held to account for the crime; "sale" by coercion – forcing something totally useless on the buyer, and taking his money "in payment for the goods"; or vice versa, when something valuable is taken by force from the "seller" and only token "compensation" is paid.

When people are abused but society considers it just business as usual, this is *chamas*. Such a society must die, because their deeds are not recognized as crimes, and therefore the impulse to repent never arises. That is why the crime of *chamas* has such terrible consequences.

An example of *chamas* can be seen in the story of Sodom. The dominant crime of the people of Sodom was not that they performed robbery and murder (for this happens everywhere). Rather, the gravity of the crime was that such acts were deemed in that society to be perfectly normal. Had there been individuals among them bemoaning Sodom's sins and calling others to repentance, the situation could have been salvaged. Even if those reformers were not heard at that moment, repentance would have been possible in principle at least, and the city could have been spared from death.

Even in evil societies there were righteous individuals: Lot in Sodom, and Noah in the generation of the Flood. But Lot and Noah kept silent, for they were personally incapable of denouncing the crimes of their fellow citizens or standing up to them, and they therefore could not save their respective societies.

And so, says the Midrash, Noah too deserved death, and was spared only by God's mercy. "But Noah found favor with the Lord" (6:8). Noah was saved only because he found *favor* with God, and not because he deserved to be saved as a matter of strict justice. Noah did not himself effect salvation – he was only the object of salvation, because he was indispensable for the next stage of human development.

## 10.11. Noah and Abraham: Two Kinds of Righteousness (6:9)

ט אֵלֶּה תּוֹלְדֹת נֹחַ נֹחַ אִישׁ צַדִּיק תָּמִים הָיָה בְּדֹרֹתָיו אֶת־הָאֱלֹהִים הִתְהַלֶּךְ־נֹחַ:

*[9] This is the line of Noah. – Noah was a righteous man; he was blameless in his age; Noah walked with God.*

When we compare Noah to other righteous men in the Torah, we see a huge difference. We are told repeatedly about Abraham, Isaac, Jacob, and Moses that they have "merit" – a huge legacy of righteousness that continues to exert positive influence on us today, even after almost four thousand years. But with Noah the situation is different. He was saved not on his own merits, but only because the Almighty condescended to spare him. Noah deserved to die in the Flood, and was saved only by God's grace.

As we have already noted, Abraham walked "before (that is, ahead of) God" (17:1, see commentary). But Noah only "walked *with* God," alongside Him.

Noah "walked with God" – as a child walks alongside the parent, veering neither to the right nor to the left. The Midrash notes that Noah refused to communicate with the evildoers of his generation. Indeed, he fulfilled the letter of the law, but no more than that. Noah was concerned only with his own personal righteousness. He was not engaged in correcting the outside world.

Jewish tradition calls this kind of person "a righteous man in a fur coat" (in Yiddish, *tsaddik im peltz*). Instead of building a fire to warm himself and everyone else – as Abraham did when he carried the idea of God to humanity – a *tsaddik im peltz* dons a fur coat, thus warming only himself. The "righteous man in a fur coat" is by no means an egoist – he will of course not refuse anyone who appeals to him for help, although on his own initiative he shows little zeal for the sake of others. But the Torah expects such self-sacrifice from those who have been given the distinction of being considered righteous.

When God tells Noah to build the Ark for himself and his family, Noah fully obeys the order. He is not indignant on behalf of the human race; he does not argue with God. He does not say: "What do you mean? Are you really going to destroy the entire human race? No, let's instead help them mend their ways." Noah does or says nothing of the kind, he simply accepts the Divine Judgment. Because God is great, right? And His decisions are therefore always just.

That kind of passivity is the approach of the "righteous man in a fur coat." It is the sin of the righteous.

Abraham behaves differently. When God informs Abraham of His intentions to destroy Sodom, Abraham raises his objections to God – vehemently and persistently! "Will You sweep away the innocent along with the guilty? What if there should be fifty innocent within the city; will You then wipe out the place and not forgive it for the sake of the innocent fifty who are in it? Far be it from You to do such a thing, to bring death upon the innocent as well as the guilty, so that innocent and guilty fare alike. Far be it from You! Shall not the Judge of all the earth deal justly? ... What if the fifty innocent should lack five? Will You destroy the whole city for want of the five?" ... "What if forty should be found there?" ... What if thirty should be found there?" ... What if twenty should be found there?" ... What if ten should be found there?" (18:23-32).

Abraham argues with God, but Noah passively and docilely accepts everything God tells him. Abraham therefore walks "before God," but Noah is only "with God." By demanding the Almighty to show mercy, Abraham actively brings salvation to the world; he is himself the initiator and the cause of salvation. But Noah does nothing but obey. Noah is therefore only the "object" of salvation.

Of course, God is just and all His decisions are just. But He has also given us morally sensitive souls for the very purpose of arguing with God when we feel that the issues warrant it. When a person argues persuasively, God changes his decision, because when man steps up to argue, that itself shows that change has already taken place in the world. We see an example of this in God's dialogue with Moses in the incident of the Golden Calf (Exodus 32:14). This is the only way that God can raise us, as human beings, to ever higher levels of personal development – by encouraging and requiring us to debate, disagree, and discuss.

## 10.12. Building the Ark as an Attempt to Influence Humanity

Noah's Ark is described in the Torah as follows: "The length of the ark shall be three hundred cubits, its width fifty cubits, and its height thirty cubits. Make an opening for daylight in the ark, and terminate it within a cubit of the top … make it with bottom, second, and third decks" (6:15).

Thus, Noah's ark was no ordinary ship, but a floating three-story pyramid. The Midrash describes the ark as a completely autonomous structure. The lower level was where foodstuffs were kept, and animal waste was stored. The animals inhabited the middle level, and the upper level is where Noah and his family lived.

Clearly, the purpose of the ark was not only to save Noah and the animals. God commanded Noah to build that huge floating hulk as a last attempt to save all of humanity from annihilation.

God informed Noah of the upcoming flood 120 years in advance. "The Lord said, "My breath shall not abide in man forever, since he too is flesh; let the days allowed him be one hundred and twenty years" (6:3). He then immediately ordered Noah to begin building the ark. For all those 120 years Noah was engaged in a highly unusual job, during which time he also had to answer questions from perplexed citizens about the future flood that would destroy humanity because it was leading an unseemly life.

Noah's actions created conflict and placed him at the center of public debate. Thus, the purpose of constructing the ark was not only to rescue Noah; rather (and even more so), it was an attempt to reeducate the people. God charged Noah with going out to the people, and making efforts to reform humanity.

The futility of that attempt was not a foregone conclusion by any means. Quite the contrary, the attempt was fraught with hope that the people would listen to Noah and try to improve, and then there would have been no need for a flood. According to the Midrash, the Almighty had predetermined that a very great abundance of water would pour down on the earth that year. The only question was, would it be waters of blessing and Torah wisdom (for the Torah is compared to water), or would it be flood waters that would purge and destroy? The answer depended only on what mankind would choose - righteousness or evil.

## 10.13. Why did the Flood last an entire year? (7:23-24)

כג וַיִּמַח אֶת־כָּל־הַיְקוּם | אֲשֶׁר | עַל־פְּנֵי הָאֲדָמָה מֵאָדָם עַד־בְּהֵמָה עַד־רֶמֶשׂ וְעַד־עוֹף הַשָּׁמַיִם וַיִּמָּחוּ מִן־הָאָרֶץ וַיִּשָּׁאֶר אַךְ־נֹחַ וַאֲשֶׁר אִתּוֹ בַּתֵּבָה: כד וַיִּגְבְּרוּ הַמַּיִם עַל־הָאָרֶץ חֲמִשִּׁים וּמְאַת יוֹם:

*[23] All existence on earth was blotted out—man, cattle, creeping things, and birds of the sky; they were blotted out from the earth. Only Noah was left, and those with him in the ark.*
*[24] And when the waters had swelled on the earth one hundred and fifty days,*

In addition to the many decades Noah spent constructing the ark, the time that the ark continued to sail on the floodwaters also served the same purpose of reeducating Noah. An hour would have been quite sufficient for the Flood to destroy all living things on earth, but the flood lasted much, much longer - almost a year. Why, after all life outside the ark had already been destroyed, did Noah have to sail the waves for almost another whole year? And what was Noah doing in the ark all that time?

We have already noted that the word "ah," "only," used in verse 23 can also mean "hardly," or "barely," The verse can thus be translated differently: "Noah just barely remained alive with others who were in the ark." Noah himself was barely alive, and could easily have died.

The Midrash explains that Noah and his family spent an entire year in the ark tending to the needs of the animals. They ran up and down the levels of the ark, carrying food to the animals and cleaning up behind them. Noah delayed on one occasion and was late in feeding the lion, whereupon the lion became incensed and mauled Noah almost to the point of death.

Thus, the ark was for Noah not only a refuge from the Flood, but a place of correction resembling a forced-labor camp. For Noah, a righteous man preoccupied exclusively with himself, the primary aspect of the correction was the lesson of taking responsibility for the entire world (which at that time was the ark). When Noah learned this lesson, after living in the ark for a full year, the Flood ended.

## 10.14. Suspension of Life in the Ark and the Reeducation of Noah

וּיח וַהֲקִמֹתִי אֶת־בְּרִיתִי אִתָּךְ וּבָאתָ אֶל־הַתֵּבָה אַתָּה
וּבָנֶיךָ וְאִשְׁתְּךָ וּנְשֵׁי־בָנֶיךָ אִתָּךְ:

*(6:18) But I will establish My covenant with you, and you shall enter the ark, with your sons, your wife, and your sons' wives.*

זיג בְּעֶצֶם הַיּוֹם הַזֶּה בָּא נֹחַ וְשֵׁם־וְחָם וָיֶפֶת בְּנֵי־נֹחַ
וְאֵשֶׁת נֹחַ וּשְׁלֹשֶׁת נְשֵׁי־בָנָיו אִתָּם אֶל־הַתֵּבָה:

*(7:13) That same day Noah and Noah's sons, Shem, Ham, and Japheth, went into the ark,*

*with Noah's wife and the three wives of his sons –*

ח:טז צֵא מִן־הַתֵּבָה אַתָּה וְאִשְׁתְּךָ וּבָנֶיךָ וּנְשֵׁי־בָנֶיךָ
אִתָּךְ:

*(8:16) "Come out of the ark, together with your
wife, your sons, and your sons' wives.*

ח:יח וַיֵּצֵא־נֹחַ וּבָנָיו וְאִשְׁתּוֹ וּנְשֵׁי־בָנָיו אִתּוֹ:

*(8:18) So Noah came out, together with his sons,
his wife, and his sons' wives.*

ט:א וַיְבָרֶךְ אֱלֹהִים אֶת־נֹחַ וְאֶת־בָּנָיו וַיֹּאמֶר לָהֶם פְּרוּ
וּרְבוּ וּמִלְאוּ אֶת־הָאָרֶץ:

*(9:1) God blessed Noah and his sons, and said to
them, "Be fertile and increase, and fill the earth.*

The Flood was more than just water covering the earth.
The flood suspended the normal functioning of the entire
world, a hiatus that was necessary for transforming the world
and for creating a whole new "breed" of man. This finds
expression, specifically, in the cessation of married family life
in the ark. We have already mentioned that men and women
had to enter the ark separately (6:18). And as long as they
were in the ark, the men lived separately from the women.

But when the time came to leave the ark, the men and
women were told to do so together (8:16). Thus, intimate
relations that had to be suspended during the Flood
were now once again permitted. However, although God
instructed Noah and his family to emerge from the ark in

pairs, they were afraid of returning to normal family life, and they therefore left the Ark just as they had lived in it (8:18) – men and women separately. God therefore renewed for them the Divine command to "be fruitful and multiply" (9:1).

Another aspect of the suspension of nature during the Flood is derived by the Midrash from the following verse: "So long as the earth endures, seedtime and harvest, cold and heat, summer and winter, day and night shall not cease" (8:22). The Midrash explains that the normal cycles of time would never cease *after* the Flood, but during the Flood those cycles – summer and winter, day and night, and so on – were in fact suspended.

The normal rhythms of life were suspended even inside the ark, for as already mentioned, the women neither conceived nor gave birth inside the ark, just as summer and winter, night and day were suspended outside of it. Noah and his family were reeducated in the ark, and the nature of the earth was suspended and reorganized outside the ark.

Food was first stored on the ground floor, which is where Noah also dumped animal waste. He could not simply throw that waste off the ark, because the ark was an autonomous entity, completely separated from the outside world. The whole world was reduced to the size of an ark, so that Noah could learn to take care of others.

When the whole world found itself literally "in the same boat" with him, Noah was able to realize the importance of loving one's neighbor. In the ark, Noah gained a new understanding of righteousness as responsibility for others. Only after that did the space of the ark expand back to the full size of the earth.

The verse preceding the end of the Flood says: "God remembered Noah and all the beasts and all the cattle that were with him in the ark" (8:1). What is the meaning of "God remembered"? Does God ever forget anything? Obviously not. But "remembered" means, simply, that the time had come for God to have Noah exit from the ark onto dry land, since Noah had now sufficiently corrected himself such that any new flood could be avoided.

## 10.15. After the Flood (8:20-21)

**כ** וַיִּבֶן נֹחַ מִזְבֵּחַ לַיי וַיִּקַּח מִכֹּל ׀ הַבְּהֵמָה הַטְּהֹרָה וּמִכֹּל הָעוֹף הַטָּהוֹר וַיַּעַל עֹלֹת בַּמִּזְבֵּחַ: **כא** וַיָּרַח יי אֶת־רֵיחַ הַנִּיחֹחַ וַיֹּאמֶר יי אֶל־לִבּוֹ לֹא־אֹסִף לְקַלֵּל עוֹד אֶת־הָאֲדָמָה בַּעֲבוּר הָאָדָם כִּי יֵצֶר לֵב הָאָדָם רַע מִנְּעֻרָיו וְלֹא־אֹסִף עוֹד לְהַכּוֹת אֶת־כָּל־חַי כַּאֲשֶׁר עָשִׂיתִי:

*[20] Then Noah built an altar to the Lord and, taking of every clean animal and of every clean bird, he offered burnt offerings on the altar.*
*[21] The Lord smelled the pleasing odor, and the Lord said to Himself: "Never again will I doom the earth because of man, since the devisings of man's mind are evil from his youth; nor will I ever again destroy every living being, as I have done.*

After leaving the ark, Noah, before doing anything else, offered a sacrifice.

The Torah distinguishes between several different types of sacrifices. Here Noah's sacrifice is "burnt offerings" that are entirely burned on the altar. This kind of sacrifice is brought as a sign of "replacing oneself," a symbol of understanding that the person himself should have been sacrificed, rather than the animal, and that only the mercy of the

Almighty allows him to continue to live.

Thus the burnt offering testifies that Noah was aware that his salvation was an act of Divine mercy. Noah understood that he was not saved on his own merits, nor as a reward for having executed divine orders. He is not saved because of something he did in the past, but for the sake of something that lay in the future - creating a new humanity, for whom life is impossible without concern for one's fellow man. Now that Noah understands this, he can be allowed to leave the ark.

**[21] The Lord smelled the pleasing odor**. God confirmed that Noah had reached the required level of understanding.

**[21] Never again will I doom the earth.** The high level of connection with the earth that man previously had is no more. In Noah was realized (albeit in a completely different way than was originally expected) the prophetic prayer of his father Lamech: to comfort, simplify, and reconcile with the world. Noah realized his name by making the world more "simple and convenient." But the price that had to be paid for this simplicity was the Flood.

Perhaps the lesson for us today is that we should not complain about life being too complicated. The desire to have an easier life can lead directly to a Flood or some other catastrophe.

### 10.16. The Meaning of the Word mabbul, "Flood" (6:17)

יז וַאֲנִי הִנְנִי מֵבִיא אֶת־הַמַּבּוּל מַיִם עַל־הָאָרֶץ לְשַׁחֵת
כָּל־בָּשָׂר אֲשֶׁר־בּוֹ רוּחַ חַיִּים מִתַּחַת הַשָּׁמָיִם כֹּל אֲשֶׁר־
בָּאָרֶץ יִגְוָע:

*[17] "For My part, I am about to bring the Flood*
*– waters upon the earth – to destroy all flesh*
*under the sky in which there is breath of life;*
*everything on earth shall perish."*

**[17] I am about to bring the Flood-waters upon the earth.**
After the word "Flood" there is an addition for the sake of
refinement, "water on the earth." This means that the *mab-*
*bul*, the Flood, is not the same as any other simple inundation of water. Water is only one of the parameters, and the
Flood itself is something quite unique.

In Hebrew, *mabbul* is associated with the root *beit-lamed*,
from which are derived, for example, the words *balal* and
*bilbel* – "confuse" and "mix," as well as the name *Bavel*, Babylon ("because there the Lord confounded the speech of
the whole earth" – 11:9), and the verb *bala* – to decay.

What is the significance of the concept of decay? When
a thing is new, it has both coarse and fine structure. Take
clothing as an example. It has not only sleeves and pock-
ets, but also finishing, details, and patterns. When clothing
decays, it retains a coarse structure, but loses its subtleties
and details, and becomes more "simple." This loss of fine
structure, which results in the intermingling of everything
into one confused mass, is the general meaning of the *bet-*
*lamed* root.

Thus, the *mabbul*, the Flood, is the destruction of the
"fine structure" of the Universe. The fine structure of the
earth means its susceptibility to the level of human righteousness. This is what was destroyed in the Flood. Inundation by water was only a means to realizing the Flood
itself. Only the water was predetermined. But it then turned
into death by causing drowning, because of the sins of the
people.

Since the Flood destroyed man's spiritual influence on the earth, God will have no need to destroy the world again, and He promises that there will be never be another flood. We can now understand the meaning of "Never again will I doom the earth because of man, since the devisings of man's mind are evil from his youth" (8:21). Although man is still prone to evil even after the Flood, he no longer has such a formidable ability to influence the world. Because the "thin structure" of man's interaction with the earth is no longer effective, the world cannot be completely destroyed, and a situation requiring almost total destruction of humanity is no longer possible.

## 10.17. The Rainbow in the Cloud (9:13-17)

יג אֶת־קַשְׁתִּי נָתַתִּי בֶּעָנָן וְהָיְתָה לְאוֹת בְּרִית בֵּינִי וּבֵין הָאָרֶץ: יד וְהָיָה בְּעַנְנִי עָנָן עַל־הָאָרֶץ וְנִרְאֲתָה הַקֶּשֶׁת בֶּעָנָן: טו וְזָכַרְתִּי אֶת־בְּרִיתִי אֲשֶׁר בֵּינִי וּבֵינֵיכֶם וּבֵין כָּל־נֶפֶשׁ חַיָּה בְּכָל־בָּשָׂר וְלֹא־יִהְיֶה עוֹד הַמַּיִם לְמַבּוּל לְשַׁחֵת כָּל־בָּשָׂר: טז וְהָיְתָה הַקֶּשֶׁת בֶּעָנָן וּרְאִיתִיהָ לִזְכֹּר בְּרִית עוֹלָם בֵּין אֱלֹהִים וּבֵין כָּל־נֶפֶשׁ חַיָּה בְּכָל־בָּשָׂר אֲשֶׁר עַל־הָאָרֶץ: יז וַיֹּאמֶר אֱלֹהִים אֶל־נֹחַ זֹאת אוֹת־הַבְּרִית אֲשֶׁר הֲקִמֹתִי בֵּינִי וּבֵין כָּל־בָּשָׂר אֲשֶׁר עַל־הָאָרֶץ:

*[13] I have set My bow in the clouds, and it shall serve as a sign of the covenant between Me and the earth.*
*[14] When I bring clouds over the earth, and the bow appears in the clouds,*
*[15] I will remember My covenant between Me and you and every living creature among all flesh, so that the waters shall never again*

*become a flood to destroy all flesh.*
*[16] When the bow is in the clouds, I will see it*
*and remember the everlasting covenant between*
*God and all living creatures, all flesh that is on*
*earth.*
*[17] "That," God said to Noah, "shall be the sign*
*of the covenant that I have established between*
*Me and all flesh that is on earth."*

The rainbow in particular is chosen as a sign of the covenant, because its colors are the entire spectrum from red to indigo-violet. In Hebrew, *adom*, "red," is associated with the word *adamah*, "earth," which represents the lower levels of being, or materiality. The indigo-violet *techelet*, which is also associated with the word *tachlit*, "goal" (striving toward something higher), is the color of the sky, and also the color of the blue thread that must be woven as tassels on the corners of four-cornered garments (Num. 15:37 ff.), symbolizing the goal that leads a person to the Almighty (See Numbers 15:37 and commentaries there).

The rainbow extends from *adom* to *techelet*, from the low, material level to the high and spiritual, and thus symbolizes many facets of the new post-Flood humanity. It is as if the Almighty were saying: "I have reconciled with man's imperfections. I have removed his special powers; now let him be multi-faceted. There are the evildoers and there are the righteous. For the sake of the righteous I must not destroy the evildoers. Humanity is now a multi-faceted, polychromatic community."

An important question arises in this connection: Where was the rainbow *before* the Flood? Were rainbows perhaps not seen then at all? Or did they appear, but were simply not yet a symbol of God's covenant? Although in Jewish tradition we find both approaches, most opinions agree that before the Flood rainbows did not exist.

The world before the Flood was, in a sense, black and white. Evil was then so powerful that every human being was either a villain or a righteous man. And Noah, who was righteous but only relatively speaking, was nonetheless in the world of all black and white considered completely pure. But at the same time, he was truly limited.

After the Flood, the world went from monochrome to color, and everything was far less unambiguous. The rainbow is a symbol of this diversity.

## 10.18. Noah and His Sons in the New World (9:20-23)

כ וַיָּחֶל נֹחַ אִישׁ הָאֲדָמָה וַיִּטַּע כָּרֶם: כא וַיֵּשְׁתְּ מִן־הַיַּיִן וַיִּשְׁכָּר וַיִּתְגַּל בְּתוֹךְ אָהֳלֹה: כב וַיַּרְא חָם אֲבִי כְנַעַן אֵת עֶרְוַת אָבִיו וַיַּגֵּד לִשְׁנֵי־אֶחָיו בַּחוּץ: כג וַיִּקַּח שֵׁם וָיֶפֶת אֶת־הַשִּׂמְלָה וַיָּשִׂימוּ עַל־שְׁכֶם שְׁנֵיהֶם וַיֵּלְכוּ אֲחֹרַנִּית וַיְכַסּוּ אֵת עֶרְוַת אֲבִיהֶם וּפְנֵיהֶם אֲחֹרַנִּית וְעֶרְוַת אֲבִיהֶם לֹא רָאוּ:

*[20] Noah, the tiller of the soil, was the first to plant a vineyard.*
*[21] He drank of the wine and became drunk, and he uncovered himself within his tent.*
*[22] Ham, the father of Canaan, saw his father's nakedness and told his two brothers outside.*
*[23] But Shem and Japheth took a cloth, placed it against both their backs and, walking backward, they covered their father's nakedness; their faces were turned the other way, so that they did not*

*see their father's nakedness.*

**[20] Noah, the tiller of the soil, was the first to plant a vineyard.** Noah began with an action that what was fully permissible – we could even say it was a positively motivated action. He planted a vineyard, made wine, and drank. All of that is permissible. But then he quickly met his downfall, for his actions crossed the line into the unlawful.

The problem was that Noah could not hold his own in a multicolored world, where there is a sea of intermediate shades and everything is ambiguous. Noah could remain righteous only in the simplest possible world, where everything is unambiguously either black or white.

**[23] But Shem and Japheth took a cloth, placed it against both their backs and, walking backward, covered their father's nakedness; their faces were turned the other way, so that they did not see their father's nakedness.** Shem and Japheth, unlike their father Noah, are people of a different, new world. What's going on here? A son hears that his father lies naked in his tent. What should be done? It all seems simple enough: grab a cloth and go and cover him. Shem and Japheth, however, do not act "simply." They give thought to the details and the consequences, they check their own behavior, and they therefore walk backwards, turning their faces away.

Noah's sons understand that in a complex, ambiguous world it is very easy to gravitate from what is right to what is wrong. Thus, they personify a new kind of righteousness that has staying power in this new, more complex, multifaceted world.

## 10.19. The Flood and the Land of Israel

According to the Midrash, although the Flood affected the entire world, there was one place that was untouched by the ravages of the Flood: the Land of Israel. Yes, there was an inundation of water there, even a flood, but there was no *mabbul* (see 13.16) in the Holy Land that muddled and erased the "fine structure." To this very day, the Land of Israel remains an "antediluvian" country.

This means that the pre-Flood ability of the earth to respond to the spiritual state of society has been preserved in the Land of Israel (and only there). And precisely in this does the sanctity of the Holy Land lie. Although this property does not manifest itself as clearly as it did everywhere before the Flood, here the earth itself perceives the holiness of society and of man, and materializes it.

If the Jewish people – to whom alone the Land of Israel truly reacts – start to behave incorrectly, then the Earth stops producing crops, and it proceeds to expel its inhabitants (a circumstance that is analogous to God's expulsion of humanity from the earth during the Flood). Only when the Jews in exile correct their behavior does the land take them back and restore their crops.

# Chapter 11

# Descendants of Noah's Sons

## 11.1. The Descendants of Japheth (10:1-5)

א וְאֵלֶּה תּוֹלְדֹת בְּנֵי־נֹחַ שֵׁם חָם וָיָפֶת וַיִּוָּלְדוּ לָהֶם בָּנִים
אַחַר הַמַּבּוּל: ב בְּנֵי יֶפֶת גֹּמֶר וּמָגוֹג וּמָדַי וְיָוָן וְתֻבָל
וּמֶשֶׁךְ וְתִירָס: ג וּבְנֵי גֹּמֶר אַשְׁכְּנַז וְרִיפַת וְתֹגַרְמָה: ד וּבְנֵי
יָוָן אֱלִישָׁה וְתַרְשִׁישׁ כִּתִּים וְדֹדָנִים: ה מֵאֵלֶּה נִפְרְדוּ אִיֵּי
הַגּוֹיִם בְּאַרְצֹתָם אִישׁ לִלְשֹׁנוֹ לְמִשְׁפְּחֹתָם בְּגוֹיֵהֶם:

*[1] These are the lines of Shem, Ham, and Japheth, the sons of Noah: sons were born to them after the Flood.*
*[2] The descendants of Japheth: Gomer, Magog, Madai, Javan, Tubal, Meshech, and Tiras.*
*[3] The descendants of Gomer: Ashkenaz, Riphath, and Togarmah.*
*[4] The descendants of Javan: Elishah and Tarshish, the Kittim and the Dodanim.*
*[5] From these the maritime nations branched out. [These are the descendants of Japheth] by their lands - each with its language - their clans and their nations.*

**[1] Sons were born to them after the Flood.** This is not mere chronological information (since we already know that before the Flood Noah's sons had no children). Rather, it is an indication of the new, post-Flood character of the new humanity.

**[5] By their lands – each with its language – their clans and their nations.** The dispersal of nations occurred immediately after the Flood, even before the incident of the Tower of Babel. Already then, every nation had its own land and its own language. The same is said about the sons of Ham and Shem (10:20 and 10:32).

## 11.2. The Descendants of Ham (10:6-20)

ו וּבְנֵי חָם כּוּשׁ וּמִצְרַיִם וּפוּט וּכְנָעַן: ז וּבְנֵי כוּשׁ סְבָא
וַחֲוִילָה וְסַבְתָּה וְרַעְמָה וְסַבְתְּכָא וּבְנֵי רַעְמָה שְׁבָא
וּדְדָן: ח וְכוּשׁ יָלַד אֶת־נִמְרֹד הוּא הֵחֵל לִהְיוֹת גִּבֹּר
בָּאָרֶץ: ט הוּא־הָיָה גִבֹּר־צַיִד לִפְנֵי יי עַל־כֵּן יֵאָמַר
כְּנִמְרֹד גִּבּוֹר צַיִד לִפְנֵי יי: י וַתְּהִי רֵאשִׁית מַמְלַכְתּוֹ בָּבֶל
וְאֶרֶךְ וְאַכַּד וְכַלְנֵה בְּאֶרֶץ שִׁנְעָר: יא מִן־הָאָרֶץ הַהִוא
יָצָא אַשּׁוּר וַיִּבֶן אֶת־נִינְוֵה וְאֶת־רְחֹבֹת עִיר וְאֶת־כָּלַח:
יב וְאֶת־רֶסֶן בֵּין נִינְוֵה וּבֵין כָּלַח הִוא הָעִיר הַגְּדֹלָה:
יג וּמִצְרַיִם יָלַד אֶת־לוּדִים וְאֶת־עֲנָמִים וְאֶת־לְהָבִים
וְאֶת־נַפְתֻּחִים: יד וְאֶת־פַּתְרֻסִים וְאֶת־כַּסְלֻחִים אֲשֶׁר
יָצְאוּ מִשָּׁם פְּלִשְׁתִּים וְאֶת־כַּפְתֹּרִים: טו וּכְנַעַן יָלַד אֶת־
צִידֹן בְּכֹרוֹ וְאֶת־חֵת: טז וְאֶת־הַיְבוּסִי וְאֶת־הָאֱמֹרִי
וְאֵת הַגִּרְגָּשִׁי: יז וְאֶת־הַחִוִּי וְאֶת־הַעַרְקִי וְאֶת־הַסִּינִי:
יח וְאֶת־הָאַרְוָדִי וְאֶת־הַצְּמָרִי וְאֶת־הַחֲמָתִי וְאַחַר
נָפֹצוּ מִשְׁפְּחוֹת הַכְּנַעֲנִי: יט וַיְהִי גְּבוּל הַכְּנַעֲנִי מִצִּידֹן
בֹּאֲכָה גְרָרָה עַד־עַזָּה בֹּאֲכָה סְדֹמָה וַעֲמֹרָה וְאַדְמָה
וּצְבֹיִם עַד־לָשַׁע: כ אֵלֶּה בְנֵי־חָם לְמִשְׁפְּחֹתָם לִלְשֹׁנֹתָם
בְּאַרְצֹתָם בְּגוֹיֵהֶם:

*[6] The descendants of Ham: Cush, Mizraim, Put, and Canaan.*

*[7] The descendants of Cush: Seba, Havilah, Sabtah, Raamah, and Sabteca. The descendants of Raamah: Sheba and Dedan.*

*[8] Cush also begot Nimrod, who was the first man of might on earth.*

*[9] He was a mighty hunter by the grace of the Lord; hence the saying, "Like Nimrod a mighty hunter by the grace of the Lord."*

*[10] The mainstays of his kingdom were Babylon, Erech, Accad, and Calneh in the land of Shinar.*

*[11] From that land Asshur went forth and built Nineveh, Rehoboth-ir, Calah,*

*[12] and Resen between Nineveh and Calah, that is the great city.*

*[13] And Mizraim begot the Ludim, the Anamim, the Lehabim, the Naphtuhim,*

*[14] the Pathrusim, the Casluhim, and the Caphtorim, whence the Philistines came forth.*

*[15] Canaan begot Sidon, his first-born, and Heth;*

*[16] and the Jebusites, the Amorites, the Girgashites,*

*[17] the Hivites, the Arkites, the Sinites,*

*[18] the Arvadites, the Zemarites, and the Hamathites. Afterward the clans of the Canaanites spread out.*

*[19] (The [original] Canaanite territory extended from Sidon as far as Gerar, near Gaza, and as far as Sodom, Gomorrah, Admah, and Zeboiim, near Lasha.*

*[20] These are the descendants of Ham,*

*according to their clans and languages, by their lands and nations.*

**[8] Cush also begot Nimrod, who was the first man of might on earth.** This is the first time in the Torah that a given person is described as being superior to others.

**[9] He was a mighty hunter by the grace of the Lord.** Nimrod, at least in the beginning, saw his abilities as a gift from the Almighty. From this passage he does not appear to have "led a rebellion against God", as the Midrash depicts him.

**[10] The mainstays of his kingdom were Babylon....** Having gained an advantage over other people, Nimrod immediately became king, that is, he had power over others.

**In the land of Shinar.** A little later (11:2), we are told that the Tower of Babel was built "in the land of Shinar." The Midrash therefore identifies Nimrod as the construction manager for the Tower of Babel.

**[11] From that land Asshur went forth.** Not everyone was prepared to obey Nimrod in Babylon, which was located in the southern part of Mesopotamia. Assyria occupied its northern territory.

### 11.3. Shem's Descendants (10:21-32)

כא וּלְשֵׁם יֻלַּד גַּם־הוּא אֲבִי כָּל־בְּנֵי־עֵבֶר אֲחִי יֶפֶת הַגָּדוֹל: כב בְּנֵי שֵׁם עֵילָם וְאַשּׁוּר וְאַרְפַּכְשַׁד וְלוּד וַאֲרָם: כג וּבְנֵי אֲרָם עוּץ וְחוּל וְגֶתֶר וָמַשׁ: כד וְאַרְפַּכְשַׁד יָלַד אֶת־שָׁלַח וְשֶׁלַח יָלַד אֶת־עֵבֶר: כה וּלְעֵבֶר יֻלַּד שְׁנֵי בָנִים

שֵׁם הָאֶחָד פֶּלֶג כִּי בְיָמָיו נִפְלְגָה הָאָרֶץ וְשֵׁם אָחִיו
יָקְטָן: **כו** וְיָקְטָן יָלַד אֶת־אַלְמוֹדָד וְאֶת־שָׁלֶף וְאֶת־
חֲצַרְמָוֶת וְאֶת־יָרַח: **כז** וְאֶת־הֲדוֹרָם וְאֶת־אוּזָל וְאֶת־
דִּקְלָה: **כח** וְאֶת־עוֹבָל וְאֶת־אֲבִימָאֵל וְאֶת־שְׁבָא: **כט**
וְאֶת־אוֹפִר וְאֶת־חֲוִילָה וְאֶת־יוֹבָב כָּל־אֵלֶּה בְּנֵי יָקְטָן:
**ל** וַיְהִי מוֹשָׁבָם מִמֵּשָׁא בֹּאֲכָה סְפָרָה הַר הַקֶּדֶם: **לא**
אֵלֶּה בְנֵי־שֵׁם לְמִשְׁפְּחֹתָם לִלְשֹׁנֹתָם בְּאַרְצֹתָם לְגוֹיֵהֶם:
**לב** אֵלֶּה מִשְׁפְּחֹת בְּנֵי־נֹחַ לְתוֹלְדֹתָם בְּגוֹיֵהֶם וּמֵאֵלֶּה
נִפְרְדוּ הַגּוֹיִם בָּאָרֶץ אַחַר הַמַּבּוּל:

[21] Sons were also born to Shem, ancestor of
all the descendants of Eber and older brother
of Japheth.
[22] The descendants of Shem: Elam, Asshur,
Arpachshad, Lud, and Aram.
[23] The descendants of Aram: Uz, Hul, Gether,
and Mash.
[24] Arpachshad begot Shelah, and Shelah begot
Eber.
[25] Two sons were born to Eber: the name of
the first was Peleg, for in his days the earth was
divided; and the name of his brother was Joktan.
[26] Joktan begot Almodad, Sheleph,
Hazarmaveth, Jerah,
[27] Hadoram, Uzal, Diklah,
[28] Obal, Abimael, Sheba,
[29] Ophir, Havilah, and Jobab; all these were
the descendants of Joktan.
[30] Their settlements extended from Mesha as
far as Sephar, the hill country to the east.
[31] These are the descendants of Shem
according to their clans and languages, by their
lands, according to their nations.

*[32] These are the groupings of Noah's descendants, according to their origins, by their nations; and from these the nations branched out over the earth after the Flood.*

**[21] Sons were also born to Shem, ancestor of all the descendants of Eber.** Although Eber was only one of Shem's great-grandchildren, his strong connection with Shem, which will become apparent in the history of Abraham's family, is emphasized here.

**[32] And from these the nations branched out over the earth after the Flood.** The Torah once again emphasizes that immediately after the Flood, even before the "mingling of tongues" at the Tower of Babel, there are different nations, each with its own language, and they are settled over the entire earth.

Chapter 12

# The Generations of the Tower of Babel

## 12.1. The Building of the Tower of Babel (11:1-4)

א וַיְהִי כָל־הָאָרֶץ שָׂפָה אֶחָת וּדְבָרִים אֲחָדִים: ב וַיְהִי
בְּנָסְעָם מִקֶּדֶם וַיִּמְצְאוּ בִקְעָה בְּאֶרֶץ שִׁנְעָר וַיֵּשְׁבוּ שָׁם:
ג וַיֹּאמְרוּ אִישׁ אֶל־רֵעֵהוּ הָבָה נִלְבְּנָה לְבֵנִים וְנִשְׂרְפָה
לִשְׂרֵפָה וַתְּהִי לָהֶם הַלְּבֵנָה לְאָבֶן וְהַחֵמָר הָיָה לָהֶם
לַחֹמֶר: ד וַיֹּאמְרוּ הָבָה ׀ נִבְנֶה־לָּנוּ עִיר וּמִגְדָּל וְרֹאשׁוֹ
בַשָּׁמַיִם וְנַעֲשֶׂה־לָּנוּ שֵׁם פֶּן־נָפוּץ עַל־פְּנֵי כָל־הָאָרֶץ:

*[1] Everyone on earth had the same language
and the same words.*
*[2] And as they migrated from the east, they
came upon a valley in the land of Shinar and
settled there.*
*[3] They said to one another, "Come, let us make
bricks and burn them hard" – Brick served them
as stone, and bitumen served them as mortar.*
*[4] And they said, "Come, let us build us a city,
and a tower with its top in the sky, to make a*

*name for ourselves; else we shall be scattered*
*all over the world."*

**[1] Everyone on earth had the same language and the same words.** As noted earlier (10:5, 20, 32), the nations split apart immediately after the Flood, even before the building of the Tower. How, then, is that to be reconciled with the one language for all mentioned here? The answer is that the word "language" is being used in two different senses.

Hebrew has two different words for "language": *lashon*, which also means "tongue" (the organ inside the mouth), and *safah*, which also means "lip." The expression in 0, "branched out each with its language," uses the word *lashon*, but in "Everyone on earth had the same language" here in 1, the Hebrew word is *safah*.

Just as the tongue is inside the human body, while the lips are outside, the two forms of language represented by those same words are likewise not at all identical. *Lashon*, the "language for internal use," is a system of concepts for describing reality that is needed to formulate models of the surrounding world, and which forms the basis of a functioning society. Each nation had such an internal language specific to it that it used to describe its affairs in terms of its own specific culture. But there was also a single "external communication language," *safah*, common to all the nations of the earth, which they used for intercommunication. In the aftermath of the incident of the Tower of Babel it was this language of external communication that disintegrated, leaving each nation with its own conception of the world, as the nations were dispersed to their respective countries.

**And the same words.** Literally, "and few words." The

existence of a common communication language, in addition to the independent, individual language of each nation and culture, is not *per se* a bad thing. The problem is only that such a language is poor, having only "few words." Due to the poverty and the primitive nature of this common language, it was impossible to build anything except a rigid "vertical of power" and a simple command structure. It was impossible to express fine-grained thoughts in that language, nor could it be used to describe cultural subtleties or to establish genuine mutual understanding among nations; it served only as the language of government. In other words, the people had so perverted this means of communication that it no longer had any right to exist.

**[3] They said to one another, "Come, let us make bricks and burn them hard." - Brick served them as stone, and bitumen served them as mortar.** This monumental technological revolution, homogeneous bricks instead of a motley assortment of stones, was bound together with a new connecting element (tar is far more adhesive than clay) and led to drastically improved construction quality and human living conditions. These new achievements, however, were used for an entirely different purpose.

**[4] And they said, "Come, let us build us a city, and a tower with its top in the sky, to make a name for ourselves; else we shall be scattered all over the world."** The goal of building the tower was not to reach the heavens, which, although a feature of the project, was not its actual objective. That goal, as clearly stated, was different –namely, to prevent the break-up of mankind. After the departure of Assyria (10:11), whose example could easily have set a precedent, Nimrod is determined to strengthen his kingdom in order to prevent the departure of yet other nations. To accomplish this he needs to create a unifying idea: "To make a name for ourselves." The construction of the great "city, and a tower with its top in the sky" became that idea; that is, it was envisioned as a project that would draw all nations into a shared undertaking and effect cohesion among the nations.

**A tower with its top in the sky.** The goal had to be a colossal, but also unattainable one. Only such an enormous, unrealizable project could consistently maintain the intensity needed to ensure universal involvement in the process. Captivating a population with grandiose designs is far easier than directing them to solve practical tasks of much smaller scale.

### 12.2. The Destruction of the Tower of Babel (11:5-9)

ה וַיֵּרֶד יי לִרְאֹת אֶת־הָעִיר וְאֶת־הַמִּגְדָּל אֲשֶׁר בָּנוּ בְּנֵי הָאָדָם: ו וַיֹּאמֶר יי הֵן עַם אֶחָד וְשָׂפָה אַחַת לְכֻלָּם וְזֶה הַחִלָּם לַעֲשׂוֹת וְעַתָּה לֹא־יִבָּצֵר מֵהֶם כֹּל אֲשֶׁר יָזְמוּ לַעֲשׂוֹת: ז הָבָה נֵרְדָה וְנָבְלָה שָׁם שְׂפָתָם אֲשֶׁר לֹא יִשְׁמְעוּ אִישׁ שְׂפַת רֵעֵהוּ: ח וַיָּפֶץ יי אֹתָם מִשָּׁם עַל־פְּנֵי כָל־הָאָרֶץ וַיַּחְדְּלוּ לִבְנֹת הָעִיר: ט עַל־כֵּן קָרָא שְׁמָהּ בָּבֶל כִּי־שָׁם בָּלַל יי שְׂפַת כָּל־הָאָרֶץ וּמִשָּׁם הֱפִיצָם יי עַל־פְּנֵי כָּל־הָאָרֶץ:

[5] *The Lord came down to look at the city and tower that man had built,*
[6] *and the Lord said, "If, as one people with one language for all, this is how they have begun to act, then nothing that they may propose to do will be out of their reach.*
[7] *Let us, then, go down and confound their*

*speech there, so that they shall not understand one another's speech."*

*[8] Thus the Lord scattered them from there over the face of the whole earth; and they stopped building the city.*

*[9] That is why it was called Babel, because there the Lord confounded the speech of the whole earth; and from there the Lord scattered them over the face of the whole earth.*

**[5] The Lord came down to look at the city and tower that man had built.** This descent can be understood as Divine judgment, but also as Divine revelation (cf., "And the Lord came down on Mount Sinai," Exodus 19:20). By virtue of this descent the people attained such spiritual heights as would have been impossible through "the same language and few words" alone. Thus, it was that Divine revelation specifically that led to mutual miscomprehension, and consequently, to their abandonment of the primitive common command language, and to their ceasing construction of the Tower.

That approach, which understands God's descent as mercy (revelation) rather than judgment, is indicated by the use in this entire passage of the Divine Name ("The Lord," the Tetragrammaton), which is traditionally understood as expressing the attribute of mercy, as opposed to *Elohim* ("God"), which is associated with rigor and judgment.

**[6] And the Lord said, "If, as one people.** Above (10:32, and earlier, where the Torah describes the division of nations after the Flood, which preceded the account of the Tower of Babel), *goy* is the word used to denote the concept of "nation." Here, however, the Hebrew word is *am*, which means "people" in the sense of a political state. Mankind at that time was already a multitude of established ethnic groups, politically united into one Babylonian kingdom. Once this political unity collapsed, those ethnic groups diverged into their respective countries.

**With one language for all, this is how they have begun to act.** Having a common channel of communication, they began using it improperly.

**Then nothing that they may propose to do will be out of their reach.** The unattainable was not the building of the "tower with its top in the sky." (Reaching the sky is of course impossible, and the ancients were no more foolish than we are.) But building the tower was only a means toward implementing the plan, whose goal was to not "be scattered all over the world"; that is, to remain under a unified Babylonian power. That goal, with the endless building of the tower, was completely realizable.

Such unity wholly impedes the advancement and development of society. The task envisioned by God for humanity is in development and diversification, surely not in homogeneity. Development requires that different nations and cultures compete, rather than execute a common project. God therefore confounds their languages and drives off the nations in different directions.

Upon experiencing the Divine manifestation, a person can express his new, complex feelings and impressions only through *lashon*. Each nation has its own – a language that is rich, but incomprehensible to others. A poor common language is insufficient for describing the reality in which God is revealed. Each nation feels its own unique aspect of this revealed Divinity, which becomes for it more valuable than the common language and whatever importance it had previously acquired.

**[7] So that they shall not understand one another's speech.** In a technical sense the common language might not have completely disappeared, and they continued to understand each other's words, but nonetheless could come to no true mutual understanding. The level reached by individual cultures so exceeded the ability of a limited common language to express it that intercommunication became almost impossible. The result was their complete disseverance.

**[8] Thus the Lord scattered them from there over the face of the whole earth.** This scattering was actually a positive circumstance, for it laid the foundations for the further development and progress of humanity.

## 12.3. The Genealogy of Shem, Through Abraham (11:10-27)

י אֵלֶּה תּוֹלְדֹת שֵׁם שֵׁם בֶּן־מְאַת שָׁנָה וַיּוֹלֶד אֶת־
אַרְפַּכְשָׁד שְׁנָתַיִם אַחַר הַמַּבּוּל: **יא** וַיְחִי־שֵׁם אַחֲרֵי
הוֹלִידוֹ אֶת־אַרְפַּכְשָׁד חֲמֵשׁ מֵאוֹת שָׁנָה וַיּוֹלֶד בָּנִים
וּבָנוֹת: **יב** וְאַרְפַּכְשַׁד חַי חָמֵשׁ וּשְׁלֹשִׁים שָׁנָה וַיּוֹלֶד
אֶת־שָׁלַח: **יג** וַיְחִי אַרְפַּכְשַׁד אַחֲרֵי הוֹלִידוֹ אֶת־שֶׁלַח
שָׁלֹשׁ שָׁנִים וְאַרְבַּע מֵאוֹת שָׁנָה וַיּוֹלֶד בָּנִים וּבָנוֹת: **יד**
וְשֶׁלַח חַי שְׁלֹשִׁים שָׁנָה וַיּוֹלֶד אֶת־עֵבֶר: **טו** וַיְחִי־שֶׁלַח
אַחֲרֵי הוֹלִידוֹ אֶת־עֵבֶר שָׁלֹשׁ שָׁנִים וְאַרְבַּע מֵאוֹת שָׁנָה
וַיּוֹלֶד בָּנִים וּבָנוֹת: **טז** וַיְחִי־עֵבֶר אַרְבַּע וּשְׁלֹשִׁים שָׁנָה
וַיּוֹלֶד אֶת־פָּלֶג: **יז** וַיְחִי־עֵבֶר אַחֲרֵי הוֹלִידוֹ אֶת־פֶּלֶג
שְׁלֹשִׁים שָׁנָה וְאַרְבַּע מֵאוֹת שָׁנָה וַיּוֹלֶד בָּנִים וּבָנוֹת: **יח**
וַיְחִי־פֶלֶג שְׁלֹשִׁים שָׁנָה וַיּוֹלֶד אֶת־רְעוּ: **יט** וַיְחִי־פֶלֶג

אַחֲרֵי הוֹלִידוֹ אֶת־רְעוּ תֵּשַׁע שָׁנִים וּמָאתַיִם שָׁנָה וַיּוֹלֶד
בָּנִים וּבָנוֹת: **כ** וַיְחִי רְעוּ שְׁתַּיִם וּשְׁלשִׁים שָׁנָה וַיּוֹלֶד
אֶת־שְׂרוּג: **כא** וַיְחִי רְעוּ אַחֲרֵי הוֹלִידוֹ אֶת־שְׂרוּג שֶׁבַע
שָׁנִים וּמָאתַיִם שָׁנָה וַיּוֹלֶד בָּנִים וּבָנוֹת: **כב** וַיְחִי שְׂרוּג
שְׁלשִׁים שָׁנָה וַיּוֹלֶד אֶת־נָחוֹר: **כג** וַיְחִי שְׂרוּג אַחֲרֵי
הוֹלִידוֹ אֶת־נָחוֹר מָאתַיִם שָׁנָה וַיּוֹלֶד בָּנִים וּבָנוֹת:
**כד** וַיְחִי נָחוֹר תֵּשַׁע וְעֶשְׂרִים שָׁנָה וַיּוֹלֶד אֶת־תָּרַח: **כה**
וַיְחִי נָחוֹר אַחֲרֵי הוֹלִידוֹ אֶת־תֶּרַח תְּשַׁע־עֶשְׂרֵה שָׁנָה
וּמְאַת שָׁנָה וַיּוֹלֶד בָּנִים וּבָנוֹת: **כו** וַיְחִי־תֶרַח שִׁבְעִים
שָׁנָה וַיּוֹלֶד אֶת־אַבְרָם אֶת־נָחוֹר וְאֶת־הָרָן: **כז** וְאֵלֶּה
תּוֹלְדֹת תֶּרַח תֶּרַח הוֹלִיד אֶת־אַבְרָם אֶת־נָחוֹר וְאֶת־
הָרָן וְהָרָן הוֹלִיד אֶת־לוֹט:

[10] This is the line of Shem. Shem was 100 years
old when he begot Arpachshad, two years after
the Flood.
[11] After the birth of Arpachshad, Shem lived
500 years and begot sons and daughters.
[12] When Arpachshad had lived 35 years, he
begot Shelah.
[13] After the birth of Shelah, Arpachshad lived
403 years and begot sons and daughters.
[14] When Shelah had lived 30 years, he begot
Eber.
[15] After the birth of Eber, Shelah lived 403 years
and begot sons and daughters.
[16] When Eber had lived 34 years, he begot Peleg.
[17] After the birth of Peleg, Eber lived 430 years
and begot sons and daughters.
[18] When Peleg had lived 30 years, he begot Reu.
[19] After the birth of Reu, Peleg lived 209 years
and begot sons and daughters.
[20] When Reu had lived 32 years, he begot Serug.

*[21] After the birth of Serug, Reu lived 207 years
and begot sons and daughters.
[22] When Serug had lived 30 years, he begot
Nahor.
[23] After the birth of Nahor, Serug lived 200
years and begot sons and daughters.
[24] When Nahor had lived 29 years, he begot
Terah.
[25] After the birth of Terah, Nahor lived 119 years
and begot sons and daughters.
[26] When Terah had lived 70 years, he begot
Abram, Nahor, and Haran.
[27] Now this is the line of Terah: Terah begot
Abram, Nahor, and Haran; and Haran begot Lot.*

Only a partial family tree is provided, the line from Shem to the family of Abraham, around which the story will continue to unfold.

But here we must return to Eber, about whom it was said above (10:21): "Shem, father of all the sons of Eber." It is from Eber that the word *ivri*, "Hebrew," is derived. We shall see later how important that Hebrew (in this case proto-Jewish) identity has itself become. Both Abraham and Joseph are called Hebrews (14:13, 41:12), while the entire country is called the "land of the Hebrews" (40:15). The Midrash explains that Noah, Shem, and Eber were "early monotheists" – "the first Patriarchs," as it were – and Abraham, Isaac, and Jacob continued to advance their legacy.

The passage "Eber had two sons, the name of one Peleg, because in his days the land was divided" (10:25) is a reference to the story of the Tower of Babel. To Eber, the division of the nations was an experience so compelling that he named his son "Peleg" (which means "division"), as if to say, "may this division lead to multiplication." One kind of division occurs when everything irrevocably falls apart. But there is another kind of division that is the result of multiplication. The name "Peleg" expresses Eber's hope for a division of the latter type.

Because the hopes of the "early monotheists" for the improvement of mankind were based on its unity and common language, the scattering of peoples that occurred was nothing less than a tragedy for Eber. After their division into nations, these lonely monotheists could have no influence, because the new reality was that it was necessary to be a people in order to influence others. Although their own attempts were fruitless, they bequeathed to us the word *ivrim*, "Hebrews," which tells us that their heritage is very much alive. They were the teachers of Abraham, Isaac and Jacob, who were the progenitors of the "chosen people," a people capable of improving other communities of humankind.

### 12.4. The History of the Family of Abraham (11:28-32)

כח וַיָּמָת הָרָן עַל־פְּנֵי תֶּרַח אָבִיו בְּאֶרֶץ מוֹלַדְתּוֹ בְּאוּר כַּשְׂדִּים: כט וַיִּקַּח אַבְרָם וְנָחוֹר לָהֶם נָשִׁים שֵׁם אֵשֶׁת־אַבְרָם שָׂרָי וְשֵׁם אֵשֶׁת־נָחוֹר מִלְכָּה בַּת־הָרָן אֲבִי־מִלְכָּה וַאֲבִי יִסְכָּה: ל וַתְּהִי שָׂרַי עֲקָרָה אֵין לָהּ וָלָד: לא וַיִּקַּח תֶּרַח אֶת־אַבְרָם בְּנוֹ וְאֶת־לוֹט בֶּן־הָרָן בֶּן־בְּנוֹ וְאֵת שָׂרַי כַּלָּתוֹ אֵשֶׁת אַבְרָם בְּנוֹ וַיֵּצְאוּ אִתָּם מֵאוּר כַּשְׂדִּים לָלֶכֶת אַרְצָה כְּנַעַן וַיָּבֹאוּ עַד־חָרָן וַיֵּשְׁבוּ שָׁם: לב וַיִּהְיוּ יְמֵי־תֶרַח חָמֵשׁ שָׁנִים וּמָאתַיִם שָׁנָה וַיָּמָת תֶּרַח בְּחָרָן:

*[28] Haran died in the lifetime of his father Terah, in his native land, Ur of the Chaldeans.*

*[29] Abram and Nahor took to themselves wives, the name of Abram's wife being Sarai and that of Nahor's wife Milcah, the daughter of Haran, the father of Milcah and Iscah.*

*[30] Now Sarai was barren, she had no child.*

*[31] Terah took his son Abram, his grandson Lot the son of Haran, and his daughter-in-law Sarai, the wife of his son Abram, and they set out together from Ur of the Chaldeans for the land of Canaan; but when they had come as far as Haran, they settled there.*

*[32] The days of Terah came to 205 years; and Terah died in Haran.*

**[28] Haran died in the lifetime of his father Terah, in his native land, Ur of the Chaldeans.** From the fact that Ur of the Chaldeans is mentioned as the place of birth of Haran, we can infer that Terah's older children were not born there; that is, Terah's family arrived in Ur of the Chaldeans somewhat earlier, and Terah himself was born in Charan (where Nahor continued to reside), or perhaps even in Canaan, the Land of the Hebrews (40:15). For that reason, he later wishes to return there.

**Ur of the Chaldeans.** In Hebrew, *ur kasdim*. It is a city in Lower Mesopotamia. But *ur* literally means "furnace," so the verse can be read as, "and Haran died … in the Chaldean furnace." The midrashim about Abraham's childhood (see below) are based on this point.

**[29] Abram and Nahor took to themselves wives, the name of Abram's wife being Sarai and that of Nahor's**

**wife Milcah, the daughter of Haran, the father of Milcah and Iscah.** This mention of Iscah seems to have no actual relevance to the story. The Midrash therefore identifies her with Sarah, which would mean that Nahor and Abraham married nieces, the two daughters of Haran. Later (20:12) we learn that Sarah was Abraham's step (not full) sister / niece. In other words, Terah had two wives. Abram and Nahor were born from the one, and Haran from the other.

**[30] Now Sarai was barren, she had no child.** The apparent redundancy here of "barren, she had no children" is apparently meant to tell us that Abraham and Sarah had made peace with being childless, seeing their continuation therefore in their disciples, and not in their descendants.

**[31] Terah took his son Abram, his grandson Lot the son of Haran, and his daughter-in-law Sarai, the wife of his son Abram.** Nahor is not mentioned among those whom Terah took with him (probably because he continued to live in Charan). But Sarah is mentioned specifically, to tell us that she is an independent personality in her own right.

**And they set out together from Ur of the Chaldeans for the land of Canaan; but when they had come as far as Haran, they settled there.** Thus, Terah had intentions to "go to the land of Canaan" even before Abraham received such instructions from God (12:1). We shall see very soon why this point is significant.

# Weekly Portion
# Lech Lecha

# Chapter 13

# Chosenness, Faith, and Monotheism

## 13.1. Chosenness for a Purpose (12:1-3)

א וַיֹּאמֶר יי אֶל־אַבְרָם לֶד־לְךָ מֵאַרְצְךָ וּמִמּוֹלַדְתְּךָ
וּמִבֵּית אָבִיךָ אֶל־הָאָרֶץ אֲשֶׁר אַרְאֶךָּ: ב וְאֶעֶשְׂךָ לְגוֹי
גָּדוֹל וַאֲבָרֶכְךָ וַאֲגַדְּלָה שְׁמֶךָ וֶהְיֵה בְּרָכָה: ג וַאֲבָרֲכָה
מְבָרְכֶיךָ וּמְקַלֶּלְךָ אָאֹר וְנִבְרְכוּ בְךָ כֹּל מִשְׁפְּחֹת הָאֲדָמָה:

*[1] The Lord said to Abram, "Go forth from your
native land and from your father's house to the
land that I will show you.
[2] I will make of you a great nation, And I will
bless you; I will make your name great, And you
shall be a blessing.
[3] I will bless those who bless you, And curse him
that curses you; And all the families of the earth
shall bless themselves by you."*

The story of Abraham begins with God urging him to

undertake the creation of a people needed for the spiritual perfection of all mankind.

The reasons that God chose only Abraham for this mission are not explained in Scripture. The Midrash tells many stories about Abraham's youth, his righteousness, and his merits, but these find no expression in the Torah text itself. This contrasts starkly with, for example, God's choosing Noah for being "righteous and blameless" (7:9). The reason that God chose Abraham is concretely explained by the Torah much later (18:19), when God says, "For I have singled him out, that he may instruct his children and his posterity to keep the way of the Lord by doing what is just and right."

Here we see several aspects of God's choosing Abraham. Firstly, it is based on action ("doing what is just and right"), and not merely on "faith in God." Secondly, God's reason for choosing Abraham is not Abraham's past merits, but the promise that his future holds (or, more precisely, that of his descendants). Abraham, like the Jewish people in general, is chosen for the objective he is charged to accomplish – that is, not as a reward for actions he has already performed, but for the sake of his potential, which will be revealed only in the future.

God wants to help mankind draw nearer to Him, to realize the "kingdom of God on earth." For this, He needs helpers who will pass on Divine principles to humanity. God chooses Abraham because he and his descendants, the Jewish people, are capable of accomplishing this.

## 13.2. Existence Determined by the Future

The idea of favoring the future over the past, and believing that the cardinal events of our lives primarily occur not merely "for a reason" but "for the sake of a goal" permeates the entire Jewish perception of the world.

That idea can be found, for example, in the following midrash about the exodus from Egypt. When at the splitting of the Red Sea the Egyptians were close to drowning, Egypt's guardian angel turned to God with the following complaint: "Judge of the world! You are unfair, you play favorites among your children. Why do you allow the Egyptians to drown, but you rescue the Jews? Neither practiced idolatry in Egypt any less than the other!" God answered him: "It is true that in Egypt they behaved in many ways the same. For the Jews, however, I grant a miraculous salvation outside the natural course of events, because of their potential to soon accept the Torah on Mount Sinai (and bring that Torah to humanity). For the Egyptians I perform no such miracle, leaving them subject to only the natural course of events, for they have no such potential. And so they perish under the waves."

Indeed, in some ways the Jews behaved in Egypt no better than the Egyptians themselves. They deserved the Exodus and the salvation at the Red Sea not for their prior merit, but for the mission that they would accomplish in the future.

Likewise, God has given the Jewish people today the opportunity to build and develop the State of Israel only for the sake of the future Jewish mission, not because of its past merits. The primary force that drives the Jewish people today, as in antiquity, is in the future, not in the past. It is rooted in projected purpose rather than historical causation.

## 13.3. Faith as the Sense of Purpose and Meaning in the Creation

The distinction between the materialistic (atheistic) and

monotheistic religious views of the world is not limited to the questions of whether God exists or what He is. (Such questions are for the most part so complex and theoretically abstract that we are hard-pressed to consider any answer satisfactory.) In concrete, practical terms the difference between the religious and materialistic worldviews is that materialists view the world as driven by cause and effect (they reduce the entire movement of the universe to principles of physical causation), whereas a religious person sees the world teleologically, believing that the universe is moving, first and foremost, toward the fulfillment of its goals (although the presence of physical causes is of course also not denied). Because it is the Almighty Who has established these goals for the world, our dialogue with God becomes the fundamental substance of our lives.

This essential difference of approaches to how one sees the world is not just abstract theory, but is inextricably linked with our entire essence, the Jewish way of life.

Let us try to further elucidate this issue.

In everyday life, we explain the processes occurring all around us in two different ways: causally and teleologically. For example, in response to the question "Why is the car travelling down the road?" two answers are possible: a causal answer (the driver's foot presses the gas pedal, fuel enters the engine, the wheels spin and push off the ground, and the car moves), and a teleological one (the car moves because the driver wants to go somewhere). That goal – the pursuit of the future – is the primary answer to our original question of why the car moves. For it is that goal that initiates the chain of physical causes, due to which the automobile begins to move.

At the same time, the driver's wish to travel in one direction and not the other cannot be fully predicted, even if one knows all the material factors motivating him. Because that driver is a person and (unlike the car) he has freedom of choice, rather than being a slave to circumstances.

In ordinary life, if we want to perceive the world adequately, we use both types of explanations. When dealing with inanimate objects we can limit ourselves to causative explanations. But when we need to understand the behavior of living beings and, especially, human beings, then only teleological explanations will suffice (he has desires and motivations that cause him to act in a particular way).

The concept of purpose, and the concept of meaning that is inseparably connected with it as the highest goal, are extremely important for understanding human behavior. Personality cannot be reduced to causation, nor can a person live without that sense of meaning in everything that happens.

But if we consider more global, socio-historical processes in society and in the course of history generally (the entire universe as a whole), we must ask ourselves: Are there only "causes", or does each of these historical processes have also a purpose and a meaning? The materialist and the religious person will disagree on this issue.

For a materialist, only causation drives the world as a whole. But a monotheistically religious person believes that the history of humankind in general, and our own lives in particular, have purpose and meaning.

Of course, neither the one nor the other viewpoint can be proved or scientifically substantiated; the choice between them is entirely our own.

On this issue note that the idolaters side with the materialists: they see in life only causes, even if those causes are of a "supernatural" quality, such as karma or rock. The concept of "purpose and meaning," on the other hand, becomes relevant only when we believe that behind all phenomena in the world stands a monotheistic God, the Being who created all humans in His image and likeness, and with whom we are in constant dialogue.

Abraham's belief in ethical monotheism consisted precisely in that – his sense of goal and meaning, which to him implied also his moral responsibility to realize his own potential and purpose. It was that faith that Abraham wanted to teach to all of humanity.

## 13.4. Abraham as Chesed, and the Spreading of Monotheism

Abraham devoted his life to spread ethical monotheism among humankind. As we noted earlier, he was by no means the first to profess this religion, for Noah, Shem, and Eber were monotheists even before Abraham was. But Abraham was the first to actively disseminate this idea by initiating a process that continues to this day. Throughout his life, Abraham was active as an itinerant: "And he built there an altar to the Lord and invoked the Lord by name" (12:8, 13:4, 13:18, 14:22, 21:33). This thirst for proliferation is one of the aspects of *chesed* (acts of kindness) – the desire to give, as already mentioned (above 5.4).

*Chesed* is the cardinal principle fundamental to any creation, from the creation of the world to the creation of a people. Abraham, the progenitor of all Jews, therefore had to possess this quality in the extreme, as it pertains both to love of God (the spread of monotheism) and to the love of one's fellow humans. Abraham, however, besides spreading the idea of performing acts of kindness, also perfected that very attribute of kindness that then became the foundation for the future life of the Jewish people. Abraham's tests and difficulties were therefore related precisely to that attribute of kindness, as we shall discuss in detail below.

## 13.5. The Essence of Monotheism as Dialogue with God

Let us define more clearly what was the nature of Abraham's faith, and why it changed all of humankind.

In defining the faith of Abraham as ethical monotheism we often fail to comprehend what the term "monotheism" really means. Why is monotheism so important, and what real difference does it make if we believe in one God, or in several? Why did the adoption of monotheism and the rejection of "polytheism" so strongly influence the world that, practically speaking, it created Western civilization?

The misunderstanding relates firstly to the widespread misconception that the entire essence of monotheism is "faith in one God." Of course, monotheism asserts that God is the one and the only. But that is only the beginning, and not even the primary essence of monotheism, nor is it the basis for the revolution that it created in the world.

In principle, the Supreme Power of any religious system is always the one and only, besides being also supreme. And even if there were several, the "all-inclusive, highest law of the universe" would have to dominate them all to preserve world balance and the unity of the laws of nature. The difference between monotheistic culture (represented in ancient times by Judaism alone, but today by all of Western civilization) and idolatrous, polytheistic culture (in ancient times all of humankind, and today the "Eastern religions" – Hinduism, Buddhism and Confucianism) is not in quantitative indicators, but in the nature of this Supreme Power. As understood by polytheism, that supreme power is "rock," "universal law," the "law of Heaven," the "law of Karma," and so on – that is, an impersonal power, a world law that dominates absolutely everything, but cannot be addressed, nor can one engage with it in dialogue. This force will not participate in dialogue; it dominates, and an individual is personally of no importance to it.

However, in the monotheistic Abrahamic religions, the supreme power is a personal God who created man in His own image and likeness. He is therefore not indifferent to mankind; on the contrary, He loves every human being, wants good for him, cares about him, and seeks to bring him closer to Himself. All the difficulties and problems in our lives are the tasks that God gives us so that by solving them we can advance both ourselves and the rest of the world. This approach leads a person to a completely different worldview, already enshrined in the linguistic apparatus of Western cultures. The very concept of a Supreme Power, that is, God, does not exist with a capital letter in the language of Eastern religions; there are only "gods" there.

It would therefore be more correct to characterize the clash of religions in world history not as monotheism against polytheism, but as personal-monotheistic religions against karmic religions.

Monotheism proclaims that God, having created man in His own image and likeness, endowed him with freedom of choice, diverse skills and abilities, and a mind and feelings, and that He still today engages with man in dialogue. God's creating man "in his image and likeness" was necessary for that dialogue to be feasible, for, as we know, dialogue is possible only between like interlocutors. All our thoughts and actions are our words in dialogue with God, while everything that happens around us and everything that happens to us – the way the world responds to us – are God's words addressed to us. Only such a personal monotheism allows you to feel how disparate phenomena occurring in the world have as their cause a single Being and are not random results of the interactions of dissimilar forces.

Ethical monotheism thus views the entire surrounding world as a zone of dialogue between man and God. In this dialogue God demands from each of us ethical, responsible behavior – responsibility before Him. (This feeling is varyingly called responsibility to conscience, to life, to one's national history, or to humankind. But in practice all these are almost equivalent concepts. It is this global responsibility that forms the basis of all ethics.) In this dialogue, a person throughout his life attains for himself, and reveals for others, diverse manifestations of the Divine light.

The faith that Abraham preached was just such an ethical monotheism. He did not achieve it straightaway; rather, it took time, his own efforts, and Divine support and revelation. By the time he was seventy years old, however – the point where the book of Genesis begins its story of God's choosing Abraham (12:1) – he was already imbued with that faith.

The spread of faith, however, is not enough to save humanity. Abraham had to create the Jewish people, because only a nation can improve other nations (that is, improve human existence at the social, and not only the individual level). The Torah now proceeds to tell of the trials that the Patriarchs experienced on their way to creating a people.

# Chapter 14

# The Dynamics of the Patriarchs as Corrections to the Sefirot

## 14.1. The Lives of the Patriarchs as the Process of Faceting the Sefirot

As mentioned earlier, in the course of the Torah's narrative each of the Patriarchs (and his *sefirah* with him) must undergo the dynamics of his correction.

The term "dynamics of correction" means that the *sefirah*, like a diamond in the rough, must be properly cut if it is to serve its intended purpose. This "cutting" means trimming off any excess to yield the correct shape. For example, if *chesed*, as the desire to give, to share, to show mercy and grace, goes unchecked beyond all limits, the world will collapse. (As an example at the simplest social level, suppose that for the realization of mercy and grace we were to offer social benefits, sufficient to guarantee a good and easy life to all, free for the asking. An enormous number of people would then stop working, and civilization would perish.) *Chesed* must therefore be restricted. Abraham learned how to accomplish that, and the process of limiting *chesed* is Abraham's personal dynamic. Abraham's process of restricting his own *chesed*, and similar processes for Isaac and Jacob, are carried out with the help of *nisayon*, trials.

The tests of the Patriarchs did not consist in requiring them to exhibit always positive inclinations and never negative ones. We would consider that just a completely normal and common level of difficulty, whereas the Patriarchs were incomparably more advanced. The trials of the Patriarchs are situations in which each has to serve God while correcting himself by working *against* that positive attribute that was unique to him. The result is a "cut," a proper restricting of the given attribute. Each of the Patriarchs initially resembles a rough diamond, which only after cutting – the removal of excess material – becomes a true jewel whose value and price steadily increase. For only a cut diamond can serve its intended purpose. Likewise, if we need a large stone of a desired shape and size to be incorporated into the foundation of a building, we will first need to find an even much larger, irregularly shaped stone, and only after its cutting will we have a large, smooth and even stone suitable for use in construction.

Abraham limits *chesed* by learning to act against *chesed*. Abraham is by nature the very embodiment of *chesed*, who longed to show favor to all. God demands that he act against *chesed*, but only so that Abraham would learn to restrict that attribute. Likewise, Isaac and Jacob in the course of their respective tests learn to limit the qualities inherent in them.

Applying the basic ideas of Kabbalah to an analysis of the lives of the Patriarchs is widespread in Western culture today. Through Hasidism especially, many of these ideas are elucidated in a multitude of books and other publications, thus entering the consciousness of a wide-ranging public. The teachings of Rabbi Y. L. Ashkenazi-Manitou, on which our approach is based, unveil an innovative method for tracing the "faceting" process through each actual event experienced by the Patriarchs as described in the Torah. Indeed, this allows us to achieve a completely new level of understanding.

## 14.2. The Patriarchs and the Sefirot Tree

Let us consider now in greater detail the *sefirot* tree" as it relates to the Patriarchs.

The *sefirot* tree (growing from top to bottom, from the higher worlds to our world – see the illustration in portion 5.6) begins with *keter*, the crown, corresponding to the concept of will. In Jewish thought the highest of all Divine attributes is the will of the Almighty (and not His wisdom, the *sefirah* that is *chochmah*). Since every human being is built in the image and likeness of the Almighty, willful discretion – that is, freedom of choice – is the leading force, while wisdom manifests itself only as its consequence.

Below *keter* are *chochmah*, *binah*, and *da'at*. Those three, which combine to form the concept of *sechel*, "intellect," are the three highest ("inner," hidden) *sefirot*. We refer to them also by their abbreviation *ChaBaD*.

Below them are the seven *middot* (attributes) of "quality" and "manifestation." These attributes are lower ("external"), corresponding to the seven days of the Creation, and to the seven foundational personalities that shaped the image of the Jewish people.

Directly below *ChaBaD* are *chesed*, *gevurah*, and *tiferet* (abbreviated as *ChaGaT*). These are the emotional competencies of the soul.

As noted above, the attribute of *chesed* (belonging to the right, extroverted line in the structure of the *sefirot*) means the emotion of aspiring outward, reflected by mercy and grace. On the first day of Creation G-d created light, which seeks to spread outward, "giving itself to the world"; that is, it manifests the attribute of *chesed* at the level of inanimate nature. Similarly, the primary aspiration of Abraham, the first Patriarch, was to show mercy to everyone around him, both in the material realm, by accepting travelers and helping the poor, and in the spiritual realm, by spreading the teachings of how to approach God and achieve holiness. Thus, Abraham represents the attribute of *chesed* at the structural level of the Jewish people.

The second of the *middot* (belonging to the left, introverted line in the structure of the *sefirot*) is *gevurah* – strength, power – identical with *din*, "judgment." This means striving for preservation, retention, rigidity, self-restraint, law, order, judgment, and justice. Isaac, the bearer of the attribute of *gevurah* within the structural framework of the Jewish people, devoted his life to preserving and maintaining the teachings of his father Abraham. Similarly, on the second day of the creation of the world, God created the firmament (sky), which holds water and demonstrates *gevurah* at the level of inanimate nature.

The third of the *middot* (it is found on the middle, harmonizing line) is *tiferet*, beauty or splendor. *Tiferet* is designed to maintain harmony between the attributes of *chesed* and *gevurah*, to determine when it is proper to give and to show mercy, and when to hold back, showing only the attribute of judgment.

The *tiferet* attribute is also called *emet*, truth. The leading motivation for Jacob's actions and aspirations was not "spreading" (like Abraham's) or "preserving" (like Isaac's), but finding the balance of truth in a world so full of falsehood.

The attributes of the emotional series are the product ("descent downward") of the corresponding attributes of the intellectual series. *Chochmah* is a "directing outward" at the intellectual level, and *chesed*, too, is a "directing outward," but at the emotional level. Similarly, *binah* is an intellectual directing inward, and *gevurah* is an emotional directing inward.

On the middle line, *da'at* engenders *tiferet*: only through comprehension at the *da'at* level and incorporating the knowable can one understand whether to apply mercy or judgment.

## 14.3. The Trials of the Patriarchs

Abraham, then, represents the attribute of *chesed*, the desire to give, to show mercy, to be good to all; and his *nisayon* (test) is the need, by Divine order, to act against his own nature, limiting the *chesed* within himself.

In the process of being tested, Abraham had to learn to excise from within himself "extraneous" *chesed*, the *chesed* of impurity, so that the remaining *chesed* of holiness" could become the foundation for building the Divine nation, the Jewish people.

The word *nisayon* means not only "testing," but also "gaining experience." Abraham, who is the expression of *chesed*, gained experience in its proper application. In addition, *nisayon* is linguistically related to the word *nes*, which has two meanings: "banner" (a military emblem held aloft on a pole, or other device of orientation) and "miracle" (that which runs counter to natural forces). In the Torah, therefore, *nisayon* refers to the acquisition of Divine experience, which occurs contrary to the natural course of events (a miracle) and serves as a reference point for the future (it "creates a banner").

In ordinary life, applying one's natural, positive qualities to serving God is of course the surest path, both for ordinary people and for the righteous. For the Patriarchs, however, the path to serving God was the one that went contrary to their natural positive inclinations. It was thus by virtue of the trials experienced by the Patriarchs that the Jewish people were formed (*nes* as "miracle" – the miracle of the creation of the Jewish people). These tests are described in the Torah so that subsequent generations can orient themselves by following the visual example set by the Patriarchs (carried as a banner for orientation). One of the foundations of Jewish tradition is thus the Talmudic principle that "the deeds of the ancestors serve as signals for their descendants"; that is, the narratives found in the Torah serve as examples for future generations.

Abraham is cleansed of "improper, excessive *chesed* (*chesed de-tum'ah*, "impure," i.e, "excess *chesed*") which is inherited instead by Ishmael, and "proper *chesed*" (*chesed di-kedushah*, "holy *chesed*") passes as an inheritance to Isaac, and from there on to Jacob. Similarly, "proper *gevurah*" (*gevurah di-kedushah*, "holy *gevurah*") is transmitted from Isaac to Jacob and to the Jewish people, while *gevurah de-tum'ah*, "impure *gevurah*, excess *gevurah*" goes to Esav.

Chapter 15

# Introductory Remarks on God's Choosing Abraham

## 15.1. Midrash: Stories of Abraham's childhood

To the story of Abraham's life as recorded in the Torah the Midrash adds several stories about his youth in Ur of the Chaldeans. Later we shall consider the actual meaning of these midrashim within the context of the Torah's narrative. Here we present only the text itself (in a style that approximates that of the Midrash).

### (a) The story of the vanquishing of the sun and moon

Abraham had been hidden in a cave since birth. At the age of three years Abraham left the cave, and upon seeing the world for the first time, he began to reflect on who had created the earth, the sky, and Abraham himself. Enraptured by the sight of the sun, its light and warmth, he offered prayers to the sun that entire day. But when the sun set, and the moon appeared in the sky surrounded by countless stars,

Abraham was struck by its beauty and thought, "This luminous body is obviously a deity!" All night he uttered hymns to the moon. But morning came, the moon departed in the west, and the sun reappeared in the east.

"No," said Abraham, "I was wrong. There is Someone who rules over both the sun *and* the moon. I will direct my prayers to Him."

## (b) Abraham smashes the idols

Terah, Abraham's father, was engaged in the manufacture of idols, which he then sold at the market. One day he instructed Abraham to mind the store.

A woman came and gave Abraham a bowl of flour as a gift to the idols. Abraham took a stick, smashed all the idols except one, the very largest, and placed the stick in its hand. Terah was dumbfounded upon his return.

"What is going on here? How did this happen? Who did this?"

"I will tell you," Abraham answered, "and will conceal nothing. It was like this: A woman brought a bowl of flour and asked me to present it as an offering to the idols. I was about to give them the flour, but the idols argued among themselves about who should partake first. The largest idol rose up and smashed all the others."

"Surely you mock me," Terah shouted, "how could they possibly...?"

"But what are you saying, father?! You would do well to ponder your own words."

## (c) The story of the fiery furnace

For having destroyed those idols, Abraham was brought

to judgment by Nimrod, king of Babylon.

Said Nimrod: "Bow to the fire as a deity, and I will spare you."

Abraham replied: "But water is more powerful than fire, because water extinguishes fire! Shouldn't we bow instead to the water?"

"Very well. Then, bow to the water."

"But clouds are more powerful than water, because clouds carry water! Shouldn't we bow instead to the clouds?"

"Very well. Then, bow to the clouds."

"But would it not be better to bow to the wind that disperses the clouds?"

"Then bow to the wind!"

"But doesn't man overpower even the force of the wind?"

"That's enough! I will force you to bow to the fire. ... Throw him into the fire, and we shall see whether the God whom he worships can save him."

Then they threw Abraham into the furnace, but the Almighty Himself came down and saved Abraham, and he emerged from the furnace unharmed.

Haran (Abraham's brother), who was also present at these proceedings, said: "If Abraham is saved, then he is right, and I am with Abraham. But if Abraham dies, then Nimrod is right, and I am with Nimrod."

When he saw that Abraham had been saved, Haran said: "Then I am with Abraham!" They threw him into the furnace, and he died (for he was not so deserving that God would create a miracle just for him). And this is what the Torah means when it says (11:28): "And Haran died during the lifetime of Terah his father, in the land of his birth in Ur of the Chaldeans" (*lit.*, in the Chaldean furnace).

## 15.2. Hebrews, Israel, and Jews: The Names of the Nation and its Land

The Jewish people have three characteristic names: Hebrews, Israel, and Jews. In other languages the meanings of these words are distinct. (The term "Jews" usually relates to religion, "Hebrews" to the nation, and "Israel" to a country or state.) In Hebrew, however, these words are identical in meaning. Already in the book of Esther, written two and a half thousand years ago, we find that the term "Jews" means, precisely, the entire Jewish people. Similarly, the meaning of the word "Israel" in its original sense is the people, not the country; that is, it is synonymous with the terms "Hebrews" and "Jews.." Derived from it are the phrases in the possessive form: *Eretz Yisrael* ("The Land of Israel"), *Medinat Yisrael* ("The State of Israel"), and others.

These terms, although synonymous today, developed only over time, and originally had different meanings. The word *ivrim*, "Hebrews," came first: it originally described a community much broader than the family of Abraham, namely, all the descendants of Eber.

(There is a widespread belief, based on the word "Hebrew" sharing a root with the word *ma'avar*, "transition," that Abraham is called a Hebrew because he relocated from one side of the river (Euphrates) to the other. Or, alternately, that the term "Hebrew" derives from the idea that when the entire world is on the one side, Abraham and the Jewish people are on the other. It is important to understand, however, that this is a midrash (homiletic interpretation), whereas the literal meaning of the word "Hebrew" is simply a descendant of Eber).

The word "Israel" appeared later: it was the second name of Jacob, whose descendants were called "the sons of Israel," or simply "Israel" (like many other nations in the Torah, whose names are those of their founders). And the Jews (the most recent name of the three) were originally descendants of Yehudah, i.e. one of the most prominent of the Twelve Tribes of Israel.

The ethnonym *ivri*, "Hebrew," first appears in the book of Genesis as referring to Abraham (14:13), and then later in reference to Joseph, when Potiphar's wife, coming to accuse him of a grievous offense, tells the members of her household: "He (my husband Potiphar) had to bring us a Hebrew to dally with us!" (39:14). This shows that the meaning of that ethnonym was clear to all the Egyptians present, even if they were not personally familiar with the family of Abraham. Likewise, Pharaoh's butler says: "A Hebrew youth was there with us (in prison)" (41:12). At the luncheon Joseph prepares for them, he seats his brothers, who do not yet recognize him, separate from the Egyptians, which the Torah explains as follows: "For the Egyptians could not dine with the Hebrews, since that would be abhorrent to the Egyptians" (43:32). Joseph himself tells the cupbearer how he came to be a slave with the following words: "I was kidnapped from the land of the Hebrews" (40:15). We thus see that the ethnonym *ivrim* is used in a much wider sense than the "descendants of Abraham." Moreover, Canaan was officially called the "Land of the Hebrews," otherwise Joseph could not have used that term in conversation with the butler.

All this tells us that the descendants of Eber in ancient times ruled the Holy Land. But then, most likely, the Hebrew community was destroyed, of which certain remnants, the family of Terah in particular, made their way to Ur of the Chaldeans, the city in Babylon. The Torah's story of Abraham begins from the moment that his father Terah decides to leave Ur of the Chaldeans and return to his original country, that is, to Canaan (although he gets only as far as Charan).

### 15.3. Abraham and Eber's Legacy

We shall see later that the descendants of Terah – the family of Nahor and his children – gradually assimilated among the Aramaeans and began to be called Aramaeans, after the name of the country where they took root. Thenceforth, only the family of Abraham were called "Hebrews."

Note too that according to the chronology of the Torah, Eber was still alive during Abraham's lifetime. Tradition states that Abraham, Isaac, and Jacob studied with Noah, Shem, and Eber. The latter three, however, lived apart, in a "yeshiva," so that others could come to study with them, but they did not themselves spread the teachings of monotheism.

Comparing the positions of Abraham and Eber, one can see that they differed in two respects. First, unlike Eber, Abraham was an active (one might even say militant) monotheist, The Midrash talks about how Abraham smashes idols, but about Eber it says nothing of the kind. Although a monotheist, Eber was apparently tolerant of idolatry. The Midrash describes Abraham as an uncommonly hospitable host who received all wayfarers, including idolaters, into his home. That is, he was a man of *chesed*. And yet, although he was tolerant and accepting of all people, he was harsh and intolerant towards idolatry, to the point of "smashing idols." Secondly, Abraham wanted to restore Eber's teachings precisely in the country that was the primary center of monotheism, the Land of the Hebrews, which is why he sought to live in Canaan.

Later, yet a third attribute, the most important one, came to distinguish Abraham from Eber. Namely, Abraham was the founder of a nation, albeit one that came into being only over time.

## 15.4. The Covenant of the Patriarchs

The concept of covenant occupies a prominent position in the book of Genesis, and indeed in all Jewish teachings. A covenant is an extraordinary connection with God, as opposed to that which occurs in the natural course of events. In a certain sense, God manifests Himself in our world in two opposite forms. On the one hand, all of nature and its natural laws are Divine creations and manifestations of God; in this respect the Almighty acts as the "God of nature." And yet, He is also the "God of the Covenant," which means that God establishes a special relationship with a person or people that transcends the natural course of events. In other words, that person or nation develops not as do all other persons and nations, but in an exceptional direction, while exerting a significant influence on the surrounding world.

We first encounter this concept in the covenant that God makes with Noah, when the Flood destroys all of humanity, but Noah and his family are chosen by God to alone survive. When Noah leaves the Ark after the flood, God makes a covenant with him and his descendants. "The Covenant of Noah" creates a unique status to which any of Noah's descendants can aspire. (This is a substantial, independent topic that is beyond the scope of this book.) Later we encounter the Covenant of the Patriarchs that God makes with Abraham, Isaac, and Jacob, and still later, in the book of Exodus, we see the Covenant at Sinai, made with the entire Jewish people.

The Covenant at Sinai is very different from previous covenants, for it is expressed through God's commandments. It begins with the proclamation of the Ten Commandments, followed by the remaining laws of the Torah formulated in its 613 Commandments. Unlike the Covenant at Sinai, the Covenant with the Patriarchs includes no formal laws. Within its framework, even circumcision is not a duty, but only a symbol of this covenant. In essence, it is a covenant respecting the Jewish people and the Land of Israel.

The Covenant of the Patriarchs is thus distinguished by two important characteristics. Firstly, there are no formalized commandments; these are instead replaced by ideals (mercy and justice primarily), which, while difficult to formalize, are the purpose for which the covenant is established. Secondly, the covenant is associated with the creation of a nation and a country for this people, as repeated several times in the Torah, in God's address to the Patriarchs: "I will make a nation out of you and will give you this country as your dwelling place, and I shall be your God."

Thus, the people itself and its national life in the Land of Israel are the primal substance through which God advances all of humanity. The commandments are for this people a means by which they can properly build their lives.

## Chapter 16

# The Beginning of Abraham's Journey

### 16.1. God Chooses Abraham (12:1-3)

**א** וַיֹּאמֶר יי אֶל־אַבְרָם לֶךְ־לְךָ מֵאַרְצְךָ וּמִמּוֹלַדְתְּךָ
וּמִבֵּית אָבִיךָ אֶל־הָאָרֶץ אֲשֶׁר אַרְאֶךָּ: **ב** וְאֶעֶשְׂךָ לְגוֹי
גָּדוֹל וַאֲבָרֶכְךָ וַאֲגַדְּלָה שְׁמֶךָ וֶהְיֵה בְּרָכָה: **ג** וַאֲבָרֲכָה
מְבָרֲכֶיךָ וּמְקַלֶּלְךָ אָאֹר וְנִבְרְכוּ בְךָ כֹּל מִשְׁפְּחֹת הָאֲדָמָה:

*[1] The Lord said to Abram, "Go forth from your
native land and from your father's house to the
land that I will show you.
[2] I will make of you a great nation,
And I will bless you;
I will make your name great,
And you shall be a blessing.
[3] I will bless those who bless you
And curse him that curses you;
And all the families of the earth
Shall bless themselves by you."*

**[1] The Lord said to Abram.** Abram was en route to Canaan with his father Terah even before this (11:31), for that was their family's self-motivated decision. But now the Almighty chooses Abram, and he must make his way to that land as a part of his covenant with God, making it a completely different kind of journey.

**Go forth from your native land and from your father's house.** The text literally reads: "from your native land, from your birthplace, and from your father's house." He must dissolve his old ties on three levels: by leaving his family (his father's house), his ideologically familiar community (his next closest of kin), and the social function that he had been performing in Charan. Without this break – not only with his negative past, but also with his positive past – Abram's realization of his mission would not have been possible.

**Go forth ... to the land that I will show you.** Abram understood straightaway that this meant Canaan. But the expression *ar'ekka* can be understood not only as "I will show you" (i.e., to you, with "you" as indirect object), but also as "I will show you to others" ("you" as direct object). The whole expression can thus be translated as "To the land in which I will show you [to the rest of the world]." Only when the Jewish people live in the Land of Israel can they, operating as a unit, materially influence the world. The Midrash emphasizes this point, noticing that the expression *lech lecha*, whose simple meaning is "Go thee forth," can also be translated more literally as "Go for yourself, for your own benefit," so as to say, you cannot realize your spiritual potential while living in any other place.

**[2] I will make of you a great nation.** It is a nation, not merely a religious movement. Abram abandons the framework of his former world to create a new, unprecedented reality, the chosen people. It is at this moment that the Western "Abrahamic" monotheistic tradition is born.

**I will make of you a great nation, and I will bless you; I will make your name great, and you shall be a blessing.** Note here four characteristics of chosenness: the nation's preeminence, its accomplishments, its renown, and its universal mission to all of humankind.

**[3] I will bless those who bless you, and curse him that curses you.** Abram, and the Jewish people likewise, can neither bless nor curse persons of their own choosing. Contrast this with the diametrically opposite outlook of a similar phrase used in connection with the villain Balaam (Numbers 22:6; see *Biblical Dynamics* there). Rather, the nations and peoples of the world will themselves be blessed or cursed depending on how they relate to the Jewish people: They who bless the Jews bring upon themselves a blessing, and they who curse them bring upon themselves a curse.

**And all the families of the earth shall bless themselves by you.** Here the term "families" is used (not "nations"), because the Jewish nation is charged with uniting humanity spiritually, and the cooperation between neighboring families is much tighter than among neighboring nations. In Zechariah too (14:17), the nations of the world are called "families of the earth," a term that expresses the unity of humanity from the messianic perspective.

## 16.2. God's Plan and Abraham's Plan (12:4-5)

ד וַיֵּלֶךְ אַבְרָם כַּאֲשֶׁר דִּבֶּר אֵלָיו יי וַיֵּלֶךְ אִתּוֹ לוֹט וְאַבְרָם

בֶּן־חָמֵשׁ שָׁנִים וְשִׁבְעִים שָׁנָה בְּצֵאתוֹ מֵחָרָן: ה וַיִּקַּח
אַבְרָם אֶת־שָׂרַי אִשְׁתּוֹ וְאֶת־לוֹט בֶּן־אָחִיו וְאֶת־כָּל־
רְכוּשָׁם אֲשֶׁר רָכָשׁוּ וְאֶת־הַנֶּפֶשׁ אֲשֶׁר־עָשׂוּ בְחָרָן וַיֵּצְאוּ
לָלֶכֶת אַרְצָה כְּנַעַן וַיָּבֹאוּ אַרְצָה כְּנַעַן:

*[4] Abram went forth as the Lord had
commanded him, and Lot went with him. Abram
was seventy-five years old when he left Haran.
[5] Abram took his wife Sarai and his brother's son
Lot, and all the wealth that they had amassed,
and the persons that they had acquired in Haran;
and they set out for the land of Canaan. When
they arrived in the land of Canaan.*

**[4] Abram went forth.** Surely Abram was inwardly prepared
to fulfill the mission entrusted to him (had he not been
ready, it is unlikely that God would have charged him with
that mission). That readiness, however, by no means implies
that it was an order that Abraham could take in stride. On
the contrary, God's command proved so radical that Abram
was unable to immediately assimilate and accept it.

**Abram went forth as the Lord had commanded him, and
Lot went with him... [5] Abram took his wife Sarai and his
brother's son Lot.** These passages are usually understood
simply as Abram's fulfillment of God's instructions. When
we compare the two verses, however, we see that they present a significant contradiction. In verse 12:4, "**Abram went
forth as the Lord had commanded him**" everything is
exactly as God ordered Abram, and Lot himself went along
with him. In verse 12:5, however, "**Abram took his wife Sarai
and his brother's son Lot,**" a completely different picture
is presented, prompting the question: Is it not obvious that

Abram's wife would join him? Why must this be explicitly stated? Moreover, the Torah emphasizes that Abram actively took Lot with him, which is problematic, given that he had been ordered to leave his relatives behind. Why, then, did he take not only all his wealth, but also "the souls they had acquired in Charan," of whom God had made no mention in His order?

To resolve these inconsistencies, we must consider the verses in a broader context. As noted earlier, the migration to Canaan was not initiated at all by Abram, since verse 12:5 **".. and they set out for the land of Canaan. When they arrived in the land of Canaan..."** clearly corresponds to verse 11:31: **"Terah took his son Abram, his grandson Lot the son of Haran, and his daughter-in-law Sarai, the wife of his son Abram, and they set out together from Ur of the Chaldeans for the land of Canaan; but when they had come as far as Haran, they settled there."**

Thus, in verse 12:5, Abram's journey to Canaan is presented as his continuation of the journey begun by his father Terah (11:31), and not in any sense as Abram's fulfillment of a Divine order (12:1). Terah was unable to realize his plan, for he was stranded in Charan, but Abram continued the journey and realized the original plan.

Verses 12:4 and 12:5, then, rather than merely contradicting each other, present two opposing views of the same event. On the one hand, Abram follows God's instructions in every respect, but on the other hand, he initially has his own plans and is not prepared to modify them: he journeys to Canaan to complete the project begun by his father Terah.

In other words, Abram had his own plans and, although he managed to incorporate them into his fulfillment of God's order, he did not follow God's instructions in every respect.

How and why did this come about?

## 16.3. The Transition from Cosmopolitanism to "Political Universalism"

The spiritual forefather of mankind was originally named Abram, not Abraham. Only at the end of the *Lech Lecha* portion is the Hebrew letter "heh" added to his name (in English this is represented by the h in "Abraham").

The Midrash explains the name Abram as Ab Aram – "the father of the Aramaeans," that is, the spiritual leader of the people of Mesopotamia. And the expression, "the souls they acquired in Charan" refers to Abraham's many disciples.

Earlier we cited the Midrash that tells how Abram came to monotheism while still in Ur Kasdim, smashing idols and challenging King Nimrod. Abram is thus a dissident who from his youth opposes the official ideology and exhorts the population to renounce idolatry. Later, in Charan, he has a great many disciples. Seen from this perspective, Abram's departure from Charan represents a typical Jewish dilemma: Should a Jew devote his life to advancing the morality and spirituality of the nations of the world by living among them or would he do better to tackle exclusively Jewish problems while living in the Jews' own country?

The Midrash considers this dilemma Abram's first test.

A Jew will consistently strive for universality, for interaction with all of humanity. A desire to bring a blessing upon all of humanity is quite natural for, and typical of, the Jewish national character. There is a temptation, however to equate universalism with cosmopolitanism – that is, the idea that for the sake of being truly worldly it is necessary to abandon all uniquely national interests. God's instruction to Abram was precisely the opposite: "You must adhere to the national, by striving to create your own people, because it is through the national, and never through the abandonment of it, wherein the path to the universal lies."

Upon comparing verses 12:4 and 12:5 we see that initially there are two different plans for advancing humankind towards monotheism: God's plan and Abram's plan. God's plan is to create a nation out of Abram: "I will make of you a great nation." Abram's plan, however, originally presupposed creation of a religion of ethical monotheism that would reeducate humanity while transcending all nationality. Abram therefore takes his disciples with him, notwithstanding that God had not ordered him to do so.

We shall continue our coverage of this problem below, as part of our discussion of Abraham's subsequent life crises.

## 16.4. Abraham's First Test: The Departure from Charan

Abraham's primary quality was thus *chesed*. All his life he taught ethical monotheism to the people around him.

However, Abraham's main contribution to the advancement of mankind is not merely that he cultivated enlightenment, but that he created the Jewish people, the "faceting" of *chesed*. As he underwent his tests, Abraham restricted his *chesed*, excising from within himself the extraneous components and leaving the legitimate core of *chesed* that would later serve as the basis for the soul of the Jewish nation.

Instead of the raw attribute of *chesed* – the unrestrained desire to give and show mercy – Abraham had to construct a more correct attribute of *chesed*, as he learned to give only when giving leads to good, because misplaced kindness can easily lead to evil. To this end, Abraham had to learn to act against his own nature, against *chesed*, against striving for universal grace.

From the point of view of *chesed* it seemed natural to Abraham that he should create a group of teachers for the sake of promoting his ideas. Such a group would be open to teaching all people. Promoting this same idea at the national level seems less proper, because a nation is by necessity always a restricted set: some belong to it simply by right of birth, while most others are excluded. Restricting kindness in that way seems inconsistent with the whole idea of *chesed*. God's proposal to Abraham to become the founder of a nation, and not merely of a group of disciples, was therefore itself one of Abraham's ordeals. The test here consisted not only in separating himself from his relatives and from his familiar environment, but also in transitioning to a national mindset, thereby restricting the influence of his ideas by reorienting himself away from all of humanity toward a single people.

Abraham, the spiritual leader of the people of Aram (among the most prominent civilizations of the time), had to abandon his country, whose progress he was engaged in promoting, and the people who considered him their spiritual leader. *Lech lecha*, addressed by God to Abraham, can be translated as "go for yourself, go to yourself," that is, abandon the cosmopolitan affairs that occupy you in Babylon and work for the furtherance of your own nation specifically. Restricting himself in this way was for Abraham a significant challenge.

Jewish tradition teaches an important principle: "The deeds of the ancestors serve as indicators for their descendants." The actions of the Patriarchs are archetypes, models of what happens later to the Jewish people. If we view Abraham's tests through the lens of past millennia, we see that his departure from Charan was a typically Jewish test. Jews quite often want to help all of humanity at once, but they must abandon that wish and deal instead with specifically Jewish problems.

To properly resolve such conflicts of conscience, we must realize that the transition from a cosmopolitan position to a national one is by no means a betrayal of universalism – on the contrary, it is a movement towards it. Universalism is achieved not through cosmopolitanism, but through properly oriented nationalism. The path to the universal does not lie in the abandonment of the national, but, on the contrary, through a thoroughly national orientation that is open to the world, but autonomous all the same.

Many Jews even today will see this position as far too harsh, but for Abraham it was yet much more difficult to accept the idea that universality is achieved not by spreading God's teachings at once to all, but by first creating, from the very outset, an exceptional people. Appealing to all of humankind would become possible only much later, by following the path already blazed and trodden by the Jewish people. Only gradually did Abraham come to fully accept God's plan.

## 16.5. Changing the World Requires a Nation, and not Merely Disciples

In God's command to Abraham, "Go forth to the land that I will show you, and I will make of you a great nation", the key concept is the nation. As already noted, Abraham was not the first monotheist, for even before him the idea of the One God as the basis of morality – that is, the idea of ethical monotheism – was professed by Noah, Shem and Eber. But the idea of creating nothing less than an entire monotheistic people had never been conceived before. It appears in human history only from the moment that God chose Abraham to implement that plan.

The novelty and rarity of this approach lies in the fact that it establishes the goal of achieving holiness on both the individual and national levels. Holiness is not only for righteous individuals who are "immersed in spirituality," but also for ordinary people who are involved in all aspects of material life within society. Holiness at the individual level was well-known even before then, for there certainly were exceptional, righteous personalities in every age who achieved holiness. But the idea of achieving holiness at the national level was all but unthinkable.

It should be noted that despite the progress of past millennia, pan-national holiness is still for many Jews even today something unusual, unattainable, and even downright difficult to conceive, while individual holiness, on the other hand, is a recognizable and commonplace phenomenon. But since "only like affects like," for the improvement and spiritual advancement of mankind – that is, all the peoples of the world – the required level of holiness must be achieved by an entire nation. And truly, only then "all the families of the earth shall bless themselves by you" (12:3). That is, only when the Jewish people attains national holiness can holiness then be extended to all of humanity.

## 16.6. The Lech Lecha Portion as Abraham's Transition to God's Plan

When one is trying to construct a doctrine, a religion, or a school of philosophy, what one absolutely must have are disciples; having actual children of one's own is not really necessary. But when one is trying to build a nation, the situation is completely different – one needs descendants.

We see that no legacy remains of the entire coterie of

Abraham's students (who are mentioned in the Torah only in passing). Everything that humankind received from Abraham was transmitted through his son Isaac, and then through Isaac's son Yaakov and his children.

Initially, however, Abraham did not realize this. Although he had no children, he did have pupils, and he hoped to disseminate his religious system with their help. The absence of children did not at first seem to Abraham a problem, because children are not indispensable for creating religious doctrine. Only later does Abraham come to understand the importance of progeny.

In fact, the entire *Lech Lecha* portion is about the conflict between these two enterprises: Abraham's plan to create a religion, and God's plan to create a people. By the end of that portion, Abraham finally abandons his own plan and fully transitions to realizing God's plan exclusively.

## 16.7. The Founding of the City of Shechem (12:6-7)

ו וַיַּעֲבֹר אַבְרָם בָּאָרֶץ עַד מְקוֹם שְׁכֶם עַד אֵלוֹן מוֹרֶה
וְהַכְּנַעֲנִי אָז בָּאָרֶץ: ז וַיֵּרָא יי אֶל־אַבְרָם וַיֹּאמֶר לְזַרְעֲךָ
אֶתֵּן אֶת־הָאָרֶץ הַזֹּאת וַיִּבֶן שָׁם מִזְבֵּחַ לַיי הַנִּרְאֶה
אֵלָיו:

*[6] Abram passed through the land as far as the site of Shechem, at the terebinth of Moreh. The Canaanites were then in the land.*
*[7] The Lord appeared to Abram and said, "I will assign this land to your heirs." And he built an altar there to the Lord who had appeared to him.*

**I will assign this land.** The word *zot*, "this," always refers to something visible, to which you can point. In other words, from the place where Abraham was located, the entire future Land of Israel was visible. Mount Ebal, located at 3,085 feet (940 m) above sea level in the area of Shechem, is just such a place: it affords a striking view of over 60 miles (100 km) in every direction. On this very mountain almost five hundred years after Abraham, when conquering the Holy Land, Joshua would erect an altar as a memorial to Abraham's altar (Joshua 8:30). Not too many years ago Joshua's altar was located and excavated by an Israeli archaeological expedition.

**The Canaanites were then in the land.** Describing how Abraham came to that Land, the Torah immediately informs us what kind of people were then in possession of it. That is, the situation at the time of the described events is contrasted with God's promise, "I will assign this land to your heirs." This means that the matter of state authority at the national level in the Holy Land is highly significant from God's point of view.

**Abram passed through the land as far as the site of Shechem.** Not "as far as Shechem," but "as far as the site of Shechem." When Abraham arrived there the city of Shechem apparently did not yet exist. Rather, it was the site of the future Shechem.

**I will assign this land to your heirs.** Here Abraham receives yet another prophecy, more precisely delineating the area of his activity. Earlier, when God said to Abraham, ".. I will make of you a great nation" (12:2), Abraham might still have imagined that his disciples would become the foundation of the new nation; perhaps he even considered them his adopted children. Therefore, although Abraham goes to Canaan at God's direction, he takes with him "acquired souls," intending to create a people from them, and hoping to integrate his own plans with God's instructions. But now God speaks to him in more definite terms, informing him that the nation will be built on the foundation of Abraham's descendants, and not his disciples. We therefore see later (12:8) that Abraham continues the journey with only his family.

Abraham apparently left his disciples, who then most likely founded the city of Shechem, if it did not then exist. They remained in Shechem and further developed themselves while no longer under Abraham's influence. The observation that Shechem was built and populated by Abraham's disciples, who had come from Babylon, is critical to our analysis of the history that later unfolds.

## 16.8. Babylon and Egypt

Babylon and Egypt, two fertile regions and two great civilizations framing the Land of Israel from opposite sides, were inextricably linked with it throughout the ancient era. And from those two civilizations we see, likewise, two rather different Jewish "outcomes."

Abraham's origins were in Babylon. He spends some time in Egypt and then moves on. Jacob goes to his uncle Laban in Babylon, but returns from there to Canaan. At the end of his life he and his family descend to Egypt.

Some centuries later the Jewish people made history with the Exodus from Egypt. Many more centuries after that the Babylonian captivity ensues, then ends abruptly seventy years later. At the next turn of history, now already the period we know as "antiquity," Egypt and Babylon become the primary seats of the Jewish diaspora. Its spiritual center moves to Babylon, where the Babylonian Talmud takes form.

All of ancient Jewish history was in some sense a pendulum swinging to and fro between Egypt and Babylon.

The significance of Babylon and Egypt as the primitive centers of human culture is noted at the very beginning of the Torah (Genesis 2). In the story of Adam and Eve's brief stay in the Garden of Eden, where the matter of geography would seem completely irrelevant, the Torah says: "A river issues from Eden to water the garden, and it then divides and becomes four branches. The name of the first is Pishon, the one that winds through the whole land of Havilah, where the gold is. The gold of that land is good; bdellium is there, and lapis lazuli. The name of the second river is Gihon, the one that winds through the whole land of Cush. The name of the third river is Tigris, the one that flows east of Asshur. And the fourth river is the Euphrates" (2:10-14).

These four prominent rivers symbolize the four primary orientations into which human culture diffused beyond the single "river issues from Eden." The confluence of the Tigris (Chiddekel) and the Euphrates is in Mesopotamia, although the former is associated with Assyria, and the latter with Babylon. Gihon is the Nile, which bypasses the land of Cush (Ethiopia), and symbolizes Egyptian culture. And the fourth of those rivers, Pishon, is also usually identified with the Nile – the White and Blue Nile rivers.

Because the Land of Israel lies between Egypt and Babylon, throughout the whole of ancient history the Jews found themselves caught between these two great centers of civilization, two zones of influence always in competition with one another.

At the time of the Patriarchs the boundary of that zone of influence passed through the Jordan Valley. Canaan, the mountainous part of the country, was subordinate to Egypt, while the lowland – the Jordan Valley and the vicinity of the Dead Sea, as well as the Transjordan – belonged to Babylon's sphere of influence.

The fundamental cultural difference between the ancient civilizations of Egypt and Babylon was as follows.

Egypt, with a solar calendar, was a solar civilization. It subsequently became the basis for the ancient Graeco-Roman and Christian civilizations. It manifests its legacy through the West – by expansion, rationality, and openness.

In contrast, Babylon, with its lunar calendar, was a lunar civilization. It gave rise to Islamic culture, which likewise follows a lunar calendar. Islam manifests its heritage through the East – by dreams, languor, and magic.

As we should have expected, Jewish civilization, centered in the Land of Israel midway between the other two, unites and integrates the achievements of both Egypt and Babylon, and compensates for their shortcomings. Indeed, the Jewish calendar is lunar-solar.

## 16.9. Abraham Between the Sun and the Moon

Let us turn to a midrash which we cited above (18.1) about the vanquishing of the sun and the moon. Abraham's reasoning comes across as childish and naive. After first gazing at the sun and concluding that the sun is a deity, he then turns his sights toward the moon and arrives at the same conclusion about the moon. Finally, he reasons that there must be Someone ruling over both the sun *and* the moon. The entire episode seems so very primitive. The Midrash also informs us that Abraham had emerged from a cave. What kind of cave did Abraham emerge from? And why had he been living in a cave?

To understand this Midrash we must bear in mind that it did not originate at the time of the Patriarchs, but only much later – in the Talmudic era. It is thus not a record of the actual events of Abraham's childhood, but a unique literary form through which the sages of the Talmud transmit to succeeding generations their understanding of the Torah. The cave of which the Midrash speaks here is Plato's cave – a metaphor that describes life in this world as a kind of cave-like existence. The cave's inhabitants see nothing more than shadows on the wall, which offer them only a faint impression of true life as it goes on outside the cave.

Abraham, upon emerging from that "cave" – that is, upon realizing the inadequacy of conventional perspectives – is searching for the true essence of the universe. What does he see? There is the sun and there is the moon. What is meant, of course, is not the physical sun and moon, but the world of ideas that surrounds Abraham: the Egyptian and Babylonian civilizations (the "sun" and "moon," respectively). Abraham is equally fascinated by both civilizations, for he sees for himself in each something vital. He understands that he must assimilate and incorporate something from them within himself, but at the same time transcend them in order to rise to the Almighty, who rules both the "sun" and the "moon" – that is, both of those civilizations.

Abraham therefore attempts to fashion his monotheistic abstraction so as to be identified – to a certain extent, at least – with both Babylon and Egypt, by incorporating the best of both, and then to eventually return to the source of that single river that flows forth from the Garden of Eden. Near the beginning of Abraham's sojourn in Babylon, according to the previously mentioned *aggadah*, he comes in conflict with Nimrod, king of Babylon. Precisely because Abraham considers Babylonian civilization so important, he tries to influence Nimrod, encouraging him to correct the defects of Babylonian culture. But all this ends in failure, and the Terah family departs Babylon.

In its accounts of the monotheists who preceded Abraham – Noah, Shem, and Eber – Jewish tradition mentions no instance of conflict with their surrounding society. They lived their lives privately, teaching their ideas only to those who wished to hear them. Abraham, however, was a rebel, for he could not reconcile with the idolatry that surrounded him. After his conflict with Nimrod, Abraham leaves Babylon, going first to the Land of Israel, and later to Egypt, the land of "solar" ideology. Another conflict then ensues, this time with Pharaoh; Abraham again departs, this time paving the way for his descendants' Exodus from Egypt. Thus, Abraham laid the groundwork for "extracting sparks" from both Babylon and Egypt, and integrating them into Judaism.

## 16.10. The Three Jewish Capitals: Shechem, Hebron, and Jerusalem

The dynamics of Abraham's relationship with Babylon and Egypt is also reflected in the geography of the Holy Land. First, Abraham acquires disciples in Charan, located in the region of Babylon, and he brings them with him to Canaan, but leaves them in Shechem. Thus, Shechem is the "exemplar" of Babylon in the Land of Israel. Shechem will later become the city of Joseph, the capital of Samaria, the territory of the northern tribes and the northern kingdom (the Kingdom of Israel).

Abraham then descends to Egypt, and leaves it with new supporters and followers. He settles them in Hebron, the city that is the antithesis of Shechem, and leaves them there.

Hebron is the capital of Judea, the territory of the southern tribes and the Southern (Judean) Kingdom. Hebron is thus the "exemplar" of Egypt in the Land of Israel.

The shared capital that unites Shechem and Hebron is Jerusalem, located on the boundary that divides the northern and southern tribes. Judaism spreads outward from there, for "instruction shall come forth from Zion, the word of the Lord from Jerusalem" (Isaiah 2:3). These three cities (two "inner" capitals and one "outer" capital) have been throughout history the most prominent cities of the Holy Land, and remain so to this day.

## 16.11. Abraham Proceeds to Egypt (12:8-10)

ח וַיַּעְתֵּק מִשָּׁם הָהָרָה מִקֶּדֶם לְבֵית־אֵל וַיֵּט אָהֳלֹה בֵּית־אֵל מִיָּם וְהָעַי מִקֶּדֶם וַיִּבֶן־שָׁם מִזְבֵּחַ לַיי וַיִּקְרָא בְּשֵׁם יי: ט וַיִּסַּע אַבְרָם הָלוֹךְ וְנָסוֹעַ הַנֶּגְבָּה: י וַיְהִי רָעָב בָּאָרֶץ וַיֵּרֶד אַבְרָם מִצְרַיְמָה לָגוּר שָׁם כִּי־כָבֵד הָרָעָב בָּאָרֶץ:

*[8] From there he moved on to the hill country east of Bethel and pitched his tent, with Bethel on the west and Ai on the east; and he built there an altar to the Lord and invoked the Lord by name. [9] Then Abram journeyed by stages toward the Negeb.*
*[10] There was a famine in the land, and Abram went down to Egypt to sojourn there, for the famine was severe in the land.*

**[8] And [he] pitched his tent.** The use of the verb in the singular is understood to indicate that Abraham is no longer accompanied by his numerous students. There is no one with him now but his own family.

**And invoked the Lord by name.** Having left his Babylonian disciples in Shechem, and being now disengaged of them, Abraham strengthens his connection to the land. If at Shechem he only built an altar, now he can also "invoke the Lord by name."

**Bethel on the west and Ai on the east.** Coming from the north, from Charan, Abraham arrives first at Elon Moreh, Mount Ebal, and the future Shechem. He then moves southward and stops east of Bethel – on the mountain of Baal-hazor, apparently the highest point in Samaria at 3,333 feet (1016 m) above sea level. From this mountain one can see the entire country: northward to Mount Hermon, in the south to Mitzpeh Ramon, on the west the entire coastal plain, and on the east – the plateau of the Transjordan. From here, unlike the view from Mount Ebal, you can see even Jerusalem, which sits below the surrounding mountains. Thus, from here a connection is possible with Jerusalem, the heart of the country, and here, therefore, besides erecting an altar, Abraham "invokes the Lord by name." That is, he can now disseminate ethical monotheism through the connection he has made with the Holy Land. It is here that Abraham pitches his tent, occupying this district that is the very heart of the future Land of Israel.

**[9] Then Abram journeyed by stages toward the Negeb.** The Negeb is a triangular desert region in southern Israel. But the Hebrew word "*negeb*" when used generically means, simply, "south." Abraham's wanderings take him in parallel through the spiritual and physical worlds. The future Jewish nation cannot possibly develop normally until it has assimilated within itself the culture of the world's opposite pole, Egypt. Abraham, having already absorbed from Babylon those elements of spirituality needed for creating a Jewish synthesis, now sets his sights on Egypt, and moves southward. But he has also a second objective: After failing to convert the people of Babylon to his faith, will he perhaps meet better success in Egypt?

**[10] There was a famine in the land.** Because Abraham was already progressing toward Egypt of his own accord, God likewise impels him in that direction. A severe famine ensues, and Abraham perforce descends to Egypt.

**Abram went down to Egypt to sojourn there, for the famine was severe in the land.** On the surface, God's actions appear contradictory. First God tells Abraham to make his way to the land of Canaan, but as soon as he arrives, a famine forces Abraham to depart for Egypt. The contradiction, however, is more apparent than real. In God's plan, the actual goal is neither for Abraham to live in Canaan nor to reward or punish Abraham. The goal is to develop Abraham's character. For in the process of grappling with the difficulties that God places in his path, Abraham's character achieves greater perfection.

### 16.12. Abraham and Sarah in Egypt (12:11-13)

יא וַיְהִי כַּאֲשֶׁר הִקְרִיב לָבוֹא מִצְרָיְמָה וַיֹּאמֶר אֶל־שָׂרַי
אִשְׁתּוֹ הִנֵּה־נָא יָדַעְתִּי כִּי אִשָּׁה יְפַת־מַרְאֶה אָתְּ: יב
וְהָיָה כִּי־יִרְאוּ אֹתָךְ הַמִּצְרִים וְאָמְרוּ אִשְׁתּוֹ זֹאת וְהָרְגוּ
אֹתִי וְאֹתָךְ יְחַיּוּ: יג אִמְרִי־נָא אֲחֹתִי אָתְּ לְמַעַן יִיטַב־
לִי בַעֲבוּרֵךְ וְחָיְתָה נַפְשִׁי בִּגְלָלֵךְ:

*[11] As he was about to enter Egypt, he said to his wife Sarai, "I know what a beautiful woman you are."*
*[12] If the Egyptians see you, and think, 'She is his wife,' they will kill me and let you live.*
*[13] Please say that you are my sister, that it may go well with me because of you, and that I may remain alive thanks to you."*

That Abraham would resort to calling Sarah his sister is very problematic. Some would attempt to rationalize that Abraham was a prophet and thus knew in advance that Sarah was not endangered. But this approach seems to us incorrect. If Abraham is all-knowing, then he faces no difficulty at all in arriving at any decision, nor is Abraham showing any development as a personality. And worse yet, we will derive no lesson whatsoever from any of his actions, since *we* are not all-knowing, and can therefore learn absolutely nothing from the story. The inevitable result of any such attempt to "whitewash" Abraham's actions is that the Torah will lose its meaning as a source of guidance. Let us therefore avoid any such assumptions as we try to make sense of Abraham's actions.

It should be noted that a number of Jewish commentators have criticized Abraham quite harshly for his handling of the situation. Nahmanides, for example, condemns Abraham for claiming that Sarah was his sister, and for even descending to Egypt in the first place. Nahmanides would have had Abraham remain in the land of Canaan, persevering and enduring the famine there. Overall, however, the commentaries typically have no such rigorous expectations of Abraham.

Evidently, Abraham's appeal to Sarah to pose as his sister

was based on the Code of Hammurabi, king of Babylon, which governed every sphere of life at that time and in that region. Although the Torah mentions him nowhere, we know from archeological data that Hammurabi instituted a system of laws that was widely distributed and generally accepted throughout the Middle East of that period. In the Torah, too, we can see that the behavior of the Patriarchs and their relations with their surrounding environment are likewise governed by the influence of that Babylonian legal code.

The Code of Hammurabi specifically states that if a woman has a brother or father, no man may marry her without asking and receiving their permission. If Abraham is regarded as Sarah's brother, then all parties, believing *ipso facto* that she is available for marriage, will be answerable only to Abraham for asking her hand in matrimony. And the Egyptians likewise will seek him out and ask his permission to marry Sarah. Whereas, should the Egyptians come to know that in fact he is Sarah's husband, then Abraham, seen as nothing more than an impassable hindrance to anyone who might wish to marry Sarah, could very well be killed. Thus, Abraham declares that he is Sarah's brother in order to secure his own safety during their stay in Egypt, and in order to retain control over the outcome of the situation.

Apparently, however, saving himself and his family from hunger is not Abraham's sole challenge. For we see that Abraham asks Sarah to pose as his sister not only in order that he be spared from death, but also "that it may go well with me because of you." What exactly is Abraham hoping to receive? And why is he in Egypt at all? It is ostensibly due to the famine. But even before the famine is mentioned (verse 10) the Torah states (verse 9) that "Abraham journeyed by stages toward the Negeb," that is, toward the south. In other words, the "hunger" here is twofold: an ordinary shortage of food, and Abraham's desire to acquire Egyptian wisdom. But at the same time, quite plausibly, he desires also to exert influence over the Egyptians.

By passing off Sarah as his sister, Abraham deceives an unwitting population, and quite possibly subjects Sarah to significant danger. All of this seems highly problematic from a moral point of view. In truth, however, there is profound meaning to be found here, all of which we shall discuss in greater detail below.

## 16.13. Abraham and Pharaoh (12:14-20)

יד וַיְהִי כְּבוֹא אַבְרָם מִצְרָיְמָה וַיִּרְאוּ הַמִּצְרִים אֶת־
הָאִשָּׁה כִּי־יָפָה הִוא מְאֹד: טו וַיִּרְאוּ אֹתָהּ שָׂרֵי פַרְעֹה
וַיְהַלְלוּ אֹתָהּ אֶל־פַּרְעֹה וַתֻּקַּח הָאִשָּׁה בֵּית פַּרְעֹה: טז
וּלְאַבְרָם הֵיטִיב בַּעֲבוּרָהּ וַיְהִי־לוֹ צֹאן־וּבָקָר וַחֲמֹרִים
וַעֲבָדִים וּשְׁפָחֹת וַאֲתֹנֹת וּגְמַלִּים: יז וַיְנַגַּע יי | אֶת־
פַּרְעֹה נְגָעִים גְּדֹלִים וְאֶת־בֵּיתוֹ עַל־דְּבַר שָׂרַי אֵשֶׁת
אַבְרָם: יח וַיִּקְרָא פַרְעֹה לְאַבְרָם וַיֹּאמֶר מַה־זֹּאת
עָשִׂיתָ לִּי לָמָּה לֹא־הִגַּדְתָּ לִּי כִּי אִשְׁתְּךָ הִוא: יט לָמָה
אָמַרְתָּ אֲחֹתִי הִוא וָאֶקַּח אֹתָהּ לִי לְאִשָּׁה וְעַתָּה הִנֵּה
אִשְׁתְּךָ קַח וָלֵךְ: כ וַיְצַו עָלָיו פַּרְעֹה אֲנָשִׁים וַיְשַׁלְּחוּ
אֹתוֹ וְאֶת־אִשְׁתּוֹ וְאֶת־כָּל־אֲשֶׁר־לוֹ:

[14] *When Abram entered Egypt, the Egyptians saw how very beautiful the woman was.*
[15] *Pharaoh's courtiers saw her and praised her to Pharaoh, and the woman was taken into Pharaoh's palace.*
[16] *And because of her, it went well with Abram; he acquired sheep, oxen, asses, male and female*

*slaves, she-asses, and camels.*

*[17] But the Lord afflicted Pharaoh and his household with mighty plagues on account of Sarai, the wife of Abram.*

*[18] Pharaoh sent for Abram and said, "What is this you have done to me! Why did you not tell me that she was your wife?*

*[19] Why did you say, 'She is my sister,' so that I took her as my wife? Now, here is your wife; take her and begone!"*

*[20] And Pharaoh put men in charge of him, and they sent him off with his wife and all that he possessed.*

**[15] Pharaoh's courtiers saw her and praised her to Pharaoh, and the woman was taken into Pharaoh's palace.** Sarah "was taken," that is, Pharaoh did not seek permission from Sarah's""brother." This was a scenario that Abraham could not have foreseen.

**[16] And because of her, it went well with Abram; he acquired sheep, oxen, asses, male and female slaves, she-asses, and camels.** Leaving behind the many disciples who had accompanied him from Babylon to Shechem, Abraham and his family alone go to Bethel, and then descend to Egypt. But Abraham now again, by the will of Providence, acquires a great number of souls, livestock and property.

**And ... it went well with Abram; he acquired sheep, oxen, asses, male and female slaves.** The slaves of Abraham were not slaves in the Greco-Roman sense ("talking instruments" having no rights); rather, they were his courtiers and entourage – individuals worthy of becoming his new students.

**[19] Now, here is your wife; take her and begone.** Although Pharaoh reproaches Abraham, they part on good terms. Abraham remains a confederate to Pharaoh, and this will later prove particularly significant.

The Midrash adds that among the people whom Pharaoh gave to Abraham was Hagar, the daughter of Pharaoh. Abraham, everywhere "invoking the name of God," was known as an outstanding personality. Pharaoh senses Abraham's greatness and wants their families to intermarry. For just that reason, Pharaoh had first tried to marry Sarah, Abraham's "sister," but when this proved impossible, he gave his daughter Hagar to Abraham in marriage.

We need not understand this Midrash literally, of course. The intent is that Hagar became an "exemplar" of Egyptian culture within Abraham's family. Abraham's connection with Hagar was his connection with Egypt. We will discuss this in more detail below.

Chapter 17

# Parting of the Ways with Lot and the War with the Kings

## 17.1. Abraham and Lot Part Ways (13:1-13)

א וַיַּעַל אַבְרָם מִמִּצְרַיִם הוּא וְאִשְׁתּוֹ וְכָל־אֲשֶׁר־לוֹ
וְלוֹט עִמּוֹ הַנֶּגְבָּה: ב וְאַבְרָם כָּבֵד מְאֹד בַּמִּקְנֶה בַּכֶּסֶף
וּבַזָּהָב: ג וַיֵּלֶךְ לְמַסָּעָיו מִנֶּגֶב וְעַד־בֵּית־אֵל עַד־הַמָּקוֹם
אֲשֶׁר־הָיָה שָׁם אָהֳלֹה בַּתְּחִלָּה בֵּין בֵּית־אֵל וּבֵין הָעָי:
ד אֶל־מְקוֹם הַמִּזְבֵּחַ אֲשֶׁר־עָשָׂה שָׁם בָּרִאשֹׁנָה וַיִּקְרָא
שָׁם אַבְרָם בְּשֵׁם יי: ה וְגַם־לְלוֹט הַהֹלֵךְ אֶת־אַבְרָם
הָיָה צֹאן־וּבָקָר וְאֹהָלִים: ו וְלֹא־נָשָׂא אֹתָם הָאָרֶץ
לָשֶׁבֶת יַחְדָּו כִּי־הָיָה רְכוּשָׁם רָב וְלֹא יָכְלוּ לָשֶׁבֶת יַחְדָּו:
ז וַיְהִי־רִיב בֵּין רֹעֵי מִקְנֵה־אַבְרָם וּבֵין רֹעֵי מִקְנֵה־לוֹט
וְהַכְּנַעֲנִי וְהַפְּרִזִּי אָז יֹשֵׁב בָּאָרֶץ: ח וַיֹּאמֶר אַבְרָם אֶל־
לוֹט אַל־נָא תְהִי מְרִיבָה בֵּינִי וּבֵינֶךָ וּבֵין רֹעַי וּבֵין רֹעֶיךָ
כִּי־אֲנָשִׁים אַחִים אֲנָחְנוּ: ט הֲלֹא כָל־הָאָרֶץ לְפָנֶיךָ
הִפָּרֶד נָא מֵעָלָי אִם־הַשְּׂמֹאל וְאֵימִנָה וְאִם־הַיָּמִין
וְאַשְׂמְאִילָה: י וַיִּשָּׂא־לוֹט אֶת־עֵינָיו וַיַּרְא אֶת־כָּל־כִּכַּר
הַיַּרְדֵּן כִּי כֻלָּהּ מַשְׁקֶה לִפְנֵי | שַׁחֵת יי אֶת־סְדֹם וְאֶת־
עֲמֹרָה כְּגַן־יי כְּאֶרֶץ מִצְרַיִם בֹּאֲכָה צֹעַר: יא וַיִּבְחַר־לוֹ
לוֹט אֵת כָּל־כִּכַּר הַיַּרְדֵּן וַיִּסַּע לוֹט מִקֶּדֶם וַיִּפָּרְדוּ אִישׁ

מֵעַל אָחִיו: **יב** אַבְרָם יָשַׁב בְּאֶרֶץ־כְּנָעַן וְלוֹט יָשַׁב בְּעָרֵי
הַכִּכָּר וַיֶּאֱהַל עַד־סְדֹם: **יג** וְאַנְשֵׁי סְדֹם רָעִים וְחַטָּאִים
לַיי מְאֹד:

[1] *From Egypt, Abram went up into the Negeb,
with his wife and all that he possessed, together
with Lot.*
[2] *Now Abram was very rich in cattle, silver,
and gold.*
[3] *And he proceeded by stages from the Negeb
as far as Bethel, to the place where his tent had
been formerly, between Bethel and Ai,*
[4] *the site of the altar that he had built there
at first; and there Abram invoked the Lord by
name.*
[5] *Lot, who went with Abram, also had flocks
and herds and tents,*
[6] *so that the land could not support them
staying together; for their possessions were so
great that they could not remain together.*
[7] *And there was quarreling between the
herdsmen of Abram's cattle and those of Lot's
cattle. The Canaanites and Perizzites were then
dwelling in the land.*
[8] *Abram said to Lot, "Let there be no strife
between you and me, between my herdsmen and
yours, for we are kinsmen.*
[9] *Is not the whole land before you? Let us
separate: if you go north, I will go south; and if
you go south, I will go north."*
[10] *Lot looked about him and saw how well
watered was the whole plain of the Jordan, all
of it – this was before the Lord had destroyed*

*Sodom and Gomorrah – all the way to Zoar, like the garden of the Lord, like the land of Egypt.*
*[11] So Lot chose for himself the whole plain of the Jordan, and Lot journeyed eastward. Thus they parted from each other;*
*[12] Abram remained in the land of Canaan, while Lot settled in the cities of the Plain, pitching his tents near Sodom.*
*[13] Now the inhabitants of Sodom were very wicked sinners against the Lord.*

**[1] From Egypt, Abram went up into the Negeb, with his wife and all that he possessed, together with Lot.** The entire *Lech Lecha* portion, as we have already noted, is a series of tests for Abraham, in which, instead of practicing ordinary *chesed* – sharing his teachings with any and all – he must narrow the target group through which his legacy will pass to all of humanity. Abraham first withdrew from Babylon, the country where he began his religious activity. Then, upon arriving in the Holy Land, he is separated from his disciples whom he brought from Babylon. And now, after returning from Egypt, the time has come for yet another separation – from Lot.

**(1, 2) From Egypt, Abram went up ... very rich in cattle, silver, and gold.** With this, Abraham laid the model for the Exodus of the Jewish people from Egypt "with great wealth" (15:14).

**(3, 4) And he proceeded by stages from the Negeb as far as Bethel, to the place where his tent had been formerly, between Bethel and Ai, the site of the altar that he had built there at first; and there Abram invoked the Lord**

**by name.** Upon returning from Egypt Abraham settled in his former location, the region of Bethel and Baal-hazor mountain, where he again invoked the name of the Lord by continuing to preach. But by this time he had completely changed his entourage. After leaving in Shechem the disciples he had brought from Babylon, Abraham now had servant-disciples whom he had brought from Egypt, and he himself had the status of an ally to Pharaoh.

**[5] Lot, who went with Abram.** "Going with Abram" refers not merely to the movement of related parties in unison, but to an actual ideological connection: Lot was Abraham's closest disciple and follower. Abraham says of Lot: "We are kindred people" (lit., "fraternal"), and this refers not only to lineage. Perhaps Abraham felt a particular obligation to Lot because (according to the Midrash) the death of Haran, Lot's father, was in a certain sense due to Abraham. The moment comes, however, when Abraham's further development requires that he separate from Lot.

**[6] The land could not support them staying together; for their possessions were so great that they could not remain together.** The earth was cramped for them not because there was little room for cattle grazing. No matter how large or small a common property might be, that size by itself will not interfere with joint management. No, something else is the problem – the conflict between the attitudes of Abraham and Lot, as reflected in the conflict between their respective shepherd followers.

**[7] And there was quarreling between the herdsmen of Abram's cattle and those of Lot's cattle:** Lot, too, has his "shepherds"; that is, the pupils of his own school.

**The Canaanites and Perizzites were then dwelling in the land.** The Torah's remark about the Canaanites and Perizzites seems superfluous here, for it tells us nothing informative and relevant to the storyline. The Midrash therefore sees in these words the actual topic of the dispute. Said Lot's shepherds: "Yes, the land has been promised to Abraham. But since he is childless, and the land will ultimately go to Lot, we consider it as already belonging to Lot, and we may do on this land as we please. So, go graze your cattle on someone else's fields." But Abraham's shepherds would have none of that, and thus the conflict arose between them. We see that Abraham, besides acting righteously himself, demands righteous behavior also from his shepherds, whereas Lot, although himself righteous, nevertheless allows his shepherds to behave improperly.

Abraham might at first have seen Lot as a potential heir. But the behavior of Lot's shepherds (and Lot's own attitude towards them) demonstrated the futility of that hope, and a parting of ways became the only reasonable outcome.

**[8] Abram said to Lot, "Let there be no strife between you and me."** Had Abraham undertaken to adjudicate the dispute between the shepherds, he could easily have put Lot's shepherds in their place. Any irreconcilable dispute once begun requires a forceful resolution, but Abraham, champion of the attribute of *chesed*, wants to avoid enforcing the letter of the law through extreme measures. Seeking only harmony and peace, he says: "Let there be no strife!" He therefore proposes to reach an agreement by dividing the territory, but this later becomes the source of yet greater difficulties. Abraham and Lot were both people of *chesed*, but in that situation it was Abraham's *chesed* itself that prevented him from establishing the proper working relationship with Lot and his shepherds.

**For we are kinsmen.** The Midrash understands this not merely as a statement of fact (which would make it just a restatement of the obvious), but also as a prediction for the future: Abraham and Lot must in the future be again related. Abraham sensed in Lot a certain potential that would require further development by the Jewish people, which was in fact realized later in the royal Davidic dynasty.

**Abram said to Lot ... [9] "... Let us separate: if you go north, I will go south; and if you go south, I will go north."** The literal translation is, "if you go left, I will go right; and if you go right, I will go left." The Midrash clarifies what Abraham meant: "If you are on the left, then I will be your support on the right" (and vice versa). Abraham did not wish to be removed any significant distance from Lot.

**[11] So Lot chose for himself the whole plain of the Jordan ... [12] Abram remained in the land of Canaan.** As noted earlier, the boundary between two major zones of influence ran along this line: the Jordan Valley and the lands east of it were under the influence of Babylon, while the central mountainous terrain at the center of the country and the lands to the west were the zone of Egyptian influence. (A steep and often impassable ascent up the mountain from the Jordan Valley westward was the actual border between them.) Abraham, who since the time of his visit to Egypt was a recognized ally to Pharaoh, continued living in the Egyptian zone of influence.

Abraham and his Egyptian student-servants later moved to Hebron (13:17), not too far from Sodom, where Lot settled. Hebron is the city destined to become Egypt's "paradigm" in the Land of Israel.

**[13] Now the inhabitants of Sodom were very wicked sinners against the Lord.** But despite this Lot decides to settle there. We need not fault him for this, however, for later we shall see that Lot, who holds the position of judge in Sodom, protects travelers and challenges the Sodomite order. Lot quite possibly was hoping that he could influence and re-educate the people of Sodom.

The Torah here underscores the contrast between Abraham and Lot. While Abraham, as we shall see later, is not prepared to accept "so much as a thread or a sandal strap" from Sodom, Lot has no compunctions even about living there. It is Sodom that highlights their striking differences.

Lot differs from Abraham in two respects, of which one is clearly a flaw, and the second probably even a virtue: [1] his righteousness is shaky, and his *chesed* often misdirected and "irrelevant"; but [2] he is predisposed to law and order and to promoting constructive government, because he sees in Sodom a positive core, and wishes to advance and improve it. Lot's "governmental" mindset is a manifestation of the future *sefirah* of *malchut*, "kingdom," from which his scion David will later descend.

## 17.2. Lot: Superfluous Chesed and the House of David

Lot is a righteous man, but he lacks character. He represents the attribute of improper, excessive *chesed*. Lot wants to be good to everyone, even agreeing to become a judge in Sodom, despite that city's monstrous laws. In a critical situation he is prepared, for the protection of his guests, to give the crowd free reign with his own daughters, and yet he cannot even demand proper behavior of his shepherds. Thus, Lot is in the main a good man, but he is incapable of correctly measuring the value of his own actions and those of others; there are no guiding principles on which he can properly build his *chesed*. Unlike Abraham, Lot's *chesed* has no clear ethical direction. For as we know, the mere desire to give is not, *per se*, kindness. *Chesed* must be properly used; only then will it work truly for good.

We noted earlier that Abraham takes Lot with him on his way to the land of Canaan, even in the absence of any such instruction from God. Together Lot and Abraham arrive in Egypt, and together they depart from there. And when they go their separate ways, Abraham nonetheless considers it important that he not put too much distance between himself and Lot, and that the two of them will remain in contact. When subsequently Abraham undertakes a battle against the four kings, it is only to liberate Lot. That is, for Lot's sake Abraham is willing even to risk his own life. Lot is obviously very important to Abraham.

Lot's two daughters will soon conceive from their father and each will give birth to a son, whose descendants will be the Ammonite and Moabite nations. These two nations were Abraham's antithesis, being totally devoid of the attribute of *chesed*, kindness. So much so, in fact, that the Jews were even prohibited from accepting Moabites and Ammonites as converts to Judaism. First among the reasons for this ban, the Torah itself (Deut. 23:4) explains: "No Ammonite or Moabite shall be admitted into the congregation of the Lord ... because they did not meet you with food and water on your journey after you left Egypt."

However, this ban on conversion to Judaism applies only to Moabite and Ammonite men, but not their women. Thus, the Moabitess Ruth and the Ammonitess Naamah even became part of the royal Davidic dynasty after joining the Jewish people. Ruth married Boaz, as described in detail in the biblical book of Ruth, and their great-grandson was King David, whose son Solomon married Naamah. Thus, the royal Davidic family and the *mashiach* (Messiah) of Israel are in part descendants of Lot.

Indeed, there was something about Lot that was necessary for establishing the future royal Jewish bloodline, and the shepherds were not completely mistaken in considering Lot as Abraham's rightful heir. Lot incorporated within himself an additional spark of *chesed* that was superfluous for the nation as a whole, but was necessary for` building the House of David. And Ruth became Jewish precisely because her *chesed* surpassed that of everyone else. She extracted, as it were, that exceptional spark of *chesed* from Lot, and passed it on to the royal Davidic dynasty.

The royal house always needs exceptional *chesed* as compared with the nation as a whole, in order to compensate for its exceptional *gevurah* (power, strength). Among the nations, it is most often the kings who are particularly susceptible to this manifestation of *gevurah* – power and authority – because of their need to coerce, punish, and even execute offenders. Even in childhood the king's children know that they wield enormous power over their country; this often corrupts even highly upright souls, and the royal race can thus easily undergo moral decay. If this clan is to not degenerate, it needs an additional measure of *chesed* as compared with ordinary people. The royal "spiritual genotype" must be infused with a desire to give to others that is stronger than their need to take for themselves. The royal Jewish dynasty, the House of David, received this *chesed* through Ruth, which was then reinforced through Naamah.

Consequently, the House of David has demonstrated uncommon resistance to corruption due to privilege and power, and that is a decisive factor for its special significance in Jewish history. Even in the Davidic dynasty there were villain kings, idolaters, and the like, of course, but overall it managed to uphold a generally honorable standard over the full course of its five-hundred-year reign. Among other clans to whom dominion devolves, even if their eminently righteous first representatives have been granted royal authority by virtue of actual merit, the children or grandchildren soon degrade and lose their spiritual greatness, with no hope of it being restored at any time thereafter.

This is what actually happened to the Hasmonean dynasty that the Maccabean family had founded. The first generation of Hasmoneans, who had raised a rebellion against the Greeks and occupied the royal throne, were thoroughly admirable individuals who were supported by the entire nation. Their descendants, however, forfeited that status due to power's pernicious influence. They introduced corruption and injustice into the country, and waged completely unnecessary wars of conquest; thus the Hasmoneans' former spiritual stature was lost. Due to the lofty character of the kingdom of the House of David, Jewish tradition reveres it as an ideal, and in their prayers thrice daily Jews ask God for its speedy restoration. The Hasmoneans, in contrast, are accorded no such honor.

## 17.3. The Confirmation of God's Covenant – After Lot's Departure (13:14-16)

**יד** וַיי אָמַר אֶל־אַבְרָם אַחֲרֵי הִפָּרֶד־לוֹט מֵעִמּוֹ שָׂא נָא עֵינֶיךָ וּרְאֵה מִן־הַמָּקוֹם אֲשֶׁר־אַתָּה שָׁם צָפֹנָה וָנֶגְבָּה וָקֵדְמָה וָיָמָּה: **טו** כִּי אֶת־כָּל־הָאָרֶץ אֲשֶׁר־אַתָּה רֹאֶה לְךָ אֶתְּנֶנָּה וּלְזַרְעֲךָ עַד־עוֹלָם: **טז** וְשַׂמְתִּי אֶת־זַרְעֲךָ כַּעֲפַר הָאָרֶץ אֲשֶׁר ׀ אִם־יוּכַל אִישׁ לִמְנוֹת אֶת־עֲפַר הָאָרֶץ גַּם־זַרְעֲךָ יִמָּנֶה:

*[14] And the Lord said to Abram, after Lot had parted from him, "Raise your eyes and look out from where you are, to the north and south, to the east and west,*
*[15] for I give all the land that you see to you and your offspring forever.*
*[16] I will make your offspring as the dust of the earth, so that if one can count the dust of the earth, then your offspring too can be counted.*

**[14] After Lot had parted from him.** God fully endorses that separation. From such weak material as Lot, who is sympathetic to Abraham's ideas but incapable of realizing them, it is impossible to create a chosen people.

**[15] All the land.** God's promise emphasizes the indivisibility of the land (indeed, the view from Baal-hazor, the mountain where Abraham is located at this moment, takes in the entire Land of Israel). The territorial division with Lot is only a temporary phenomenon; in the future the whole Land of Israel must belong to the descendants of Abraham. And yet, since Abraham did in fact divide the land, at different stages of the historical development of the Jewish people God will likewise bring about the Jewish people's forfeiting ownership of certain parts the land. Specifically, some chapters of the book of Genesis describe the covenant as extending only to Canaan, and then it speaks of "the land of the seven nations." But sometimes we find that the covenant includes also the lands east of the Jordan River, and then the covenant speaks of "the land of the ten nations."

## 17.4. God's Covenant with Abraham: About the Nation and the Land, but not the Commandments

As already noted, in the course of Abraham's life God makes several consecutive covenants with him. The first of those occurred in Charan, when God summoned Abraham for a journey to the Holy Land. The second covenant was made in Shechem, and the third after Lot's departure. In all of those covenants God speaks of the future nation and its land, but nowhere does He mention the Torah, in the sense of a system of commandments.

This is typical of all the covenants God made with the Patriarchs. All those covenants speak of the creation of a populous nation and of their taking possession of the land. They also speak of direct communication with God, and the integration of the ideals of mercy and justice. But the commandments – as specific rules of behavior – will be given only at Sinai through Moses; they are never mentioned in the covenants that God makes with the Patriarchs.

Thus we see the primacy in Judaism of the nation, the land and that nation's dominion over the land (to be realized through a political state), the Jewish people's connection with God, and the ideals they are to uphold. Whereas the commandments and laws of the Torah are only a means to achieving them.

This new conception of daily life in the political state as being of primary spiritual importance runs counter to the historical direction that Judaism had followed in the Diaspora. Many religious leaders in the nineteenthth century therefore opposed Zionism, which, in their opinion, aimed to replace the spiritual elements in Judaism with earthly, territorial-national values. In response, one of the leaders of Zionism articulated his own approach as follows: "Every nation has as much sky above its head as it has land beneath its feet."

## 17.5. Abraham Relocates to Hebron (13:17-18)

יז קוּם הִתְהַלֵּךְ בָּאָרֶץ לְאׇרְכָּהּ וּלְרׇחְבָּהּ כִּי לְךָ אֶתְּנֶנָּה: יח וַיֶּאֱהַל אַבְרָם וַיָּבֹא וַיֵּשֶׁב בְּאֵלֹנֵי מַמְרֵא אֲשֶׁר בְּחֶבְרוֹן וַיִּבֶן־שָׁם מִזְבֵּחַ לַיי׳:

*[17] Up, walk about the land, through its length and its breadth, for I give it to you."*
*[18] And Abram moved his tent, and came to dwell at the terebinths of Mamre, which are in Hebron; and he built an altar there to the Lord.*

**[17] Up, walk about the land, through its length and its breadth, for I give it to you.** Abraham was not to remain in one place, or even to remain generally in the central region of the country. He had to himself move about the entire country, so that his descendants could likewise take possession of it. This is an instance of the principle, "the deeds of the ancestors are indicators for their descendants." What Jewish ancestors do will extend also to their descendants. Thus, for Abraham's descendants to take possession of the land in the future, Abraham must first travel around the Land of Israel in its entirety.

This is an indicator for modern-day Israel as well. Jews must make it their priority not only to live in the Land of Israel, but also to travel its length and breadth, and to see its sights. In other words, Israeli tourism has religious significance.

**[18] And Abram moved his tent, and came to dwell at the terebinths of Mamre, which are in Hebron; and he built an altar there to the Lord.** Both Hebron and Bethel are situated on the "mountain" (the country's central mountain ridge), but much further south, closer to Sodom, where Lot settled. More importantly, however, Hebron is a royal city: David was anointed there as king, and there he began his reign. Life in Hebron will require Abraham to manifest *gevurah* (strength), a quality that God wants to develop in Abraham, because building a nation (and a state much more so) requires *gevurah*, the balancing and limiting of *chesed*.

## 17.6. The War of the Kings (14:1-16)

א וַיְהִי בִּימֵי אַמְרָפֶל מֶלֶךְ־שִׁנְעָר אַרְיוֹךְ מֶלֶךְ אֶלָּסָר כְּדָרְלָעֹמֶר מֶלֶךְ עֵילָם וְתִדְעָל מֶלֶךְ גּוֹיִם: ב עָשׂוּ מִלְחָמָה אֶת־בֶּרַע מֶלֶךְ סְדֹם וְאֶת־בִּרְשַׁע מֶלֶךְ עֲמֹרָה שִׁנְאָב ׀ מֶלֶךְ אַדְמָה וְשֶׁמְאֵבֶר מֶלֶךְ צְבֹיִּים וּמֶלֶךְ בֶּלַע הִיא־צֹעַר: ג כָּל־ אֵלֶּה חָבְרוּ אֶל־עֵמֶק הַשִּׂדִּים הוּא יָם הַמֶּלַח: ד שְׁתֵּים עֶשְׂרֵה שָׁנָה עָבְדוּ אֶת־כְּדָרְלָעֹמֶר וּשְׁלֹשׁ־עֶשְׂרֵה שָׁנָה מָרָדוּ: ה וּבְאַרְבַּע עֶשְׂרֵה שָׁנָה בָּא כְדָרְלָעֹמֶר וְהַמְּלָכִים אֲשֶׁר אִתּוֹ וַיַּכּוּ אֶת־רְפָאִים בְּעַשְׁתְּרֹת קַרְנַיִם וְאֶת־ הַזּוּזִים בְּהָם וְאֵת הָאֵימִים בְּשָׁוֵה קִרְיָתָיִם: ו וְאֶת־ הַחֹרִי בְּהַרְרָם שֵׂעִיר עַד אֵיל פָּארָן אֲשֶׁר עַל־הַמִּדְבָּר: ז וַיָּשֻׁבוּ וַיָּבֹאוּ אֶל־עֵין מִשְׁפָּט הִוא קָדֵשׁ וַיַּכּוּ אֶת־כָּל־ שְׂדֵה הָעֲמָלֵקִי וְגַם אֶת־הָאֱמֹרִי הַיֹּשֵׁב בְּחַצְצֹן תָּמָר: ח וַיֵּצֵא מֶלֶךְ־סְדֹם וּמֶלֶךְ עֲמֹרָה וּמֶלֶךְ אַדְמָה וּמֶלֶךְ צְבֹיִים וּמֶלֶךְ בֶּלַע הִוא־צֹעַר וַיַּעַרְכוּ אִתָּם מִלְחָמָה בְּעֵמֶק הַשִּׂדִּים: ט אֵת כְּדָרְלָעֹמֶר מֶלֶךְ עֵילָם וְתִדְעָל מֶלֶךְ גּוֹיִם וְאַמְרָפֶל מֶלֶךְ שִׁנְעָר וְאַרְיוֹךְ מֶלֶךְ אֶלָּסָר אַרְבָּעָה מְלָכִים אֶת־הַחֲמִשָּׁה: י וְעֵמֶק הַשִּׂדִּים בֶּאֱרֹת בֶּאֱרֹת חֵמָר וַיָּנֻסוּ מֶלֶךְ־סְדֹם וַעֲמֹרָה וַיִּפְּלוּ־שָׁמָּה וְהַנִּשְׁאָרִים הֶרָה נָּסוּ:

יא וַיִּקְחוּ אֶת־כָּל־רְכֻשׁ סְדֹם וַעֲמֹרָה וְאֶת־כָּל־אָכְלָם
וַיֵּלֵכוּ: יב וַיִּקְחוּ אֶת־לוֹט וְאֶת־רְכֻשׁוֹ בֶּן־אֲחִי אַבְרָם
וַיֵּלֵכוּ וְהוּא יֹשֵׁב בִּסְדֹם: יג וַיָּבֹא הַפָּלִיט וַיַּגֵּד לְאַבְרָם
הָעִבְרִי וְהוּא שֹׁכֵן בְּאֵלֹנֵי מַמְרֵא הָאֱמֹרִי אֲחִי אֶשְׁכֹּל
וַאֲחִי עָנֵר וְהֵם בַּעֲלֵי בְרִית־אַבְרָם: יד וַיִּשְׁמַע אַבְרָם כִּי
נִשְׁבָּה אָחִיו וַיָּרֶק אֶת־חֲנִיכָיו יְלִידֵי בֵיתוֹ שְׁמֹנָה עָשָׂר
וּשְׁלֹשׁ מֵאוֹת וַיִּרְדֹּף עַד־דָּן: טו וַיֵּחָלֵק עֲלֵיהֶם | לַיְלָה
הוּא וַעֲבָדָיו וַיַּכֵּם וַיִּרְדְּפֵם עַד־חוֹבָה אֲשֶׁר מִשְּׂמֹאל
לְדַמָּשֶׂק: טז וַיָּשֶׁב אֵת כָּל־הָרְכֻשׁ וְגַם אֶת־לוֹט אָחִיו
וּרְכֻשׁוֹ הֵשִׁיב וְגַם אֶת־הַנָּשִׁים וְאֶת־הָעָם:

[1] Now, when King Amraphel of Shinar, King
Arioch of Ellasar, King Chedorlaomer of Elam,
and King Tidal of Goiim

[2] made war on King Bera of Sodom, King
Birsha of Gomorrah, King Shinab of Admah,
King Shemeber of Zeboiim, and the king of Bela,
which is Zoar,

[3] all the latter joined forces at the Valley of
Siddim, now the Dead Sea.

[4] Twelve years they served Chedorlaomer, and
in the thirteenth year they rebelled.

[5] In the fourteenth year Chedorlaomer and the
kings who were with him came and defeated the
Rephaim at Ashteroth-karnaim, the Zuzim at
Ham, the Emim at Shaveh-kiriathaim,

[6] and the Horites in their hill country of Seir
as far as El-paran, which is by the wilderness.

[7] On their way back they came to En-mishpat,
which is Kadesh, and subdued all the territory
of the Amalekites, and also the Amorites who
dwelt in Hazazon-tamar.

[8] Then the king of Sodom, the king of

*Gomorrah, the king of Admah, the king of Zebuiim, and the king of Bela, which is Zoar, went forth and engaged them in battle in the Valley of Siddim:*

*[9] King Chedorlaomer of Elam, King Tidal of Goiim, King Amraphel of Shinar, and King Arioch of Ellasar-four kings against those five.*

*[10] Now the Valley of Siddim was dotted with bitumen pits; and the kings of Sodom and Gomorrah, in their flight, threw themselves into them, while the rest escaped to the hill country.*

*[11] [The invaders] seized all the wealth of Sodom and Gomorrah and all their provisions, and went their way.*

*[12] They also took Lot, the son of Abram's brother, and his possessions, and departed; for he had settled in Sodom.*

*[13] A fugitive brought the news to Abram the Hebrew, who was dwelling at the terebinths of Mamre the Amorite, kinsman of Eshkol and Aner, these being Abram's allies.*

*[14] When Abram heard that his kinsman had been taken captive, he mustered his retainers, born into his household, numbering three hundred and eighteen, and went in pursuit as far as Dan.*

*[15] At night, he and his servants deployed against them and defeated them; and he pursued them as far as Hobah, which is north of Damascus.*

*[16] He brought back all the possessions; he also brought back his kinsman Lot and his possessions, and the women and the rest of the people.*

**[1] Now, when King Amraphel of Shinar.** Immediately after Abraham's move to Hebron, the Torah tells of the "world war" waged by two coalitions of kings, in which Abraham was also involved. Historically and politically speaking, the cause of this war was a few kings revolting against the domination of a few others. But as concerns Abraham's dialogue with God, this war was a response from Above to Abraham's failure to establish a proper hierarchy of relations. Wishing to avoid making difficult decisions, Abraham had given a part of the land to Lot, who then settled in Sodom. The result was that Abraham was now involved in military maneuvers.

Abraham wished to avoid a very minor conflict, and in the end had to face an far more difficult one. This is common in such situations. One's reluctance to undertake immediate, tough decisions today turns into the need to fight on a larger scale tomorrow.

**[4] Twelve years they served Chedorlaomer.** Without taking up a detailed historical identification of all these kings, the geography of their kingdoms, and their battle stations, we note generally that the coalition of Chedorlaomer consisted of the kings of various regions of Babylon and the surrounding countries. The name "Shinar" is a reference to the story of the Tower of Babel (11:2). Nimrod was previously called the king of Shinar (10:11), and Amraphel is therefore associated with him.

**And in the thirteenth year they rebelled.** The kings who submitted to the Babylonians and then rebelled are the kings of the city-states located around the Dead Sea, the zones of Babylonian influence.

**[5] In the fourteenth year Chedorlaomer and the kings**

**who were with him came and defeated the Rephaim at Ashteroth-karnaim, the Zuzim....** In the course of suppressing the rebellion, the Babylonian kings wage their military campaign in the vicinity of the Dead Sea and Sodom, but they do not enter the highlands of the Land of Canaan where Abraham lives, because it is Egypt's zone of influence.

**[10] Now the Valley of Siddim was dotted with bitumen pits; and the kings of Sodom and Gomorrah, in their flight, threw themselves into them, while the rest escaped to the hill country.** The Siddim Valley is the southern region of the Dead Sea. It is quite shallow and sometimes dries up, becoming an asphalt marsh. A great many tar pits then form there; it was such pits that swallowed the kings of Sodom and Gomorrah.

The "mountain" to which the survivors fled is the region of Hebron, where Abraham was living at the time. (Because it was Egypt's zone of influence, it was possible to hide there from the Babylonian troops.) When all had fled, the Babylonian kings seized the possessions of Sodom and Gomorrah and all the foodstuffs, as well as Lot, Abraham's nephew, and began their retreat to Babylon.

We note in passing that as a result of this war, all the nations living around the Jordan River and the Dead Sea were destroyed. These areas thus became sparsely populated, and the peoples of Abraham's family settled there – the descendants of Lot, Ishmael and Esau. This is the reason that the Torah provides such a detailed listing of the characters and geography of this war.

**[13] A fugitive brought the news to Abram the Hebrew, who was dwelling at the terebinths of Mamre the Amorite, kinsman of Eshkol and Aner, these being Abram's allies.** We suddenly see Abraham in a completely unexpected light.

It turns out that he has political and military allies prepared to fight the Babylonians, and this military alliance extends to Hebron and its environs. Abraham himself also has a fairly large number of military forces, which he uses to achieve a victory.

**Brought the news to Abram the Hebrew.** This is the first instance in the Torah where the ethnonym *ivri*, "Hebrew," is used. The emphasis placed here on Abraham's ethnic origins shows that his actions are motivated by political considerations at the national level, and not only by familial ones.

However, as we see often throughout Jewish history, the main challenge of war is not in achieving the victory itself, but in putting the results of that victory to proper use.

### 17.7. Abraham and the King of Sodom (14:17-24)

יז וַיֵּצֵא מֶלֶךְ־סְדֹם לִקְרָאתוֹ אַחֲרֵי שׁוּבוֹ מֵהַכּוֹת אֶת־
כְּדָרְלָעֹמֶר וְאֶת־הַמְּלָכִים אֲשֶׁר אִתּוֹ אֶל־עֵמֶק שָׁוֵה הוּא
עֵמֶק הַמֶּלֶךְ: יח וּמַלְכִּי־צֶדֶק מֶלֶךְ שָׁלֵם הוֹצִיא לֶחֶם
וָיָיִן וְהוּא כֹהֵן לְאֵל עֶלְיוֹן: יט וַיְבָרְכֵהוּ וַיֹּאמַר בָּרוּךְ
אַבְרָם לְאֵל עֶלְיוֹן קֹנֵה שָׁמַיִם וָאָרֶץ: כ וּבָרוּךְ אֵל עֶלְיוֹן
אֲשֶׁר־מִגֵּן צָרֶיךָ בְּיָדֶךָ וַיִּתֶּן־לוֹ מַעֲשֵׂר מִכֹּל: כא וַיֹּאמֶר
מֶלֶךְ־סְדֹם אֶל־אַבְרָם תֶּן־לִי הַנֶּפֶשׁ וְהָרְכֻשׁ קַח־לָךְ: כב
וַיֹּאמֶר אַבְרָם אֶל־מֶלֶךְ סְדֹם הֲרִמֹתִי יָדִי אֶל־יי אֵל
עֶלְיוֹן קֹנֵה שָׁמַיִם וָאָרֶץ: כג אִם־מִחוּט וְעַד שְׂרוֹךְ־נַעַל
וְאִם־אֶקַּח מִכָּל־אֲשֶׁר־לָךְ וְלֹא תֹאמַר אֲנִי הֶעֱשַׁרְתִּי
אֶת־אַבְרָם: כד בִּלְעָדַי רַק אֲשֶׁר אָכְלוּ הַנְּעָרִים וְחֵלֶק
הָאֲנָשִׁים אֲשֶׁר הָלְכוּ אִתִּי עָנֵר אֶשְׁכֹּל וּמַמְרֵא הֵם יִקְחוּ
חֶלְקָם:

*[17] When he returned from defeating*

*Chedorlaomer and the kings with him, the king*
*of Sodom came out to meet him in the Valley of*
*Shaveh, which is the Valley of the King.*
*[18] And King Melchizedek of Salem brought out*
*bread and wine; he was a priest of God Most*
*High.*
*[19] He blessed him, saying,*
*"Blessed be Abram of God Most High,*
*Creator of heaven and earth.*
*[20] And blessed be God Most High,*
*Who has delivered your foes into your hand."*
*And [Abram] gave him a tenth of everything.*
*[21] Then the king of Sodom said to Abram, "Give*
*me the persons, and take the possessions for*
*yourself."*
*[22] But Abram said to the king of Sodom, "I*
*swear to the Lord, God Most High, Creator of*
*heaven and earth:*
*[23] I will not take so much as a thread or a*
*sandal strap of what is yours; you shall not say,*
*'It is I who made Abram rich.'*
*[24] For me, nothing but what my servants have*
*used up; as for the share of the men who went*
*with me-Aner, Eshkol, and Mamre-let them take*
*their share."*

This story is often understood as demonstrating Abraham's exemplary generosity, that he was free of avarice and unwilling to receive any share of Sodom's dishonestly acquired property. There is, however, a completely different way of looking at this, which we shall consider below.

**[17] When he returned from defeating Chedorlaomer and the kings with him, the king of Sodom came out to meet him.** After the victory, Abraham, who had rescued his neighbors from the invasion, became the dominant military-political figure in the region, and received all rights of power. The neighboring kings therefore welcomed Abraham and were prepared to recognize his supremacy and to give him a triumphal reception.

**In the Valley of Shaveh, which is the Valley of the King.** This is the Valley of Kidron in the vicinity of Jerusalem.

**[18] And King Melchizedek of Salem brought out bread and wine.** Salem (Hebrew, *Shalem*) is Jerusalem's original, more ancient name. As a result of the war, the territory of Abraham's influence has expanded considerably. Initially, the city of Shechem in the center of Samaria, where his disciples settled, recognized his authority. But also under control of Abraham and his allies was Hebron, the central city of the future province Judea. And now, after defeating the kings who had come from Babylon, the flourishing valley of the Jordan and the regions around the Dead Sea should likewise have come under Abraham's command. Finally, Melchizedek, king of Jerusalem – the area uniting Judea and Samaria – is willing to recognize his authority. Thus, Abraham could have become the ruler of a rather large kingdom occupying the central part of the country.

**[20] And [Abram] gave him a tenth of everything.** It would now seem that Abraham is very close to the fulfillment of the Divine promise of dominance over the land. But Abraham, who does not yet understand that he must create a people and, therefore, build a state, refuses this opportunity.

Abraham has no desire to become a political ruler, who controls the lives of his subjects with his edicts. He still believes that his primary goal is to preach, to bring people closer to God and to a worthy life based solely on their own personal choices. He therefore does not accept that power, but of its own accord it devolves upon him all the same.

The Torah emphasizes that Melchizedek is "the priest of God Most High." Had Abraham considered himself the progenitor of a nation, and thus a political leader, he would have declared himself the ruler of the land, and appointed Melchizedek as priest of the kingdom rather than giving Melchizedek "a tenth of everything." But Abraham does nothing of the kind. He behaves not as a leader but as an individual, a private citizen who gives his priest a tenth of everything acquired.

**[21] Then the king of Sodom said to Abram, "Give me the persons, and take the possessions for yourself.."** The king of Sodom understands the direction in which things are headed. The victor, as it turns out, has no interest in domination! But typical of a Sodom mentality, this arouses in him not a sense of gratitude by any means, but, on the contrary, an attitude of arrogance. He says to Abraham, "Give me the persons, and take the possessions for yourself," notwithstanding that according to the laws and conventions of war, the property of Sodom *and* its people should belong to Abraham, as victor. But the king of Sodom, instead of expressing gratitude to Abraham for his salvation and recognizing himself as Abraham's subordinate, proposes an equal division of the people and spoils, as if his and Abraham's merits in the victory are equal.

**[22] But Abram said to the king of Sodom … [24] For me, nothing.** Abraham acts honorably of course, taking nothing of the property that belongs to the king of Sodom. But was this unselfish gesture the proper response? Perhaps Abraham should have done the opposite: to declare that both the property and the persons belonged to him, and that the king of Sodom is now obliged to obey him. And then, Abraham – as commander of the entire region – could have, *inter alia*, replaced Sodom's abominable laws with more humane ones, or he could have tried at least to minimally reeducate the people of Sodom. But Abraham makes no such attempt, and the result is that Sodom comes to ruin, with Abraham indirectly to blame.

Abraham wishes to teach others a moral lesson: the rejection of dishonest money. Such behavior on the part of an ordinary citizen would be highly admirable, but is completely unbecoming and unacceptable for a king, a political leader, for whom refusing to make demands on Sodom is a sin. Abraham does not want to use political means to achieve spiritual goals, because the policy and government of the state includes violence, which Abraham, the man of *chesed*, repudiates. He wants the advancement of society to be realized through the personal spiritual growth of its members, in an atmosphere of universal love and friendship, and so he squanders the opportunity for an historic breakthrough. Building the Jewish nation and state will therefore be possible only through the higher advances in spiritual development that will be achieved by Isaac and Jacob.

# Chapter 18

# The "Covenant Between the Severed Members"

## 18.1 "Fear not Abraham": The Problem of Killing on the Battlefield (15:1)

א אַחַר הַדְּבָרִים הָאֵלֶּה הָיָה דְבַר־יי אֶל־אַבְרָם בַּמַּחֲזֶה
לֵאמֹר אַל־תִּירָא אַבְרָם אָנֹכִי מָגֵן לָךְ שְׂכָרְךָ הַרְבֵּה
מְאֹד:

*[1] Some time later, the word of the Lord came to Abram in a vision. He said, "Fear not, Abram, I am a shield to you; Your reward shall be very great."*

After the war with the kings, the Torah moves on to the "Covenant Between the Severed Members." This story begins with God addressing Abraham, which serves as a proper conclusion to the battle that Abraham had just fought.

**[1] Some time later, the word of the Lord came to Abram in a vision. He said, "Fear not, Abram...."** When a person is in danger and goes to war, it is natural that he would be afraid and in need of support. But here God addresses Abraham *after* those frightful events, when Abraham has already returned from battle. What could Abraham have feared after the victory was already won?

Perhaps Abraham feared that now he had already completely received the reward that God had promised him. God therefore reassures him, "Your reward shall be very great." Abraham might also have feared that the defeated kings could return to avenge their defeat. The Almighty therefore tells him, "I am a shield to you."

The Midrash, however, offers a profound rationale for Abraham's fear in the form of a moral problem: Abraham feared that he had killed some innocent soul in the war, for most likely there were good people among the enemy warriors who did not deserve to die. Besides such killings being a very bad thing in and of itself, to be guilty of such killings can cause a steep decline in one's spiritual level.

From both a legal and a moral perspective it is of course neither possible nor necessary in military actions to determine the ethical position of each and every enemy soldier. In war one may kill indiscriminately, although there is surely nothing praiseworthy in that. Moreover, refraining entirely from going to war is also not an option. Those being attacked must defend themselves. But at the same time, any war is itself lamentable, and can inflict real spiritual damage on anyone who fights and kills. Abraham's fears were thus not without foundation. But it is nevertheless important to note that the opposite behavior – refusing to go to war in the event of an attack on oneself or one's loved ones, and adopting a position of submission and inappropriate pacifism in the face of aggression – will cause a person far worse moral and spiritual damage than waging war ever would.

Thus, Abraham feared not the revenge of his enemies, but his own spiritual degradation due to his having been forced to kill. With the words "Fear not," God reassures Abram that this would not happen.

It must be emphasized that Abraham's dread of any unjust killing of enemies would be entirely warranted for an individual in personal conflict with an enemy, but is absolutely unacceptable for a nation and a state.

War is a social reality. Although eliminating war from our world is of course a Jewish Messianic ideal, that ideal is still very far from reality, and its application without regard for reality would be a classic case of false messianism. Were a state to advance the argument that "enemy soldiers are also human beings, each most likely an honorable family man being forced to fight against his own conscience and principles," then living in such a state would be impossible, for it would soon be destroyed along with its citizens. In other words, by showing mercy to distant strangers, that state will inflict cruelty upon its own citizens. To yield in a quarrel of individuals is indeed noble and sublime, but at the national level, when the issue is one of a state protecting its people, such capitulation would be nothing less than a crime.

Abraham understands, of course, that he was correct to go to war in order to rescue Lot. But at the same time he is troubled when he contemplates the moral and spiritual costs of victory. In a certain sense, Abraham dreads his own victories.

It should be noted that this is in a more general sense a very Jewish feeling. Today's "Abrahams" in this regard are those Israelis who win victories, but at the same time are embarrassed by their victories. Some Jews are so afraid of their victories – and all "Israeli" victories – that they embrace anti-Zionism and dream of destroying Israel, or whatever it takes to disassociate from "military force" that seems immoral to them. Such a perverted mindset was of course alien to Abraham, who, when it became necessary, did not hesitate to go to war. But he nonetheless entertains just such concerns and doubts.

Another reason, perhaps, for Abraham's apprehensions was the fact that his victory had dismantled his original plans. As discussed earlier, Abraham was acting within the framework of two competing designs: his own design, and God's design for him. Abraham's original intent was to establish universal belief in the One God, to create a cosmopolitan religious system embracing all of humanity. But God's plan for Abraham is different: to produce from him a nation that will bring monotheism to the world.

Victory in the war with the Babylonian kings has now demolished Abraham's plan for the spread of a religion that would embrace all of humanity, because Abraham was now in a sharp conflict with half of humanity – with Babylon. He has no choice but to reconsider anew God's plan for creating a people. And the problem of his own childlessness comes sharply into focus.

## 18.2. The Problem of Abraham's Posterity (15:2-3)

ב וַיֹּאמֶר אַבְרָם אֲדֹנָי יְהוִה מַה־תִּתֶּן־לִי וְאָנֹכִי הוֹלֵךְ עֲרִירִי וּבֶן־מֶשֶׁק בֵּיתִי הוּא דַּמֶּשֶׂק אֱלִיעֶזֶר: ג וַיֹּאמֶר אַבְרָם הֵן לִי לֹא נָתַתָּה זָרַע וְהִנֵּה בֶן־בֵּיתִי יוֹרֵשׁ אֹתִי:

*[2] But Abram said, "O Lord God, what can You give me, seeing that I shall die childless, and the one in charge of my household is Dammesek Eliezer!"*

*[3] Abram said further, "Since You have granted me no offspring, my steward will be my heir."*

**[2] Seeing that I shall die childless, and the one in charge of my household is Dammesek Eliezer!."** God's words "your reward is great" highlight the chasm between His promise to create a people from Abraham's descendants and the reality of Abraham's childlessness, such that not even a relative will inherit him, but only his domestic steward. (Abraham and his nephew Lot have already parted company.)

Abraham now for the first time perceives this discrepancy between the promise and the reality as an actual crisis, and so deeply that he himself raises the issue of the need for descendants. This dynamic evolution of Abraham's views, from his original idea of training disciples to the idea of building a people from progeny, is a necessary step for ensuring that Abraham will in fact finally have those descendants.

**[2] But Abram said … [3] And Abram said.** Both these verses (2 and 3) begin with questions posed by Abraham, but with no intervening response from God. By not responding immediately to Abraham, God constrains him to more clearly formulate his question, with an emphasis on the connection between offspring and heritage, in order that Abraham will more clearly understand the problem. Only after Abraham has undergone this internal advancement will his destiny change.

### 18.3. Abraham Above the Stars (15:4-5)

ד וְהִנֵּה דְבַר־יי אֵלָיו לֵאמֹר לֹא יִירָשְׁךָ זֶה כִּי־אִם אֲשֶׁר יֵצֵא מִמֵּעֶיךָ הוּא יִירָשֶׁךָ: ה וַיּוֹצֵא אֹתוֹ הַחוּצָה וַיֹּאמֶר

הַבֶּט־נָא הַשָּׁמַיְמָה וּסְפֹּר הַכּוֹכָבִים אִם־תּוּכַל לִסְפֹּר
אֹתָם וַיֹּאמֶר לוֹ כֹּה יִהְיֶה זַרְעֶךָ:

*[4] The word of the Lord came to him in reply,
"That one shall not be your heir; none but your
very own issue shall be your heir."
[5] He took him outside and said, "Look toward
heaven and count the stars, if you are able to count
them." And He added, "So shall your offspring be."*

Thus, Abraham's critical personal advancement was that
he abandoned his own plan and accepted the Divine plan.
Abraham's disciples and his nephew Lot are now separated
from him not only physically. Henceforth, Abraham no longer sees in them his continuation, and he therefore asks for
descendants.

**[5] He took him outside and said, "Look toward heaven
and count the stars.** A simple understanding of this passage
is that God took Abraham out of his tent in order to view
the stars. However, the strict meaning of the Hebrew word
*habbet* is to gaze down from above onto what is below. The
Midrash therefore explains that Abraham, who was an expert
in astrology – the "science" of those times – said to God:
"After carefully researching my horoscope I know beyond
all doubt that according to the stars (i.e., the natural course
of events, the laws of nature) I cannot have a child." God, in
response, raised Abraham higher than the heavens, allowing
him to look down on the stars from above. This way, God
gave Abraham a super-natural view of the laws of the natural
world. God told Abraham: "Your name will change (see 17:5),
and your horoscope will also change accordingly."

That "scientific" understanding of his own childlessness was perhaps one factor that drove Abraham toward his plan of creating a religion through a group of disciples. The plans that God was offering him were incomprehensible to Abraham, as if only miraculously feasible. God responds to Abraham by "taking him outside", cautioning him that one must not give absolute credence to the laws of nature. "Yes, you have in fact calculated your horoscope accurately. But you will rise *above* those stars and above the laws of nature, and from there will you bring your son into the world. There is a force higher than the stars – Divine Providence – that can alter the course of events."

This sense that the Jewish people does not – indeed cannot – possibly survive by the laws of nature alone, and that Jewish existence is the result of an ongoing miracle by which God's people "rise above the stars," has consistently accompanied the Jewish people throughout its very long history.

## 18.4. "Because he put his trust in the Lord, He reckoned it to his merit" (15:6)

ו וְהֶאֱמִן בַּיי וַיַּחְשְׁבֶהָ לּוֹ צְדָקָה:

*[6] And because he put his trust in the Lord, He reckoned it to his merit.*

Jewish tradition considers it incorrect to understand this verse as "salvation through faith": Abraham believed, and God therefore saved him – because such an understanding does not fit the context.

First, it is clear that the issue here is not faith in the

conventional sense – belief in the existence of God. Obviously, Abraham already had such faith long before this. Abraham had spoken with God many times and acted on His instructions. It is thus impossible to believe that only now Abraham suddenly "believed in God."

The Hebrew verb *"he'emin* (from which "amen" is also derived) does not mean "he believed," but, rather, "he trusted." The idea is that Abraham relied on God for the realization of His promise that was contrary to the natural course of events. It is such trust in God (and not "faith" *per se*) that is a notable religious achievement.

The second problem in understanding this verse is that the translation of the word *tzedakah* as "righteousness" is highly ambiguous. The Hebrew word *tzedakah* has two different meanings: [1] righteousness, and [2] a display of mercy, or a gift. Thus, the turn of phrase of this verse can be understood as either "He considered it righteousness," or "he considered it an act of mercy."

At the same time – and this is the third problem in understanding this verse – it is not grammatically apparent from the text who was doing the considering, and for whom – God for Abraham, or Abraham for God. If the latter, the verse should be understood differently, as follows: Abraham trusted God (i.e., that his descendants would become an innumerable people) and considered this to be Divine mercy. That is, Abraham did not believe that he could receive such descendants strictly on his own merits.

Thus, this verse admits two parallel interpretations, and incorporates for us two separate lessons: [1] A person who evinces trust in God, by actively demonstrating his awareness that the Almighty will with time provide solutions even to those problems that today seem unsolvable, is credited with having performed an act of righteousness; [2] A person who receives some benefit from God should consider it a gift of God's beneficence that greatly exceeds what he ought have received based on his merits alone.

This does not mean, of course, that our merits are irrelevant or unimportant to God, for the truth is quite the opposite. One of the reasons God has given us His many commandments is so that by keeping them we will increase our merits before Him. But at the same time, we must realize that the rewards we receive from God are not payment fully commensurate with our actual merits, but a manifestation of Divine grace.

But the idea of "salvation through faith" has no basis whatsoever in the Hebrew Bible.

## 18.5. Abraham's Lack of Trust (15:7-8)

ז וַיֹּאמֶר אֵלָיו אֲנִי יי אֲשֶׁר הוֹצֵאתִיךָ מֵאוּר כַּשְׂדִּים לָתֶת לְךָ אֶת־הָאָרֶץ הַזֹּאת לְרִשְׁתָּהּ: ח וַיֹּאמַר אֲדֹנָי יֱהוִה בַּמָּה אֵדַע כִּי אִירָשֶׁנָּה:

*[7] Then He said to him, "I am the Lord who brought you out from Ur of the Chaldeans to assign this land to you as a possession."*
*[8] And he said, "O Lord God, how shall I know that I am to possess it?"*

**[7] I am the Lord who brought you out from Ur of the Chaldeans to assign this land to you as a possession.** The purpose of Abraham's leaving Ur of the Chaldeans is precisely to create a people from the descendants of Abraham, who will then take possession of the land. The life of the Jewish people in the Land of Israel and their possession of the Land are the source of Divine light for mankind. Without it the world cannot develop normally.

**[8] And he said, "O Lord God, how shall I know that I am to possess it?"** Abraham suddenly shows a lack of trust and asks God for signs confirming the promise. But this is very strange. How is it that only a little earlier we were told that Abraham trusted in God that he would have descendants, but now he lacks trust and asks for confirmation that his descendants will possess the land and live on it?

The apparent reason for this change in Abraham's reaction to God's promise is that Divine mercy is enough for providing offspring, but an additional condition is necessary for the long-term possession of the land, namely, the specific behavior of those descendants. And for that, Divine mercy is simply not enough.

It is also possible that the very establishment of a state ("possessing the land") represents a significant moral problem for Abraham. The state tends to degrade and decompose. As a rule, it would seem, living in one's own country and possessing the land can easily lead to crisis. Not for naught does the Torah say later: "When you have begotten children and children's children and are long established in the land, should you act wickedly and make for yourselves a sculptured image in any likeness, causing the Lord your God displeasure and vexation" (Deut. 4:25 ).

"Act wickedly" – as the result of living on one's own land!? A country overflowing with vital forces is nevertheless not itself a moral being; as soon as a person takes root in his land, it can begin to eat away at his morality. This greatly worries Abraham. As an example of this Abraham has, before his very eyes, the Canaanites, who degenerated into one of the most depraved nations precisely because of their stay in the Holy Land, with its enormous vitality. The Torah therefore emphasizes: "You shall not copy the practices of the land of Egypt where you dwelt, or of the land of Canaan to which I am taking you; nor shall you follow their laws" (Lev. 18:2).

Abraham, as it were, says to God: "How wonderful that you will give me descendants, but what shall become of them in the future? Will my descendants be worthy of the gift that you wish to give them? What assurance do I have that the earth will not seize them and corrupt them? Is Your mercy toward them so very great that we can expect them to hold their own in this land?" Although Divine mercy is often given without sufficient merit, a person must nevertheless uphold a certain level of morality in order for that mercy to be granted.

The Midrash criticizes Abraham for not trusting in God's word, and even attributes the four-hundred-year exile of his descendants to that flaw. Each of Abraham's four words, *ba-mah eda ki irashennah* – "how shall I know that I am to possess it?" – corresponds to one hundred years of Egyptian exile.

It would be wrong to assume, however, that Abraham's descendants were punished simply because he lacked trust in God. More likely, the reason for that lengthy exile is that Abraham's question demonstrates an actual defect in those descendants themselves that they need to correct, namely, their own deficiency of *bitachon*, trust in the Almighty. The Jewish people needed one hundred years of correction for each of four degrees of deficiency represented by those four words.

God later responds to Abraham, mentioning (verse 17) "the smoking oven," a reference to God's opening words (verse 7) to Abraham: "I am the Lord who brought you out from Ur of the Chaldeans"; that is, it refers to that very Chaldean furnace (see 18:1(c)) from which Abraham emerged not only unharmed, but even hardened. God seems to say to Abraham: "By the strict laws of nature no one emerges from a fiery furnace unharmed. But you did, thus transcending natural law. And likewise, the four hundred years of Egyptian exile will be like a fiery furnace for your descendants, allowing them to develop supernatural qualities. Your fears are therefore unfounded. The Jewish people *will* successfully possess this land that I am giving you. No, the land will not enslave them, and as a nation they will even succeed at elevating the land."

## 18.6. The Making of a Covenant: The Course of History and the Land of the Ten Nations (15:9-21)

ט וַיֹּאמֶר אֵלָיו קְחָה לִי עֶגְלָה מְשֻׁלֶּשֶׁת וְעֵז מְשֻׁלֶּשֶׁת וְאַיִל מְשֻׁלָּשׁ וְתֹר וְגוֹזָל: י וַיִּקַּח־לוֹ אֶת־כָּל־אֵלֶּה וַיְבַתֵּר אֹתָם בַּתָּוֶךְ וַיִּתֵּן אִישׁ־בִּתְרוֹ לִקְרַאת רֵעֵהוּ וְאֶת־הַצִּפֹּר לֹא בָתָר: יא וַיֵּרֶד הָעַיִט עַל־הַפְּגָרִים וַיַּשֵּׁב אֹתָם אַבְרָם: יב וַיְהִי הַשֶּׁמֶשׁ לָבוֹא וְתַרְדֵּמָה נָפְלָה עַל־אַבְרָם וְהִנֵּה אֵימָה חֲשֵׁכָה גְדֹלָה נֹפֶלֶת עָלָיו: יג וַיֹּאמֶר לְאַבְרָם יָדֹעַ תֵּדַע כִּי־גֵר | יִהְיֶה זַרְעֲךָ בְּאֶרֶץ לֹא לָהֶם וַעֲבָדוּם וְעִנּוּ אֹתָם אַרְבַּע מֵאוֹת שָׁנָה: יד וְגַם אֶת־הַגּוֹי אֲשֶׁר יַעֲבֹדוּ דָּן אָנֹכִי וְאַחֲרֵי־כֵן יֵצְאוּ בִּרְכֻשׁ גָּדוֹל: טו וְאַתָּה תָּבוֹא אֶל־אֲבֹתֶיךָ בְּשָׁלוֹם תִּקָּבֵר בְּשֵׂיבָה טוֹבָה: טז וְדוֹר רְבִיעִי יָשׁוּבוּ הֵנָּה כִּי לֹא־שָׁלֵם עֲוֹן הָאֱמֹרִי עַד־הֵנָּה: יז וַיְהִי הַשֶּׁמֶשׁ בָּאָה וַעֲלָטָה הָיָה וְהִנֵּה תַנּוּר עָשָׁן וְלַפִּיד אֵשׁ אֲשֶׁר עָבַר בֵּין הַגְּזָרִים הָאֵלֶּה: יח בַּיּוֹם הַהוּא כָּרַת יי אֶת־אַבְרָם בְּרִית לֵאמֹר לְזַרְעֲךָ נָתַתִּי אֶת־הָאָרֶץ הַזֹּאת מִנְּהַר מִצְרַיִם עַד־הַנָּהָר הַגָּדֹל נְהַר־פְּרָת: יט אֶת־הַקֵּינִי וְאֶת־הַקְּנִזִּי וְאֵת הַקַּדְמֹנִי: כ וְאֶת־הַחִתִּי

וְאֶת־הַפְּרִזִּי וְאֶת־הָרְפָאִים: **כא** וְאֶת־הָאֱמֹרִי וְאֶת־
הַכְּנַעֲנִי וְאֶת־הַגִּרְגָּשִׁי וְאֶת־הַיְבוּסִי:

[9] He answered, "Bring Me a three-year-old heifer, a three-year-old she-goat, a three-year-old ram, a turtledove, and a young bird."

[10] He brought Him all these and cut them in two, placing each half opposite the other; but he did not cut up the bird.

[11] Birds of prey came down upon the carcasses, and Abram drove them away.

[12] As the sun was about to set, a deep sleep fell upon Abram, and a great dark dread descended upon him.

[13] And He said to Abram, "Know well that your offspring shall be strangers in a land not theirs, and they shall be enslaved and oppressed four hundred years;

[14] but I will execute judgment on the nation they shall serve, and in the end they shall go free with great wealth.

[15] As for you, You shall go to your fathers in peace; You shall be buried at a ripe old age.

[16] And they shall return here in the fourth generation, for the iniquity of the Amorites is not yet complete."

[17] When the sun set and it was very dark, there appeared a smoking oven, and a flaming torch which passed between those pieces.

[18] On that day the Lord made a covenant with Abram, saying, "To your offspring I assign this land, from the river of Egypt to the great river, the river Euphrates:

[19] *the Kenites, the Kenizzites, the Kadmonites,*
[20] *the Hittites, the Perizzites, the Rephaim,*
[21] *the Amorites, the Canaanites, the Girgashites, and the Jebusites."*

**[18] On that day the Lord made a covenant with Abram.**
This is the *berit bein ha-betarim*, the "Covenant Between the Severed Members" that God made with Abraham.

**[13] And He said to Abram, "Know well that your offspring shall be strangers in a land not theirs, and they shall be enslaved and oppressed four hundred years ... And they shall return here in the fourth generation.** God had already told Abraham earlier about the nation that would be created from his descendants, but gave him no explanation as to how this nation would further develop. Now God is inducting Abraham into the mechanism of this historical process. But the good news for Abraham, both personal and national, that "you shall be buried at a ripe old age ... and in the end they shall go free with great wealth", is integrally associated with suffering and persecution here: "Your offspring shall be strangers in a land not theirs, and they shall be enslaved and oppressed."

**[12] And a great dark dread descended upon him..** The images of the "Covenant Between the Severed Members" embrace many long eras of Jewish history, illuminating them with meaning and purpose, and engendering an overwhelming feeling of trepidation in any person aware of his own smallness. Abraham, too, experiences this trepidation, and therefore can take in the Covenant only in a sleeping state. A waking consciousness cannot withstand the tension of a collision with the enormity of history.

Each element of this vision incorporates symbolism and prophecy. Here we will mention only a small selection of those.

**[10] He brought Him all these and cut them in two, placing each half opposite the other.** The first action here is the bisection, albeit not complete, of the animals. This symbolizes that the spiritual vitality of the world – the "river issuing from the Garden of Eden" (2:10) – will be divided between different empires, first and foremost between Babylon and Egypt, to be followed later by the collapse of these same empires.

**[11] Birds of prey came down upon the carcasses, and Abram drove them away.** The Jews (Abraham) remain in the middle, passing as it were between bisected civilizations, driving off the kites from their remains, and carrying out the task of uniting those civilizations, smelting them in a single furnace.

Humanity after the Tower of Babel was fragmented; its divided parts needed to be reassembled, and that is the Jews' most essential mission. In this sense, Abraham is an *ivri*, a Hebrew, who undertakes completion of the work left undone by Eber. Israel's destiny is to restore the nations to their original unity by gathering their scattered sparks of holiness, thus making it possible for mankind to win anew its contact with God.

**[17] There appeared a smoking oven, and a flaming torch which passed between those pieces..** Later in the Torah (Deut. 4:20), Egypt is called the *kur ha-barzel*, the "iron furnace" for smelting and purifying gold. After passing through the Egyptian furnace, the descendants of Abraham will be capable of understanding the Divine word, will rise above nature, and will be worthy of inheriting the Land of Israel and passing the Divine light to all mankind.

In addition to the "smelting of the nations," exile has a second function, realized not only in Egypt but in subsequent exiles too, even up to the present day. Namely, to collect the "sparks of holiness" scattered across all nations of the world. The unification of these sparks occurs when the Jews return to the Land of Israel, after which their light, now united, spreads from Israel to all of humanity.

**[9] He answered, "Bring Me a three-year-old heifer, a three-year-old she-goat, a three-year-old ram, a turtle-dove, and a young bird."** In the four species of animals that Abraham sacrifices here, tradition sees an indication of four Jewish exiles – four kingdoms that will later rule over Israel: Babylon, Persia, Greece, and Rome. The latter is the current, ongoing exile to the countries of the West, which is, however, now ending before our own eyes.

The Talmud says: "The Almighty gave three gifts to Israel, all of which the Jews acquire through suffering: the Torah, the Land of Israel, and the World to Come." In this idea there is an apparent contradiction. If it is a gift, then why is it necessary to suffer in order to attain it?

The answer is that these gifts are so valuable precisely because they are acquired through suffering. Had they come without suffering, they would have been easily lost. Paying such a high price for those gifts is necessary for us to establish a truly integral connection with them.

**[13] And they shall be enslaved and oppressed four hundred years; [14] but I will execute judgment on the nation they shall serve.** If the servitude and suffering of the descendants of Abraham was predetermined from Above, then why are the Egyptians to be blamed for oppressing the Jews, given that they were only fulfilling the Divine will, as it were?

The Torah therefore states clearly that the oppressors *will* be judged. God grants each of us the freedom to choose. If evil comes into the world through someone, then that person will be held accountable for that.

**[16] And they shall return here in the fourth generation, for the iniquity of the Amorites is not yet complete.** That is, the Canaanite nations were not at that time sufficiently guilty of their crimes to deserve expulsion quite yet.

This means that when later the expulsion of the Canaanites did occur, it was not because the Jews had become worthy of receiving the land, but because the moment had come when these peoples were so guilty that they truly deserved to be expelled.

The right of the Jewish people to possess the Land of Israel is constant, regardless of the behavior of other nations. However, our right (which is sometimes rather a duty) to expel these peoples from our land depends solely on the behavior of these peoples themselves; that is, on whether they are righteous or sinful.

**[18] From the river of Egypt to the great river, the river Euphrates.** That is, from the borders of Egypt to the borders of Babylon. This is the territory from the easternmost branch of the "Egyptian River" (Wadi El-Arish on the Sinai Peninsula) to the closest point on the Euphrates, in the vicinity of Damascus. The Land of Israel must reach unto the borders of Egypt and Babylon without penetrating or being perceived as invading those countries.

Thus, the concept of "from the Nile to the Euphrates" embodies not only a territorial meaning, but a spiritual one as well: the unification of the Egyptian and Babylonian civilizations. And yet, the spiritual and the material meanings are inseparable. Only when the Jewish state occupies the territory that the Almighty has apportioned to it can it fulfill its world mission.

In past epochs the realms of King David and King Solomon corresponded to those boundaries exactly. Those periods left an indelible impression on humanity's collective memory, as evidenced in particular by the Psalms written in that era, and the Song of Songs and Ecclesiastes. In later times, however, the entire "land of the ten nations" was never under Jewish dominion, but only the "territory of the seven peoples" as later indicated (Deut. 7:1).

Thus, the essence of the covenant that God made with Abraham is the promise that he would have descendants, and a land through which all the tribes of the earth would be blessed. Abraham assumes the role of being both the foundation and the model for the creation of that nation.

Chapter 19

# Sarah and Hagar

## 19.1. The Discrepancy Between God's Promise and the Reality (15:18 – 16:1)

**טו:יח** בַּיּוֹם הַהוּא כָּרַת יי אֶת־אַבְרָם בְּרִית לֵאמֹר לְזַרְעֲךָ נָתַתִּי אֶת־הָאָרֶץ הַזֹּאת מִנְּהַר מִצְרַיִם עַד־הַנָּהָר הַגָּדֹל נְהַר־פְּרָת:

*(15:18) On that day the Lord made a covenant with Abram, saying, "To your offspring I assign this land ..."*

**טז:א** וְשָׂרַי אֵשֶׁת אַבְרָם לֹא יָלְדָה לוֹ וְלָהּ שִׁפְחָה מִצְרִית וּשְׁמָהּ הָגָר:

*(16:1) Sarai, Abram's wife, had borne him no children.*

In the Torah text these two verses appear in close succession, in order to emphasize the discrepancy between God's promise and Abraham's reality. We have here an instance of the often painful gap between the ideal, "true" state of affairs – in this case, God's promise to give the land of Israel to Abraham's descendants – and the reality – Sarah's failure to conceive and bear children. Such discrepancies are commonly encountered in life: Something is genuinely "true" because it has already been determined in "upper" realms, but in this lower world that we inhabit it has not yet been realized.

When we feel justified in our expectations, but they have not come to fruition, disappointment and crisis often ensue. This type of discontinuity between the expected and the actual can be a source of extreme psychological distress, often leading the persons experiencing it to commit tragically serious mistakes.

In relation to time there are generally two types of sin: the sin of being too late, and the sin of being too early. The sin of the spies (Numbers 13) is an example of the former: they tried to persuade the Jewish people not to enter the land, although the time had come to do exactly that. But more often the sin is of the other type – being prematurely zealous, when the ideal state is already striving to come true, but the reality is not yet ready for it. An example of this type of sin is the sin of Adam and Eve, who prematurely tasted the fruit of the Tree of Knowledge of Good and Evil.

Another example of sinning by "being too early" is the Jews' sin of the golden calf. While Moses was at the top of Mount Sinai, but had not yet received the tablets, the people of Israel waited patiently enough for his return. But once the tablets had already been given in Heaven (i.e., on Mount Sinai) and the time had come for Moses to present those tablets to the Jewish people, they simply could wait no longer, and demanded of Aaron: "Come, make us a god who shall go before us" (Exod. 32:1). In an ideal world Moses would have come down by then, because the tablets had already been received, and he had no more business on that mountain. But he was still in descent, as it takes some time to make that trek, and that delay led the Jews to commit the sin of the golden calf.

Note that the sin of "being too early," although more common, is less severe than the sin of "being too late." The sin of the golden calf was forgiven, but the sin of the spies was not; that entire generation died in the wilderness. To "not love" is a more grievous sin than to "love too much." As the book of Proverbs says (10:12), "Love covers up all sins."

Returning to our Torah portion, Sarah's mistake is a sin of "being too early."

The most serious problem of our lives is our lack of *bitachon*, our failing to trust in the Almighty. Fearing that a situation has no chance of improving without our impetuous intervention, we undertake improper actions, for which we ultimately pay a very steep price.

## 19.2. Hagar, Sarah's Maidservant (16:1)

א וְשָׂרַי אֵשֶׁת אַבְרָם לֹא יָלְדָה לוֹ וְלָהּ שִׁפְחָה מִצְרִית וּשְׁמָהּ הָגָר:

*[1] Sarai, Abram's wife, had borne him no children. She had an Egyptian maidservant whose name was Hagar.*

**[1] An Egyptian maidservant.** We have already noted that the Torah's concept of slave does not coincide with the Greek or Roman concepts of slave as "talking instrument" (by Aristotle's definition). Rather, the "slave" of the Torah is a "patriarchal" slave who should sooner be called a servant – a junior member of the family, as it were. Jewish law required that a slave be given living conditions that were on par with those of his master, who was also prohibited from subjecting the slave to corporal punishment of any kind, overworking him, or endangering his life or limb. The slave was obliged to rest on Shabbat, and to sit at the Passover table with all other members of the family.

In the Torah, Eliezer, who was Abraham's own servant, manages his household and chooses a wife for Abraham's son Isaac. In other words, plain and simple, a slave is a disciple. Therefore, the fact that Hagar is called a slave does not put her in the position of a mute creature, but only means that she is subordinate to Sarah.

**Whose name was Hagar: The** Midrash tells us that Hagar was the daughter of Pharaoh. After seeing the miracles that God had performed for Abraham, Pharaoh gave him his own daughter as a slave girl. We need not understand this Midrash literally, of course, but it is important to consider that Hagar has noble, even regal origins, and in the house of Abraham she is a "representative" of Egypt (even of the elite of Egypt, and of all that is spiritual in that civilization).

### 19.3. Sarah Gives Hagar to Abraham (16:2-3)

ב וַתֹּאמֶר שָׂרַי אֶל־אַבְרָם הִנֵּה־נָא עֲצָרַנִי יי מִלֶּדֶת בֹּא־
נָא אֶל־שִׁפְחָתִי אוּלַי אִבָּנֶה מִמֶּנָּה וַיִּשְׁמַע אַבְרָם לְקוֹל
שָׂרָי: ג וַתִּקַּח שָׂרַי אֵשֶׁת־אַבְרָם אֶת־הָגָר הַמִּצְרִית
שִׁפְחָתָהּ מִקֵּץ עֶשֶׂר שָׁנִים לְשֶׁבֶת אַבְרָם בְּאֶרֶץ כְּנָעַן
וַתִּתֵּן אֹתָהּ לְאַבְרָם אִישָׁהּ לוֹ לְאִשָּׁה:

*[2] And Sarai said to Abram, "Look, the Lord has kept me from bearing. Consort with my maid; perhaps I shall have a son through her." And Abram heeded Sarai's request.*

*[3] So Sarai, Abram's wife, took her maid, Hagar the Egyptian–after Abram had dwelt in the land of Canaan ten years–and gave her to her husband Abram as concubine.*

It has now been ten years since Abraham received the Divine promise that he will have descendants. After such a long interval has passed and the Divine promise is still not realized, a crisis arises.

Now desperate, Sarah resorts to extreme measures. Her confusion and lack of trust in God led to the birth of Ishmael, which becomes a serious complication for Isaac. To resolve this newer crisis, Sarah must again take steps that, although necessary, will lead to an even more dangerous global conflict in the future.

Sarah's words, "perhaps I shall have a son through her," demonstrate that she did not consider herself hopelessly barren, but only assumed that Abraham must first have children, and that once there were children in the family she too would give birth.

Or, possibly, Sarah hopes that as her reward for giving her maidservant to Abraham and adopting Hagar's newborn child, she too will be blessed with children. (Infertility sometimes ceases after the adoption of children. The presence of children in a family can exert a positive psychological influence on a woman, and can in that way effect biological changes in her as well.) But after Sarah gives Hagar to Abraham, events take an entirely different turn from what Sarah was expecting.

## 19.4. Abraham and Sarah's Childlessness

God promised offspring to Abraham, but Sarah does not give birth. Which of them is to blame for this?

Later in the Torah we will see an indication that it is Abraham who is the cause of the infertility, because it is in him that the process of spiritual growth necessary for the birth of Isaac is not yet complete. This difference in the levels of Abraham and Sarah finds expression in the different manner in which their names change. From the wording "Your name shall be Abraham..." (17:5) we see that Abraham is given a genuinely new name, but about Sarah the wording is different: "..you shall not call her Sarai, but her name shall be Sarah..." (17:5). That is, her true name, which had not been apparent previously, is now being merely revealed. Abraham has changed along with his name change, and is now no longer deficient, whereas Sarah needs only what was hidden within her to be revealed; she herself does not need to change.

However, in the course of these events involving Hagar, Abraham and Sarah themselves have no awareness of all that, and Sarah, feeling inclined to blame herself rather than her husband, says: "Look, the Lord has kept me from bearing" (16:2). Believing that she herself is to blame, Sarah wishes to improve the situation so that Abraham will have at least some descendants. At that moment she lacks the attribute of *bitachon*, trust in God, and she does what she can: She gives Hagar to Abraham.

The reason for their childlessness was not Sarah's infertility, but Abraham's being still unready for the birth of a successor, being at that time still "Abram," and not yet "Abraham." The changes that are required for the birth of Isaac need to occur in his person. But Abraham, meanwhile, does not see this, notwithstanding that God has made His promise specifically to him. Therefore, not only does he consent to Sarah's plan, but, as we shall soon see, he deems it even preferable that creating the future nation should happen through Hagar.

Other Jewish matriarchs were also childless at first, not only Sarah. Their delayed child-bearing was a part of the Divine plan – one of many indications that the people of Israel come into being not by the natural, uninterrupted flow of the birth cycle, but in the broken sequence of that reality, as something that stands above nature, having its own unique destiny.

## 19.5. The Legal Status of a Child Born of a Maidservant

We have already noted that the legal environment in which the Patriarchs lived, and in which the entire Middle East lived in antiquity, is that of the Code of Hammurabi, a Babylonian king of the 18th century BCE. Although the Code of Hammurabi is not explicitly mentioned in the Torah, it often serves as the backdrop for reported events. Without the knowledge of these laws it is sometimes difficult to correctly understand the text of the Torah.

According to the Code of Hammurabi, when a child is born to a man by his maidservant because of his wife's childlessness, there are two possible variations of that child's status. If the mistress remains childless, the maidservant's child becomes the rightful heir. But if the mistress later gives birth to a child of her own, the man's child from the maidservant loses all rights of inheritance.

In other words, the birth of Isaac will deprive Ishmael of Abraham's entire inheritance; he will remain the simple son of a slave. It is precisely this that distinguishes the conflict between Ishmael and Isaac from that between Jacob and Esau, who were clearly both rightful heirs, the dispute being only as to who holds the right of the firstborn.

Therefore, Ishmael after the birth of Isaac tries to ignore him completely, as if he does not exist.

## 19.6. Hammurabi's Code: Morality Must Precede Sanctity

Associated with Hammurabi's code is yet another important issue, around which there is a great deal of speculation. When archaeologists discovered the texts of the Code of Hammurabi in 1901, they found in it many parallels to the laws of the Torah. On that basis certain scholars wished to argue that the Torah is simply a restatement of the Code of Hammurabi. In response, certain Jewish "defenders of the Torah" took an emphatically opposite position, averring that there was no connection whatsoever between the Torah and Hammurabi's code.

The fact is, however, that from the Jewish point of view it is only normal and natural – and even necessary! – that the foundations of ethics and proper legislation would have appeared in human society *before* the giving of the Torah.

It is an essential principle of Judaism that *derech eretz* – lit., "the way of the land," or the basic humanly ethical principles – must precede the Torah. Or what amounts to the same thing: morality precedes holiness. Unless a level of universally moral and decent human behavior has been first achieved, no conditions can exist for advancing toward holiness.

This principle is usually understood at the individual level. If a person is morally depraved or dishonest, if he is a villain by ordinary human standards, no Torah study will avail to improve him.

One must first be a decent person, and then we can talk about advancing him towards holiness.

But this principle also has a historical aspect: in the history of the development of mankind, moral norms had to appear first, before any conception of holiness. Indeed, until *derech eretz* – a rudimentary but sufficient moral and legal standard – is achieved, any understanding of the Torah is in principle impossible. From this point of view it is natural that morality and justice would have appeared on a tangible human scale even before the arrival of the Patriarchs. And this was realized in the adoption, specifically, of Hammurabi's Code, which raised society to a standard of law based on a sense of justice (and not, as before, merely on force). From that time onward it was already possible for the world to receive the Torah.

Drawing these parallels between the Torah and the laws of Hammurabi is not only natural, but even essential, to a person who intuitively understands fundamental ethical laws, *derech eretz*. Universal moral and legal norms are based not on God's decrees but on the fact that it is one's conscience that allows him to distinguish right from wrong.

It is not the Torah's intent to reform villains, nor can it do so. The Torah is designed to help a person who wishes to travel the road of good to find that road and to understand its rules. Thus, morality is a prerequisite to holiness – both individually and historically.


## 19.7. Judaism and Polygamy

The Torah, in principle, allows the practice of polygamy. Abraham and Jacob had several wives; the book of Samuel begins with the story of Elkanah (father of the prophet

Samuel), who had two wives, Hannah and Peninah. And, of course, who can forget the great many wives that King David and King Solomon had.

In all these cases, however (with the exception of the kings), polygamy was a matter of necessity, not planning; the reason for it was, as a rule, the inability of a first wife to bear children. Thus, the guiding principle of the Torah regarding this matter is that polygamy is not encouraged, but it is permitted. The ideal marriage according to the Torah is monogamous, as symbolized by the marriage of Adam and Eve. However, if a woman did not have children, then it was proper for her husband to take a second wife, in order to fulfill God's commandment (Gen. 1:28) of procreation.

(The situation of the kings was entirely different: for them it was important *ex officio* to have many wives. But this was driven by political exigencies that do not apply to an ordinary citizen.)

In Jewish literature of the Talmudic era we find only isolated instances of polygamy. In the tenth century CE Rabbi Gershom of Mainz banned polygamy for Ashkenazi Jews, and that ruling then gradually spread to, and was adopted by, almost all Jewish communities everywhere.

### 19.8. Hagar as Abraham's Preferred Alternative

Feeling hopeless, Sarah gives Abraham her maidservant as a "saving grace." But it seems that Abraham sees the situation differently. Although the Torah says (16:2), "Abram heeded Sarai's request," meaning that Abram was not leading here, by all indications this flow of events was thoroughly consistent with his own sympathetic attitude toward Egypt.

Recall that originally there were two plans through which monotheism, the religion of Abraham, could reach mankind:

Abraham's original plan to establish a universal, cosmopolitan religion, and God's plan to create a monotheistic people. Although he had always inclined toward the universal approach, Abraham ultimately accepted God's plan.

Abraham might have perceived a marriage of necessity to Hagar as a shift of plans favoring the universal direction: let my nation be a conduit for the ideas of monotheism, but one that is kindred to the Egyptians, the primary civilization of mankind, all of whom together would then be a "universal world people." But if the future nation will descend from Abraham and Sarah, who are both *ivrim* (Hebrews), that nation will represent too narrow a national framework. Will such a people be able to influence all of humanity? If, however, this exceptional nation will be born of Jewish roots, but on Egyptian soil, and if Egyptian culture could be fertilized by Abraham's ideas, then that nation would have greater chances of worldly success. Or so it seemed to Abraham.

Abraham will therefore feel an especial love for Ishmael, and, as we shall soon see, he will regard the birth of Isaac as a crisis situation.

## 19.9. The Conflict Between Sarah and Hagar, and Abraham's Role (16:3-6)

ג וַתִּקַּח שָׂרַי אֵשֶׁת־אַבְרָם אֶת־הָגָר הַמִּצְרִית שִׁפְחָתָהּ מִקֵּץ עֶשֶׂר שָׁנִים לְשֶׁבֶת אַבְרָם בְּאֶרֶץ כְּנָעַן וַתִּתֵּן אֹתָהּ לְאַבְרָם אִישָׁהּ לוֹ לְאִשָּׁה: ד וַיָּבֹא אֶל־הָגָר וַתַּהַר וַתֵּרֶא כִּי הָרָתָה וַתֵּקַל גְּבִרְתָּהּ בְּעֵינֶיהָ: ה וַתֹּאמֶר שָׂרַי אֶל־אַבְרָם חֲמָסִי עָלֶיךָ אָנֹכִי נָתַתִּי שִׁפְחָתִי בְּחֵיקֶךָ וַתֵּרֶא כִּי הָרָתָה וָאֵקַל בְּעֵינֶיהָ יִשְׁפֹּט יי בֵּינִי וּבֵינֶיךָ: ו וַיֹּאמֶר אַבְרָם אֶל־שָׂרַי הִנֵּה שִׁפְחָתֵךְ בְּיָדֵךְ עֲשִׂי־לָהּ הַטּוֹב בְּעֵינָיִךְ וַתְּעַנֶּהָ שָׂרַי וַתִּבְרַח מִפָּנֶיהָ:

*[3] So Sarai, Abram's wife, took her maid, Hagar the Egyptian-after Abram had dwelt in the land of Canaan ten years-and gave her to her husband Abram as concubine.*

*[4] He cohabited with Hagar and she conceived; and when she saw that she had conceived, her mistress was lowered in her esteem.*

*[5] And Sarai said to Abram, "The wrong done me is your fault! I myself put my maid in your bosom; now that she sees that she is pregnant, I am lowered in her esteem. The Lord decide between you and me!"*

*[6] Abram said to Sarai, "Your maid is in your hands. Deal with her as you think right." Then Sarai treated her harshly, and she ran away from her.*

**[3] So Sarai, Abram's wife, took.** Sarah ever remains Abraham's wife.

**And gave her to her husband Abram as concubine.** The Hebrew word here is *ishah*, which means, simply, "wife." Thus Hagar's status increases dramatically. Sarah gives her to Abram not as a concubine, but as a wife. The difference between the relative standings of Sarah and Hagar now becomes less pronounced, and Hagar entertains the illusion that that difference has dissipated altogether.

**[5] Now that she sees that she is pregnant, I am lowered in her esteem.** Having now conceived, Hagar concludes that her own merits outweigh Sarah's merits - and she begins to behave inappropriately.

**The Lord decide between you and me!"** In such a situation as Sarah finds herself she petitions Abraham using legal terminology. Sarah in general manifests the attribute of judgment, *gevurah* within Abraham's *chesed*. This quality of hers – to be an "internal attribute of judgment" – will make itself known much more clearly later, since without Abraham she cannot bear Isaac, who is "righteous in the attribute of the court."

**[6] Abram said to Sarai, "Your maid is in your hands. Deal with her as you think right."** Abraham again avoids making harsh legal decisions. Being the embodiment of *chesed*, he is not inclined to implement the attribute of the court. He therefore defers to Sarah, for whom the attribute of the court is natural.

But in fact this was a test that Abraham could not pass. He neglected his obligation, now that Hagar was his wife, to establish of his own accord Hagar's subordinate status vis-à-vis Sarah. Abraham's failure to apply the attribute of the court has led to an imbalance between the court and mercy, and has exacerbated the conflict.

**Then Sarai treated her harshly.** The Hebrew *va-te'anneha sarai* means, literally, "Sarai oppressed her." The Midrash explains that Sarah burdened Hagar with a usual work regimen, disregarding her special needs as occasioned by her pregnancy (itself the source of Hagar's supercilious attitude). That is, Sarah realized too harshly the attribute of the court. The Torah regards this behavior as "oppression" and condemns Sarah for acting so.

### 19.10. God's Question to Hagar (16:7-8)

...**וַתִּבְרַח** מִפָּנֶיהָ: **ז** וַיִּמְצָאָהּ מַלְאַךְ יי עַל־עֵין הַמַּיִם בַּמִּדְבָּר עַל־הָעַיִן בְּדֶרֶךְ שׁוּר: **ח** וַיֹּאמַר הָגָר שִׁפְחַת שָׂרַי

אֵי־מִזֶּה בָאת וְאָנָה תֵלֵכִי וַתֹּאמֶר מִפְּנֵי שָׂרַי גְּבִרְתִּי
אָנֹכִי בֹּרַחַת:

*[6] ... and she ran away from her.*
*[7] An angel of the Lord found her by a spring of*
*water in the wilderness, the spring on the road*
*to Shur,*
*[8] and said, "Hagar, slave of Sarai, where have*
*you come from, and where are you going?" And*
*she said, "I am running away from my mistress*
*Sarai."*

**[6] ... and she ran away from her. [7] An angel of the Lord found her.** Superficially Hagar seems to flee simply to escape Sarah's oppression. But actually she is seeking greater clarity in ascertaining her own status, and for that she is now deserving of Divine assistance.

**[8] And said, "Hagar, slave of Sarai ....** When Hagar can no longer bear the uncertainty of her position, God sends her a clarification. Simply through his manner of addressing Hagar, the angel restores her understanding of her subordinate status in relation to Sarah.

**... Where have you come from, and where are you going?"** The angel's question to Hagar – which is actually the Almighty's question – is reminiscent of God's question to Adam: "Where are you?" (3:9) and to Cain: "Where is Abel, your brother?" (4:9). Throughout history God has continuously posed to humankind this essential question, whose purpose is to induce each of us to understand our place in the world.

God wants to help us to find the right path on our own.

Rather than exerting pressure, He acts through allusions.

**I am running away from my mistress Sarai.** Hagar takes the hint and acknowledges her slave status. By correcting her earlier mistakes she becomes worthy of the Divine blessing.

### 19.11. The Problem of "Wilderness Religion"

ז וַיִּמְצָאָהּ מַלְאַךְ יי עַל־עֵין הַמַּיִם בַּמִּדְבָּר עַל־הָעַיִן
בְּדֶרֶךְ שׁוּר

**[7] An angel of the Lord found her by a spring of water in the wilderness, the spring:** God appears to Hagar not at home, but in the wilderness. In the future, likewise, the place of revelation for the descendants of Hagar and Ishmael is the desert.

The type of theology that develops in the desert completely subordinates man to the Divine; it is the theology of submission, or in Arabic, "Islam." The desert is by no means a place of freedom; on the contrary, it is a place where one is keenly aware of his insignificance, a place where one feels abandoned and forgotten by all. Living in the wilderness, one is aware of the smallness of man and the greatness of God. Accordingly, Islam, the religion of the desert, emphasizes the predominance of Divine predestination, where there is practically no room for any freedom of choice.

This kind of experience – repression by God – occurred in Judaism when the Torah was given in the wilderness at Mount Sinai. The Midrash says that God lifted up the mountain and suspended it over the Jewish people, threatening to drop it on them unless they would agree to accept the Torah. However, according to Jewish tradition the event at

Sinai was only the "preliminary" giving of the Torah, in no way affording ideal conditions for a complete connection with God. So long as we have accepted the burden of the commandments under duress, we will never stop feeling a sense of having suffered an injustice at the hands of Heaven. And therefore, after receiving the Torah a lengthy "treatment" is required for us to be cured of the "side effects."

At Sinai the Jews accepted the Torah through compulsion. We therefore had to "re-receive" the Torah in repeated renewals of our Covenant with God that have taken place throughout the full length of Jewish history, beginning with the covenant in the city of Shechem after the Jews crossed the Jordan River with Joshua into the Land of Israel, and continuing with the story of Purim, and even unto the present day.

As Islam continues to evolve, it might likewise have to pass through similar stages of development.

### 19.12. Hagar and Ishmael's Status, and their Roles (16:9-16)

ט וַיֹּאמֶר לָהּ מַלְאַךְ יי שׁוּבִי אֶל־גְּבִרְתֵּךְ וְהִתְעַנִּי תַּחַת יָדֶיהָ: י וַיֹּאמֶר לָהּ מַלְאַךְ יי הַרְבָּה אַרְבֶּה אֶת־זַרְעֵךְ וְלֹא יִסָּפֵר מֵרֹב: יא וַיֹּאמֶר לָהּ מַלְאַךְ יי הִנָּךְ הָרָה וְיֹלַדְתְּ בֵּן וְקָרָאת שְׁמוֹ יִשְׁמָעֵאל כִּי־שָׁמַע יי אֶל־עָנְיֵךְ: יב וְהוּא יִהְיֶה פֶּרֶא אָדָם יָדוֹ בַכֹּל וְיַד כֹּל בּוֹ וְעַל־פְּנֵי כָל־אֶחָיו יִשְׁכֹּן: יג וַתִּקְרָא שֵׁם־יי הַדֹּבֵר אֵלֶיהָ אַתָּה אֵל רֳאִי כִּי אָמְרָה הֲגַם הֲלֹם רָאִיתִי אַחֲרֵי רֹאִי: יד עַל־ כֵּן קָרָא לַבְּאֵר בְּאֵר לַחַי רֹאִי הִנֵּה בֵין־קָדֵשׁ וּבֵין בָּרֶד: טו וַתֵּלֶד הָגָר לְאַבְרָם בֵּן וַיִּקְרָא אַבְרָם שֶׁם־בְּנוֹ אֲשֶׁר־ יָלְדָה הָגָר יִשְׁמָעֵאל: טז וְאַבְרָם בֶּן־שְׁמֹנִים שָׁנָה וְשֵׁשׁ שָׁנִים בְּלֶדֶת־הָגָר אֶת־יִשְׁמָעֵאל לְאַבְרָם:

*[9] And the angel of the Lord said to her, "Go back to your mistress, and submit to her harsh treatment."*

*[10] And the angel of the Lord said to her, "I will greatly increase your offspring, And they shall be too many to count."*

*[11] The angel of the Lord said to her further, "Behold, you are with child And shall bear a son; You shall call him Ishmael, For the Lord has paid heed to your suffering.*

*[12] He shall be a wild ass of a man; His hand against everyone, And everyone's hand against him; He shall dwell alongside of all his kinsmen."*

*[13] And she called the Lord who spoke to her, "You Are El-roi", by which she meant, "Have I not gone on seeing after He saw me!"*

*[14] Therefore the well was called Beer-lahai-roi; it is between Kadesh and Bered.*

*[15] Hagar bore a son to Abram, and Abram gave the son that Hagar bore him the name Ishmael.*

*[16] Abram was eighty-six years old when Hagar bore Ishmael to Abram.*

**[9] Go back to your mistress**: Recognition of Sarah's superiority is a requisite for Hagar herself. So long as her self-determination is false, no blessing can be hers.

**[11] Behold, you are with child and shall bear a son.** But when Hagar acknowledges her status as maidservant and corrects her behavior, she is blessed.

**You shall call him Ishmael, for the Lord has paid heed to your suffering.** The role of Ishmael and his descendants, the Arabs, in world history is highly significant, and is also a feature of Abraham's legacy. In relation to Sarah and the Jewish people, Hagar and Ishmael's position is ambivalent. On the one hand, they have subordinate status, but on the other hand, they must not be oppressed. The very name Ishmael means "God hears," that is, He hears the sufferings of Hagar and her descendants. Maintaining a balance between these two aspects is not easy, and in daily life we often see that some Jews emphasize much more the need for Ishmael's subordination, while others put greater emphasis on the commandment to not oppress him. In truth, however, only by learning to integrate both of these principles can we expect to normalize our relations with the descendants of Hagar.

It should be noted that Jewish tradition generally sees Hagar in a positive light despite her conflict with Sarah, as a person of rather high spiritual attainments. At the end of portion *Chayei Sarah* the Torah relates how after the death of Sarah, Abraham took a wife named Keturah. The Talmud maintains that Keturah is Hagar; Hagar, who was expelled by Abraham (as we will read below), did not marry, but waited until Abraham called her back. Which indeed he did, after which Hagar bore yet more children to Abraham. At the same time, the change of name from Hagar to Keturah shows a change in her identity, and her ability to overcome her former complexes.

Hagar's problem is that her spiritual potential allows her to rise to the level of one of the "spiritual leaders of the nations of the world," but not to become a spiritual leader of the Jewish people. Among her descendants are people who can become the Righteous of the Nations, and fulfill an important spiritual function in the world, but they are not included among the chosen people.

**[12] He shall be a wild ass of a man; he shall dwell alongside of all his kinsmen.** Although here it means "savage," the strict meaning of the Hebrew word *pere* is "a wild ass that refuses to accept the yoke." A yoke does in fact limit freedom, but mostly it represents the opportunity to work productively. Ishmael wants to be free, but he has a problem with doing constructive work.

**His hand against everyone, and everyone's hand against him.** The Hebrew literally translated is, "His hand in everyone, and everyone's hand in him." He needs all, and all need him. He will have no independent existence, but while he remains dependent, he too will have something that everyone needs.

Over the course of history this blessing apparently found fulfillment in the fact that, although the creative role of Islamic countries themselves in the development of civilization has been fairly minor, their "transmissional contribution" – in culture, commerce, and the like – has been nonetheless quite high. The constant danger that Islam poses to the West fulfills its historically mandated role of "threatening savage."

**[13] And she called the Lord who spoke to her, "You Are El-roi", by which she meant, "Have I not gone on seeing after He saw me!."** God says to Hagar: "I am listening" (16:11), as in "Come to me, I am ready for dialogue." But Hagar says of God that He sees – he oversees everything and controls everything, no one can hide from Him. Here we have the essential conflict within Islam. The inability to engage in dialogue with God gives rise to the inability to engage in dialogue with people. And the yearning to obey God by blindly executing Divine orders, but not deliberating with Him, creates a mindset of issuing orders and dictating to other people, rather than entering into dialogue with them.

**[16] Abram was eighty-six years old when Hagar bore Ishmael to Abram.** Abraham left Haran and came to the land of Canaan when he was seventy-five years old. After ten years, when Abraham is eighty-five, Sarah gives him Hagar, who one year later, when Abraham is eighty-six years of age, bears him a son, Ishmael. The news of the future birth of Isaac comes when Abraham is ninety-nine years old. Ishmael, who is thirteen years old, has now come of age. This is an essential point concerning Ishmael's stage of development at that time, as we shall see.

# Chapter 20

# The Covenant of Circumcision

## 20.1. "Walk in My Ways" (17:1-2)

א וַיְהִי אַבְרָם בֶּן־תִּשְׁעִים שָׁנָה וְתֵשַׁע שָׁנִים וַיֵּרָא יי
אֶל־אַבְרָם וַיֹּאמֶר אֵלָיו אֲנִי־אֵל שַׁדַּי הִתְהַלֵּךְ לְפָנַי
וֶהְיֵה תָמִים: ב וְאֶתְּנָה בְרִיתִי בֵּינִי וּבֵינֶךָ וְאַרְבֶּה אוֹתְךָ
בִּמְאֹד מְאֹד:

*[1] When Abram was ninety-nine years old, the
Lord appeared to Abram and said to him, "I am
El Shaddai. Walk in My ways and be blameless.
[2] I will establish My covenant between Me and
you, and I will make you exceedingly numerous."*

**[1] When Abram was ninety-nine years old.** Ishmael had
now reached his thirteenth birthday, and Abraham must have
realized that Ishmael was not capable of continuing his work.

**[2] I will establish My covenant between Me and you.** This reorientation from Ishmael to Isaac is associated with the renewal of the covenant between God and Abraham.

Previously the covenant was simply a promise that Abraham would have offspring who would inherit the land. "On that day the Lord made a covenant with Abram, saying, 'To your offspring I assign this land ...'" (15:18). But that covenant now finds its completion in circumcision, a change of name, and Abraham's spiritual advancement. The Torah therefore says "I will establish My covenant" using the future tense.

**Walk in My ways and be blameless.** Here we hear echoes of the Torah's description of Noah (Gen. 6:9), who "was blameless in his age and walked with God." And yet, the formulation here is somewhat different. Jewish tradition compares and contrasts Abraham and Noah in the two kinds of righteousness they represent. Noah's integrity is, temporally speaking, only local – "in his age" – while the integrity of Abraham is global – for all ages and all times.

The words *hithalech lefanai* ("walk in My ways") translate literally as "walk before Me." Noah walks "*with* God," never departing from Him, and executing all His orders, namely, to build the ark and thus to survive the flood, while the rest of humankind perishes. Abraham, however, walks "*before* God," that is to say, ahead of Him, sometimes even objecting and disagreeing with Him – as we will see, for example, when Abraham challenges God to spare the wicked city of Sodom for the sake of even just a few righteous individuals who might be living there.

Thus, Noah was "saved" while Abraham is himself a savior. While Noah is the forefather of humanity, Abraham is the teacher of nations. Noah is the "righteous man in a fur coat," who counteracts the cold by donning a fur coat for his own warmth, but does nothing to help others who share the same predicament. By contrast, Abraham, forefather of the Jewish nation, kindles a fire to warm all of humanity.

## 20.2. "But your name shall be Abraham" (17:3-8)

ג וַיִּפֹּל אַבְרָם עַל־פָּנָיו וַיְדַבֵּר אִתּוֹ אֱלֹהִים לֵאמֹר: ד
אֲנִי הִנֵּה בְרִיתִי אִתָּךְ וְהָיִיתָ לְאַב הֲמוֹן גּוֹיִם: ה וְלֹא־
יִקָּרֵא עוֹד אֶת־שִׁמְךָ אַבְרָם וְהָיָה שִׁמְךָ אַבְרָהָם כִּי אַב־
הֲמוֹן גּוֹיִם נְתַתִּיךָ: ו וְהִפְרֵתִי אֹתְךָ בִּמְאֹד מְאֹד וּנְתַתִּיךָ
לְגוֹיִם וּמְלָכִים מִמְּךָ יֵצֵאוּ: ז וַהֲקִמֹתִי אֶת־בְּרִיתִי בֵּינִי
וּבֵינֶךָ וּבֵין זַרְעֲךָ אַחֲרֶיךָ לְדֹרֹתָם לִבְרִית עוֹלָם לִהְיוֹת
לְךָ לֵאלֹהִים וּלְזַרְעֲךָ אַחֲרֶיךָ: ח וְנָתַתִּי לְךָ וּלְזַרְעֲךָ
אַחֲרֶיךָ אֵת | אֶרֶץ מְגֻרֶיךָ אֵת כָּל־אֶרֶץ כְּנַעַן לַאֲחֻזַּת
עוֹלָם וְהָיִיתִי לָהֶם לֵאלֹהִים:

*[3] Abram threw himself on his face; and God spoke to him further,*

*[4] "As for Me, this is My covenant with you: You shall be the father of a multitude of nations.*

*[5] And you shall no longer be called Abram, but your name shall be Abraham, for I make you the father of a multitude of nations.*

*[6] I will make you exceedingly fertile, and make nations of you; and kings shall come forth from you.*

*[7] I will maintain My covenant between Me and you, and your offspring to come, as an everlasting covenant throughout the ages, to be God to you and to your offspring to come.*

*[8] I assign the land you sojourn in to you and your offspring to come, all the land of Canaan, as an everlasting holding. I will be their God."*

**[3] Abram threw himself on his face.** Until Abraham is circumcised and receives his new name, he cannot remain standing when the Lord reveals Himself through the ineffable Divine four-letter name, the "Tetragrammaton," which is always pronounced by Jews as "the Lord" and translated likewise. (It is the name used in 17:1.) God therefore conducts further dialogue with Abraham (see 17:3) at the level of *Elohim*, "God," a term of a somewhat lower Divine status (as indicated by its additional carrying of profane meanings, e.g., false gods and human judges).

**[5] And you shall no longer be called Abram, but your name shall be Abraham.** Although the meaning of the name Abraham is clearly explained in these verses as *av hamon goyim*, "father of a multitude of nations," the etymology of the name itself is not obvious. The Hebrew letter *he* that God added to the name "Abram" to make it "Abraham" is derived in the Midrash from the word *hamon*, "multitude."

But the expression *av hamon goyim* contains no letter *resh* that would correspond to that letter in the name *Avraham* (the "r" of the English transliteration "Abraham"). One explanation for the unexpected letter *resh* in "Abraham" is that it was carried over from the former name, "Abram," *ab aram*, "father of Aram." (Another suggested translation is "father of the sublime.")

Others point out that there is an older Semitic root preserved in the ancient Arabic language, where the word for "multitude" is *raham*, notwithstanding that that root with its additional *resh* has not been preserved in Hebrew. "Abraham" could then mean, quite precisely, "father of the multitude."

**I make you the father of a multitude of nations.** Earlier in this book (0) the Torah enumerated those "nations" in the ethnic sense of the word, as those who descended from each of the sons of Noah: Shem, Ham and Japheth. But the nations that will descend from Abraham will be "nations" in the religious sense, "members of the Abrahamic religions."

Those religions gradually spread to all mankind. Abraham is therefore the "father of a multitude of nations" not only in the sense that several ethnic groups will come from him, but also that his ideas and ideals will gradually spread to all of humanity.

**[7] I will maintain My covenant between Me and you, and your offspring to come ... to be God to you and to your offspring to come. [8] I assign the land you sojourn in.** As in all the covenants that God made with the Patriarchs, three aspects stand out here: creating a nation from Abraham's descendants, giving them the Land of Israel, and the promise that they will be God's people. Here God reveals His intention to create a nation as a political reality, as a national-state entity in its land, through which God will be revealed to the world. There is no mention here of the commandments or the laws of the Torah. We will hear much about them later, at the revelation at Sinai as described in the book of Exodus.

Thus, the nationalist element is not fundamentally alien to Judaism, as some would have it; on the contrary, it is the commandments of the Torah that should be understood as a supplemental aspect of the process of forming a nation, rather than an integral part of it. For this very reason, Rashi, in his commentary on this passage, explains that "living outside the Land of Israel is equivalent to having no God." And conversely, one who lives in Israel, even if there is nothing very "religious" about him, has an encounter with God on a daily basis.

The commandments are of course essential to normative Jewish life. We must bear in mind, however, that the primary

content of the covenant – the part that will change all of
humanity – is not the Torah commandments *per se*, but the
national-political existence of the Jewish people.

## 20.3. Circumcision as a Sign of the Covenant (17:9-14)

ט וַיֹּאמֶר אֱלֹהִים אֶל־אַבְרָהָם וְאַתָּה אֶת־בְּרִיתִי
תִשְׁמֹר אַתָּה וְזַרְעֲךָ אַחֲרֶיךָ לְדֹרֹתָם: י זֹאת בְּרִיתִי אֲשֶׁר
תִּשְׁמְרוּ בֵּינִי וּבֵינֵיכֶם וּבֵין זַרְעֲךָ אַחֲרֶיךָ הִמּוֹל לָכֶם כָּל־
זָכָר: יא וּנְמַלְתֶּם אֵת בְּשַׂר עָרְלַתְכֶם וְהָיָה לְאוֹת בְּרִית
בֵּינִי וּבֵינֵיכֶם: יב וּבֶן־שְׁמֹנַת יָמִים יִמּוֹל לָכֶם כָּל־זָכָר
לְדֹרֹתֵיכֶם יְלִיד בָּיִת וּמִקְנַת־כֶּסֶף מִכֹּל בֶּן־נֵכָר אֲשֶׁר לֹא
מִזַּרְעֲךָ הוּא: יג הִמּוֹל | יִמּוֹל יְלִיד בֵּיתְךָ וּמִקְנַת כַּסְפֶּךָ
וְהָיְתָה בְרִיתִי בִּבְשַׂרְכֶם לִבְרִית עוֹלָם: יד וְעָרֵל | זָכָר
אֲשֶׁר לֹא־יִמּוֹל אֶת־בְּשַׂר עָרְלָתוֹ וְנִכְרְתָה הַנֶּפֶשׁ הַהִוא
מֵעַמֶּיהָ אֶת־בְּרִיתִי הֵפַר:

*[9] God further said to Abraham, "As for you, you
and your offspring to come throughout the ages
shall keep My covenant.*

*[10] Such shall be the covenant between Me
and you and your offspring to follow which
you shall keep: every male among you shall be
circumcised.*

*[11] You shall circumcise the flesh of your
foreskin, and that shall be the sign of the
covenant between Me and you.*

*[12] And throughout the generations, every male
among you shall be circumcised at the age of
eight days. As for the homeborn slave and the
one bought from an outsider who is not of your
offspring,*

*[13] they must be circumcised, homeborn, and
purchased alike. Thus shall My covenant be
marked in your flesh as an everlasting pact.
[14] And if any male who is uncircumcised fails to
circumcise the flesh of his foreskin, that person
shall be cut off from his kin; he has broken My
covenant."*

**[9] You and your offspring to come throughout the ages
shall keep My covenant.** The Torah stresses here that
although the descendants of Abraham will become "a multitude of nations," the covenant will be made exclusively
through the Jewish people.

**[10] Such shall be the covenant ... which you shall keep: every
male among you shall be circumcised.** God's covenant with
Abraham considers circumcision not just one of many commandments, but a sign of the covenant – its visible expression.

The main idea that circumcision signifies is that "natural
man" as he is born is by no means perfect. In this lies the critical difference between the Jewish and Greek worldviews.
The Greeks considered "natural man" the embodiment of
harmony and the measure of all things, and they therefore
despised circumcision (as did the Romans), because they
saw it as an assault on nature. When the Hellenistic Seleu-
cid empire began to persecute the Jews (events that led up
to the story of Hanukkah), the prohibition of circumcision
was one of the main demands of the Greeks. Judaism, on the
other hand, rejects the idea of "perfection by nature," arguing that a person is perfect only in his potential, and that he
has a long road of development to travel before he can hope
to even approach such perfection.

The Greeks saw the natural world as perfectly complete. Judaism, in contrast, believes that when one becomes aware of nature's lack of perfection, this is the point at which man's union with the Divine, which transcends nature, can begin.

This is especially important in the context of human pro-creation, development, and advancement. And that is why circumcision is done on the organ of reproduction.

### 20.4. "For Sarah is Her Name" (17:15-16)

טו וַיֹּאמֶר אֱלֹהִים אֶל־אַבְרָהָם שָׂרַי אִשְׁתְּךָ לֹא־תִקְרָא אֶת־שְׁמָהּ שָׂרָי כִּי שָׂרָה שְׁמָהּ: טז וּבֵרַכְתִּי אֹתָהּ וְגַם נָתַתִּי מִמֶּנָּה לְךָ בֵּן וּבֵרַכְתִּיהָ וְהָיְתָה לְגוֹיִם מַלְכֵי עַמִּים מִמֶּנָּה יִהְיוּ:

*[15] And God said to Abraham, "As for your wife Sarai, you shall not call her Sarai, but her name shall be Sarah.*
*[16] I will bless her; indeed, I will give you a son by her. I will bless her so that she shall give rise to nations; rulers of peoples shall issue from her."*

**[15] You shall not call her Sarai, but her name shall be Sarah.** Originally her name was Sarai, "my ruler," but now she is simply "ruler," that is, a world leader. Earlier the Torah says of Abraham (17:5), "And you shall no longer be called Abram, but your name shall be Abraham." That is, his name has been changed. For Sarah, however, we read in this verse as it would be literally translated: "But, rather, Sarah is her name." That is, her name had always been Sarah, but only now is that name revealed. In other words, Sarah all along had been at a level suitable for bearing Isaac, but Abraham still needed to reach that level. When Abraham received from God the commandment of circumcision, it was an indicator that he had attained the required level.

**[16] I will bless her; indeed, I will give you a son by her. I will bless her so that she shall give rise to nations; rulers of peoples shall issue from her.."** There are two parts to this blessing. The first is that a son will be born, and the second is that nations and kings will come from him. Thus, Sarah's son, besides being Abraham's physical descendant, will also continue his father's work.

**I will bless her; indeed, I will give you a son by her.** Sarah will be blessed in that Abraham's successor will come from her. Both of his parents must be *ivrim*, Hebrews, in order to facilitate God's plan to create the chosen people on a profoundly "national" basis. This people must stand apart from other nations, since it is this separation that creates the prerequisites for the realization of a universal Jewish destiny.

### 20.5. Proper Nationalism as the Foundation of Universalism

The European humanist tradition maintains that nationalism is antithetical to universalism, because that tradition believes that any preservation of a distinct national identity isolates a nation from the rest of humanity. But the Torah's position is quite the opposite: to become truly universal, you must first realize your uniquely national potential; only then can you offer something to the rest of the world. Thus, when Abraham undergoes circumcision, and focuses on his

Jewish identity, God gives Abram and Sarai new names that emphasize their universal purpose.

Abraham's ideas could not find their way to the rest of humanity until a unique people was created to transmit them.

Thus, the foundation of universalism is a proper nationalism, the realization of one's own national specificity, rather than a cosmopolitanism that is the rejection of any national orientation.

## 20.6. Division of the Inheritance Between Isaac and Ishmael (17:17-22)

יז וַיִּפֹּל אַבְרָהָם עַל־פָּנָיו וַיִּצְחָק וַיֹּאמֶר בְּלִבּוֹ הַלְבֶן מֵאָה־שָׁנָה יִוָּלֵד וְאִם־שָׂרָה הֲבַת־תִּשְׁעִים שָׁנָה תֵּלֵד: יח וַיֹּאמֶר אַבְרָהָם אֶל־הָאֱלֹהִים לוּ יִשְׁמָעֵאל יִחְיֶה לְפָנֶיךָ: יט וַיֹּאמֶר אֱלֹהִים אֲבָל שָׂרָה אִשְׁתְּךָ יֹלֶדֶת לְךָ בֵּן וְקָרָאתָ אֶת־שְׁמוֹ יִצְחָק וַהֲקִמֹתִי אֶת־בְּרִיתִי אִתּוֹ לִבְרִית עוֹלָם לְזַרְעוֹ אַחֲרָיו: כ וּלְיִשְׁמָעֵאל שְׁמַעְתִּיךָ הִנֵּה | בֵּרַכְתִּי אֹתוֹ וְהִפְרֵיתִי אֹתוֹ וְהִרְבֵּיתִי אֹתוֹ בִּמְאֹד מְאֹד שְׁנֵים־עָשָׂר נְשִׂיאִם יוֹלִיד וּנְתַתִּיו לְגוֹי גָּדוֹל: כא וְאֶת־בְּרִיתִי אָקִים אֶת־יִצְחָק אֲשֶׁר תֵּלֵד לְךָ שָׂרָה לַמּוֹעֵד הַזֶּה בַּשָּׁנָה הָאַחֶרֶת: כב וַיְכַל לְדַבֵּר אִתּוֹ וַיַּעַל אֱלֹהִים מֵעַל אַבְרָהָם:

*[17] Abraham threw himself on his face and laughed, as he said to himself, "Can a child be born to a man a hundred years old, or can Sarah bear a child at ninety?"*
*[18] And Abraham said to God, "O that Ishmael might live by Your favor!"*
*[19] God said, "Nevertheless, Sarah your wife*

*shall bear you a son, and you shall name him*
*Isaac; and I will maintain My covenant with*
*him as an everlasting covenant for his offspring*
*to come.*
*[20] As for Ishmael, I have heeded you. I hereby*
*bless him. I will make him fertile and exceedingly*
*numerous. He shall be the father of twelve*
*chieftains, and I will make of him a great nation.*
*[21] But My covenant I will maintain with Isaac,*
*whom Sarah shall bear to you at this season*
*next year."*
*[22] And when He was done speaking with him,*
*God was gone from Abraham.*

**[17] And laughed**. Abraham's laughter and his words that follow demonstrate that although he perceives God's words
as a gift and a miracle, the prospect of having a son born to
Sarah is very problematic for him. As mentioned earlier, Ishmael, the son of Hagar, representing the great civilization
of Egypt, is in Abraham's eyes more preferred for becoming
the progenitor of the chosen people than is Sarah's son, who
is ethnically only a Hebrew. Abraham believed that through
his connection with Egypt it would be easier to influence
the larger world. Perhaps he even saw Divine Providence
in the fact that Sarah had no children, and that his son was
born of Hagar.

**[18] "O that Ishmael might live by Your favor!."** Hearing from God that Sarah will give birth to a son, Abraham
becomes confused. Does God really wish to return him to
that narrowly ethnic plan, from which Abraham, thanks to
Ishmael's birth, thought he had been liberated? Abraham is

still hoping that God will backtrack from His peculiar decision and settle instead on Ishmael.

Abraham prefers Ishmael to Isaac for two reasons. Firstly, by marrying Hagar, Abraham had sought to forge a connection with Egypt, the leading world civilization of the time, and that desire has remained with him ever since. Secondly, Ishmael's character is *chesed*, and even if it is an improper *chesed*, it is still closer and more comprehensible to Abraham than Isaac's character, *gevurah*.

**[19] God said, "Nevertheless, Sarah your wife shall bear you a son, and you shall name him Isaac; and I will maintain My covenant with him as an everlasting covenant for his offspring to come**. God is emphatic, as if to say: "No, it is Sarah – despite all of your objections."

**[20] As for Ishmael, I have heeded you ... I will make him fertile and exceedingly numerous ... [21] But My covenant I will maintain with Isaac.** Abraham's preference for Ishmael led to a bifurcation of his legacy. The promise of "I will multiply your offspring" (16:10) is to be fulfilled in Ishmael, but the covenant and the promise of the land is to be fulfilled in Isaac. Although later both Isaac and Jacob will receive from God the promise of numerically abundant offspring, the quantitative ratio between the descendants of Isaac and the descendants of Ishmael as fundamentally given here favors Ishmael.

**I will make of him a great nation.** When it comes to faith, the Arab people are "a great nation," occupying a central place among the peoples of the world. Islam in the first centuries of its existence developed its philosophy of Abrahamic monotheism with a clarity and inner consistency that Jewish religious philosophers were able to develop only in subsequent centuries. The problem with Islam, however, is that its adherents' faith does not sufficiently reflect on their interpersonal relationships. The fact remains that mere acceptance of the principle of the unity of God and submission to Him is not by itself enough. Real life must have as its foundations the unity of ideals and a system of commandments.

To achieve that, it is not enough to be a child of Abraham. One must be also the child of Sarah. The nation that Abraham created was chosen not only to disseminate the theological and philosophical ideas of the One God, but also to show mankind the path to God through "doing what is just and right" (18:19). Therefore, Ishmael himself is not able to create a civilization. He can only "camp alongside his kinsmen" (16:12), that is, serve as a counterweight and a regulating force that compensates for the defects of other Abrahamic religions.

**[22] And when He was done speaking with him, God was gone from Abraham.** God interrupts the conversation and departs from Abraham, even putting some distance between them. It would seem that the Almighty is even angry with Abraham and says to him, as it were: "What I originally wished to give to your offspring from Sara will now be divided into two parts. Because you pleaded on Ishmael's behalf, the blessing of becoming a numerous people will be his. But, needless to say, my covenant remains only with Isaac." Later on, this division will make it very difficult for Isaac's descendants to fulfill their mission.

## 20.7. The Circumcision of Abraham's Household (17:23-27)

כג וַיִּקַּח אַבְרָהָם אֶת־יִשְׁמָעֵאל בְּנוֹ וְאֵת כָּל־יְלִידֵי בֵיתוֹ
וְאֵת כָּל־מִקְנַת כַּסְפּוֹ כָּל־זָכָר בְּאַנְשֵׁי בֵּית אַבְרָהָם וַיָּמָל

אֶת־בְּשַׂר עׇרְלָתָם בְּעֶצֶם הַיּוֹם הַזֶּה כַּאֲשֶׁר דִּבֶּר אִתּוֹ
אֱלֹהִים: **כד** וְאַבְרָהָם בֶּן־תִּשְׁעִים וָתֵשַׁע שָׁנָה בְּהִמֹּלוֹ
בְּשַׂר עׇרְלָתוֹ: **כה** וְיִשְׁמָעֵאל בְּנוֹ בֶּן־שְׁלֹשׁ עֶשְׂרֵה שָׁנָה
בְּהִמֹּלוֹ אֵת בְּשַׂר עׇרְלָתוֹ: **כו** בְּעֶצֶם הַיּוֹם הַזֶּה נִמּוֹל
אַבְרָהָם וְיִשְׁמָעֵאל בְּנוֹ: **כז** וְכָל־אַנְשֵׁי בֵיתוֹ יְלִיד בָּיִת
וּמִקְנַת־כֶּסֶף מֵאֵת בֶּן־נֵכָר נִמֹּלוּ אִתּוֹ:

*[23] Then Abraham took his son Ishmael, and all his homeborn slaves and all those he had bought, every male in Abraham's household, and he circumcised the flesh of their foreskins on that very day, as God had spoken to him.*
*[24] Abraham was ninety-nine years old when he circumcised the flesh of his foreskin,*
*[25] and his son Ishmael was thirteen years old when he was circumcised in the flesh of his foreskin.*
*[26] Thus Abraham and his son Ishmael were circumcised on that very day;*
*[27] and all his household, his homeborn slaves and those that had been bought from outsiders, were circumcised with him.*

**[24] Abraham was ninety-nine years old ... [25] and his son Ishmael was thirteen years old when he was circumcised in the flesh of his foreskin.** The enumeration of their ages is superfluous here, given that they have already been reported above (17:1). Note, too, that the laws of circumcision require that that commandment be performed on the eighth day from birth (17:12). Thus, the Torah is emphasizing here that since neither Abraham nor Ishmael met this requirement; only Isaac is the first "authentic Jew from birth."

# Weekly Portion
## Vayera

Chapter 21

# The Visit of the Three Angels and Abraham Challenging God About Sodom

### 21.1. The Relationship of the Weekly Portions Lech Lecha and Vayera

As already noted, the weekly portions in the Book of Genesis are a series of pairs. Just as the Torah relates the opening history of mankind in two weekly portions, *Bereshit* and *Noah*, so the story of Abraham is told to us in two weekly portions: *Lech Lecha* and *Vayera*.

The *Lech Lecha* ("Go thee forth") portion tells of Abraham's "departure." In addition to leaving not only his father's house and his former life, Abraham also experiences a gradual shift from his original plan of creating a universal religion to accepting God's plan of creating a unique, monotheistic nation as a strict prerequisite to spreading that universal idea to all of humanity.

In the course of his travels through the Land of Israel, Abraham gradually comes to realize that the continuation of his teachings can be accomplished not through Eliezer,

Lot, or Ishmael, but only through his son born to him from Sarah. Eliezer, Lot, and Ishmael were all close associates of Abraham and followers of his teachings, but that was not sufficient for any of them to become his successors.

To continue Abraham's teachings, it was necessary not only to know and understand what he taught, but also to have enormous creative potential. With Abraham, the creation of the nation and of Judaism has only just begun; thus, his successor must not merely duplicate Abraham's accomplishments, but must continue to also blaze his own trail. Only a son born of both Abraham and Sarah could be a personality strong and bright enough to further Abraham's work.

In the *Lech Lecha* portion Abraham undergoes the transition from his level of individual understanding to the level of national understanding; that is, from Abram to Abraham.

From this turning point, a new weekly portion of the Torah begins, the *Vayera* portion ("The Lord appeared to him"). In this portion, the Almighty reveals himself to Abraham as none other than the founder of a nation. The main event here is the birth of Isaac. Abraham, the epitome of righteousness – the attribute of *chesed* – has begun to realize (as difficult as this is for him) that his successor would be a person of completely different attitudes than himself, a righteous person of a different type – the attribute of *gevurah*. Abraham should have understood and accepted that *chesed*, rather than operating in isolation, requires integration with other attributes, primarily with *gevurah*.

The *Lech Lecha* portion tells of Abraham's beginnings. Portion *Vayera* covers Abraham's relationship with Isaac, because it is vital not only to have one's own achievements, but also to find a successor to continue those accomplishments. This story begins with the prediction of the birth of Isaac, and ends with the *akedat yitzchak*, "the sacrificing of

Isaac," as the pinnacle of mutual understanding between Abraham and Isaac.

Isaac could be born only after Ishmael had grown up, because in the process of Ishmael's birth and upbringing, a certain *kelippah* ("shell" or "husk") was lifted from Abraham that had been hindering his development. (This is Ishmael's "unclean *chesed*," to be discussed below.) Abraham's formation as ancestor of the Jewish people now begins. Only after his circumcision and the change of his name could Abraham become the progenitor of a nation.

### 21.2. Revelation in the Afternoon: First Steps Toward the Attribute of Gevurah (18:1)

א וַיֵּרָא אֵלָיו יי בְּאֵלֹנֵי מַמְרֵא וְהוּא יֹשֵׁב פֶּתַח־הָאֹהֶל
כְּחֹם הַיּוֹם:

*[1] The Lord appeared to him by the terebinths of Mamre; he was sitting at the entrance of the tent as the day grew hot.*

**[1] The Lord appeared to him.** God had already appeared to Abraham not long before (17:1), but Abraham during this time has changed much by circumcising himself and his family. Abraham therefore no longer "falls on his face" when meeting with the Almighty, but conducts direct dialogue with Him.

**By the terebinths of Mamre.** This is the city of Hebron (13:18), where Abraham has lived since the time of the war with the kings (14:13). The *sefirah* – Kabbalistic attribute – of Hebron within the Land of Israel is *malchut*, "kingdom."

This is the attribute of realization, the attribute of David who will reign in Hebron. But the attribute of Abraham is *chesed*, and the quality of *malchut* is therefore alien to him. Abraham has not yet built a nation, but has only just begun the enormous task of creating it.

The structure of the Jewish nation, according to the *sefirot* tree, tends toward *malchut*, to David, and to the Messiah, the descendant of David. In Abraham are only the beginnings of its growth. Abraham settles in Hebron, the royal city (see 20:5), because internally he wants to move towards *malchut*; he wants to start learning this attribute. However, as becomes apparent below, Abraham cannot find his place in Hebron, so he goes to Gerar, and then on to Beersheba. Only Isaac and Jacob, his son and grandson, will later return to Hebron.

**As the day grew hot.** Afternoon is the time of the *gevurah* attribute, - reckoning and judgment - while dawn, the early morning, is the time of grace, *chesed*, the attribute of Abraham. Afternoon, *gevurah*, is the time of Isaac. (Night, as we shall see later, is *tiferet* - "adornment" or "splendor" - the time of Jacob.)

When light reappears in the morning, we perceive it as a Divine gift to the world after the darkness of the night. God restores every man's soul to him after sleep, so that we can renew our lives each day. In *shacharit*, the daily morning prayer, a Jew rejoices that he is awake, having received anew the gift of life. All this is the attribute of *chesed*.

By the time afternoon arrives the sun is shining hot, and being exposed to it is difficult; this is the attribute of law and judgment. Accordingly, in *minchah*, the afternoon prayer, a person gives an account to God for the work he has accomplished so far that day. Thus he justifies his existence by accounting for his accomplishments in relation to the opportunities that he has been given. Such is the character of Isaac.

Abraham's vision, which begins here in the afternoon, in the heat of the day, and not early in the morning, is itself an indicator of the coming birth of Isaac, the righteous exemplar of the attribute of judgment.

**He was sitting at the entrance of the tent as the day grew hot.** At this time of day one would normally seek refuge inside his tent from the sweltering heat. Sitting at the tent's entrance in such heat is unnatural. The Midrash explains that Abraham did so as an expression of his eagerness to invite travelers into his home.

### 21.3. The Three "Men" as the Unification of Abraham, Isaac, and Jacob (18:2-5)

ב וַיִּשָּׂא עֵינָיו וַיַּרְא וְהִנֵּה שְׁלֹשָׁה אֲנָשִׁים נִצָּבִים עָלָיו
וַיַּרְא וַיָּרָץ לִקְרָאתָם מִפֶּתַח הָאֹהֶל וַיִּשְׁתַּחוּ אָרְצָה: ג
וַיֹּאמַר אֲדֹנָי אִם־נָא מָצָאתִי חֵן בְּעֵינֶיךָ אַל־נָא תַעֲבֹר
מֵעַל עַבְדֶּךָ: ד יֻקַּח־נָא מְעַט־מַיִם וְרַחֲצוּ רַגְלֵיכֶם
וְהִשָּׁעֲנוּ תַּחַת הָעֵץ: ה וְאֶקְחָה פַת־לֶחֶם וְסַעֲדוּ לִבְּכֶם
אַחַר תַּעֲבֹרוּ כִּי־עַל־כֵּן עֲבַרְתֶּם עַל־עַבְדְּכֶם וַיֹּאמְרוּ כֵּן
תַּעֲשֶׂה כַּאֲשֶׁר דִּבַּרְתָּ:

*[2] Looking up, he saw three men standing near him. and, bowing to the ground,*
*[3] he said, "My lords, if it please you, do not go on past your servant As soon as he saw them, he ran from the entrance of the tent to greet them.*
*[4] Let a little water be brought; bathe your feet and recline under the tree.*

*[5] And let me fetch a morsel of bread that you
may refresh yourselves; then go on-seeing that
you have come your servant's way." They replied,
"Do as you have said."*

**[2] Three men standing near him.** Who were these three
"men" whom Abraham meets here? The story begins with the
fact that "the Lord appeared to him" (verse 1), but we do not
find that God actually speaks to Abraham here; the text cuts
over immediately to the three "men." Later, the Torah says of
Abraham's visitors: "The men ... looked down toward Sodom
... and the two angels arrived in Sodom" (18:16, 19:1). So, with
what kind of "men" was Abraham actually communicating?

Tradition provides several different ways of understanding
this passage. They might have been three ordinary travelers,
sent by God on a mission to Abraham. Or perhaps they were
angels. Or perhaps it was the Almighty Himself, revealed to
Abraham in a vision. In different periods, Jewish commentators emphasized those aspects of their understanding of
this story that they felt were important for their generation.

For our generation today, the most significant interpretation is that of the Zohar, which says that the three men
whom Abraham saw were images of the three Patriarchs.
In other words, it is Abraham himself in the company of his
son and grandson Isaac and Jacob. This means that Abraham
recognized himself not only as a distinct personality representing the attribute of *chesed* independently of the other
*sefirot*, but also as a link in the chain of generations, as part
of the overall picture of the development of the nation in
both the physical and spiritual senses. Abraham was coming
to understand that the attribute of *chesed* cannot work in
isolation; that it is impossible to improve humanity and the

universe by love, kindness, and grace alone. Abraham now understood that he was himself only the first link in the chain of Patriarchs who would continue the work he had started. Understanding that his own *sefirah* must be complemented by those of Isaac and Jacob is a major advance for Abraham.

**As soon as he saw them, he ran from the entrance of the tent to greet them.** Abraham saw his connection to the attributes of Isaac and Jacob, and willingly accepted that connection. The Hebrew word *ratz* ("he ran") is related in Hebrew to the word *ratzon*, "desire," which causes one to run after what is desired. Thus, Abraham is open to the idea of unification, for he now realizes that the founder of the nation must be not just a single Patriarch, but all three of them as a unit. Or, the same idea differently stated: All the attributes together and not only *chesed* must form the foundation of the Jewish people. This is Abraham's "dynamic" – his enormous spiritual advancement.

Having achieved this understanding, Abraham is now prepared for the birth of Isaac. Being now circumcised, Abraham understands his "specialness," but he has now advanced even further, realizing that he is only the first in a chain of multiple stages of development. Therefore, he can now father his son Isaac, a righteous man of a direction different from his own. Until he had passed through this stage of development Abraham could not give birth to Isaac; he could be the father of only Ishmael, who in a sense is merely a "weak copy" of early Abraham.

### 21.4. Overcoming Fanaticism

A person will normally consider his own ideas and views the most significant and valid. This is natural and necessary, for otherwise we would not be able to defend our ideas and views, and that would make it impossible for us to realize our mission in the world. On the other hand, however, it is dangerous for a person to become such a fanatical supporter of a certain idea that he believes it to be the sole panacea for all the world's problems. And this is true even when the idea itself is not *per se* unwholesome. Take, for example, love, beauty and social justice. These values are vital for human existence. But if one begins to absolutize them, declaring that "only love will save the world," or "only beauty will save the world," or "only social justice will save the world," this is evil, for it is only a destructive fanaticism.

A higher level of human awareness for that person would be to continue actively supporting that concept or idea, but at the same time to be capable of seeing it as only one component of the overall picture. It is essential to admit that your favorite idea must also have its spiritual antithesis, and that in the end this spiritual antithesis will only benefit it.

It would be wrong, of course, for me to renounce my own views; rather, I should argue and defend them. For who will do so for me if I will not? As Hillel said (Mishnah, Avot 1:14): "If I am not for myself, who will be for me?" It is vital, however, that I not consider my own particular direction the only valid one.

Fanaticism is thus not a characteristic of a person's views, be they left or right, extreme or moderate. Fanaticism is a characteristic of one's attitude toward other people when he neither sees, nor wants to see, anything except his own ideas. One who does not see the world around him cannot develop properly.

Any positive thing or idea can be legitimate, provided it remains in its proper place. If it attempts to overstep its boundaries without limit, then by definition it is out of place, and cannot possibly function properly. The Kabbalah calls such a myopic view an *olam hanekudim*, a "world of points", where each *sefirah* (an attribute that is good and proper in itself) wants to absorb all the surrounding Divine light. Bursting from an excess of internal pressure, it explodes and shatters.

That is what the Kabbalah calls *shevirat kelim*, shattering of vessels. Any system that tries to suppress the opposing viewpoint will *ipso facto* lose its balance and inevitably collapse. The *tikkun* (correction) consists in finding the necessary balance. The effect of Abraham's transition from total preoccupation with *chesed* to an understanding of the importance of harmonizing the attributes of all three "men" who appeared to him is to prevent any potential fanaticism, the most important step towards improving the world.

### 21.5. The "Unclean" Chesed of Ishmael

When we say that Ishmael is "a weak copy of early Abraham," we mean that Ishmael, like Abraham, is also a person of *chesed*, but he incorrectly orients that *chesed*, which in Kabbalistic terminology is therefore called *chesed de-tum'ah* ("unclean *chesed*"). However, since Ishmael too is the embodiment of *chesed*, he in this sense resembles Abraham, who understands Ishmael even with all his faults. But Isaac, who is *gevurah*, neither resembles Abraham nor is comprehensible to him. This is one of the reasons that Abraham loves Ishmael more than he loves Isaac. Getting his inner self in touch with Isaac will be a difficult job for Abraham.

The way Jewish tradition sees this manifestation of Ishmael's impure *chesed* can be discerned in the words of the Torah, "His hand against everyone, and everyone's hand against him" (16:12), which indicates a lack of any sense of boundaries; it is this attitude towards one's neighbor that turns that *chesed* into something "unclean." Similarly, the Hebrew word *metzachek* that the Torah uses to describe Ishmael's "mocking" Isaac (21:9) is understood by the Midrash as indicating a propensity for sexual aspirations without a sense of boundaries. The word *metzachek*, to mock or dally amorously, has clear sexual connotations in the Torah (see 26:9).

"Unclean *chesed*" inclines Ishmael to apply that *chesed* inwardly to himself: he tends to be all-permissive, which explains why the flip side of Middle Eastern hospitality is the mass murder of infidels. That is why the descendants of Ishmael, for the sake of balance, choose Islam, which typifies the opposite attribute, *gevurah*, with its minimalist monotheism and a very harshly restrictive system of religion.

As we shall have occasion to observe later, the descendants of Esau, whose attribute is *gevurah*, likewise feel the need to counter their natural inclinations, and they have therefore embraced Christianity, the religion of *chesed* and love.)

As previously noted, we can learn a great deal about a civilization from how it envisions paradise, because those images reflect the deepest aspirations of the people's "collective soul." Or, to paraphrase an oft-quoted maxim about the friends we choose: "Tell me what your paradise looks like, and I will tell you who you are."

It is by no mere happenstance that in the minds of Ishmael's descendants, paradise is the place where "every man will be attended by seventy-two virgins." Such ideas demonstrate the inclination of the Arab soul and its inner desire for lewdness. Aware of this inclination, Islam introduces extremely tough "anti-debauchery" measures into everyday life as a means of self-preservation. Its women are thus required to cover themselves from head to toe, so that no man will possibly be seduced by them.

Abraham had to be cleansed of all this "unclean *chesed*" precisely in order that the Jewish people could then inherit *chesed* only in its purified form.

## 21.6. The Nature and Roles of Angels

If we perceive Abraham's three guests as angels, especially in light of what the Torah says later, "The two angels arrived in Sodom," we must ask why there would be three or two angels, and not just one. The Midrash explains that every angel has its own particular role to fulfill, and no angel can fulfill two or more roles. One of the angels who came to Abraham was the "angel of good tidings" (Michael), who came to inform Sarah of the birth of Isaac. The second was the "angel of healing" (Raphael), who healed Abraham from the after-effects of his circumcision. (He later also brought Lot out of Sodom before its destruction, since healing and rescue are considered one and the same role.) And the third was the "angel of judgment" (Gabriel), charged with destroying Sodom.

Here we see an expression of the Jewish understanding of an angel as the will of the Almighty that has assumed a certain bounded and finite form, in some sense separated from Him and descended into lower worlds. An angel according to this understanding is the materialized or "concentrated" will of God sent to the lower world for the fulfillment of a specific mission.

Such a manifestation of the will of the Almighty can be a one-time, ad hoc occurrence, or it can be an ongoing and permanent assignment, as when it takes the form of some law of nature.

From this point of view, it should be noted, all forces of evil are likewise angels. In particular, Satan, in the Jewish view, is one of the angels performing the functions entrusted to him by God; he is not by any means an autonomous "force that opposes God." Satan's job is to act as prosecutor, to accuse and challenge human beings with difficulties and trials. But these are all tasks assigned to him by God; Satan himself is not an "adversary of God" in any sense.

## 21.7. Abraham's Hospitality as a Religious Value (18:6-8)

ו וַיְמַהֵר אַבְרָהָם הָאֹהֱלָה אֶל־שָׂרָה וַיֹּאמֶר מַהֲרִי שְׁלֹשׁ סְאִים קֶמַח סֹלֶת לוּשִׁי וַעֲשִׂי עֻגוֹת: ז וְאֶל־הַבָּקָר רָץ אַבְרָהָם וַיִּקַּח בֶּן־בָּקָר רַךְ וָטוֹב וַיִּתֵּן אֶל־הַנַּעַר וַיְמַהֵר לַעֲשׂוֹת אֹתוֹ: ח וַיִּקַּח חֶמְאָה וְחָלָב וּבֶן־הַבָּקָר אֲשֶׁר עָשָׂה וַיִּתֵּן לִפְנֵיהֶם וְהוּא־עֹמֵד עֲלֵיהֶם תַּחַת הָעֵץ וַיֹּאכֵלוּ:

*[6] Abraham hastened into the tent to Sarah, and said, "Quick, three seahs of choice flour! Knead and make cakes!"*
*[7] Then Abraham ran to the herd, took a calf, tender and choice, and gave it to a servant-boy, who hastened to prepare it.*
*[8] He took curds and milk and the calf that had been prepared and set these before them; and he waited on them under the tree as they ate.*

**[6] Abraham hastened into the tent to Sarah, and said, "Quick...."** Hospitality is nothing unusual for us today. But at that time the situation was different, and such conduct was not generally accepted at all. For Abraham, however, hospitality was a routine expression of his religiosity, and he sought to make it as widespread a practice as possible.

The essence of monotheism, as preached by Abraham, is love of God, expressed through love of one's fellow man as the image of God on earth. The essential feature of monotheism is not that God is One, but that man is created in His image and likeness. Abraham, by receiving travelers and showing them love, actualizes his religious values.

As a relative and disciple of Abraham, Lot too is hospitable, but Sodom, as Abraham's opposite, is the very antithesis of hospitality, and it therefore has no right to exist. Because of Sodom's failure to be hospitable toward other people, God is "inhospitable" toward them.

**[8] He took curds and milk and the calf that had been prepared and set these before them.** The righteous do much more than they promise, as the Talmud points out, citing Abraham here as an example. He promised only water and a piece of bread (18:5), but he gives meat and milk as well.

**Curds and milk and the calf.** In the Patriarchal era the commandments of the Torah did not yet exist. Thus, there were no laws of *kashrut* (kosher and non-kosher food), such as the prohibition of eating an admixture of meat and dairy, or consuming both of those at the same meal.

### 21.8. The Cave of Machpelah: Jewish Tradition Begins with Adam

The Midrash connects the story of the angels' visit with Abraham's discovery of the cave of Machpelah. In the verse

18:7, "Then Abraham ran to the herd ... ," the preposition *el* ("in the direction of") is used, a rather atypical usage which means not "(run) to" but rather "(run) after." Thus, the passage should be translated as "Then Abraham ran after the herd..." The Midrash, based on the above grammatical observation, tells us that the calf he planned to have slaughtered ran away from Abraham, and into the cave of Machpelah (recall that Abraham at that time was living in Hebron). Chasing the calf, Abraham saw the light of the Garden of Eden emanating from the cave, and realized that it was the tomb of Adam and Eve. He later decided to purchase that cave and make it his family tomb.

The lesson of this Midrash is not only the idea that hospitality will be rewarded, but also the fact that Adam is buried in the cave of Machpelah, the tomb of the Patriarchs, which means that the Jewish traditions of that cave hark back not only as far as Abraham, but even unto Adam; that is, to the very dawn of mankind. The Torah wishes to emphasize that Jewish traditions are universally relevant. The purpose of Jewish tradition is to bring the Divine light to all of humanity, and not only to the Jewish people.

## 21.9. Ishmael's Adulthood and His Test (18:7)

ז וְאֶל־הַבָּקָר רָץ אַבְרָהָם וַיִּקַּח בֶּן־בָּקָר רַךְ וָטוֹב וַיִּתֵּן
אֶל־הַנַּעַר וַיְמַהֵר לַעֲשׂוֹת אֹתוֹ:

*[7] Then Abraham ran to the herd, took a calf, tender and choice, and gave it to a servant-boy, who hastened to prepare it.*

**[7] And gave it to a servant-boy.** Since the boy is not named, tradition seeks to identify him with one of the aforementioned characters, and claims that he was Ishmael. As we know, Ishmael was thirteen years old at that time, standing on the very threshold of adulthood, the age of responsible decision making. Abraham must wait until Ishmael becomes an adult for Isaac's birth to happen, because accepting and acknowledging Isaac was to be a test for Ishmael.

The test that God places before Ishmael is to recognize his subsidiary position in the family hierarchy, and to acknowledge that Isaac is Abraham's full heir in every sense, while he, Ishmael, is only a junior member of the family. Only by passing this test, by acknowledging the truth of that hierarchy, will Ishmael receive his portion of the inheritance, just as Hagar received her rightful reward only after recognizing Sarah's primacy and her own slave status. Prior to that she was driven off, on account of her overinflated pretensions.

It is therefore vital that Ishmael learn all these lessons as early as possible, and all the better if he will do so while Isaac is still only "in the pipeline," in order to condition himself in advance to what lies ahead. To undergo that kind of restructuring Ishmael must have reached the age of adulthood – thirteen years old. And then, being already capable of making responsible decisions, he can choose whether to agree or disagree with his new position in the family.

In the end, Ishmael could not pass this test and was driven away. But God did give him the opportunity initially to make that choice.

On the other hand, Abraham himself also needed to feel convinced that Ishmael was not a suitable heir to his legacy. In order for Ishmael to show his true self and for Abraham to understand this, Ishmael had to be an adult. Only then could his behavior convince Abraham that his other son Isaac was the son worthy of continuing his work.

## 21.10. Sarah's Laughter: Not Lack of Faith, but Overcoming Gevurah (18:9-15)

ט וַיֹּאמְרוּ אֵלָיו אַיֵּה שָׂרָה אִשְׁתֶּךָ וַיֹּאמֶר הִנֵּה בָאֹהֶל: י וַיֹּאמֶר שׁוֹב אָשׁוּב אֵלֶיךָ כָּעֵת חַיָּה וְהִנֵּה־בֵן לְשָׂרָה אִשְׁתֶּךָ וְשָׂרָה שֹׁמַעַת פֶּתַח הָאֹהֶל וְהוּא אַחֲרָיו: יא וְאַבְרָהָם וְשָׂרָה זְקֵנִים בָּאִים בַּיָּמִים חָדַל לִהְיוֹת לְשָׂרָה אֹרַח כַּנָּשִׁים: יב וַתִּצְחַק שָׂרָה בְּקִרְבָּהּ לֵאמֹר אַחֲרֵי בְלֹתִי הָיְתָה־לִּי עֶדְנָה וַאדֹנִי זָקֵן: יג וַיֹּאמֶר יי אֶל־אַבְרָהָם לָמָּה זֶּה צָחֲקָה שָׂרָה לֵאמֹר הַאַף אֻמְנָם אֵלֵד וַאֲנִי זָקַנְתִּי: יד הֲיִפָּלֵא מֵיי דָּבָר לַמּוֹעֵד אָשׁוּב אֵלֶיךָ כָּעֵת חַיָּה וּלְשָׂרָה בֵן: טו וַתְּכַחֵשׁ שָׂרָה | לֵאמֹר לֹא צָחַקְתִּי כִּי | יָרֵאָה וַיֹּאמֶר | לֹא כִּי צָחָקְתְּ:

[9] They said to him, "Where is your wife Sarah?" And he replied, "There, in the tent."
[10] Then one said, "I will return to you next year, and your wife Sarah shall have a son!" Sarah was listening at the entrance of the tent, which was behind him.
[11] Now Abraham and Sarah were old, advanced in years; Sarah had stopped having the periods of women.
[12] And Sarah laughed to herself, saying, "Now that I am withered, am I to have enjoyment–with my husband so old?"
[13] Then the Lord said to Abraham, "Why did Sarah laugh, saying, 'Shall I in truth bear a child, old as I am?'

*[14] Is anything too wondrous for the Lord? I will*
*return to you at the time next year, and Sarah*
*shall have a son."*
*[15] Sarah lied, saying, "I did not laugh", for she*
*was frightened. But He replied, "You did laugh."*

At a superficial glance, here is what we see. Sarah demon-strates a lack of faith, not believing in any possibility of a miracle. God faults her for this, but she is unwilling to admit that her faith is deficient.

We should infer from this the importance of believing in the possibility of receiving miracles from the Almighty. Even if Sarah did not consider those guests to be angels, she nonetheless should have felt a desire to see their promises fulfilled, rather than deeming them impossible.

However, as we delve deeper into our analysis of this dia-logue, we will see that it must be understood in an entirely different way.

**[12] Am I to have enjoyment, with my husband so old?** As ordinarily understood, Sarah's words here refer to Abraham. Sarah is saying that bearing a child is not possible, because she and Abraham are both too old. When repeating Sarah's words to Abraham, God paraphrases them "in order to keep the peace" (between husband and wife) – that is, so that Abraham will not feel offended on Sarah's account. How-ever, there are a number of problems with this interpretation.

First, if Sarah is too old to bear children, one good rea-son is sufficient, and adding words about Abraham's old age makes no sense.

Secondly, forty years later, after Sarah dies, Abraham will marry Keturah, who will bear him many children (see 25:1).

It is evident, then, that Abraham's ability to have children is unimpaired.

But something else, too, is unclear. If the words "Sarah laughed to herself" mean that she laughed quietly, and not out loud, then why does God ask Abraham, "Why did Sarah laugh?" If Abraham had not even heard Sarah laughing, how would he be able to explain that laughter? But still more troublesome is God's criticizing of Sarah to Abraham. Could anything constructive have been achieved by that?

Thus, the usual understanding of this passage is firstly inconsistent with the text and secondly depicts Abraham and Sarah's dialogue with God as monstrously primitive, as only a series of petty reproaches and quibbles. This is in no way consistent with the true image of these personalities in the Torah.

Evidently, we must completely revise our understanding of Sarah's words and God's response, by suggesting that Sarah's actual words were "and my Lord is old," referring to God, and not "and my lord is old," referring to Abraham. (There are no uppercase letters in Hebrew.)

In referring to God's "old age," Sarah means that He no longer interferes with the natural flow of events. "Old age" here means the cessation of variability, the loss of dynamism. And this understanding that Sarah has corresponds perfectly to God's answer: Instead of addressing Abraham's purported old age, God says: "Is anything too wondrous for the Lord?"

Moreover, if we understand Sarah to be speaking of God's "old age," her phrasing now becomes much more logical, as if to say: "I have myself already grown old, and God, too, no longer intervenes in the world. Everything that happens now follows the immutable laws of nature. Therefore I cannot give birth."

With that understanding we can grasp the deeper essence

of the problem. Sarah's attribute in relation to Abraham is *gevurah*. And since the desire to observe laws, including the laws of nature, is the most important quality of *gevurah*, Sarah's words very clearly express the essence of these attributes.

Recall that *chesed* is not just kindness, but the desire to change the status quo. And *gevurah*, likewise, is not just justice and law, but the desire to preserve and protect social order. Abraham is *chesed*, and Sarah, as a member of Abraham's family, is "the *gevurah* that is within *chesed*." When they act as a family, Sarah and Abraham together perform *chesed*, influencing others to have faith in the One God, to receive and care for travelers, and so on. But in her relationship with Abraham, Sarah's attribute is *gevurah* within the family.

That is why the laws of nature seem inviolable to Sarah, and why it is difficult for her to accept that God would alter them according to His will. But the Almighty challenges her, saying that even His altering of the laws of nature is entirely within the realm of possibility.

**[14] Is anything too wondrous for the Lord?.** Based on the above interpretation, the answer of God becomes clear. His objective is not to cavil and reproach, but to help Sarah in her spiritual advancement: He seeks to teach Sarah to entertain the possibility of miraculous changes in the world and in life.

Even so, while God addresses both Sarah and Abraham as one, He highlights His appeal to Abraham as an appeal to the attribute of *chesed*.

In response to Sarah's position that "after God created the world and initiated its processes, he will never again alter its natural course," the Almighty expresses his willingness to override the laws of even an already functioning world.

With these words he challenges the concept of the universe to which Sarah has grown accustomed. It is this change in Sarah's consciousness – that is to say, the dynamic development and refinement of the attribute of *gevurah* – that is God's objective in speaking these words, and not merely to make Abraham aware of Sarah's laughter. Sarah's laughter here plays a very essential role.

## 21.11. The Role of Laughter Within a Religious Worldview

What is the meaning of laughter in general? And what is its role within a religious worldview in particular?

We laugh when events or narratives develop unexpectedly, illogically, or unpredictably, but when at the same time we are given the opportunity to see more complex connections between events and phenomena than we had originally supposed. Thus, the essence of laughter is the joy we experience when, by transcending logic and being elevated above it, we manage to perceive a higher level of world harmony. This liberation from the shackles of logic can be found in the surprise punchline of a joke, in a logical paradox, or in the sudden unraveling of a problem that previously had seemed all but intractable.

When we manage to surmount the barriers created by our past limitations and our excessively primitive, logical understanding of how the world works, this is for us a source of great pleasure, and we express our joy with laughter. None of us really loves prescription and logical inevitability. We want to be free, to be liberated from the confines of predestination. Freedom, not compulsion, is a Divine quality, and laughter is a feeling of approaching God, who laughs too, of course. Of God's laughter we read in the Psalms (2:4, 37:13, 104:26), and also quite often in the Talmud and Midrashim.

In other words, laughter is the joy we experience when we overpower *gevurah*. Laughter, then, is Sarah's *sefirah* correction. And as for Isaac, who embodies *gevurah*, even his very name speaks of laughter. ("Isaac" means "he will laugh.")

*Gevurah*, in its essence, always accepts life as it is. It is the belief that God has arranged everything in the best possible way, and that praying for change is therefore completely unnecessary and pointless. Therefore, Sarah cannot believe that God will intervene to change her life. Sarah's main problem – her disbelief in miracles – arises not from a failure to believe in God's omnipotence, but because she does not believe in the need for miracles. Thus, Sarah and Isaac, who both represent *gevurah* – rigidity, law, "correctness" – are tested in situations where the world develops illogically, unpredictably, and unexpectedly. As a person it is good to be "correct," but being *too* correct is ridiculous, because the world itself is not entirely correct, which is what makes it so remarkable.

The subconscious joy of transcending logic – this is Sarah's laughter, but it is at first only "internal." That is, Sarah herself is not aware of it yet. In Sarah, the state of transcending nature is still in progress, and God, speaking clearly to her about her laughter (by calling on Sarah to acknowledge Him) helps her in this advancement. (Note that Abraham, who is *chesed*, does not have this problem; he laughs immediately and openly [Gen 17:17].)

Thus, Sarah's laughter in this situation in no way indicates a disregard for the prophecy she has heard, but her sensing within herself the possibility of a breakthrough. At a conscious level, however, she does not yet believe it, because she knows that physiologically she cannot give birth. Therefore, she is herself unaware of her own subconscious joy – her laughter.

And that is why in all sincerity she denies it: "Sarah lied, saying, 'I did not laugh,' for she was frightened" (18:15). It would be too primitive, of course, to suggest that Sarah simply feared punishment or reprimand for laughing at the words of angels. No, there is something else at work here. Sarah is afraid to admit to *herself* that she had laughed, that she believes in any possibility of an illogical, abnormal procession of events. No less than anyone else, Sarah fears the total collapse of her perceived world order. And so she is afraid to acknowledge her own laugh.

(For a further discussion of Isaac's laughter, see 36.11.)

### 21.12. God Supports Sarah in Her Laughter

As soon as the angel promises Sarah the birth of a son, the soul of Isaac begins to descend into the world. Sarah already feels Isaac being born inside her, but she still feels this only subconsciously, in her deepest essence. A new reality is already entering the world, even if it is not yet a physical one. Sarah already feels this reality, for her subconscious now acknowledges and accepts the unlikely eventuality of motherhood.

Sarah's laughter expresses hope – the first step in accepting the possibility of the unexpected. Therefore, when Sarah is pessimistic about her old age and about the old age of her "master," she laughs at this, but only subconsciously and in her own mind. God does not reproach Sarah for this, however; on the contrary, He explains to her that she needlessly fears her own laughter, because nothing is beyond the Lord's capabilities, including that she can indeed give birth to a son.

God supports Sarah in her laughter and wants her to believe in a new opportunity, to not be afraid to laugh, and to recognize that all of this is nothing out of the ordinary. By virtue of all of that, she will achieve a new level of personal advancement. And that is why God ends the dialogue by telling Sarah, "No, you did laugh!"

In fact, the dialogue continues, but only later, when Sarah calls her son *Yitzchak* ("he will laugh"), saying that "everyone who hears will laugh with me" (21:6).

By calling her son "Isaac," Sarah responds positively to God's words. Besides coming to realize that her laughter was necessary, and that *gevurah* must be restricted, Sarah also invites others to join with her in her laughter. Only by accepting Sarah's laughter as a positive response can we understand the meaning of the name *Yitzchak*. For if God had considered her laughter inappropriate and blamed her for it, surely she would not have named her son *Yitzchak*, "he will laugh."

Just as Abraham's development consists of limiting his own *chesed*, Sarah's development consists of limiting her own *gevurah*. We will continue our discussion of this topic later, in the chapters dealing with Isaac himself.

### 21.13. Abraham Escorts the Angels (18:16)

**טז** וַיָּקֻמוּ מִשָּׁם הָאֲנָשִׁים וַיַּשְׁקִפוּ עַל־פְּנֵי סְדֹם
וְאַבְרָהָם הֹלֵךְ עִמָּם לְשַׁלְּחָם:

*[16] The men set out from there and looked down toward Sodom, Abraham walking with them to see them off.*

**[16] The men ... looked down.** *Lehashkif* means "to look judgmentally" – in this case, with the intention of judging Sodom. This is an expression of the attribute of *gevurah*, judgment. The destruction of Sodom is tightly integrated with the news of Isaac's birth. Precisely because a righteous individual who personifies the attribute of judgment will soon be born, that very attribute is now increasing, congealing – and this means that the time has come for Sodom to stand in judgment.

**Abraham walking with them to see them off.** He accompanies *gevurah*, because he already feels a desire to follow the events unfolding in order to understand the attribute of judgment – how it is implemented, and how to deal with it properly. Abraham is not quite ready to fully accept the attribute of judgment, but he is already moving in that direction.

## 21.14. God Invites Abraham to the Trial of Sodom (18:17-19)

**יז** וַיי אָמָר הַמְכַסֶּה אֲנִי מֵאַבְרָהָם אֲשֶׁר אֲנִי עֹשֶׂה: **יח** וְאַבְרָהָם הָיוֹ יִהְיֶה לְגוֹי גָּדוֹל וְעָצוּם וְנִבְרְכוּ־בוֹ כֹּל גּוֹיֵי הָאָרֶץ: **יט** כִּי יְדַעְתִּיו לְמַעַן אֲשֶׁר יְצַוֶּה אֶת־בָּנָיו וְאֶת־בֵּיתוֹ אַחֲרָיו וְשָׁמְרוּ דֶּרֶךְ יי לַעֲשׂוֹת צְדָקָה וּמִשְׁפָּט לְמַעַן הָבִיא יי עַל־אַבְרָהָם אֵת אֲשֶׁר־דִּבֶּר עָלָיו:

*[17] Now the Lord had said, "Shall I hide from Abraham what I am about to do,*
*[18] since Abraham is to become a great and populous nation and all the nations of the earth are to bless themselves by him?*
*[19] For I have singled him out, that he may*

*instruct his children and his posterity to keep the way of the Lord by doing what is just and right, in order that the Lord may bring about for Abraham what He has promised him."*

Why does God say that He cannot "hide" His plans from Abraham? In what way do the Divine plans regarding Sodom concern Abraham, and what is it that Abraham needs to know about God's plan?

God could have destroyed Sodom without Abraham's knowledge or participation, of course. But God is involving Abraham in the judgment of Sodom as a necessary part of Abraham's education, in order to acquaint him with the attribute of *gevurah*.

## 21.15. Chosenness for a Purpose: The Covenant with Abraham as "the Way of the Lord"

יט כִּי יְדַעְתִּיו לְמַעַן אֲשֶׁר יְצַוֶּה אֶת־בָּנָיו וְאֶת־בֵּיתוֹ אַחֲרָיו וְשָׁמְרוּ דֶּרֶךְ יי לַעֲשׂוֹת צְדָקָה וּמִשְׁפָּט לְמַעַן הָבִיא יי עַל־אַבְרָהָם אֵת אֲשֶׁר־דִּבֶּר עָלָיו:

**[19] For I have singled him out, that he may instruct his children and his posterity to keep the way of the Lord by doing what is just and right.** In this verse, the Almighty explains His reason for choosing Abraham. Let us highlight several of its aspects.

We note first that God chose Abraham not as recompense for something he had already done in the past, but to achieve something new in the future. In other words, Abraham was chosen for mission, not merit. There are many worthy people in this world deserving of a reward, but Abraham's chosen-ness is not a reward – it is the burden and the mission of the Jewish people in relation to the rest of humanity.

Secondly, Abraham is chosen "that he may instruct his children and his posterity." As great as Abraham is, his house-hold and descendants are even more important, because of the nation that they will become, and the direction in which that nation will develop.

Finally, "to keep the way of the Lord" is an incomparably broader concept than mere observance of the command-ments. We have already explored the two stages of God's covenant with the Jewish people:

1. The covenant with Abraham and the other Patriarchs, and
2. The covenant with Moses and the Jewish nation at Sinai.

Although Jewish tradition views these covenants as a sin-gle unit, they are nonetheless very different. God's covenant with Abraham is "the way of the Lord" – the first stage in the development of Judaism, which determines its foundation and establishes its ideals and its general direction. But there are still no formalized commandments. It is only the second stage, the covenant through Moses at Sinai, that includes concrete commandments and instructions.

At the Patriarchs' stage of development a system of com-mandments does not yet exist. It appears only much later, soon after the Exodus from Egypt. It is therefore essential for us to understand that the initial, fundamental stage of Judaism is all about ideals; the commandments are only second in importance to those. If we forget that Judaism is, before anything else, a religion of ideals, and if we perceive it instead as only a system of commandments, we will reduce Judaism to primitivism, rendering it repugnant to both the Jewish people and all of humanity.

## 21.16. The Jewish Ideal: Integration of Mercy and Justice

**[19] To keep the way of the Lord by doing what is just and right.** The "way of the Lord" is a combination of *tzedakah* and *mishpat*, mercy and justice. These correspond to the attributes of *chesed* and *gevurah*, benevolence and law.

The conflict between these ideals must be resolved not by choosing one to the detriment of the other, but by integrating the two. Effecting such a union is extremely difficult, but in Judaism it is the ideal. Moreover, there are no exact instructions for the realization of such a synthesis, nor can there be. Every person, in the multitude of different situations that constantly arise in life, must apply his own moral and religious intuition in order to achieve it.

It is important to note, that unlike the system of commandments, which cannot entertain contradictions (and, if they do occur, they must be resolved through legislative action), a system of ideals not only can, but inevitably will, entail contradictions and inconsistencies. We will give this issue more detailed coverage in its own portion.

## 21.17. Sodom's Perverted Justice

The Midrash describes Sodom as a city-state where the rule of law is acknowledged supreme. But it is a law that perverts justice and flouts mercy. Everyone gets exactly what he deserves. If one is rich, it means that he is worthy, and has every right to oppress anyone less fortunate. The latter's poverty shows that he is not deserving of wealth, and that he has only himself to blame for that.

Consider this example. The people of Sodom organized a "herd cooperative," to relieve each individual cattle owner of the trouble of constantly feeding his own animals. But at the same time, any owner of just one cow was considered "insufficiently invested" in the cooperative, and was therefore required to contribute two days of work for every day of work required of an owner of two cows.

The people of Sodom also passed a law that prohibited giving alms to the poor who came to the city; the intent was to prevent the poor from coming to Sodom and disquieting its inhabitants. For Sodom was a wealthy city, and had no use for beggars from the countryside.

However, in order to create the appearance of being charitable, and to avoid being disparaged in the eyes of neighboring cities, the Sodomites enacted that every citizen would receive a bogus coin inscribed with his own name. Only these coins and no others could be given to the poor. Thus, when a scrounger begged for help in the Sodom town square, coins were hurled at him from every direction – but these coins were worthless for purchasing anything at all. The poor man would die of starvation even while surrounded by all of that "money," after which the Sodomites would just take back their coins and get on with their lives.

If one person struck another in Sodom, the victim was ordered to pay the offender "the going rate of a bloodletting." Eliezer, Abraham's servant, was walking one day in Sodom and was attacked by a local resident. When Eliezer apprehended the culprit and dragged him to court, the judge ordered Eliezer to pay the offender "for his professional bloodletting services." Eliezer then beat the judge and told him, "Now you can just pay him the money that you owe me."

And yet another story: A traveler passing through Sodom rented a room for the night. Fearing thieves as he had no security protection of his own, the man entrusted to the inn-keeper for safekeeping an expensive carpet from among his belongings before turning in for the night. When he came to claim his carpet in the morning, the innkeeper informed him that he knew nothing about a carpet, nor had he received anything for safekeeping. Said the traveler, "Well, of course there was a carpet! It is multicolored, with tassels." And the innkeeper answered, "Heave-ho with your multicolors, and with your tassels I wish you only the best. Is it not enough for you that I have interpreted your dream? Begone!" The traveler dragged the owner to the judge, who ruled, "This man is a respected citizen of Sodom, and you are nobody. Pay your host for deciphering your dream, and be on your way!"

Any visitor to Sodom seeking overnight lodging would be given the "standard-issue, one-size-fits-all" Sodom bed. If he was too tall for the bed, they would amputate his legs; if too short, they would stretch him on the rack. But come now – how could any traveler dare to be anything but an exact fit for those magnificent, even "ideal" Sodom beds! Such arrogance on the part of a traveler required that he be subjected to the proper Sodom "correction."

Thus, the Midrash presents Sodom as a place of law and order, but where those "laws" are so horrific that they are nothing less than actual crimes. But much worse than merely breaking the law is committing crimes in the name of the "law." For as long as people have normal laws and a posi-tive moral attitude, even if they violate those laws, they can still mend their ways when their conscience awakens and gets the better of them. But once they have enshrined their crimes as law in a grotesque legislative system, and they now accept that as normal behavior, they are already beyond all hope of ever repenting.

Sodom, by its very existence, is destroying the world. The Almighty therefore decides to obliterate Sodom.

## 21.18. The Trials of Sodom, Lot, and Abraham (18:20-22)

כ וַיֹּאמֶר יי זַעֲקַת סְדֹם וַעֲמֹרָה כִּי־רָבָּה וְחַטָּאתָם
כִּי כָבְדָה מְאֹד: **כא** אֵרְדָה־נָּא וְאֶרְאֶה הַכְּצַעֲקָתָהּ
הַבָּאָה אֵלַי עָשׂוּ | כָּלָה וְאִם־לֹא אֵדָעָה: **כב** וַיִּפְנוּ מִשָּׁם
הָאֲנָשִׁים וַיֵּלְכוּ סְדֹמָה וְאַבְרָהָם עוֹדֶנּוּ עֹמֵד לִפְנֵי יי:

*[20] Then the Lord said, "The outrage of Sodom and Gomorrah is so great, and their sin so grave! [21] I will go down to see whether they have acted altogether according to the outcry that has reached Me; if not, I will take note." [22] The men went on from there to Sodom, while Abraham remained standing before the Lord.*

**[20] Then the Lord said, "The outrage of Sodom and Gomorrah is so great, and their sin so grave!.** These are God's words to Abraham, informing him of the necessity of bringing Sodom to judgment.

**[21] I will go down to see.** God "goes down" to Sodom. Specifically, He sends angels to perform a final check, to ascertain whether the time has come to destroy the city or perhaps not yet. God invites Abraham to "go down to see" with Him, for the purpose of bringing Sodom to judgment. In other words, the entire situation is meant to serve as a lesson and a test not only for Sodom and for Lot, but for Abraham as well.

**[22] The men went on from there to Sodom, while Abraham remained standing before the Lord.** Abraham accepts the challenge. But while the angels are already on their way to Sodom, Abraham is still "standing before the Lord." Rather than departing, he is preparing to argue. God provokes Abraham to argue with Him, to object and to be combative, because each of us, in order to advance in our understanding, must learn to think independently, to formulate our thoughts and to defend our point of view. Disputing with God, struggling with God, is the most important feature of the Jewish spiritual paradigm.

**[21] Whether they have acted altogether according to the outcry that has reached Me.** An alternate translation is, "If they have acted according to the outcry that has reached Me, then this is their end." In order to teach Abraham this lesson, and to move him toward accepting the integration of mercy and justice, the Almighty puts him in a situation where he must raise an immediate objection. To that end, God tells Abraham that the final decision on Sodom must be made forthwith.

**If not, I will take note.** Sodom's main test is Lot, who, as the Midrash informs us, had been appointed a municipal judge there.

Not by mere chance had Sodom become a prosperous and affluent city. There are also positive elements in its culture: its inhabitants want to be a legitimate society

and live in a city with a well-organized and highly developed infrastructure. Yet, Sodom is so morally corrupt that
even positive ideas are thoroughly perverted there. And
yet, the people of Sodom are not completely hopeless.
Having appointed a person of Lot's caliber as their judge,
the Sodomites now have the opportunity to effect positive
change. Lot's appointment as judge in Sodom is the city's
final chance to change and be saved.

This situation is of course a test also for Lot himself. Which
path will he choose – Sodom's "justice" or Abraham's mercy?

Thus, all are being tested here – Abraham, Lot, and the
people of Sodom. These tests provide an opportunity for
advancement and improvement, but they might just as easily
bring death in their wake. Ultimately Sodom will completely
fail its tests and be destroyed. Lot passes his tests relatively
speaking, albeit not completely. But Abraham, thanks to his
tests, has now achieved significant spiritual advancement.

### 21.19. The Destruction of Sodom and Purification of the Gevurah Attribute

We have already noted the connection between the
destruction of Sodom and the birth of Isaac. Outwardly, this
connection is expressed in the fact that as Isaac prepares to
descend into the world, the attribute of *gevurah* is increasing
in the universe. As a result, the Almighty destroys Sodom,
summoning Abraham to the trial of that perverted city, so
that Abraham can learn to integrate mercy and judgment.
But there is yet another connection. Before Isaac could be
born, a certain purification of the quality of *gevurah* had
to occur, and that happened when Sodom was destroyed.

As noted earlier, the main sin of Sodom was not sexual

perversion, for that was only one of its external manifestations. Sodom's primary characteristic was the law "going
wild" – *gevurah* "busting out." The people of Sodom
approached human existence with all the severity of a strict
legal code. Every person must earn his living; anyone who
is poor – and all the more so, who goes begging – is a par-
asite who doesn't deserve to live. In Sodom's estimation,
God did not create people to go begging, for that is unworthy human behavior. "We live in this fertile valley," the Sodomites used to say, "having earned the good life by the toil
of our own hands. Now some needy bastards show up, and
we are expected to corrupt the world by supporting them?!"

For those same reasons the Sodomites outlawed all hospitality and mercy. Really now, if God has made a person poor, or
sick and unable to afford treatment, then evidently this is the
will of God; what right do we have to help such a person and
interfere with the Divine will? Let every person earn his own
living, support himself, heal himself, and take care of himself.

Note that although there is some element of truth in
these arguments, they are on the whole quite appalling. We
cannot know what God really wants for the poor – that they
should remain poor, or that we should help them. Nor do we
know whether God wants the sick to remain so, or rather to
be cured, and He has just for that reason given the doctor
the expertise and opportunity to heal.

If by his own choice a person does not wish to earn a living and to take care of himself, then, of course, outside help
is of no benefit to him, and will only corrupt him. But on the
other hand, a great many people find themselves in serious
predicaments due only to external circumstances. Our help
can allow them to get back on their feet.

Indeed, unbounded *chesed* corrupts and can even destroy the
world. But unmitigated *gevurah* is even worse. If no one receives

sustenance beyond what he himself earns, then the world – and any such society in particular – has no right to exist. For even our ability to earn our keep and feed ourselves is Divine *chesed*, and if we will not show mercy to our neighbor, then we ourselves deserve no mercy from God. No one can survive in a world that operates solely on the attribute of judgment.

Isaac, who is *gevurah*, exists only because he is the son of Abraham, who is *chesed*. Yes, a person must of course earn his own bread, but we must also help him in that undertaking. Better than giving him money outright, we should help him build for himself a means to a livelihood, so that our initial jumpstart will enable him eventually to provide for himself.

*Gevurah* – as the realization that a person must earn a living on his own – is a necessary quality. But it is needed precisely to emphasize God's kindness and mercy, which are so great that God not only feeds us, but also gives us the opportunity to support ourselves and to thereby feel the dignity of being the sources of our own livelihood. This is the path of the unity of *chesed* and *gevurah*.

*Gevurah* is positive as an adjunct to *chesed*, but in isolation it only leads to death. Likewise, *chesed* that overruns its boundaries turns into debauchery; this is what led to the Flood. An overabundance of *gevurah* makes the very existence of human society impossible.

Thus, the imminent birth of Isaac as a carrier of proper *gevurah* requires that Sodom's perverted *gevurah* be eliminated from the world.


## 21.20. Abraham Argues with God (18:23-25)

**כג** וַיִּגַּשׁ אַבְרָהָם וַיֹּאמַר הַאַף תִּסְפֶּה צַדִּיק עִם־רָשָׁע: **כד** אוּלַי יֵשׁ חֲמִשִּׁים צַדִּיקִם בְּתוֹךְ הָעִיר הַאַף תִּסְפֶּה וְלֹא־

תִּשָּׂא לַמָּקוֹם לְמַעַן חֲמִשִּׁים הַצַּדִּיקִם אֲשֶׁר בְּקִרְבָּהּ: **כה** חָלִלָה לְּךָ מֵעֲשֹׂת | כַּדָּבָר הַזֶּה לְהָמִית צַדִּיק עִם־רָשָׁע וְהָיָה כַצַּדִּיק כָּרָשָׁע חָלִלָה לָּךְ הֲשֹׁפֵט כָּל־הָאָרֶץ לֹא יַעֲשֶׂה מִשְׁפָּט:

*[23] Abraham came forward and said, "Will You sweep away the innocent along with the guilty? [24] What if there should be fifty innocent within the city; will You then wipe out the place and not forgive it for the sake of the innocent fifty who are in it?*

*[25] Far be it from You to do such a thing, to bring death upon the innocent as well as the guilty, so that innocent and guilty fare alike. Far be it from You! Shall not the Judge of all the earth deal justly?"*

**[23] Abraham came forward and said.** When entering into a dispute with God, Abraham moves in closer to God, rather than distancing himself from Him. Discussion of the justice or injustice of the Almighty's actions will be constructive if a person asks questions in order to strengthen his connection with God, and not as an excuse for breaking that connection. The latter is what happens when a person says: "How could God allow such a thing? I reject any notion of faith."

**Will You sweep away the innocent along with the guilty?.** Sodom is the very embodiment of disdain for all people, of being inhospitable and inconsiderate of one's fellow man. The Sodomites are thus Abraham's antithesis in every sense. Abraham's coming to their defense is therefore quite unexpected.

**[25] Far be it from You to do such a thing ... Far be it from You!.** The word *chalilah* is used twice here. It means "unacceptable" or "unworthy," and is a very harsh term (as seen, for example, in the expression *chillul ha-shem*, desecration of God's name). Such powerful words cannot be called a mere "plea for mercy"; Abraham is making a serious accusation here. And so we must understand: What makes Abraham so sure of himself, to believe that his own position is correct and good? How does he even dare speak out against what God has said and has decided to do? Is such behavior at all acceptable?

For many religious people any "disputation with God" is completely unimaginable, and the idea of challenging a Divine decision is nothing less than monstrous. It seems to them that since man's relationship with God is built entirely on divine grace, and everything received from God is only a gift and an expression of His mercy, for no person on his own merits is deserving of anything at all – so given that, no argumentation is ever possible, because we know that we must "never look a gift horse in the mouth."

The Jewish concept is rather different, however. Judaism maintains that it is not only possible, but even *necessary*, to argue with God. Abraham and Moses argued with the Almighty; Jacob even received his second name, "Israel," for just such a dispute. That name, which is also the name of the entire Jewish people, means, literally, "the one who does battle with God." Such disputation with the Almighty is perceived as the normal process of establishing a dialogue with God and approaching Him; in no way is it seen as rebellion against God.

The Jewish approach recognizes, of course, that "whatever God does is always for the best," but it also legitimizes disagreeing with God and engaging in disputation with

Him. Moreover, Judaism believes that the Almighty Himself encourages us to have just this type of relationship with Him. The Talmudic account of one such "dispute with God" ends with God remarking with a satisfied smile, "My children have defeated Me."

Note that our relationship with our children and with other people will usually very closely parallel our approach to our relationship with God. For example, if we believe that all God does is give orders to people that they cannot possibly understand and are forbidden to debate, and that our only business is to be submissive and obedient, then we, too, will be inclined to give orders to others and dictate our will to them. And likewise, if we go on the premise that "God is love" and that God's attitude toward mankind is exclusively one of unearned mercy, then the main thing that is expected from us as God's children will be love and obedience, and submission will be the central value.

The Jewish approach, however, sees the world differently. Of course, God wants from us both love and compliance, and sometimes also submission. But above all and most importantly, He wants us to grow up. From God's point of view, the objective of His engaging in dialogue with humans is not that we will agree with God and abandon our own position, but, rather, that we will become capable of engaging in dialogue and skilled at being opponents. In order to be able to argue and have the courage to disagree, an opponent must be independent and self-sufficient.

In the same way, in order to rise to the level of dialogue with the Almighty, and to the level of collaboration in running the world, we must not merely love and agree with Him. Rather, we must argue and defend our point of view sometimes, which requires that we be able to think critically. It is not by chance that the Jews, who since ancient times argued with the Almighty, became accustomed to thinking critically also about themselves and everyone else with whom they came in contact. The desire to debate and to disagree thus became characteristically national Jewish traits.

## 21.21. The Divinity Within Us as Justification for Arguing with God

But how does Abraham justify arguing with God and telling him, "It is unacceptable for You to do such and such"? That is, what is the religious and moral foundation for the arguments he wishes to advance? Is God not the ultimate source of morality, kindness, and justice? How then does Abraham undertake to determine for himself what is right and proper and what is not, what is good and what is evil? If this is merely Abraham's personal opinion, how can it possibly compete with God's word?

Abraham's justification for arguing with God, it would seem, is yet another form of Divinity – that Divinity that is within himself. To argue with Divinity, one must juxtapose it with yet another Divinity. And since man is created "in the image and likeness of God," God is to us not just an "external" reality; He is also "within us." In this sense, Adam, Abraham, and each of us possesses "godly" in us.

It is the Divine spark within us that allows us to disagree with God. In other words, it is a dispute between two kinds of Divinity: "transcendental Divinity," the manifestation of God that addresses us from outside (for Abraham these are the words of God as revealed to him in a vision, but for us today it is the Divine tradition that has come down to us from Sinai), and immanent Divinity, the manifestation of the Divine spark in the ethical sensibility that is within each of us. The conflict between these two manifestations of Divinity: moral and ethical awareness, that is, immanent Divinity, and halachic teachings and traditions, which is transcendental Divinity, has been the most significant impetus for the development of Judaism in all ages of its existence.

## 21.22. Abraham's Chesed and the Salvation of the Wicked

Abraham's fundamental position in his dispute with God is that strictly applying the attribute of judgment is impossible, because any such attempt will lead to injustice. And how can the Judge of all the land, Who Himself *is* that very attribute of justice, fail to do justice? That is, how can God allow innocent people to be punished?

Abraham does not ask God to pardon the people of Sodom; rather, he formulates his arguments in terms of justice. But in essence he does not speak of justice. What do we mean by that?

Justice would require that the righteous be rewarded and the wicked punished. In this case, that could be accomplished by removing the righteous from the city, and then destroying the wicked. But Abraham completely ignores this option for saving the righteous. Instead he insists that for those fifty (or forty-five, forty, thirty, twenty, or ten) righteous individuals the entire city should be spared. In other words, Abraham's goal is not merely to save the righteous and achieve justice. His goal is to save everyone, including the wicked. He wants *chesed* – universal grace, mercy – and he uses the presence of the righteous as an argument to save the wicked!

Nor does Abraham ask God to wait and see whether the

wicked might repent. Had he wanted to wait for the repentance of the wicked, he would have said: "Do not destroy the city now, give them some time ..." But Abraham takes a different position.

The Midrash puts into Abraham's mouth the following words: "If it is Judgment that You want, then the world cannot exist (i.e., the world will be destroyed). If you want the world to continue to exist, then do not apply the attribute of judgment." Seen this way, there is no place for the attribute of judgment in the world at all. For no matter how carefully the destruction of evil is carried out, something good will also perish in the process. Consequently, evil cannot not be destroyed.

Abraham represents here a position that is in fact quite far from the ethics of Judaism. He says to God as follows: "Because it is Your essence always to give, and You Yourself created people with the freedom to choose to be wicked, You must bear responsibility for what You have created, and You must not destroy them."

Abraham is still absolutely unprepared for the idea of integrating mercy and justice. He still feels that the two are too different to allow their unification. Moreover, the establishment of justice would be an unworthy affair, because the righteous would perish with the sinners.

In our own time, people with such views oppose having any real battles with terrorist organizations, because of the possibility that innocent people will suffer. A balanced Jewish view (that of Abraham, Isaac, and Jacob) understands that any such approach is incorrect, and will lead to the destruction of the world. But Abraham, who is pure *chesed*, represents the Jewish path only in its incipient stages. In the future, that path will need to be supplemented and counterbalanced by Isaac and Jacob.

## 21.23. Sodom as Abraham's Spiritual Failure

There is another important motivation behind Abraham's defense of Sodom that is not quite obvious from reading the text.

Sodom is Abraham's exact opposite – his antipode. If Abraham receives guests and is benevolent to all, then Sodom, on the contrary, refuses to receive guests and is unfriendly to all. Abraham strives for kindness; Sodom forbids any show of kindness.

But even so, Abraham has a very long history of relationships with Sodom: Lot's settlement there, and the war of the kings, which included the king of Sodom and from which Abraham emerged victorious. Later, Ruth and Naamah, descendants of Moab and Ammon who are born to Lot by his daughters, will join this long-standing relationship through their role in establishing the royal house of David, from which the Messiah himself will later descend. And that means that he, too, must be born with the sparks of Sodom incorporated within him.

There is another reason that Abraham intercedes on Sodom's behalf: he feels that he is himself to blame for Sodom's impending destruction. We noted after Abraham's victory in the the war of the kings that he could have leveraged that victory to become the ruler of Sodom, and to rebuild the life of that city. But Abraham had no interest in wielding such authority; he wanted to bring people to God and to a just life only by their free choice. And this is now the result.

At the conclusion of the war of the kings, the king of Sodom proposed to Abraham (14:21): "Give me the persons, and take the possessions for yourself." That means that in the given situation, deciding the Sodomites' fate was entirely Abraham's prerogative. He could have forced the king of

Sodom to obey, and thus he could have established just laws in the city. But Abraham did nothing of the kind, because he was loathe to use power, *gevurah*.

And now Sodom is condemned to annihilation, the cause of which was, *inter alia*, Abraham's inaction. Sodom's punishment is a reproach to Abraham. Therefore now, when God is about to destroy Sodom, He summons Abraham, as it were, to the sentencing, as if to say, "Look what you have done; observe the consequences of your actions." When Abraham, in turn, argues and negotiates with God over the number of righteous people in the city, he is motivated not only by *chesed*, but also by his own personal involvement in the impending catastrophe.

The downfall of Sodom is in many ways a personal tragedy for Abraham.

## 21.24. The Responsibility of the Righteous for the Misfortunes of Their Generation

A righteous person is called to account not only for himself, but also for the people of his immediate circle.

There is a big difference between being "righteous" and being merely "not wicked." A non-wicked person is simply someone who does not commit crimes. But being righteous is a completely different category. The job of the righteous is to improve and rehabilitate others. If others behave in an unworthy manner, it means that the righteous man is falling short of his own obligations.

However, teaching is only one aspect of the responsibility that a righteous person bears for his generation. Another aspect of the guilt of the righteous in the misfortunes of their generation is that the attribute of *gevurah* intensifies because of them, even if they have no actual intent that this should happen.

Rabbi Pinchas of Korets in his book *Midrash Pinchas* writes: "Why must the righteous in every generation pray for the entire generation? Because they are complicit in the calamities that befall other people."

The mere existence of a righteous person in the world is a condemnation of the wicked. No one before Noah was described as being righteous. But as soon as Noah appeared, a flood engulfed the earth. When the righteous Abraham arrives on the scene, disaster strikes Sodom and Gomorrah. The mere appearance of the righteous, the fact that he has managed to achieve a level that others could not, is a condemnation of those around him. A righteous person must therefore exercise great care to assure that his righteousness does not bring judgment on others, because he will then be held accountable in part for their punishment. Righteousness should be uplifting. One must strive to bring people to repentance, but this should not be done in a manner that highlights their sins or shortcomings.

### 21.25. A Righteous Individual Within the city (18:26)

**כו** וַיֹּאמֶר יי אִם־אֶמְצָא בִסְדֹם חֲמִשִּׁים צַדִּיקִם בְּתוֹךְ הָעִיר וְנָשָׂאתִי לְכָל־הַמָּקוֹם בַּעֲבוּרָם:

*[26] And the Lord answered, "If I find within the city of Sodom fifty innocent ones, I will forgive the whole place for their sake."*

**[26] I will forgive the whole place for their sake.** God

unexpectedly acknowledges that Abraham is right, and says that He is willing to change His decision, but only subject to certain conditions.

Abraham asks God to save the entire city for the sake of any righteous persons who live there. It is not enough that the righteous will themselves be saved; their presence must save the whole city. The Almighty, responding to Abraham, generally agrees with this principle, but significantly refines it, emphasizing two important points as follows.

**Fifty innocent ones.** First, the city cannot be saved by a single righteous person, but only by a community, a group. Indeed, if there are fifty righteous people in a city of villains, this means that the citizens on the whole are not all that wicked; for if they were truly wicked, they would have killed off the righteous. And this means that there is still hope that the city can be reformed. Moreover, even while the Almighty makes concessions to Abraham, in order for the city to be saved He requires the presence of at least ten righteous individuals, since this is the minimum number necessary to form a community.

**If I find within the city of Sodom.** Secondly, that community of righteous individuals must be "within the city," that is, they must be officially recognized by the city's other inhabitants. The righteous who simply exist in their own little corner, doing no harm to others, but also going unnoticed by anyone else, cannot save the city. Rather, those righteous must form a kind of social stratum, however minimal, but noticeable within the city, and the other residents must allow them to exist openly and unharmed.

After all, the idea that the righteous can save not only themselves, but the entire city, is predicated on the hope that the righteous will reform the wicked. And that is possible only if the righteous have been given the opportunity to influence the city. If there is no social stratum of righteous people, or if the inhabitants suppress or expel their righteous neighbors, then in a crisis situation there is no one who can save that city.

## 21.26. Reducing the Required Minimum of Righteous (18:27-33)

**כז** וַיַּעַן אַבְרָהָם וַיֹּאמַר הִנֵּה־נָא הוֹאַלְתִּי לְדַבֵּר אֶל־
אֲדֹנָי וְאָנֹכִי עָפָר וָאֵפֶר: **כח** אוּלַי יַחְסְרוּן חֲמִשִּׁים
הַצַּדִּיקִם חֲמִשָּׁה הֲתַשְׁחִית בַּחֲמִשָּׁה אֶת־כָּל־הָעִיר
וַיֹּאמֶר לֹא אַשְׁחִית אִם־אֶמְצָא שָׁם אַרְבָּעִים וַחֲמִשָּׁה:
**כט** וַיֹּסֶף עוֹד לְדַבֵּר אֵלָיו וַיֹּאמַר אוּלַי יִמָּצְאוּן שָׁם
אַרְבָּעִים וַיֹּאמֶר לֹא אֶעֱשֶׂה בַּעֲבוּר הָאַרְבָּעִים: **ל** וַיֹּאמֶר
אַל־נָא יִחַר לַאדֹנָי וַאֲדַבֵּרָה אוּלַי יִמָּצְאוּן שָׁם שְׁלֹשִׁים
וַיֹּאמֶר לֹא אֶעֱשֶׂה אִם־אֶמְצָא שָׁם שְׁלֹשִׁים: **לא** וַיֹּאמֶר
הִנֵּה־נָא הוֹאַלְתִּי לְדַבֵּר אֶל־אֲדֹנָי אוּלַי יִמָּצְאוּן שָׁם
עֶשְׂרִים וַיֹּאמֶר לֹא אַשְׁחִית בַּעֲבוּר הָעֶשְׂרִים: **לב** וַיֹּאמֶר
אַל־נָא יִחַר לַאדֹנָי וַאֲדַבְּרָה אַךְ־הַפַּעַם אוּלַי יִמָּצְאוּן
שָׁם עֲשָׂרָה וַיֹּאמֶר לֹא אַשְׁחִית בַּעֲבוּר הָעֲשָׂרָה: **לג** וַיֵּלֶךְ
יְיָ כַּאֲשֶׁר כִּלָּה לְדַבֵּר אֶל־אַבְרָהָם וְאַבְרָהָם שָׁב לִמְקֹמוֹ:

*[27] Abraham spoke up, saying, "Here I venture to speak to my Lord, I who am but dust and ashes:*
*[28] What if the fifty innocent should lack five? Will You destroy the whole city for want of the five?" And He answered, "I will not destroy if I find forty-five there."*
*[29] But he spoke to Him again, and said,*

*"What if forty should be found there?" And He answered, "I will not do it, for the sake of the forty."*

*[30] And he said, "Let not my Lord be angry if I go on: What if thirty should be found there?" And He answered, "I will not do it if I find thirty there."*

*[31] And he said, "I venture again to speak to my Lord: What if twenty should be found there?" And He answered, "I will not destroy, for the sake of the twenty."*

*[32] And he said, "Let not my Lord be angry if I speak but this last time: What if ten should be found there?" And He answered, "I will not destroy, for the sake of the ten."*

*[33] When the Lord had finished speaking to Abraham, He departed; and Abraham returned to his place.*

**[27] Here I venture to speak to my Lord, I who am but dust and ashes ... [30] Let not my Lord be angry.** Abraham maintains distance and reverence, but remains adamant.

**[28] What if the fifty innocent should lack five?**: Rather than asking God, "Why would you not have mercy on forty-five?", Abraham formulates the question more pointedly: "Would you really destroy the whole city for the lack of a mere five righteous individuals?"

**And He answered, "I will not destroy if I find forty-five there."** Despite Abraham's increasing demands, God continues to engage with him in dialogue, reinforcing his resolve to argue with God.

**[33] When the Lord had finished speaking to Abraham, He departed.** It is not Abraham who stops talking, but God Who interrupts the conversation with Abraham and withdraws from him. Like the conversation as a whole, this withdrawal should be understood as a means employed by the Almighty to educate Abraham. To destroy Sodom, God obviously did not require Abraham's sanction. He only wanted Abraham to understand that there are limits, beyond which the wicked must be judged and destroyed.

**And Abraham returned to his place.** He now returned to the same place where he had been earlier. Abraham did not agree with God's position, for he was not willing to recognize that there is a place in the world for the attribute of strict judgment. Only later, by virtue of his dialogue with Isaac, did Abraham grasp the meaning of the attribute of *gevurah*. Thus, by inviting Abraham to debate the fate of Sodom, the Almighty is preparing Abraham for the birth of Isaac and for further advancement toward *gevurah*.

As a result of this lengthy process, although Abraham remains, as ever, a champion of *chesed*, he does gradually desist from his "*chesed* fanaticism" – an important stage in correcting the attribute of *chesed* in the soul of the Jewish people. In our own lives too, it is important that we support love and peace, but being fanatical about either of those is destructive.

# Chapter 22

# The Destruction of Sodom and the Incident of Lot's Daughters

## 22.1. Lot as Judge of Sodom (19:1)

אֲ וַיָּבֹאוּ שְׁנֵי הַמַּלְאָכִים סְדֹמָה בָּעֶרֶב וְלוֹט יֹשֵׁב בְּשַׁעַר־
סְדֹם וַיַּרְא־לוֹט וַיָּקָם לִקְרָאתָם וַיִּשְׁתַּחוּ אַפַּיִם אָרְצָה:

*[1] The two angels arrived in Sodom in the evening, as Lot was sitting in the gate of Sodom. When Lot saw them, he rose to greet them and, bowing low with his face to the ground,*

The fact that Sodom is ripe for destruction means that the spark contained within Sodom is ripe for release. It is time to conduct the trial, to separate the positive spark from the collective evil of Sodom. For we know that the very concept of "judgment", *gevurah*, is associated with distinguishing and separating.

**[1] The two angels arrived in Sodom in the evening.** One of the functions of an angel is to perform verification, but at the same time to serve as an ordeal – a person's "training ground." An encounter with an angel is a challenge sent to test one's internal constitution. In the process of conversing with the angels, Abraham and Sarah were raised to a higher level. Lot, too, in meeting with the angels passes his test, albeit with difficulty. But as for Sodom – it will be their utter downfall.

**He rose to greet them and, bowing low with his face to the ground.** Unlike Abraham, who ran towards the angels, Lot merely rises and bows to them. Abraham actively strives toward union and synthesis, for he is in a state of constant development. But Lot is spiritually static; he does not thirst for inner development, but reacts only when under pressure from the outside (by the angels, his daughters, and so on). He therefore pays a steep price for his advancement.

**Lot was sitting in the gate of Sodom.** In biblical texts, "sitting at the gate" usually means "judging" – serving in the capacity of a judge. Here, the word *yoshev,* "sitting," is written without the letter vav, which the Midrash therefore understands as *yashav,* the perfect past tense of that verb. That is, only very recently had Lot "sat down at the gates of Sodom" as judge.

It seems that after Abraham's war with the kings, Lot became a man of note – "internationally renowned." The Sodomites, wanting to create a positive image for themselves, formally appointed Lot to one of the city's prominent judicial posts. Lot was hoping that he could revamp the legal system and rehabilitate Sodom. Even when besieged by the city's inhabitants, Lot probably believed that since he now enjoyed such an exalted status, he would be obeyed, but the people of Sodom, of course, had in mind no such thing, and only mocked him, saying, "The fellow came here as an alien, and already he is acting like a judge" (19:9).

The trial of Sodom takes place in Lot's house, who was not only a judge as an honorary title, but a real judge of Sodom in all respects. In Sodom, Lot is a righteous man (against his background the sin of Sodom is much more apparent), and at the same time its judge. Sodom is therefore condemned to destruction as a result of Lot's presence there. The Sodomites considered Lot's appointment as judge a mere formality. But from the Almighty's point of view, Lot had been "appointed" a true judge in Sodom. Thus, it was the events involving Lot that finally sealed the fate of the city.

In a certain sense, every Sodom has its Lot, who determines its fate. Of course, every Sodom is also in conflict with its Lot, but so long as the residents cooperate with him and at least minimally obey him, Sodom lives on. But when Sodom revolts against Lot, this becomes the deciding factor in their imminent destruction.

## 22.2. Conscience and Legislation (19:2-3)

ב וַיֹּאמֶר הִנֶּה נָּא־אֲדֹנַי סוּרוּ נָא אֶל־בֵּית עַבְדְּכֶם וְלִינוּ
וְרַחֲצוּ רַגְלֵיכֶם וְהִשְׁכַּמְתֶּם וַהֲלַכְתֶּם לְדַרְכְּכֶם וַיֹּאמְרוּ
לֹא כִּי בָרְחוֹב נָלִין: ג וַיִּפְצַר־בָּם מְאֹד וַיָּסֻרוּ אֵלָיו וַיָּבֹאוּ
אֶל־בֵּיתוֹ וַיַּעַשׂ לָהֶם מִשְׁתֶּה וּמַצּוֹת אָפָה וַיֹּאכֵלוּ:

*[2] He said, "Please, my lords, turn aside to your servant's house to spend the night, and bathe your feet; then you may be on your way early."*

*But they said, "No, we will spend the night in the square."*

*[3] But he urged them strongly, so they turned his way and entered his house. He prepared a feast for them and baked unleavened bread, and they ate.*

**[2] Turn aside to your servant's house to spend the night ... [3] But he urged them strongly.** Lot, in violation of the laws of Sodom, urges travelers to not spend the night on the street. At the same time, the Midrash notes that the meaning of the phrase "turn aside to your servant's house" is not, simply "enter" but "go in a roundabout way." Lot, as it were, is saying to his guests, "I will only tell you where my house is. And you see to it that somehow, through the back alleyways, you will get to me."

When Lot sees that the travelers have nowhere to go, he invites them to stay with him, for hospitality is one of the central religious values of Abraham's family. God is testing Lot, as a judge in Sodom, for his readiness to put morality above state law. His moral choice becomes his decisive spiritual achievement, although Lot takes precautions while exercising that choice.

We mentioned earlier that Lot contains within himself the attribute of *malchut*, "kingdom." Everything that pertains to the functioning of the state and, in particular, strict compliance with the law, is critical to this attribute. We have also noted that the tests of the Patriarchs are associated with the "limiting and faceting" of their inherent attributes. The tests of Abraham, who is *chesed*, teach him that *chesed* must sometimes be withheld. Isaac is *gevurah*, and his tests consist in limiting *gevurah*. And likewise Lot, as a representative of the *malchut* attribute, which incorporates duty, order, and execution of the law of the state, must come to understand that those laws are not to be implemented at all costs, that principles of morality must be held above state law.

## 22.3. Lot – Righteous by Sodom Standards

Lot, though in many ways duplicating the actions of Abraham, carries them out at a lower level. Abraham runs to meet the guests; Lot only rises and bows. Abraham gives the guests "curds and milk and the calf he had prepared"; Lot only bakes unleavened bread for them. Lot has to "urge the travelers strongly" to enter his house; Abraham, who radiates hospitality, does not need to importune them to enter. It is true that Abraham has complete freedom to receive travelers, while Lot risks many an unpleasantness by doing so. But those are conditions that Lot has chosen for himself, by deciding to settle in Sodom.

Lot is righteous by Sodomite standards. He does not wish to live near Abraham, because that would create demands on him that he would be unable to meet. In Sodom he feels more comfortable.

Lot has moral principles, but he is not steadfast in them. He is righteous, but "spineless." He wants to be good, but he lacks the resolve to achieve it. Once inside the world of Sodom, Lot falls under its influence, as evidenced in particular by his proposal to share his daughters with the Sodomites.

Lot's position is ambiguous. On the one hand, he personally wants to do good. But on the other hand, he is a "conductor" of evil, because once he becomes a judge in Sodom, he is an instrument for implementing their laws.

Lot, as it were, is an exemplar of "semi-Jewishness", a prototype of those many Jews who by fate depart from the Jewish people, having decided to integrate into the surrounding non-Jewish space. Lot is talented, and finding himself in Sodom, he occupies a high position there. But in the end, his Jewish character leads to conflict with Sodom and to the disintegration of his original hopes.

## 22.4. The Inhabitants of Sodom Against Lot (19:4-11)

ג וַיִּפְצְרוּ־בָם מְאֹד וַיָּסֻרוּ אֵלָיו וַיָּבֹאוּ אֶל־בֵּיתוֹ וַיַּעַשׂ לָהֶם מִשְׁתֶּה וּמַצּוֹת אָפָה וַיֹּאכֵלוּ: ד טֶרֶם יִשְׁכָּבוּ וְאַנְשֵׁי הָעִיר אַנְשֵׁי סְדֹם נָסַבּוּ עַל־הַבַּיִת מִנַּעַר וְעַד־זָקֵן כָּל־הָעָם מִקָּצֶה: ה וַיִּקְרְאוּ אֶל־לוֹט וַיֹּאמְרוּ לוֹ אַיֵּה הָאֲנָשִׁים אֲשֶׁר־בָּאוּ אֵלֶיךָ הַלָּיְלָה הוֹצִיאֵם אֵלֵינוּ וְנֵדְעָה אֹתָם: ו וַיֵּצֵא אֲלֵהֶם לוֹט הַפֶּתְחָה וְהַדֶּלֶת סָגַר אַחֲרָיו: ז וַיֹּאמַר אַל־נָא אַחַי תָּרֵעוּ: ח הִנֵּה־נָא לִי שְׁתֵּי בָנוֹת אֲשֶׁר לֹא־יָדְעוּ אִישׁ אוֹצִיאָה־נָּא אֶתְהֶן אֲלֵיכֶם וַעֲשׂוּ לָהֶן כַּטּוֹב בְּעֵינֵיכֶם רַק לָאֲנָשִׁים הָאֵל אַל־תַּעֲשׂוּ דָבָר כִּי־עַל־כֵּן בָּאוּ בְּצֵל קֹרָתִי: ט וַיֹּאמְרוּ | גֶּשׁ־הָלְאָה וַיֹּאמְרוּ הָאֶחָד בָּא־לָגוּר וַיִּשְׁפֹּט שָׁפוֹט עַתָּה נָרַע לְךָ מֵהֶם וַיִּפְצְרוּ בָאִישׁ בְּלוֹט מְאֹד וַיִּגְּשׁוּ לִשְׁבֹּר הַדָּלֶת: י וַיִּשְׁלְחוּ הָאֲנָשִׁים אֶת־יָדָם וַיָּבִיאוּ אֶת־לוֹט אֲלֵיהֶם הַבָּיְתָה וְאֶת־הַדֶּלֶת סָגָרוּ: יא וְאֶת־הָאֲנָשִׁים אֲשֶׁר־פֶּתַח הַבַּיִת הִכּוּ בַּסַּנְוֵרִים מִקָּטֹן וְעַד־גָּדוֹל וַיִּלְאוּ לִמְצֹא הַפָּתַח:

*[4] They had not yet lain down, when the townspeople, the men of Sodom, young and old– all the people to the last man–gathered about the house.*
*[5] And they shouted to Lot and said to him,*

*"Where are the men who came to you tonight? Bring them out to us, that we may be intimate with them."*

*[6] So Lot went out to them to the entrance, shut the door behind him,*

*[7] and said, "I beg you, my friends, do not commit such a wrong.*

*[8] Look, I have two daughters who have not known a man. Let me bring them out to you, and you may do to them as you please; but do not do anything to these men, since they have come under the shelter of my roof."*

*[9] But they said, "Stand back! The fellow", they said, "came here as an alien, and already he acts the ruler! Now we will deal worse with you than with them." And they pressed hard against the person of Lot, and moved forward to break the door.*

*[10] But the men stretched out their hands and pulled Lot into the house with them, and shut the door.*

*[11] And the people who were at the entrance of the house, young and old, they struck with blinding light, so that they were helpless to find the entrance.*


**[4] They had not yet lain down.** The Midrash tells us that Lot's wife was very well assimilated into Sodomite life. She might have even herself come from Sodom. (Over twenty years had passed from the moment Lot had gone to Sodom and achieved a position of prominence there, and his children had grown up there.) Lot's wife went begging to the neighbors for salt, saying, "my insufferable husband has invited guests to our home, who must be fed, but we are all out of salt." The neighbors spread the news around the city, and rose up against Lot. This is why Lot's wife was subsequently punished by becoming a pillar of salt (19:26).

**The townspeople, the men of Sodom, young and old – all the people to the last man – gathered about the house.** Sodom, for all its repugnance, projects the image of a highly organized society.

**[7] My friends, do not commit such a wrong.** The word that Lot uses is *achai*, literally, "my brothers." Lot calls the Sodomites "brothers" because he still firmly believes that he can influence them. But very soon thereafter he seems to have lost his mind, offering those people his two unmarried daughters.

**[8] Look, I have two daughters who have not known a man. Let me bring them out to you, and you may do to them as you please.** There are two possible explanations for Lot's behavior. Either he was hoping that his two daughters would escape unharmed, because they too were Sodomites after all, or alternatively he had already so lost his moral bearings that he no longer had any sense of proper boundaries.

It should be noted that by declaring its society ideal, Sodom has a major influence on others. We will see later that even the angels, once in Sodom, become confused and unable to assess the true situation. Lot is of course a relative and disciple of Abraham himself, but because he has lived so long in Sodom, his morality has become perverted. Unable to develop independently and find correct solutions to new problems, Lot reduces righteousness to the simple list of items he has inherited from his youth. Because he knows so well that travelers must be invited in, he selflessly does so. But when he has to confront a rambunctious crowd, Lot is completely lost.

Having lived so long in Sodom, Lot has lost the spontaneous, intuitive understanding of righteousness. The principles and attitudes of the city and state where we live exert a powerful influence on us. A person should not – especially alone with only his family – settle in a wicked place in the hope of reforming it. Rather, one should settle only where the righteous live, in order to improve himself and his family, for that is the surest way to become a positive influence on the world.


## 22.5. The Origins of Mashiach in the Depths of Sodom

We noted above that Sodom, for all its repugnance, gives the appearance of a highly ordered society. And that such an "independent social organization" in that era, 20th century BCE, was a significant state achievement.

In fact, the Midrash depicts Sodom as a form of false messianism. Sodom and Gomorrah were among the most prosperous cities in the world ("Lot looked about him and saw how well watered was the whole plain of the Jordan, all of it – this was before the Lord had destroyed Sodom and Gomorrah – all the way to Zoar, like the garden of the Lord, like the land of Egypt" [13:10]). Sodom, reminiscent of the Garden of Eden, was a place of such abundance that its inhabitants reached the pinnacle of material affluence. But this prosperity also had a downside.

The people of Sodom proclaimed material prosperity the goal of life, which only led to their complete spiritual downfall. However, from a religious and spiritual point of view, material abundance is in no way a bad thing. In fact, it is even a distinctive feature of the Messianic era. The problem of Sodom was that it absolutized that criterion ("economic messianism"), and believed that the size of an ideal society is properly determined by the limits of one's own city.

It is a truism that the essence of any false messianic doctrine is, precisely, the absolutization of one solitary feature of messianism, to the exclusion of all other features. Sodom's perversion of messianic ideas in just this way made it, in a certain sense, the first false messianic society that the world had known.

The Sodomites claimed that their society represented the pinnacle of human development – which is just another way of telling us that their objective was to improve the world. But that is absurd and offensive. Hence the Sodomite ban on giving alms: any need for charity can only mean that the world is not doing well, and this is an insult to Sodomite sensibilities. The prophet Ezekiel (16:49) describes Sodom as follows: "Only this was the sin of your sister Sodom: arrogance! She and her daughters had plenty of bread and untroubled tranquility; [precisely for that reason] she did not support the poor and the needy."

Who could be begging for alms in a society of such abundance? Only aliens, strangers. Selfishness in Sodom was thus realized at the social level. The people of this city hated strangers, and behaved in such a way that no one would want to ask for hospitality there.

Sodom became the center of evil, but the Messiah must come from Sodom in order that he will himself be affected. The purpose of the Messiah is to fix everything that is broken in the world, which includes reforming the wicked. But you cannot fix anything unless you, too, have some connection with it; otherwise, what understanding could you have of it in the first place? Therefore, to be capable of reforming Sodom a person must himself have a spark of Sodom within his soul; he must contain something of this place within himself, and be in some sense implicated in their wrong-doings. King David is such a man, as is his descendant, the Messiah, because David (through Ruth and Moab) descends from Sodom.

That the reality of our world includes the element of Sodom cannot be denied. Therefore, the Messiah, whose job it is to heal all the world's ills, must also carry that spark within himself.

Acting through *chesed* alone, it is impossible to reform Sodom. David, however, represents the attribute of *malchut*, "kingdom," and he is therefore qualified to reform Sodom. The people of Sodom, who strive to create a socialized structure, cannot be rehabilitated without clear laws and strict enforcement measures. Therefore, it is not by chance that the attribute of *malchut* itself – David – is born through the agency of Sodom.

A little later the angel addresses Lot: "Take your two daughters who are here" (19:15). The Midrash connects these words with the verse in the Psalms (89:21): "I have found David, My servant; anointed him with My sacred oil." Says the Midrash: Where did God find David? He found him in Sodom. Lot's two daughters were that "find" that made David and the Messiah possible.

The path of the Messiah is always – *ab initio* and by its very nature – "on the edge", through events that are, from a moral point of view, "borderline." (E.g., Lot's daughters who bore children from their own father, the story of Judah and Tamar, the story of Ruth, and the relationship of David and Bathsheba.) The Messiah must himself experience all these dilemmas in order to feel them from the inside, learning thereby to correct them.

The Mashiach ascends from below - morally and geographically. Sodom is not by mere chance the lowest place on earth.

## 22.6. The Angels Lead Lot Out of Sodom (19:12-16)

יב וַיֹּאמְרוּ הָאֲנָשִׁים אֶל-לוֹט עֹד מִי-לְךָ פֹּה חָתָן וּבָנֶיךָ
וּבְנֹתֶיךָ וְכֹל אֲשֶׁר-לְךָ בָּעִיר הוֹצֵא מִן-הַמָּקוֹם: יג כִּי-
מַשְׁחִתִים אֲנַחְנוּ אֶת-הַמָּקוֹם הַזֶּה כִּי-גָדְלָה צַעֲקָתָם
אֶת-פְּנֵי יי וַיְשַׁלְּחֵנוּ יי לְשַׁחֲתָהּ: יד וַיֵּצֵא לוֹט וַיְדַבֵּר ׀
אֶל-חֲתָנָיו ׀ לֹקְחֵי בְנֹתָיו וַיֹּאמֶר קוּמוּ צְּאוּ מִן-הַמָּקוֹם
הַזֶּה כִּי-מַשְׁחִית יי אֶת-הָעִיר וַיְהִי כִמְצַחֵק בְּעֵינֵי
חֲתָנָיו: טו וּכְמוֹ הַשַּׁחַר עָלָה וַיָּאִיצוּ הַמַּלְאָכִים בְּלוֹט
לֵאמֹר קוּם קַח אֶת-אִשְׁתְּךָ וְאֶת-שְׁתֵּי בְנֹתֶיךָ הַנִּמְצָאֹת
פֶּן-תִּסָּפֶה בַּעֲוֹן הָעִיר: טז וַיִּתְמַהְמָהּ ׀ וַיַּחֲזִיקוּ
הָאֲנָשִׁים בְּיָדוֹ וּבְיַד-אִשְׁתּוֹ וּבְיַד שְׁתֵּי בְנֹתָיו בְּחֶמְלַת יי
עָלָיו וַיֹּצִאֻהוּ וַיַּנִּחֻהוּ מִחוּץ לָעִיר:

*[12] Then the men said to Lot, "Whom else have you here? Sons-in-law, your sons and daughters, or anyone else that you have in the city–bring them out of the place.*
*[13] For we are about to destroy this place; because the outcry against them before the Lord has become so great that the Lord has sent us to destroy it."*
*[14] So Lot went out and spoke to his sons-in-law, who had married his daughters, and said, "Up, get out of this place, for the Lord is about to destroy the city." But he seemed to his sons-in-law as one who jests.*

*[15] As dawn broke, the angels urged Lot on, saying, "Up, take your wife and your two remaining daughters, lest you be swept away because of the iniquity of the city."*
*[16] Still he delayed. So the men seized his hand, and the hands of his wife and his two daughters-in the Lord's mercy on him-and brought him out and left him outside the city.*

We have here three processes occurring in parallel. On the one hand, the city is destroyed. On the other hand, all righteous people (even if only potentially righteous) are saved, namely, Lot's entire family. But there is yet a third, hidden process: preparation for the future birth of the Mashiach. Except that in order for that to happen, it is necessary not only to remove Lot from Sodom, but also to "remove Sodom from Lot." Lot's spark must be purified over a very long period before it can be united with the Jewish people.

**[12] Then the men said to Lot, "Whom else have you here?."** The angels invite Lot to think for himself: Is there anything else of value left in Sodom? What could you possibly be looking for in a city where the behavior of its inhabitants is so heinous? Any connection of some inhabitant of Sodom with Lot would mean that that person is not hopeless, that there is hope for his salvation – and the angels emphasize this point. But Lot's connection with Sodom, on the contrary, is becoming his downfall, and Lot must break this connection within himself. And yet, he could not influence even his own household. Lot's wife had become so attached to Sodom that she could not restrain herself from looking behind her, and she paid the price with her life.

**[14] So Lot went out and spoke to his sons-in-law, who had married his daughters.** Besides the two unmarried daughters who lived with him, Lot also had two married daughters. Lot went to persuade their husbands to flee with him. These two remained at home and of course did not join in the assault on Lot's house, but neither did they try to stop any of the townspeople from doing so. As concerns everything that is tied to Sodom, if it cannot find the strength within itself to break that connection, it loses its chance for salvation.

**But he seemed to his sons-in-law as one who jests.** They thought he was joking, and they laughed at his words. It's amusing to them, because it never enters their mind to imagine how anything untoward could happen in such a magnificent place. But the Torah mention this laughter not just tangentially, for it is actually an echo of a different laughter – God's laughing over Sodom. (We shall discuss the important concept of God's "laughter" in more detail below.) The laughter of Lot's Sodomite sons-in-law was therefore not an absolute blunder on their part; they were sensing a reflection of the metaphysical, supremely Divine laughter, which is why they, too, felt a desire to laugh. Except that they were unable to correctly interpret it.

Laughter is an integral part of the geulah, the Messianic redemption, because the Messianic process never proceeds as originally expected. This laughter intensifies, becoming one with the Divine laughter, as described in the Talmud (Avodah Zarah 3b): "There is no complete laughter before the Holy One Blessed be He, except on the Day of the Redemption." When Lot leaves Sodom, a breakthrough toward the *geulah* begins: King David's soul begins its descent into the world. That the Messiah would have his origins in the depths of Sodom's evil contravenes conventional logic, and is therefore quite "funny." Laughter represents the triumph over the laws of logic that is associated with the irradiance of a new light.

**[15] As dawn broke.** Night is the time of preparation for Exodus. But the actual exit from Sodom itself occurs only at the crack of dawn, for it reflects the beginning of the geulah.

**Lest you be swept away because of the iniquity of the city.** If you do not separate yourself from Sodom, you will go down with it, even if you are not personally guilty.

**The angels urged Lot on ... [16] Still he delayed.** Lot is not able to recognize his own role in the Messianic process. He hesitates to leave, because it is not in his nature to move forward on his own; he must be "taken by the hand" and brought out by force.

**[16] So the men seized his hand, and the hands of his wife and his two daughters–in the Lord's mercy on him – and brought him out.** While the night drags on, Lot can still linger in Sodom. But once dawn has broken (that is, the *geulah* has begun), anyone who delays in participating in the Exodus is in serious danger of perishing.

**In the Lord's mercy on him.** Lot was not himself deserving of salvation; he was taken out of Sodom only because the future David otherwise could not have been born.

**And left him outside the city.** Encouraging him to move forward on his own.

## 22.7. Do not Look Behind You (19:17-26)

יז וַיְהִי כְהוֹצִיאָם אֹתָם הַחוּצָה וַיֹּאמֶר הִמָּלֵט עַל־נַפְשֶׁךָ
אַל־תַּבִּיט אַחֲרֶיךָ וְאַל־תַּעֲמֹד בְּכָל־הַכִּכָּר הָהָרָה הִמָּלֵט
פֶּן־תִּסָּפֶה: יח וַיֹּאמֶר לוֹט אֲלֵהֶם אַל־נָא אֲדֹנָי: יט
הִנֵּה־נָא מָצָא עַבְדְּךָ חֵן בְּעֵינֶיךָ וַתַּגְדֵּל חַסְדְּךָ אֲשֶׁר עָשִׂיתָ
עִמָּדִי לְהַחֲיוֹת אֶת־נַפְשִׁי וְאָנֹכִי לֹא אוּכַל לְהִמָּלֵט הָהָרָה
פֶּן־תִּדְבָּקַנִי הָרָעָה וָמַתִּי: כ הִנֵּה־נָא הָעִיר הַזֹּאת קְרֹבָה
לָנוּס שָׁמָּה וְהִוא מִצְעָר אִמָּלְטָה נָּא שָׁמָּה הֲלֹא מִצְעָר
הִוא וּתְחִי נַפְשִׁי: כא וַיֹּאמֶר אֵלָיו הִנֵּה נָשָׂאתִי פָנֶיךָ גַּם
לַדָּבָר הַזֶּה לְבִלְתִּי הָפְכִּי אֶת־הָעִיר אֲשֶׁר דִּבַּרְתָּ: כב מַהֵר
הִמָּלֵט שָׁמָּה כִּי לֹא אוּכַל לַעֲשׂוֹת דָּבָר עַד־בֹּאֲךָ שָׁמָּה עַל־
כֵּן קָרָא שֵׁם־הָעִיר צוֹעַר: כג הַשֶּׁמֶשׁ יָצָא עַל־הָאָרֶץ וְלוֹט
בָּא צֹעֲרָה: כד וַיי הִמְטִיר עַל־סְדֹם וְעַל־עֲמֹרָה גָּפְרִית
וָאֵשׁ מֵאֵת יי מִן־הַשָּׁמָיִם: כה וַיַּהֲפֹךְ אֶת־הֶעָרִים הָאֵל
וְאֵת כָּל־הַכִּכָּר וְאֵת כָּל־יֹשְׁבֵי הֶעָרִים וְצֶמַח הָאֲדָמָה: כו
וַתַּבֵּט אִשְׁתּוֹ מֵאַחֲרָיו וַתְּהִי נְצִיב מֶלַח:

*[17] When they had brought them outside, one said, "Flee for your life! Do not look behind you, nor stop anywhere in the Plain; flee to the hills, lest you be swept away."*
*[18] But Lot said to them, "Oh no, my lord!*
*[19] You have been so gracious to your servant, and have already shown me so much kindness in order to save my life; but I cannot flee to the hills, lest the disaster overtake me and I die.*
*[20] Look, that town there is near enough to flee to; it is such a little place! Let me flee there–it is such a little place–and let my life be saved."*
*[21] He replied, "Very well, I will grant you this favor too, and I will not annihilate the town of which you have spoken.*

*[22] Hurry, flee there, for I cannot do anything until you arrive there." Hence the town came to be called Zoar.*

*[23] As the sun rose upon the earth and Lot entered Zoar,*

*[24] the Lord rained upon Sodom and Gomorrah sulfurous fire from the Lord out of heaven.*

*[25] He annihilated those cities and the entire Plain, and all the inhabitants of the cities and the vegetation of the ground.*

*[26] Lot's wife looked back, and she thereupon turned into a pillar of salt.*

**[17] One said, "Flee for your life!."** The angels remove Lot from the city, but instead of leading him to a safe place, they only explain the further action he must himself undertake: "Do not look behind you, nor stop anywhere in the Plain; flee to the hills."

This is a test for Lot. If even now that he is already outside Sodom he is unable to proceed on his own, then he cannot be saved. A person cannot be saved by force; he must act independently. Now that Lot has been brought out from Sodom, he needs to continue at least some short distance on his own. Lot is capable of that – albeit minimally – but his wife is not, and she turns back.

**Flee to the hills, lest you be swept away.** The more literal translation is "Flee to the *mountain*, lest you be swept away." Sodom is the lowest place on earth, both geographically (1378 ft / 420 m below sea level) and morally. Abraham lives fairly closeby, in Hebron, but on a rather high mountain (3018 ft / 920 m above sea level). This difference in altitude of 4396 ft (1340 m) symbolizes moral ascent. Thus, when the angel offers Lot to be saved on the "mountain," geographically speaking, we should also understand this to mean that Lot is expected to advance toward Abraham in the moral sense.

**[19] I cannot flee to the hills, lest the disaster overtake me and I die.** Aware of his own moral deficiency, Lot wants to avoid living in close proximity to Abraham, for although he is righteous against the backdrop of Sodom, compared to Abraham he can be considered wicked. Abraham's moral achievements are Lot's condemnation. Thus it often happens in life that those who are "righteous," but only like Lot, who appear downright worthy against the background of Sodom, prefer to keep their distance from the truly righteous of Abraham's caliber.

**[20] Look, that town there is near enough to flee to; it is such a little place!.** Lot seeks to find a place for himself apart from both Sodom and Abraham. For this, he needs a small town on the border of "Sodom County," located geographically – and morally – somewhat higher than Sodom, but not by much. Like Lot himself, Zoar is a borderline city – in terms of its location as well as its spiritual level.

**Let me flee there–it is such a little place–and let my life be saved.** Lot believes that although he could not influence Sodom in all its enormity, he will be able to influence tiny Zoar, and he asks for this chance. Lot is not capable of climbing immediately from the Sodomite lowland up to the mountain. He needs an "intermediate station," which Zoar becomes for him. (The next such station will be a cave midway up the mountain.) This shows that Lot has a certain positive moral dynamic, which is why he is in fact saved. The angel agrees to give him that opportunity.

**[26] Lot's wife looked back, and she thereupon turned into a pillar of salt.** A man who is half righteous and half wicked has no right to watch the death of the wicked from the sidelines, pretending that he has nothing to do with them. For it is indeed quite possible that he too is deserving of that same punishment, but is saved by God's grace alone. Therefore, if such a weakly righteous person gazes upon the punishment of the wicked, he too will perish with them. Only one who is completely righteous can observe the death of the wicked without bringing harm upon himself.

By looking back, Lot's wife demonstrates that her connection to Sodom is stronger than her connection to the future Messianic process. It is possible, however, that God was not punishing her individually; she was simply restored to her former, natural status as one of the Sodomites, and therefore met her end with them.

## 22.8. Abraham Gazes at the Destruction of Sodom (19:27-29)

**כז** וַיַּשְׁכֵּם אַבְרָהָם בַּבֹּקֶר אֶל־הַמָּקוֹם אֲשֶׁר־עָמַד שָׁם אֶת־פְּנֵי יי: **כח** וַיַּשְׁקֵף עַל־פְּנֵי סְדֹם וַעֲמֹרָה וְעַל־כָּל־פְּנֵי אֶרֶץ הַכִּכָּר וַיַּרְא וְהִנֵּה עָלָה קִיטֹר הָאָרֶץ כְּקִיטֹר הַכִּבְשָׁן: **כט** וַיְהִי בְּשַׁחֵת אֱלֹהִים אֶת־עָרֵי הַכִּכָּר וַיִּזְכֹּר אֱלֹהִים אֶת־אַבְרָהָם וַיְשַׁלַּח אֶת־לוֹט מִתּוֹךְ הַהֲפֵכָה בַּהֲפֹךְ אֶת־הֶעָרִים אֲשֶׁר־יָשַׁב בָּהֵן לוֹט:

*[27] Next morning, Abraham hurried to the place where he had stood before the Lord,*
*[28] and, looking down toward Sodom and Gomorrah and all the land of the Plain, he saw the smoke of the land rising like the smoke of a kiln.*

*[29] Thus it was that, when God destroyed the*
*cities of the Plain and annihilated the cities*
*where Lot dwelt, God was mindful of Abraham*
*and removed Lot from the midst of the upheaval.*

**[29] God was mindful of Abraham and removed Lot from the midst of the upheaval.** The Torah reiterates that Lot did not for his own sake deserve to be saved, but that salvation was necessary for the future development of Abraham's descendants.

**[27] Next morning.** Morning is related to the attribute of *chesed*, which is typical of Abraham.

**To the place where he had stood before the Lord.** It is the place where he argued with God about the fate of Sodom, and where, from the mountaintop, he could see the Jordan Valley and the region of the Dead Sea. Abraham now himself returns to this place of *gevurah*, for he feels that *chesed* alone is not enough.

**[28] And, looking down toward Sodom and Gomorrah and all the land of the Plain.** Unlike Lot, Abraham is allowed to observe the destruction of Sodom. Moreover, this is necessary in order for him to understand God's ways in running the world.

**Smoke of the land rising like the smoke of a kiln.** A kiln is a place where everything is burned and completely destroyed. After Lot's departure from Sodom, nothing at all remains there, which means there is no hope of recovery.

And therefore, a little later we will learn that Abraham has left Hebron for Gerar. According to the Midrash, Abraham left Hebron because people no longer traveled the road through Hebron after the destruction of Sodom, and there was no one that Abraham could influence there. It is striking that thanks to the wicked city of Sodom, Hebron, the city of the righteous Abraham, was given the opportunity to influence the world. The destruction of Sodom, which eliminated the purpose of Abraham's life in Hebron, had now become a reproach of unrealized opportunities.

## 22.9. Lot's Daughters Resolve to Bear Children from Him (19:30-31)

ל וַיַּעַל לוֹט מִצּוֹעַר וַיֵּשֶׁב בָּהָר וּשְׁתֵּי בְנֹתָיו עִמּוֹ כִּי יָרֵא לָשֶׁבֶת בְּצוֹעַר וַיֵּשֶׁב בַּמְּעָרָה הוּא וּשְׁתֵּי בְנֹתָיו: **לא** וַתֹּאמֶר הַבְּכִירָה אֶל־הַצְּעִירָה אָבִינוּ זָקֵן וְאִישׁ אֵין בָּאָרֶץ לָבוֹא עָלֵינוּ כְּדֶרֶךְ כָּל־הָאָרֶץ:

*[30] Lot went up from Zoar and settled in the hill country with his two daughters, for he was afraid to dwell in Zoar; and he and his two daughters lived in a cave.*
*[31] And the older one said to the younger, "Our father is old, and there is not a man on earth to consort with us in the way of all the world.*

**[30] Lot went up from Zoar.** Zoar escaped destruction, but the catastrophe itself so affected Lot that he decided to distance himself from anything related to Sodom, even if only indirectly.

**And settled in the hill country.** Not on the mountain nor at the foot of the mountain, but midway up the mountain and inside of it, in a cave isolated from the rest of humanity. Between the mountain peak – Abraham – and the lowest point on earth – Sodom; midway between good and evil.

**And he ... lived in a cave.** The Hebrew word *va-yeshev* normally carries some connotation of permanence. Here, too, Lot was by now living in that cave permanently. Lot's potential has been exhausted, and he is unable to move forward.

**[31] Our father is old.** We therefore cannot expect him to solve the problem of creating posterity. We must ourselves take that initiative.

**There is not a man on earth.** It is very strange that they would think that. Lot's daughters cannot possibly believe that there are no people left in the entire world. At very least, they know that the city of Zoar was not destroyed.

**To consort with us.** The literal translation is, "There is no man on earth to come onto us." This, too, is an oddly constructed phrase. When referring to intimate relations the Torah will usually say *lavo el*, a man "entering unto" a woman, but here it uses a different expression, *lavo 'al*, "coming onto" (or "upon"). This expression is found only once more in the Torah, in Deuteronomy (25:5), in the discussion of levirate marriage: "When brothers dwell together and one of them dies and leaves no son, the wife of the deceased shall not be married to a stranger, outside the family. Her husband's brother shall unite with her (*yavo 'aleha*): he shall take her as his wife." The preposition *'al* is usually understood here as implying an addition. That is, in addition to the deceased husband, her levir shall cohabit with her and take her as his wife.

Lot's daughters would adopt the terminology of levirate marriage only if they saw themselves as "widows" of the "deceased" Sodom, and they viewed intimate relations with their father as their opportunity to "restore the seed" of Sodom.

Since their father is "old," Sodom cannot by its own efforts be reborn. But some hope of extracting sparks from it must remain, otherwise the Messianic dynasty, which must be born from Sodom, will not happen. Lot, their father, carries the essential Sodomite spark that will allow the Messianic process to continue.

Had Lot still had energy, he could well have found a new wife, had children with her, and found husbands for his daughters. The Messianic process would thus have properly progressed. But Lot can no longer act on his own. His daughters' words "there is no man on earth" mean that apart from Lot there is no man left for a "levirate marriage" with them, that there is no one else who is able to extract the spark of Sodom.

We have noted that in the course of his long stay in Sodom, Lot had lost his natural moral sensibilities, which is how he could come up with the wild idea of appeasing a crowd of lecherous Sodomites by giving them his daughters. In the literal sense of the text no such outcome ever materialized, but in a somewhat deeper sense, Lot did in fact "marry off his daughters to Sodom." And now, after the death of the city, they have become its "widows." Lot's daughters therefore now consider it their moral obligation to resurrect Sodom. Moreover, they are so strongly attached to Sodom that they are prepared even to cohabit with their own father, the only surviving Sodomite, in order to make that happen.

A true ideological Sodomite is not just a criminal, a greedy and heartless resident of that city, but one who considers the positive component of the Sodomite ideology a prototype of the future – who believes, despite the destruction of the city, in its potential messianism. Lot's daughters need just that kind of person to continue the race.

At first glance, this of course seems monstrous. From a more conventional point of view, however, what Lot's daughters did was not an atrocity, because within the culture of that time, connection between a father and his daughters, although discouraged, was not strictly forbidden. Moreover, any relative, and not only the deceased husband's brother, could conclude a levirate marriage. (Tamar, for example, seduces her father-in-law, Judah, with just that objective in mind [38:13 ff].) After the giving of the Torah such connections were outlawed, but in the days of the Patriarchs they were still allowed.

Paradoxically, the daughters of Lot want to perform a *chesed* for Sodom – a city that was the embodiment of the very denial of all *chesed*. It is not by chance that this happened only when they were already outside Sodom and midway up the mountain, "halfway to Abraham." The positive spark contained within Sodom could not be extracted from it until Sodom was destroyed.

## 22.10. Lot is Made Drunk with Wine (19:32-35)

**לב** לְכָה נַשְׁקֶה אֶת־אָבִינוּ יַיִן וְנִשְׁכְּבָה עִמּוֹ וּנְחַיֶּה מֵאָבִינוּ זָרַע: **לג** וַתַּשְׁקֶיןָ אֶת־אֲבִיהֶן יַיִן בַּלַּיְלָה הוּא וַתָּבֹא הַבְּכִירָה וַתִּשְׁכַּב אֶת־אָבִיהָ וְלֹא־יָדַע בְּשִׁכְבָהּ וּבְקוּמָהּ: **לד** וַיְהִי מִמָּחֳרָת וַתֹּאמֶר הַבְּכִירָה אֶל־ הַצְּעִירָה הֵן־שָׁכַבְתִּי אֶמֶשׁ אֶת־אָבִי נַשְׁקֶנּוּ יַיִן גַּם־

הַלַּיְלָה וּבֹאִי שִׁכְבִי עִמּוֹ וּנְחַיֶּה מֵאָבִינוּ זָרַע: לה
וַתַּשְׁקֶיןָ גַּם בַּלַּיְלָה הַהוּא אֶת־אֲבִיהֶן יָיִן וַתָּקָם
הַצְּעִירָה וַתִּשְׁכַּב עִמּוֹ וְלֹא־יָדַע בְּשִׁכְבָהּ וּבְקֻמָהּ:

[32] *Come, let us make our father drink wine,
and let us lie with him, that we may maintain
life through our father."*
[33] *That night they made their father drink
wine, and the older one went in and lay with
her father; he did not know when she lay down
or when she rose.*
[34] *The next day the older one said to the
younger, "See, I lay with Father last night; let
us make him drink wine tonight also, and you
go and lie with him, that we may maintain life
through our father."*
[35] *That night also they made their father drink
wine, and the younger one went and lay with
him; he did not know when she lay down or when
she rose.*

**[32] Let us make our father drink wine.** Wine is an essential component for implementing this plan. Lot upholds
certain moral principles and normally would not agree to
having relations with his daughters, but he is unstable and
easily made drunk. However, in a deeper sense, this really
means that Lot in a state of sober consciousness cannot
accomplish anything at all.

The Midrash says something truly astonishing: that the
wine that Lot's daughters brought to the cave came from
*Gan Eden*, the Garden of Eden, and had been kept on hand
since the Creation of the World specifically for this occasion.

That wine was earmarked for the daughters of Lot, for the express purpose of getting their father drunk and bearing him sons. As bad as this incident may appear, it is an essential component of the Messianic process. This means that what happened here, although it was Lot's daughters' personal sin, was in fact the realization of a path that was essential for the proper development of the universe.

Once again we are confronted with the principle that the Messianic process often seems aberrant, not "as things are meant to be," and always takes place on the very edge of what is acceptable. If Lot could have behaved properly, then this "borderline of what is acceptable" would have passed not through him, but through Zoar (whose inhabitants were also "Sodomites" to a certain extent, because of their close proximity to Sodom), whence husbands for his daughters would have come. But Lot lost the will to advance. It did not enter his mind that, as a father, he was expected to make efforts to marry off his daughters. The necessary process therefore had to be accomplished directly through him instead.

## 22.11. Moab and Ammon, the Sons of Lot's Daughters (19:36-38)

לו וַתַּהֲרֶיןָ שְׁתֵּי בְנוֹת־לוֹט מֵאֲבִיהֶן: לז וַתֵּלֶד הַבְּכִירָה בֵּן וַתִּקְרָא שְׁמוֹ מוֹאָב הוּא אֲבִי־מוֹאָב עַד־הַיּוֹם: לח וְהַצְּעִירָה גַם־הִוא יָלְדָה בֵּן וַתִּקְרָא שְׁמוֹ בֶּן־עַמִּי הוּא אֲבִי בְנֵי־עַמּוֹן עַד־הַיּוֹם:

*[36] Thus the two daughters of Lot came to be with child by their father.*
*[37] The older one bore a son and named him*

*Moab; he is the father of the Moabites of today.*
*[38] And the younger also bore a son, and she*
*called him Ben-ammi; he is the father of the*
*Ammonites of today.*

**[37] The older one bore a son and named him Moab.** Moab
translates, literally, as *me-av*, "from the father." The eldest
daughter regards the relationship with her father, though
it is not quite an ordinary one, as a Levirate marriage, and,
without hesitating, she declares this to the whole world.

**[38] And the younger also bore a son, and she called him
Ben-ammi.** Lot's younger daughter is more bashful. Having conceived and given birth not by her own independent
decision, but at the direction of her older sister, she gives her
son the neutral name "Ben-Ammi," "the son of my people."

Subsequently, Lot's daughters' descendants settled near
Canaan: Moab on the eastern shore of the Dead Sea, and
Ammon to the north, on the east bank of the Jordan River.
The capital of the Ammonites, Rabbath Ammon (see Deut
3:11; 2 Sam. 11:1), today known as Amman, is the capital of
Jordan.

**He is the father of the Ammonites of today.** The Midrash
takes the position that the merit of the elder sister was
greater than that of the younger, because the elder initiated
the connection with their father and was not ashamed to do
so. In the merit of that, her descendant, Ruth the Moabite,
David's great-grandmother, will be first to have a role in the
creation of the Jewish kingdom. Only later will the younger
sister's descendant, Naamah the Ammonite, become Solomon's wife.

Thus, our sages deemed this act a credit to the daughters of Lot, as it was motivated by their yearning for Divine deliverance and for the arrival of the Messiah. The fact that in order to restore the spark of Sodom they had to conceive and give birth from their own father was, in the sages' view, more an instance of self-sacrifice for the sake of an ideal than an actual crime.

### 22.12. Moabites and Ammonites: Nations Who Lack Chesed

The peculiarities of their origin made the Moabites and Ammonites two "anomalous" nations that straddle the boundary between the righteousness of Abraham and the wickedness of Sodom.

It is noble to strive for the preservation of one's native lineage. Lot's daughters' desire to restore their city and their family line was therefore a positive phenomenon. Their wish was completely unselfish and idealistic: they wanted to reform Sodom, and only for that reason they allowed themselves to become pregnant from their own father. The very concept of "allowing" belongs to the attribute of *chesed*. But even so, the decision to do something like that is a manifestation of "unclean *chesed*."

We already know that *chesed*, like any other spiritual attribute, can be "clean" or "unclean," and its excess can lead to evil. It is unlikely that Lot was twice so drunk that he really "did not know" (v. 33 and 35) what his daughters were doing to him. Not that he deliberately went looking to cohabit with his own daughters, but he allowed himself to do so. This, too, was a manifestation of "excessive, impure *chesed*." There is a specific kind of *chesed* in Lot that is superfluous for Abraham and the entire Jewish people (which is why Lot had to be separated from Abraham), but because of that latent spark within him, proper *chesed* – Ruth the Moabite and Naamah the Ammonite – can manifest in the future.

Lot's daughters performed a *chesed* on behalf of a city that was the very antithesis of *chesed*; thus they combined the qualities of Abraham with the qualities of Sodom. But because these are opposite forces that repel each other, the Moabites and Ammonites cannot exist "in the middle" by living in an intermediate state, being not so righteous as Abraham but not so wicked as Sodom, as other nations do. For them this is impossible, which means that the Moabites and the Ammonites can either rise high or fall low.

In the end, the Ammonites and the Moabites gravitated toward the Sodomite direction; they failed to bestow elementary mercy on the Jewish people as they passed through the wilderness. Because the Sodomite instinct prevailed in them, the Torah says: "No Ammonite or Moabite shall be admitted into the congregation of the Lord; none of their descendants, even in the tenth generation, shall ever be admitted into the congregation of the Lord, because they did not meet you with food and water on your journey after you left Egypt" (Deut. 23:4-5).

But what is so terrible about this "not meeting with bread and water"? There were other nations who even actively fought the Jews, but accepting proselytes from among them was not forbidden. It is obvious that the Egyptians treated the Jews incomparably worse than the Ammonites and the Moabites did, but an Egyptian could become Jewish by undergoing *giyyur* (conversion). Edom threatened the Jews with war (Num. 20:18). But of both Egypt and Edom the Torah says, "Children born to them may be admitted into the congregation of the Lord in the third generation" (ibid. 23:9).

Although the Ammonites and the Moabites did not initiate wars, the crime of these nations is that they showed absolute indifference, and just for that reason they are forever deprived of the opportunity to join the Jewish community. Such a harsh punishment was imposed on Ammon and Moab because only two diametrically opposite paths are open to them: being like Abraham or being like Sodom. By repudiating hospitality – that is, by not emulating Abraham – they have made their choice in favor of Sodom.

Sodom was notorious for its total indifference to the needs of others, the result of Sodom's over-confident self-sufficiency and their contempt for their fellow humans, a manifestation of their definitive "anti-*chesed*." Therefore, in addition to "No Ammonite or Moabite shall be admitted into the congregation of the Lord," Scripture also says, "Moab shall become like Sodom and the Ammonites like Gomorrah" (Zephaniah 2:9).

However, the women of these nations, unlike the men, are permitted to join the Jewish people by undergoing conversion. The ban does not apply to them, because going forth to meet wayfarers is incumbent upon men, but inappropriate for women. The Ammonite and Moabite women were thus not guilty of the sin of being inhospitable and indifferent to the Jewish nation, and are therefore given the opportunity to join the Jewish people. Moreover, some of the women among them demonstrate even super-*chesed*, and participate in the birth of the Messianic dynasty.

Chapter 23

# Abraham and Abimelech in Gerar

## 23.1. Abraham in Gerar (20:1)

א וַיִּסַּע מִשָּׁם אַבְרָהָם אַרְצָה הַנֶּגֶב וַיֵּשֶׁב בֵּין־קָדֵשׁ וּבֵין שׁוּר וַיָּגָר בִּגְרָר:

*[1] Abraham journeyed from there to the region of the Negeb and settled between Kadesh and Shur. While he was sojourning in Gerar,*

**[1] Abraham journeyed from there.** Abraham is not moving toward any desired goal by doing so; his only objective here is to leave Hebron in order to distance himself from Sodom and from Lot.

Lot's departure from Sodom was the beginning of the descent of the Mashiach's soul into the world, and Abraham could not help but feel that a providentially historical event of utmost significance was taking place. Why, then, does Abraham journey away from here instead of maintaining contact with that spark of holiness that has now been created in Lot's family?

Apparently, it was not yet time to bring this spark to the Jewish people. Some things require a lengthy cleansing process before they can be united with holiness. Any premature attempt to make that happen can mean the loss of those things and also of the holiness itself. Therefore, Abraham had to withdraw from Lot's family at that moment.

**He was sojourning in Gerar.** We have already mentioned (19:28) the reason given by the Midrash for Abraham's departure from Hebron. Namely, that after the destruction of Sodom there were few if any wayfarers passing through Hebron, and Abraham no longer had anyone to influence there. (Geographically, Sodom is the Dead Sea's southern extremity, which passes through the Hebron region and is connected with Gerar by the east-west highway.)

However, we can also view this from the opposite direction. Hebron, the capital of the future Judea, is *malchut*, the "kingdom" attribute, which Abraham is still unable to master. Sodom, located east of Hebron, is the original and potential source of that attribute, which the Sodomites strove to implement in its improper form. But Gerar, located west of Hebron, is Sodom's opposite: a highly developed Philistine trading kingdom, located on the coast in the very thick of civilization and culture. (The primary channel of communication between nations was over the sea.) Perhaps Abraham migrated to this kingdom in order to advance himself there toward the attribute of *malchut*.

Abraham's departure from Hebron is yet another breakdown of hope, and all this happens even before the birth of Isaac. There is yet another lesson that Abraham must learn before he can have a true heir.

## 23.2. Abraham Again Calls Sarah His Sister (20:2)

ב וַיֹּאמֶר אַבְרָהָם אֶל־שָׂרָה אִשְׁתּוֹ אֲחֹתִי הִוא וַיִּשְׁלַח
אֲבִימֶלֶךְ מֶלֶךְ גְּרָר וַיִּקַּח אֶת־שָׂרָה:

*[2] Abraham said of Sarah his wife, "She is my
sister." So King Abimelech of Gerar had Sarah
brought to him.*

What had happened in Egypt is now repeated in Gerar.
It is as if Abraham is only coming back to the same point he
had passed through long before.

A simple explanation of Abraham's actions – that just as had
happened in Egypt, he fears that he may be attacked in order
to take Sarah from him – seems strange. After all, only recently
Abraham had a whole army at his disposal, and had defeated
an entire coalition of kings. So why is he now defenseless?

The apparent answer is that Abraham had once again left
all his disciples behind, and had gone to Gerar alone with
his family. Recall that much earlier, near the beginning of
his journey, Abraham had brought his Babylonian disciples
into the land and settled them in Shechem, only to leave
them there and depart for Egypt alone. Then, upon leaving
Egypt, again with slave-disciples, Abraham settled in Hebron,
waged war, and moved on. But now, leaving those disciples
in Hebron, he and his family, again unaccompanied, depart
for the land of the Philistines. Thus, Shechem and Hebron
remained settlements of Babylonian and Egyptian "representatives" within the Land of Israel.

So Abraham is now alone and again confronts a difficult
situation regarding Sarah. But this time, as we shall soon see,
Abraham is already able to manifest the attribute of *gevurah*.

It is for him a difficult challenge, but gradually he is learning this attribute – he is learning to act more severely.

However, when Abraham calls Sarah his sister, there is now an additional aspect that is apparent. Subconsciously, Abraham even now does not feel completely that Sarah is his wife, the future mother of his children. Even now he seems to consider her more as his "comrade-in-arms" for spreading monotheism among the surrounding population. Abraham does not yet have any deep-rooted sense that Sarah's purpose, rather than helping him to educate disciples, is to produce a nation from him. It therefore feels natural to him to call Sarah his sister. Abraham will now receive a lesson that continuing to treat Sarah as a sister is unacceptable.

Abraham needed to understand at long last, through the incident of Abimelech, that Sarah was his true wife. Only then could Isaac be born.

### 23.3. Abimelech's Guilt (20:3-6)

ג וַיָּבֹא אֱלֹהִים אֶל־אֲבִימֶלֶךְ בַּחֲלוֹם הַלָּיְלָה וַיֹּאמֶר לוֹ
הִנְּךָ מֵת עַל־הָאִשָּׁה אֲשֶׁר־לָקַחְתָּ וְהִוא בְּעֻלַת בָּעַל: ד
וַאֲבִימֶלֶךְ לֹא קָרַב אֵלֶיהָ וַיֹּאמַר אֲדֹנָי הֲגוֹי גַּם־צַדִּיק
תַּהֲרֹג: ה הֲלֹא הוּא אָמַר־לִי אֲחֹתִי הִוא וְהִיא־גַם־הִוא
אָמְרָה אָחִי הוּא בְּתָם־לְבָבִי וּבְנִקְיֹן כַּפַּי עָשִׂיתִי זֹאת: ו
וַיֹּאמֶר אֵלָיו הָאֱלֹהִים בַּחֲלֹם גַּם אָנֹכִי יָדַעְתִּי כִּי בְתָם־
לְבָבְךָ עָשִׂיתָ זֹּאת וָאֶחְשֹׂךְ גַּם־אָנֹכִי אוֹתְךָ מֵחֲטוֹ־לִי עַל־
כֵּן לֹא־נְתַתִּיךָ לִנְגֹּעַ אֵלֶיהָ:

*[3] But God came to Abimelech in a dream by night and said to him, "You are to die because of the woman that you have taken, for she is a married woman."*

*[4] Now Abimelech had not approached her. He said, "O Lord, will You slay people even though innocent?*
*[5] He himself said to me, 'She is my sister!' And she also said, 'He is my brother.' When I did this, my heart was blameless and my hands were clean."*
*[6] And God said to him in the dream, "I knew that you did this with a blameless heart, and so I kept you from sinning against Me. That was why I did not let you touch her.*

**[5] He himself said to me, 'She is my sister!'.** Abimelech emphasizes that he is innocent in the strict sense. He feels confident that he has broken no laws, nor tried to expropriate anyone's wife. Nevertheless, the Sages say that he deserved to die not for violating the prohibition of adultery, but for violating universal moral standards. The general principle is that the nations of the world are punished when they violate the obligations that they have themselves assumed.

From Abraham's answer below (verse 11) we understand that he called Sarah his sister as a protection from the danger he was facing. When upon arriving as an unknown in that place Abraham is questioned about the woman who is with him, it is only natural that he would feel endangered. (This mode of questioning, as used here in Gerar, is further elaborated later in the Torah, in the similar incident of Isaac and Rebecca [26:7 ff.]). The sin committed in making such inquiries is the sin of violating universal moral norms. Abimelech, being a king, is responsible for sanctioning an atmosphere of danger that would force guests visiting his city to lie.

**"When I did this, my heart was blameless and my hands were clean." [6] And God said to him in the dream, "I knew that you did this with a blameless heart."** God acknowledges that Abimelech had done it "with a blameless heart" – but not "with cleanliness of hands."

**[6] "So I kept you from sinning against Me. That was why I did not let you touch her."** God protected Abimelech from a worse crime. But he is nonetheless responsible for the atmosphere in Gerar, and therefore cannot be considered innocent.

### 23.4. The Intrinsic Relationship Between Prophecy and Prayer (20:7)

ז וְעַתָּה הָשֵׁב אֵשֶׁת־הָאִישׁ כִּי־נָבִיא הוּא וְיִתְפַּלֵּל בַּעַדְךָ וֶחְיֵה וְאִם־אֵינְךָ מֵשִׁיב דַּע כִּי־מוֹת תָּמוּת אַתָּה וְכָל־ אֲשֶׁר־לָךְ:

*[7] Therefore, restore the man's wife–since he is a prophet, he will intercede for you–to save your life. If you fail to restore her, know that you shall die, you and all that are yours."*

**[7] Since he is a prophet, he will intercede for you.** In this verse the words "prophet" and "pray" appear for the first time in the Torah. Whenever prayer is further mentioned in the Tanakh, it is often associated with prophets. In ancient times there was an inextricable link between prayer and prophecy. The ability to pray was one of the functions of a prophet.

This concept is unfamiliar to us, because today anyone can pray. In ancient times, however, people doubted their own ability to turn directly to God. They sensed such a vast abyss, such an enormous distance, between themselves and God, that they had no idea how to bridge that gap.

Within the context of religious education it is usual and customary to hear that prayer is a completely natural thing. It is taken for granted that every person has a path for turning to God. But we see that in the Torah this is absolutely not the case.

In the *Shulchan Aruch*, the Code of Jewish Law, we read: "A person who prays must understand in his heart the meaning of the words that his mouth utters, and must imagine that he is standing before the *Shechinah*, the very presence of God. He must drive away all distracting thoughts so that the meaning he puts into the words will be worthy of prayer. Certainly, if he were speaking before a king of flesh and blood, he would arrange his words and give them meaning, so as not to err or falter; how much more so should he behave accordingly before the King of Kings, Who probes all our thoughts. So did the pious do long ago. After secluding themselves, they would concentrate on the meaning of their prayers to such an extent that they were liberated from materiality, and approached the level of prophecy."

Thus we see that in order to pray, a person must approach the degree of prophecy.

In ancient times it was believed that only prophets could pray; that in order to turn to God, one first needs God to turn to him, and until that happens, one has no right to pray.

The essence of that approach is that when turning to God, it is critical not only to perceive with whom you are engaging in dialogue, but also to find the right words and the proper form of address. This is because one of the most important problems of prayer is that, in a certain sense, it borders on magic. Doesn't God Himself know what we need? Does He really need us to tell Him that? And, more generally, how can a person believe that he is able to influence God?

It is precisely to avoid confusing prayer with magic that prayer requires a prophet. For he understands the relationship between the human and the Divine.

There is an episode in the book of Samuel (I Sam. 12) where the prophet Samuel attempts to admonish the people and appeals to the Lord. It is mid-summer, and rain begins to fall. (Rain during the harvest season endangers the entire crop.) When the people ask Samuel to beseech God for the rain to stop, Samuel replies: "Have no fear, God loves you, and I, too, will not stop praying for you." Samuel concludes his prayer, and the rain stops. But through all of this it never occurs to any of the people that they should themselves pray; they only ask the prophet to do so on their behalf.

The example of the famous prayer of Hannah, mother of the prophet Samuel, is also interesting in this regard. Jewish tradition counts Hannah among the Prophets, and her prayer (I Sam. 2) is a prime example of prayer-prophecy. But the high priest Eli, who sees Hannah whispering silently to herself as she enters the Temple (1:13), takes her for a drunk, because he implicitly assumes that no ordinary person could possibly be praying.

As concerns our liturgy, it was established by the Men of the Great Assembly in the era when prophecy was still extant. The last of the prophets, aware that all prophecy would soon cease, felt that the people were in very serious danger of losing their sense of direct connection with God. The Men of the Great Assembly therefore established the liturgy and the proper order of our prayers, by compiling a text that incorporated the entire scope of prophetic experience.

That formulation of prayer, which in some measure reduced the distance between man and God, was something only a prophet would be able to do.

Only after the last prophets had composed a fixed prayer text could praying become a universal practice. Various guidelines for prayer also exist, indicating how one can achieve that state of mind that brings a person closer to the level of prophecy.


## 23.5. Prayer and Sacrifice – Their Similarities and Differences

It is important to note that praying and bringing a sacrifice are completely different religious experiences. Prayer, by its very nature, can even be seen as the opposite of sacrifice. Sacrifice, which is designed to preserve the existing order of the world, is an expression of gratitude to God for what *is*. The purpose of prayer, on the other hand, is to effect change in the world. A person prays because he wants to improve the world: to heal the sick, to render aid to the poor, to resurrect the ruins of Jerusalem, and so on.

While the Temple stood in Jerusalem there were two forms of Jewish religious service: prayer and sacrifice. Even when prayer became a universal practice toward the end of the Second Temple period, those two forms of service remained distinct.

Only after the destruction of the Second Temple did prayer assume the additional role of replacing sacrifice – in a sense it became itself a sacrifice, and incorporated both of those functions. The Sages accomplished this by precisely establishing the order of the prayers and the proper times of day for reciting them, which paralleled those of the sacrificial service in the Temple in Jerusalem, which those prayers replaced.

The prophets said of the Third Temple to be built in the future that "it shall be called a house of prayer for all peoples" (Isaiah 56:7). The onset of the Messianic era must not be understood to mean that people will be living in a state of absolute perfection, that God will have nothing to ask of us, and that nothing in the world will need to be changed. On the contrary, a world where nothing needs to change would be death, not life. The Messianic times will be the times of life enhanced, an era of further active correction in the world, and of drawing closer to God. That process is endless.

## 23.6. The End of the Conflict over Sarah (20:8-18)

ח וַיַּשְׁכֵּם אֲבִימֶלֶךְ בַּבֹּקֶר וַיִּקְרָא לְכָל־עֲבָדָיו וַיְדַבֵּר אֶת־
כָּל־הַדְּבָרִים הָאֵלֶּה בְּאָזְנֵיהֶם וַיִּירְאוּ הָאֲנָשִׁים מְאֹד: ט וַיִּקְרָא אֲבִימֶלֶךְ לְאַבְרָהָם וַיֹּאמֶר לוֹ מֶה־עָשִׂיתָ לָּנוּ וּמֶה־חָטָאתִי לָךְ כִּי־הֵבֵאתָ עָלַי וְעַל־מַמְלַכְתִּי חֲטָאָה גְדֹלָה מַעֲשִׂים אֲשֶׁר לֹא־יֵעָשׂוּ עָשִׂיתָ עִמָּדִי: י וַיֹּאמֶר אֲבִימֶלֶךְ אֶל־אַבְרָהָם מָה רָאִיתָ כִּי עָשִׂיתָ אֶת־הַדָּבָר הַזֶּה: יא וַיֹּאמֶר אַבְרָהָם כִּי אָמַרְתִּי רַק אֵין־יִרְאַת אֱלֹהִים בַּמָּקוֹם הַזֶּה וַהֲרָגוּנִי עַל־דְּבַר אִשְׁתִּי: יב וְגַם־אָמְנָה אֲחֹתִי בַת־אָבִי הִוא אַךְ לֹא בַת־אִמִּי וַתְּהִי־לִי לְאִשָּׁה: יג וַיְהִי כַּאֲשֶׁר הִתְעוּ אֹתִי אֱלֹהִים מִבֵּית אָבִי וָאֹמַר לָהּ זֶה חַסְדֵּךְ אֲשֶׁר תַּעֲשִׂי עִמָּדִי אֶל כָּל־הַמָּקוֹם אֲשֶׁר נָבוֹא שָׁמָּה אִמְרִי־לִי אָחִי הוּא: יד וַיִּקַּח אֲבִימֶלֶךְ צֹאן וּבָקָר וַעֲבָדִים וּשְׁפָחֹת וַיִּתֵּן לְאַבְרָהָם וַיָּשֶׁב לוֹ אֵת שָׂרָה אִשְׁתּוֹ: טו וַיֹּאמֶר אֲבִימֶלֶךְ הִנֵּה אַרְצִי לְפָנֶיךָ בַּטּוֹב בְּעֵינֶיךָ שֵׁב: טז וּלְשָׂרָה אָמַר הִנֵּה נָתַתִּי אֶלֶף כֶּסֶף לְאָחִיךְ הִנֵּה הוּא־לָךְ כְּסוּת עֵינַיִם לְכֹל אֲשֶׁר אִתָּךְ וְאֵת כֹּל וְנֹכָחַת: יז וַיִּתְפַּלֵּל אַבְרָהָם אֶל־הָאֱלֹהִים וַיִּרְפָּא

אֱלֹהִים אֶת־אֲבִימֶלֶךְ וְאֶת־אִשְׁתּוֹ וְאַמְהֹתָיו וַיֵּלֵדוּ: **יח** כִּי־עָצֹר עָצַר יי בְּעַד כָּל־רֶחֶם לְבֵית אֲבִימֶלֶךְ עַל־דְּבַר שָׂרָה אֵשֶׁת אַבְרָהָם:

*[8] Early next morning, Abimelech called his servants and told them all that had happened; and the men were greatly frightened.*

*[9] Then Abimelech summoned Abraham and said to him, "What have you done to us? What wrong have I done that you should bring so great a guilt upon me and my kingdom? You have done to me things that ought not to be done."*

*[10] "What, then," Abimelech demanded of Abraham, "was your purpose in doing this thing?"*

*[11] "I thought," said Abraham, "surely there is no fear of God in this place, and they will kill me because of my wife.*

*[12] And besides, she is in truth my sister, my father's daughter though not my mother's; and she became my wife.*

*[13] So when God made me wander from my father's house, I said to her, 'Let this be the kindness that you shall do me: whatever place we come to, say there of me: He is my brother.'"*

*[14] Abimelech took sheep and oxen, and male and female slaves, and gave them to Abraham; and he restored his wife Sarah to him.*

*[15] And Abimelech said, "Here, my land is before you; settle wherever you please."*

*[16] And to Sarah he said, "I herewith give your brother a thousand pieces of silver; this will serve you as vindication before all who are with you, and you are cleared before everyone."*

*[17] Abraham then prayed to God, and God
healed Abimelech and his wife and his slave girls,
so that they bore children;
[18] for the Lord had closed fast every womb of
the household of Abimelech because of Sarah,
the wife of Abraham.*

**[9] Then Abimelech summoned Abraham and said to him
... [10] Abimelech demanded of Abraham.** At first Abraham
does not answer Abimelech. He seems to be feel uncomfortable in the given situation, and Abimelech needs to ask
a second time.

**[11] "I thought ... surely there is no fear of God in this
place, and they will kill me because of my wife.** Abraham
explains that the general atmosphere in the kingdom compelled him to deception. Rather than justifying himself, he
accuses Abimelech of improper behavior. Thus, Abraham
has begun, if only in small measure, to use the attribute of
judgment; this is essential for the birth of Isaac.

**[12] And besides, she is in truth my sister.** We see that Abraham did actually regard Sarah as a sister, that he was deficient
in regarding Sarah as his wife. But now that he has offered
Abimelech this rationale, Abraham can no longer maintain
that kind of attitude towards Sarah. And this, too, is a critical aspect of Abraham's advancement to the level that the
birth of Isaac requires.

**My father's daughter though not my mother's.** Abraham
now also clarifies an important detail of his relationship with
Sarah, of which we had no knowledge previously. It turns out

that Terah, Abraham's father, had two wives, one of which bore him Abraham and Nahor, and the other – Haran, whose children are Lot, Milcah (the wife of Nahor), and Iscah, which is another name for Sarah, the wife of Abraham. Thus, Abraham and Nahor both married their nieces – but they were half-nieces, actually – from Terah's second wife.

Terah's second wife carries a special "gene," apparently, that Abraham lacks, but that Sarah and Lot share, whence it passes through Ammon and Moab to Ruth and the House of David. This is the "redness gene," so important to David (see I Sam. 16:12 and commentaries there). Rebekah, Isaac's wife (being a descendant of Nahor from his wife Milcah) likewise carries that "redness" gene, which will appear in her son Esau, who is called Edom, from *adom*, "red." Redness represents the attribute of judgment in the aspect of power, violence, and severity. This is *gevurah*, which for Abraham is realized through Sarah.

Perhaps it was because of this quality that Sarah possessed, but Abraham lacked, that he kept his distance from her. And partly because he lacked this quality, Abraham in the course of his journey with Sarah asks her to pose as his sister. This was, on the one hand, Abraham's means of protecting himself in the face of a threat, and on the other hand, a subconscious assumption on his part that there might be another wife for him who would give him descendants. When God commanded Abraham to create a Jewish nation, Abraham was completely incredulous that this was to be realized through Sarah.

So long as Abraham still perceives Sarah as his sister, she cannot bear him a son, and the blame for Sarah's failure to conceive and bear a child lies only with Abraham. In Egypt and in Gerar, God teaches Abraham that he must stop treating Sarah as his sister; Abimelech's reproach of Abraham is actually a reproach coming from God. (We note in passing that often in life, even in the words of people completely distant from us and alien to us we must learn to hear the Divine voice teaching and admonishing us.) The danger that Abraham sensed was very real, and he had entirely valid reasons to call Sarah his sister. Indeed those reasons were found to be satisfactory, but nonetheless the situation ultimately required him to reconsider his position. Because Abraham has modified his approach, Isaac can now be born.

**[14] Abimelech took sheep and oxen, and male and female slaves, and gave them to Abraham.** The considerable value of these gifts underscores Abimelech's respect for Sarah, which within the social system of those times was an indicator of Sarah's total vindication.

**[16] And to Sarah he said, "... This will serve you as vindication before all who are with you, and you are cleared before everyone."** Sarah is "vindicated before all" not only in the sense that she has received the recognition of Abimelech, but also because Abraham now finally understands her importance to him as a wife. Previously, Sarah struggled constantly just to maintain her rightful position. In her attempt to establish a family, she gave Hagar to Abraham, quarreled with Abraham, and then drove Hagar away. But now that she has finally been vindicated and her status was acknowledged, the family can progress to the next stage of its development. This highly essential advancement in Abraham's relationship with Sarah came about as a result of the incident with Abimelech.

Moreover, Abraham for yet a third time (as previously in Charan and in Egypt) acquires abundant possessions and servants. In view of Abraham's esteem and renown he can no longer remain a private citizen; he must seek for himself a more appropriate place in the social hierarchy. As we shall soon see, Abraham therefore moves to Beersheba, a city at the desert's edge.

**[17] Abraham then prayed to God, and God healed Abimelech and his wife and his slave girls, so that they bore children.** The community that raised a hand to Abraham was made barren, and were healed of that affliction only after Abraham prayed on their behalf.

# Chapter 24

# The Birth of Isaac and the Expulsion of Ishmael

## 24.1. The birth of Isaac (21:1-5)

א וַיי פָּקַד אֶת־שָׂרָה כַּאֲשֶׁר אָמָר וַיַּעַשׂ יי לְשָׂרָה כַּאֲשֶׁר
דִּבֵּר: ב וַתַּהַר וַתֵּלֶד שָׂרָה לְאַבְרָהָם בֵּן לִזְקֻנָיו לַמּוֹעֵד
אֲשֶׁר־דִּבֶּר אֹתוֹ אֱלֹהִים: ג וַיִּקְרָא אַבְרָהָם אֶת־שֶׁם־בְּנוֹ
הַנּוֹלַד־לוֹ אֲשֶׁר־יָלְדָה־לּוֹ שָׂרָה יִצְחָק: ד וַיָּמָל אַבְרָהָם
אֶת־יִצְחָק בְּנוֹ בֶּן־שְׁמֹנַת יָמִים כַּאֲשֶׁר צִוָּה אֹתוֹ אֱלֹהִים:
ה וְאַבְרָהָם בֶּן־מְאַת שָׁנָה בְּהִוָּלֶד לוֹ אֵת יִצְחָק בְּנוֹ:

*[1] The Lord took note of Sarah as He had promised,
and the Lord did for Sarah as He had spoken.
[2] Sarah conceived and bore a son to Abraham
in his old age, at the set time of which God had
spoken.
[3] Abraham gave his newborn son, whom Sarah
had borne him, the name of Isaac.
[4] And when his son Isaac was eight days
old, Abraham circumcised him, as God had
commanded him.*

*[5] Now Abraham was a hundred years old when his son Isaac was born to him.*

**[1] The Lord took note of Sarah as He had promised, and the Lord did for Sarah as He had spoken. [2] Sarah conceived and bore a son.** God's two actions, "took note" and "did" correspond to Sarah's two events, "conceived" and "bore a son." Here we see two levels of change in Sarah – with respect to Abraham, and with respect to their child.

**[4] And when his son Isaac was eight days old, Abraham circumcised him, as God had commanded him.** Isaac is the first child ever circumcised at the appointed time, on the eighth day following birth. Because Isaac is already from birth the beneficiary of God's Covenant, he is to some extent superior to even his father Abraham..

While this is a major advantage, it is also creates a problem. When a self-made man who has endured an arduous personal journey achieves a Covenant with God through his own efforts exclusively, that is for him a major accomplishment. But when a person is born into the Covenant, there is no achievement to speak of. It is therefore always challenging for "the righteous, the son of the righteous" even merely to hold on to his past achievements, not to mention further augmenting them with new ones.

Isaac solves this problem by faceting – cutting and shaping – the attribute of *gevurah*. As we shall see below, this process of faceting is closely associated with laughter and in particular with the name "Isaac" which means, "he will laugh."

### 24.2. The Laughter Concerning Isaac (21:6-8)

וַתֹּאמֶר שָׂרָה צְחֹק עָשָׂה לִי אֱלֹהִים כָּל־הַשֹּׁמֵעַ יִצְחַק־
לִי: ז וַתֹּאמֶר מִי מִלֵּל לְאַבְרָהָם הֵינִיקָה בָנִים שָׂרָה כִּי־
יָלַדְתִּי בֵן לִזְקֻנָיו: ח וַיִּגְדַּל הַיֶּלֶד וַיִּגָּמַל וַיַּעַשׂ אַבְרָהָם
מִשְׁתֶּה גָדוֹל בְּיוֹם הִגָּמֵל אֶת־יִצְחָק:

*[6] Sarah said, "God has brought me laughter;*
*everyone who hears will laugh with me."*
*[7] And she added, "Who would have said to*
*Abraham*
*That Sarah would suckle children!*
*Yet I have borne a son in his old age."*
*[8] The child grew up and was weaned, and*
*Abraham held a great feast on the day that Isaac*
*was weaned.*

**[6] God has brought me laughter; everyone who hears
will laugh with me.** Anyone hearing what has happened to
Sarah will laugh for joy, upon realizing that miraculous inter-
ventions do occur in our lives.

At this stage Sarah is no longer ashamed of laughing, for
she now understands that even before, there was nothing
improper about her laughter.

Sarah represents the attribute of *gevurah* within Abraham; a miracle is therefore for her an occasion for laughter.
Her individual advancement is that she now believes in miracles – that is, she has learned to laugh.

Isaac too is associated with laughter. His most important task is the preservation of tradition (which is likewise
the attribute of *gevurah*). Thus, he teaches us to laugh at
ourselves, at our own excessive correctness, and even at
our customs and traditions. Such laughter overcomes the
"excessive attribute of *gevurah*."

Yes, we must laugh at our own solemn religious beliefs, because all our ideas about the universe are correct only to a point; in the strict sense they cannot be absolutely true. Even in the field of Torah our perception is always imprecise, and always involves some minor transgressions, at least. No idea or belief should ever be treated with fanatical seriousness. If you cannot laugh at your ideas and beliefs, your own dogmatic pedantry can easily be your undoing.

## 24.3. Ishmael's Mocking Laughter (21:9-10)

ט וַתֵּרֶא שָׂרָה אֶת־בֶּן־הָגָר הַמִּצְרִית אֲשֶׁר־יָלְדָה לְאַבְרָהָם מְצַחֵק: י וַתֹּאמֶר לְאַבְרָהָם גָּרֵשׁ הָאָמָה הַזֹּאת וְאֶת־בְּנָהּ כִּי לֹא יִירַשׁ בֶּן־הָאָמָה הַזֹּאת עִם־בְּנִי עִם־יִצְחָק:

*[9] Sarah saw the son whom Hagar the Egyptian had borne to Abraham playing.*
*[10] She said to Abraham, "Cast out that slave-woman and her son, for the son of that slave shall not share in the inheritance with my son Isaac."*

And yet, when it comes to laughter, things are not quite that simple. Abraham's laughter, Sarah's laughter, and God's laughter ("God has brought me laughter") are all constructive. But when it comes to Ishmael, his laugh is deemed so destructive that Ishmael is driven out of the house because of it. Here is where we must begin to distinguish between proper and improper laughter.

As we have noted, to laugh means to overcome the attribute of *gevurah*, to go beyond the limits of the law, beyond the norm and the boundaries of correctness. (The Hebrew word *tzechok*, laughter, can be interpreted as *tzei chok* – "go beyond the law.") This means a situation where a person sees events unfolding in a manner completely unexpected and contrary to reason, but he sees in this "not quite right" a higher level of harmony and beauty, a greater meaning and spirituality than if everything had happened in the ordinary way. The joy of triumph over the usual order of things is expressed through laughter.

But at the same time, going beyond the limits of the norm and of correctness is problematic. You can rise above the norm, but you might also fall below it. It is critical that we learn to distinguish the laughter of a righteous man rising above the law from the laughter of a villain falling below the law.

Proper laughter arises from one's ability to see that harmony of the world that stands above simple logic. Those who know how to laugh at themselves – Abraham, Sarah and Isaac – can laugh at the world, and their laughter is constructive. (Note in particular that in "Jewish jokes" it is the Jews who are laughing at themselves. This is essential for Jewish survival.) An improper laugh is a mocking laugh that seeks to destroy someone or something. It is the laughter of people who are not able to laugh at themselves. Such is Ishmael's laugh.

That laughter is destructive for him and also for those in his company. Ishmael must therefore be expelled.

**[9] Playing.** The more literal translation would be "mocking." Ishmael's derisive action is indicated by the verb *metzachek* in the present tense, as we shall now explain.

Through Isaac the world learns to distinguish between proper and improper laughter, because Isaac is associated not only with laughter in general, but with future-oriented laughter specifically. The name "Isaac" means "he will laugh," with the future tense indicating hope for the future, as if to say: "Laugh we will! Don't be discouraged, everything will turn out fine."

Mocking laughter, on the other hand, is all in the present tense, because its essence is ridiculing unrealized hopes. Since the present is always imperfect, hope for the future is the source of everything good. The destruction of that hope is therefore the source of evil.

The Midrash notes that the verb *metzachek*, to "jeer" or "revel boisterously," has a connotation of adultery (39:17), of idolatry (Ex. 32:60), and of murder (II Sam. 2:14). Thus, this word serves as an indicator of the kinds of dangers that emanated from Ishmael, and explains why Sarah decided to deal with him so harshly.

**[10] Cast out that slave-woman and her son.** Sarah attributes Ishmael's behavior, his ridiculing Isaac, to his being "the son of a maidservant." A penchant for mocking others is one of the features of a slave mentality.

**Cast out … her son.** Ishmael (Islam), as a lunar civilization, lives largely in an illusory world. The only way to correct Ishmael's laughter that mocks Isaac is to expel him from his family, giving him the opportunity to face reality independently, without the presence of Isaac.

Sarah therefore wishes to expel Ishmael, for this was the only way to rehabilitate him, and to protect Isaac from his influence.

## 24.4. Development Within the Hierarchy

Ishmael could not remain in Abraham's family, but this was not a foregone conclusion from the outset. The birth of Isaac did not *per se* require the expulsion of Ishmael.

Had Ishmael been able to comprehend his own status – which was not the highest, but also far from the lowest – he would have understood his intermediate position within the family hierarchy and correctly structured his behavior. In that case, the story would then have been quite different. Hagar, too, is an example of this. When she acknowledged her place in the family and her status as maidservant of Sarah, then besides continuing to live in the house of Abraham, she also received a unique Divine blessing. But as soon as Hagar ceased to acknowledge Sarah as her mistress, she was immediately expelled.

And so it is with Ishmael. By acknowledging Isaac's superiority, he can have a normal life. But if he cannot do so, he must be expelled from the family. In fact, Ishmael is banished because he is psychologically incapable of occupying a place where he will be constructive, and consequently he becomes a destructive force.

Destructiveness, in essence, means nothing more than the "inability to occupy one's proper place." Such a place does not necessarily have to be the boss's chair – not every person can and should lead. If an unworthy individual seeks to occupy a leading position, that attempt will end in failure, and will also prevent him from occupying even the place that is right for him.

Your true place in life is the place where you bring positive development to the world. You will derive pleasure from living in that place, and others will treat you with respect as well, because you are changing the world for the better.

In this situation Ishmael could not receive his share of Abraham's legacy – not because the others in his circle did not allow it, but because of his own inability to realize his true mission. Sarah does not wish to deprive Ishmael of his share, but she feels that since Ishmael is unable to inherit his share while living together with Isaac, he must be expelled.

## 24.5. Why Ishmael Had to Be Born Before Isaac

This conflict between Ishmael and Isaac arose because Ishmael, who was born first, is now being displaced by Isaac, thus depriving Ishmael of his status as Abraham's heir. Had Ishmael been younger than Isaac, there would have been no conflict. What, then, is the meaning of Ishmael's "premature" birth? What is the spiritual justification for this conflict?

On the one hand, Ishmael became the firstborn as the result of Sarah's mistake. Having lost hope of giving birth to a son of her own, she gave her maidservant Hagar to Abraham to bear him a son. On the other hand, however, Abraham acquired some highly essential experience in the process of expelling Ishmael; namely, Abraham now understood that God's chosen people could not be created from origins in Egyptian civilization.

Abraham had to abandon the Egyptian scenario of his own volition, for a person can completely reject a certain path only by personally feeling and understanding its unsuitability. It was, in a sense, "a mistake that had to be made." Or, to use Kabbalistic terminology: there was a *kelippah*, an "unclean shell," associated with the birth and upbringing of Ishmael, from which Abraham needed to be liberated in order for Isaac to be born.

Likewise, it was necessary psychologically for Sarah to follow the path of error when she gave Hagar to Abraham, for only in this way could she overcome her excess *gevurah*.

There are mistakes in life that we must make, because those mistakes teach us important lessons. Although the historical price that we pay for those mistakes can be quite steep, we cannot avoid making them.

### 24.6. Sarah Corrects Abraham (21:11-13)

יא וַיֵּרַע הַדָּבָר מְאֹד בְּעֵינֵי אַבְרָהָם עַל אוֹדֹת בְּנוֹ: יב
וַיֹּאמֶר אֱלֹהִים אֶל־אַבְרָהָם אַל־יֵרַע בְּעֵינֶיךָ עַל־הַנַּעַר
וְעַל־אֲמָתֶךָ כֹּל אֲשֶׁר תֹּאמַר אֵלֶיךָ שָׂרָה שְׁמַע בְּקֹלָהּ
כִּי בְיִצְחָק יִקָּרֵא לְךָ זָרַע: יג וְגַם אֶת־בֶּן־הָאָמָה לְגוֹי
אֲשִׂימֶנּוּ כִּי זַרְעֲךָ הוּא:

*[11] The matter distressed Abraham greatly, for it concerned a son of his.*
*[12] But God said to Abraham, "Do not be distressed over the boy or your slave; whatever Sarah tells you, do as she says, for it is through Isaac that offspring shall be continued for you.*
*[13] As for the son of the slave-woman, I will make a nation of him, too, for he is your seed."*

**[12] Whatever Sarah tells you, do as she says, for it is through Isaac that offspring shall be continued for you.** God not only supports Sarah's position on this issue, but also commands Abraham to obey her completely. An enormous change in the hierarchy of Abraham's family is about to occur, because the first stage – Abraham's own advancement – has already taken place. At the second stage of Abraham's family life, the important thing is for him to build his relationship with Isaac, and on that issue Sarah's opinion is the most decisive.

**It is through Isaac that offspring shall be continued for you.** Sarah insists on expelling Ishmael, because otherwise they cannot properly raise Isaac. Given that Isaac and the survival of the Jewish people are at issue, all other considerations are secondary.

Sarah's role is paramount in the family, for her position corrects the errors in Abraham's worldview. As the father of a multitude of nations (17:3), Abraham strives for universality and cosmopolitanism. He loves Ishmael because Ishmael too is his son. But Sarah redirects Abraham from these more general considerations to the specific task at hand, creating the Jewish nation. Sarah is the force that keeps Abraham focused on the primary objective, putting everything else aside, at least for now.

**[13] As for the son of the slave-woman, I will make a nation of him, too, for he is your seed.** Although God confirms Ishmael's significant role in history, that role can be realized only after Isaac's potential is realized. (In particular, we see this in the fact that the Arabs – the descendants of Ishmael – forgot Abraham's monotheism until Muhammad brought them back to it, relying as he did on the Jewish, not the Arab, tradition.) Isaac's education must therefore be made the priority.

### 24.7. Hagar and Ishmael in the Desert (21:14-21)

יד וַיַּשְׁכֵּם אַבְרָהָם ׀ בַּבֹּקֶר וַיִּקַּח־לֶחֶם וְחֵמַת מַיִם וַיִּתֵּן אֶל־הָגָר שָׂם עַל־שִׁכְמָהּ וְאֶת־הַיֶּלֶד וַיְשַׁלְּחֶהָ וַתֵּלֶךְ וַתֵּתַע בְּמִדְבַּר בְּאֵר שָׁבַע: טו וַיִּכְלוּ הַמַּיִם מִן־הַחֵמֶת וַתַּשְׁלֵךְ אֶת־הַיֶּלֶד תַּחַת אַחַד הַשִּׂיחִם: טז וַתֵּלֶךְ וַתֵּשֶׁב לָהּ מִנֶּגֶד הַרְחֵק כִּמְטַחֲוֵי קֶשֶׁת כִּי אָמְרָה כִּי אָמְרָה אַל־אֶרְאֶה

בְּמֹת הַיֶּלֶד וַתֵּשֶׁב מִנֶּגֶד וַתִּשָּׂא אֶת־קֹלָהּ וַתֵּבְךְּ: **יז** וַיִּשְׁמַע אֱלֹהִים אֶת־קוֹל הַנַּעַר וַיִּקְרָא מַלְאַךְ אֱלֹהִים | אֶל־הָגָר מִן־הַשָּׁמַיִם וַיֹּאמֶר לָהּ מַה־לָּךְ הָגָר אַל־תִּירְאִי כִּי־שָׁמַע אֱלֹהִים אֶל־קוֹל הַנַּעַר בַּאֲשֶׁר הוּא־שָׁם: **יח** קוּמִי שְׂאִי אֶת־הַנַּעַר וְהַחֲזִיקִי אֶת־יָדֵךְ בּוֹ כִּי־לְגוֹי גָּדוֹל אֲשִׂימֶנּוּ: **יט** וַיִּפְקַח אֱלֹהִים אֶת־עֵינֶיהָ וַתֵּרֶא בְּאֵר מָיִם וַתֵּלֶךְ וַתְּמַלֵּא אֶת־הַחֵמֶת מַיִם וַתַּשְׁקְ אֶת־הַנָּעַר: **כ** וַיְהִי אֱלֹהִים אֶת־הַנַּעַר וַיִּגְדָּל וַיֵּשֶׁב בַּמִּדְבָּר וַיְהִי רֹבֶה קַשָּׁת: **כא** וַיֵּשֶׁב בְּמִדְבַּר פָּארָן וַתִּקַּח־לוֹ אִמּוֹ אִשָּׁה מֵאֶרֶץ מִצְרָיִם:

[14] Early next morning Abraham took some bread and a skin of water, and gave them to Hagar. He placed them over her shoulder, together with the child, and sent her away. And she wandered about in the wilderness of Beer-Sheba.
[15] When the water was gone from the skin, she left the child under one of the bushes,
[16] and went and sat down at a distance, a bowshot away; for she thought, "Let me not look on as the child dies." And sitting thus afar, she burst into tears.
[17] God heard the cry of the boy, and an angel of God called to Hagar from heaven and said to her, "What troubles you, Hagar? Fear not, for God has heeded the cry of the boy where he is.
[18] Come, lift up the boy and hold him by the hand, for I will make a great nation of him."
[19] Then God opened her eyes and she saw a well of water. She went and filled the skin with water, and let the boy drink.
[20] God was with the boy and he grew up; he dwelt in the wilderness and became a bowman.
[21] He lived in the wilderness of Paran; and his

*mother got a wife for him from the land of Egypt.*

**[14] In the wilderness of Beer-Sheba.** After solving his problems with Abimelech, Abraham apparently left Gerar and moved to the Beersheba region. Later we will discuss this issue in greater detail.

**And she wandered about.** She was wandering and lost, not only physically, but also spiritually and psychologically.

**And she wandered about in the wilderness of Beer-Sheba.** After leaving Abraham's house, Hagar decided to go south, to return to Egypt, her former world.

**[15] When the water was gone from the skin, she left the child under one of the bushes.** Sensing the loss of the life-giving water she had carried from Abraham's house, Hagar despaired of any solution and abandoned the child.

**[16] And sitting thus afar, she burst into tears.. ... [17] God heard the cry of the boy.** God heard the boy's cry, not Hagar's cry. Hagar cannot help Ishmael, but he can help himself. Ishmael was banished because of his own bad behavior, but when he turns to God, the Almighty hears him.

**[17] For God has heeded the cry of the boy where he is.** The literal translation is, "God has heeded the boy's voice." Ishmael "voiced" his admission that he was wrong. The level "where he was" then sufficed for him to be saved.

**[19] Then God opened her eyes and she saw a well of water.** Hagar was dying not for lack of a well. There was in fact a well, but she did not see it – because she was "wandering" in the desert, moving towards Egypt. She therefore could no longer correctly perceive the surrounding reality.

Fundamentally, Hagar is psychologically dependent. Being torn away from Abraham's house is for her nothing less than a catastrophe. Ishmael, however, has the opposite character. He can learn to see the world correctly only by being expelled and left alone in the wilderness with his reality. Only when he has no one else to blame for his problems (as he could do in Abraham's home) does he begin to perceive the actual state of affairs. Thanks to Ishmael's despair, which forces him to seek help from God, salvation comes also to Hagar. She sees the well, and they both survive.

**[20] God was with the boy and he grew up; he dwelt in the wilderness.** After settling in the desert, apart from Isaac, Ishmael finds himself and takes his true place in life – and only then does he receive Divine support. In such a setting Ishmael can understand the family hierarchy and acknowledge his subordinate position in relation to Isaac. For someone who has acquired self-knowledge, this is not a problem. Later, at Abraham's funeral, we will see that Ishmael will be standing next to Isaac, but as a subordinate to him (25:9). In other words, if Ishmael is reined in tightly, there will be no issues with him; otherwise, he begins to lay claim to what is not his, and he destroys the world.

**[21] He lived in the wilderness of Paran; and his mother got a wife for him from the land of Egypt.** The Midrash says that Abraham, rather than losing contact with Ishmael, continued to communicate with him even after he had been expelled. Abraham would come to his son's tent, to see what kind of wife he had taken, and how he was getting along.

Abraham ever remains "the father of a multitude of nations," (17:5) demonstrating the same universality as before. He is not only the forefather of the Jews, but also the spiritual ancestor of the whole world, and he therefore cares for the entire world – in particular, by conveying to the world a part of his heritage, through Ishmael.

# Chapter 25

# Abraham and Abimelech in Beersheba

## 25.1. Abimelech Visits Abraham (21:22-23)

**כב** וַיְהִי בָּעֵת הַהִוא וַיֹּאמֶר אֲבִימֶלֶךְ וּפִיכֹל שַׂר־צְבָאוֹ אֶל־אַבְרָהָם לֵאמֹר אֱלֹהִים עִמְּךָ בְּכֹל אֲשֶׁר־אַתָּה עֹשֶׂה: **כג** וְעַתָּה הִשָּׁבְעָה לִּי בֵאלֹהִים הֵנָּה אִם־תִּשְׁקֹר לִי וּלְנִינִי וּלְנֶכְדִּי כַּחֶסֶד אֲשֶׁר־עָשִׂיתִי עִמְּךָ תַּעֲשֶׂה עִמָּדִי וְעִם־הָאָרֶץ אֲשֶׁר־גַּרְתָּה בָּהּ:

*[22] At that time Abimelech and Phicol, chief of his troops, said to Abraham, "God is with you in everything that you do.*
*[23] Therefore swear to me here by God that you will not deal falsely with me or with my kith and kin, but will deal with me and with the land in which you have sojourned as loyally as I have dealt with you.""*

## [22] At that time Abimelech and Phicol, chief of his

**troops, said to Abraham, "God is with you in everything that you do."** Abraham settled in Beersheba, on the edge of the desert – within the boundaries of Abimelech's dominion, but far removed from the capital. He now receives recognition as a "righteous man living apart." Abimelech notices Abraham's extraordinary success and recognizes that the reason for this success is God's support. That is, Abimelech recognizes Abraham as a spiritual authority. Therefore, Abimelech, accompanied by his military leader Phicol, pays Abraham a state visit as a sign of respect.

**[23] Therefore swear to me here by God that you will not deal falsely with me or with my kith and kin.** Because Abimelech perceives Abraham as a strategic threat, he wants to make an alliance with him that will extend also to his descendants.

**As loyally as I have dealt with you.** Abimelech exaggerates his own merits.

**You ... will deal with me and with the land in which you have sojourned as loyally.** While at the same time, he refers to Abraham using the verb *gar*, "to live as a stranger, without rights." Abraham, however, ignores these inconsistencies and the fact that God had promised to give *him* the entire land, and agrees to conclude the alliance.

Because Abraham had no right to promise any part of the country to Abimelech, the Midrash views this story as a sin on Abraham's part, and believes that this was one of the reasons behind the *Akedah* (the Sacrifice of Isaac). However, the intent here is not to draw a connection between these events in terms of sin and punishment; rather it is a matter of shortcomings and their correction.

Abimelech, a king and politician, sees the situation more clearly than Abraham does. Because he sees Abraham's immense potential, and understands that in the future his descendants will rule over the land, Abimelech wants to receive guarantees from Abraham concerning their children and grandchildren. For Abraham, however, this aspect is less significant, because he has not yet himself created a nation. It is more important to him to be a teacher to the people and to disseminate his views. Although he knows that his descendants will become a nation, he does not yet feel it deeply enough. Only the *Akedah* that still lies just ahead will force Abraham to modify his approach.

Abraham accepts Abimelech's offer to grant him the status of a respected religious leader within his political territory. ("Abraham planted a tamarisk at Beer-Sheba, and invoked there the name of the Lord, the Everlasting God" [verse 33].) The Philistines of that period were noted for their accomplishments in maritime trade and economic and technological development. (Later, in the Book of Samuel, we learn that the Philistines already had iron, while the Israelites were still using weapons of bronze.) Abraham therefore sees in his alliance with the Philistine state an opportunity to influence the world.

Abraham seems to prefer life under Abimelech over his troublesome military-political independence in Hebron. And therefore, "Abraham resided in the land of the Philistines a long time" (verse 34). Only Sarah will later restore the family to Hebron.

## 25.2. Judaism as the Synthesis of Abraham, Isaac and Jacob

If we distill from Abraham's teachings the pure

"Abrahamic" line – universal love, *chesed*, grace, cosmopolitanism, universalism, rejection of political aspirations, correction without coercion, and striving for an alliance with Egypt (the leading civilization of the day) – that is, if we separate Abraham from Isaac and Jacob, we get something that is very far from Judaism.

Likewise, if we distill from Isaac the pure "Isaacian" line – *gevurah*, self-isolation, severity, readiness for self-sacrifice, acceptance of the world as it is with no desire to "improve" it, and strict adherence to the received heritage – we will not be true to Judaism also.

It is precisely the synthesis of all three Patriarchs – Abraham, Isaac, and Jacob – that produced Judaism as it is known and practiced.

## 25.3. The Alliance Between Abraham and Abimelech (21:24-28)

כד וַיֹּאמֶר אַבְרָהָם אָנֹכִי אִשָּׁבֵעַ: כה וְהוֹכִחַ אַבְרָהָם אֶת־
אֲבִימֶלֶךְ עַל־אֹדוֹת בְּאֵר הַמַּיִם אֲשֶׁר גָּזְלוּ עַבְדֵי אֲבִימֶלֶךְ:
כו וַיֹּאמֶר אֲבִימֶלֶךְ לֹא יָדַעְתִּי מִי עָשָׂה אֶת־הַדָּבָר הַזֶּה
וְגַם־אַתָּה לֹא־הִגַּדְתָּ לִּי וְגַם אָנֹכִי לֹא שָׁמַעְתִּי בִּלְתִּי הַיּוֹם:
כז וַיִּקַּח אַבְרָהָם צֹאן וּבָקָר וַיִּתֵּן לַאֲבִימֶלֶךְ וַיִּכְרְתוּ שְׁנֵיהֶם
בְּרִית: כח וַיַּצֵּב אַבְרָהָם אֶת־שֶׁבַע כִּבְשֹׂת הַצֹּאן לְבַדְּהֶן:

*[24] And Abraham said, "I swear it."*
*[25] Then Abraham reproached Abimelech for the well of water which the servants of Abimelech had seized.*
*[26] But Abimelech said, "I do not know who did this; you did not tell me, nor have I heard of it until today."*

*[27] Abraham took sheep and oxen and gave them
to Abimelech, and the two of them made a pact.
[28] Abraham then set seven ewes of the flock
by themselves,*

**[25] Then Abraham reproached Abimelech.** *Even after concluding the alliance, Abraham cannot fail to notice that there
are still unresolved issues between himself and Abimelech.*

**For the well of water which the servants of Abimelech had
seized**: *Only after the fact does the discrepancy come to light
between Abimelech's claim of "dealing loyally" with Abraham,
and Abimelech's slaves having seized Abraham's well.*

**[26] But Abimelech said, "I do not know who did this; you
did not tell me, nor have I heard of it until today."** Rather
than responding to the issue itself, Abimelech simply denies
having any knowledge of the whole affair. But he promises
to make good on everything... And all Abraham can do is to
rely on that promise.

This is yet another lesson for Abraham – to not demonstrate infinite *chesed*, but instead to demand, at very least,
that which belongs to him by right. He therefore now undertakes at least to protect his well in Beersheba from the
attempts of Abimelech's slaves to seize it.

### 25.4. The Essence of Beersheba (21:29-34)

**כט** וַיֹּאמֶר אֲבִימֶלֶךְ אֶל־אַבְרָהָם מָה הֵנָּה שֶׁבַע כְּבָשֹׂת
הָאֵלֶּה אֲשֶׁר הִצַּבְתָּ לְבַדָּנָה: **ל** וַיֹּאמֶר כִּי אֶת־שֶׁבַע
כְּבָשֹׂת תִּקַּח מִיָּדִי בַּעֲבוּר תִּהְיֶה־לִּי לְעֵדָה כִּי חָפַרְתִּי

אֶת־הַבְּאֵר הַזֹּאת: **לא** עַל־כֵּן קָרָא לַמָּקוֹם הַהוּא בְּאֵר
שָׁבַע כִּי שָׁם נִשְׁבְּעוּ שְׁנֵיהֶם: **לב** וַיִּכְרְתוּ בְרִית בִּבְאֵר
שָׁבַע וַיָּקָם אֲבִימֶלֶךְ וּפִיכֹל שַׂר־צְבָאוֹ וַיָּשֻׁבוּ אֶל־אֶרֶץ
פְּלִשְׁתִּים: **לג** וַיִּטַּע אֶשֶׁל בִּבְאֵר שָׁבַע וַיִּקְרָא־שָׁם בְּשֵׁם
יי אֵל עוֹלָם: **לד** וַיָּגָר אַבְרָהָם בְּאֶרֶץ פְּלִשְׁתִּים יָמִים
רַבִּים:

*[29] and Abimelech said to Abraham, "What
mean these seven ewes which you have set
apart?"*
*[30] He replied, "You are to accept these seven
ewes from me as proof that I dug this well."*
*[31] Hence that place was called Beer-Sheba, for
there the two of them swore an oath.*
*[32] When they had concluded the pact at
Beer-Sheba, Abimelech and Phicol, chief of his
troops, departed and returned to the land of the
Philistines.*
*[33] [Abraham] planted a tamarisk at Beer-
Sheba, and invoked there the name of the Lord,
the Everlasting God.*
*[34] And Abraham resided in the land of the
Philistines a long time.*

**[30] "You are to accept these seven ... [31] Hence that place
was called Beer-Sheba, for there the two of them swore
an oath.** The word *sheva* means "seven" and also "oath." The
name Beersheba can therefore be translated both as "the
well of the oath," and "the well of seven."

**[33] He planted a tamarisk at Beer-Sheba, and invoked
there the name of the Lord, the Everlasting God.** Thus,

the alliance between the political authority and the spiritual leader is now concluded, and Abraham has complete freedom to disseminate his ideas.

**[34] And Abraham resided in the land of the Philistines a long time.** That is, he felt no desire to move from there to any other place. Abraham was quite satisfied with his status of spiritual leader while living in a remote area of the Philistine territory, under the rule of Abimelech.

After finally reaching the apex of his personal development, Abraham now needs to build his connection with Isaac. This connection is important not only for Abraham, but also for Isaac himself, and for this reason it must wait for Isaac to grow up. Abraham lives all this time in Beersheba, "the well of the oath of seven."

The number seven is associated with the seven days of Creation, and always indicates the seven *middot* – the seven lower *sefirot*. In this case, these seven *sefirot* are born from the "well of the seven" -their source, according to the scheme of the *sefirot*, is the attribute of *binah* (understanding). *Binah* is a structure of rigidity and logic, but it is a "hidden" *sefirah* that found its position on the *sefirot* tree even before the Seven Days of Creation.

Beersheba is therefore located not in plain sight of all, but on the edge of the desert. Abraham, in communion with Sarah and Isaac, goes through a certain path of development hidden from prying eyes. Until Isaac grows up, this new potential cannot be manifested openly.

Chapter 26

# Akedat Yitzchak, "The Sacrifice of Isaac"

## 26.1. Lessons from the "Binding of Isaac"

In Jewish tradition, what happened on Mount Moriah is called *akedat yitzchak*, "the binding of Isaac", but in the Christian (European) tradition it is known as "the sacrifice of Isaac." The Christian approach focuses on the intent (to sacrifice Isaac), while the Jewish one emphasizes what actually happened (Isaac was bound, but not sacrificed).

The story of *Akedat Yitzchak* is psychologically a very difficult one for us. Many see its meaning in glorifying the greatness of Abraham: God told him to sacrifice his son, and he proceeded to carry out the order, showing no mercy for his son. Such an interpretation cannot be called "wrong," but it is far from sufficient. It emphasizes Abraham's obedience, yet obedience is not at all his characteristic quality, and besides, this is not the main point of the story of *Akedah*.

Others see the meaning of the *Akedah* to be the lesson that the Almighty does not want human sacrifice. Of course, this is true, but it is again insufficient for understanding the details of this complex story.

Following the approach of *Biblical Dynamics*, in which the Patriarchs are viewed as personalities who undergo constant dynamic development, the very question of the meaning of this story must be phrased differently: How did Abraham evolve as a person during these events and due to them?

With this approach, the *Akedah*, "the binding," is viewed as a process of establishing contact with, and the proper relationship between, *chesed*-Abraham and *gevurah*-Isaac.

The *Akedah* is the last story of this *Va-yera'* portion. The portion began with Abraham receiving the news of the future birth of Isaac, and ends (in the *Akedah*) with Abraham establishing a dialogue with Isaac. Thus, the *Va-yera'* portion as a whole is devoted to the transition from "Abraham only" to the system of "Abraham plus his son Isaac," which makes possible the future creation of the Jewish people.

In Hebrew, the word *ben*, "son," is closely related to the verb *b-n-h*, forming the basis for *livnot*, "to build." A person's future, his family line, and his occupation are all built through his son – and he fully becomes what he is meant to be only upon realizing his relationship with his son. Only by building a relationship with Isaac – *gevurah* – will Abraham be able to complete the purification and creation of the attribute of *chesed*.

### 26.2. "God Put Abraham to the Test" (22:1)

א וַיְהִי אַחַר הַדְּבָרִים הָאֵלֶּה וְהָאֱלֹהִים נִסָּה אֶת־
אַבְרָהָם וַיֹּאמֶר אֵלָיו אַבְרָהָם וַיֹּאמֶר הִנֵּנִי:

*[1] Some time afterward, God put Abraham*

*to the test. He said to him, "Abraham," and he*
*answered, "Here I am."*

**[1] Some time afterward.** In the Torah text, this phrase that introduces the *Akedah* is expressed as *ahar ha-devarim ha-eleh*, "after these events." The first thing the Torah wants us to know about the *Akedah* is that it must be understood in the context of, and in connection with, the events that led up to it. Jewish tradition offers two possibilities for understanding this connection.

The first of these interprets the story of the *Akedah* as a response to the immediately preceding event – the making of an alliance between Abraham and Abimelech. In response to the misplaced benevolence that Abraham bestowed on Abimelech, God judges Abraham, as if to say, "I have given you a son to inherit and possess the land. If you don't need that land, then give me back your son."

*Davar* – whence the plural, *devarim* – in *ahar ha-devarim ha-eleh* ("after these events") can mean "event" or "deed," but at least as often means "word."

The second approach therefore interprets the given phrase not as "after these events," but as "after these utterances" (i.e., of Ishmael). The Torah itself reports not a single dialogue between Ishmael and Isaac, but the Midrash puts into Ishmael's mouth the following words spoken to Isaac: "You were circumcised at infancy, when others made that choice for you. Whereas I, unlike you, could have refused to be circumcised, but I nevertheless consented. Therefore, my sacrifice, and thus my merit, are both greater than yours."

Isaac, however, instead of explaining to Ishmael that being circumcised entails no sacrifice to begin with, answers Ishmael hotly: "Well, I, as it happens, would gladly make an even far greater sacrifice than you did. You sacrificed only a single body part. But I, if God should so command me, would gladly offer *my entire self* as a sacrifice upon the altar!"

Once Isaac had spoken these words (which he, of course, should never have done), God followed through by holding Isaac literally to his pledge.

This story cautions us against an excess of "enthusiastic fanaticism," and the impropriety of speaking too freely of one's readiness to die for one's ideals.

There is, however, a third approach, which makes no attempt to connect the *Akedah* with any specific event that preceded it. "After these events" can also mean that the *Akedah* situation developed simply because "Abraham resided in the land of the Philistines a long time" (21:34).

**God put Abraham to the test.** It is here that the Torah first introduces the concept of a test, or trial. We have already noted earlier that *nisayon* actually means not "testing," but rather "experience" – the purpose of a test is to "gain experience." The trials of the Patriarchs in the Torah are always intended to help them overcome their base inclinations; *nisayon* is can thus be thought of as the education through the acquisition of experience in the process of solving complex problems that run contrary to the nature of the individual being tested.

Moreover, the word *nisayon* is also phonetically related to the root *naso*, "to lift" or "to elevate." Thus, the phrase can be translated as "God elevated Abraham." God elevated Abraham by giving him a new dimension of understanding.

**God put Abraham to the test.** Why does the Torah not mention that God tested Isaac too? After all, Isaac, now already an adult, went to the sacrifice voluntarily and fully aware of what was supposed to happen. Was it not Isaac's test as well?

The reason is that Abraham, whose essence is *chesed*, had to go against his nature and against his deep-seated inclinations during these events. He was being asked not to give, but to take away – an incredibly difficult assignment for Abraham, because it threatened to demolish his entire value system.

Within Isaac's coordinate system – as for the attribute of *gevurah* which he represents – as difficult as it is to sacrifice oneself, doing so is not an unbearable challenge. It is for him not an ordeal, but only an experience, albeit a highly challenging one. *Gevurah* is the desire for everything to happen according to the laws of justice. If that attribute senses that it is guilty of any wrongdoing, it wants to bear the punishment for that.

In a sense, then, *gevurah* has "a penchant for self-flagellation." Therefore, as Isaac sees it, since he has not lived up to his ideal, sacrificing himself is not unreasonable. It is as though he says, "Since I have been found deficient, I have only myself to blame, and perhaps I do therefore actually deserve to die." Surely Isaac wants to live, but, above all, he wants justice to be served. If *gevurah*, which is the attribute of judgment, requires you to die, then you must die.

Since everything is created imperfectly, everyone and everything will always be guilty if measured by an ideal standard. This is one of the key problems of *gevurah*, which judges the world with standards that are in reality unattainable. A person completely immersed in *gevurah* may even begin to hate the whole world (and himself too) for its shortcomings. Therefore, it is very important to limit *gevurah*, which is what the *Akedah* accomplished.

**And he answered, "Here I am."** Abraham's answer, *hineni*, means not only "here I am", but "I am all at attention." This expression plays a crucial role in the story of *Akedah*: it is found again in Abraham's response to Isaac (22:7) and in Abraham's response to God (22:11). This phrase expresses readiness to answer a question with every ounce of one's being. If Abraham will not reveal his soul, and will offer any lesser response, creating a connection of any kind between himself and Isaac will be impossible.

### 26.3. "Take Your Son" (22: 2)

ב וַיֹּאמֶר קַח־נָא אֶת־בִּנְךָ אֶת־יְחִידְךָ אֲשֶׁר־אָהַבְתָּ אֶת־
יִצְחָק וְלֶךְ־לְךָ אֶל־אֶרֶץ הַמֹּרִיָּה וְהַעֲלֵהוּ שָׁם לְעֹלָה עַל
אַחַד הֶהָרִים אֲשֶׁר אֹמַר אֵלֶיךָ:

*[2] And He said, "Take your son, your favored one, Isaac, whom you love, and go to the land of Moriah, and offer him there as a burnt offering on one of the heights that I will point out to you."*

[2] **Take your son.** The Hebrew includes the word *na*, usually translated as "please" – *please* take your son. God does not command, but only requests, and Abraham must decide for himself whether to comply. Otherwise it would not be a test.

**Your son, your favored one, whom you love, Isaac.** The Midrash explains this elaborate enumeration not as God's monologue, but as a dialogue between Him and Abraham. To the command, "take your son," Abraham replies, "But I have two sons: Isaac and Ishmael." God specifies, "Your favored one" – literally, "your one and only." Abraham responds,

"But each one is his mother's one and only." God specifies, "Whom you love." Abraham answers, "But I love both." Only then God finally specifies unequivocally, "Isaac."

God does not express immediately what he wants, because Abraham must first continue to advance through graded stages of understanding and recognition that his only heir is Isaac.

We recall that ever since the birth of Isaac there has been an ongoing dispute between Sarah and Abraham over who is Abraham's true son. God repeatedly points out to Abraham that that son is Isaac; while Ishmael, the son of a maidservant, is "seed" but not a "son." "Seed" inherits some of the qualities of his father, and may even receive his blessing, but cannot be the successor to his father's life work.

But now that Abraham has, as it were, already accepted this relationship between his children, the situation is suddenly reversed.

## 26.4. From Back-to-Back Connection to Face-to-Face Connection

In the course of the *Akedah*, Abraham changes his attitude towards Isaac as his heir, which evolves from recognition due to pressure from Above to recognition by his own choice. In order for this transition to take place, God must first release Abraham from the decision that he made under pressure regarding Isaac as his heir.

This spiritual mechanism is known in the Kabbalah by the term *nesirah*, "sawing." A classic example of sawing is the creation of Eve from Adam. Initially there was the dual Adam, in which both male and female attributes were combined back-to-back. God separated the "edge" (rib) from him and rebuilt it into a woman, after which Adam and Eve, as independent entities, could already be connected independently and by their own choice, "face to face."

So long as the two are "connected back-to-back," perforce, by the fact of kinship, they are unable to see each other as distinct personalities. Parents in general are a familiar example of this. Because their child is inseparable from themselves, they cannot fully acknowledge it as a distinct entity. A child cannot reveal himself as a fully-fledged, independent personality in his communication with his parents; this can happen only after the child marries, and has a face-to-face relationship with his spouse. And Adam likewise, in order to be united "face-to-face" with Eve, needed first to break his back-to-back connection with her. This is *nesirah*, "sawing."

Abraham, forced to accept Isaac as his heir, was united with the idea of such an inheritance as a "back-to-back" relationship. God forcibly instructed Abraham that no one but Isaac was suitable for this role. Abraham then acknowledged the Divine order, but such a violent communication is incomplete, and for the continuation of the development of a nation it is necessary to unite *hesed* and *gevurah* with an absolute connection. For this to happen, that *hesed* must first be "faceted" and limited, so that it becomes proper *hesed*. (It is in this that all of Abraham's prior personal advancement consists.) And this purified *hesed* must then be united with *gevurah*.

For the emergence of an absolute connection between *hesed* and *gevurah*, Abraham and Isaac must build their connection as between two independent personalities. For that to happen, Abraham must first get past his acceptance of the idea that Isaac is his heir under "pressure from above," by freely embracing that idea on his own. This is the meaning of the story of *Akedat Yitzchak*: God puts Abraham in a situation where the question of inheritance, for all its apparent certainty, suddenly becomes incomprehensible and ambiguous.

### 26.5. "And Offer Him There as a Burnt Offering" (22:2)

וְלֶךְ־לְךָ אֶל־אֶרֶץ הַמֹּרִיָּה וְהַעֲלֵהוּ שָׁם לְעֹלָה עַל
אַחַד הֶהָרִים אֲשֶׁר אֹמַר אֵלֶיךָ׃

*[2] ... and go to the land of Moriah, and offer him there as a burnt offering on one of the heights that I will point out to you."*

**[2] And go.** The Hebrew is *lech lecha*, the very same expression with which God addressed Abraham at the very beginning of his journey (12:1). This can hardly be accidental. It means that we have here the continuation of movement previously begun. But we struggle to understand how we can possibly reconcile the words there (12:2), "I will make of you a great nation," spoken at that original *lech lecha*, with God's order here to sacrifice Isaac. These two moments seem incompatible, and this contradiction sets the tone for the entire event.

**On one of the heights.** There is uncertainty in both of these *lech lecha* instances. In the initial *lech lecha* God tells Abraham, "Go forth ... to the land that I will show you" (12:1), and here, "Offer him there ... on one of the heights that I will point out to you." In both cases the destination is left unspecified. This uncertainty is materially connected with the turning points in Abraham's life to which the two verses refer. Uncertainty is itself an integral component of any task that God commands us to perform, and is also a necessary condition for our own advancement.

God told Abraham, "Take your son, your favored one, whom you love, Isaac." Isaac's status as Abraham's only true heir would appear to be fully defined here. Even earlier, from the very beginning of his arrival in the land, God repeatedly made it clear to Abraham that no one but Isaac could be his successor – neither Lot, nor Ishmael, nor Eliezer, nor Abraham's Babylonian or Egyptian disciples.

But now, when Abraham has already agreed to all that, the entire situation is turned on its head. God suddenly orders that Isaac be sacrificed, and Abraham again finds himself in a state of utter confusion. But all this is necessary, because the confusion of feelings and situational ambiguity provide the required impetus for further advancement.

**To the land of Moriah.** Although it is called "Moriah" from the very beginning, only at the end of the *Akedah* will we learn what the meaning of this name is. (And only later will we learn that this is one of the names of Jerusalem.)

The meaning of many geographical names in the Torah becomes clear only after the fact. For example, we have seen that when Abimelech comes to Abraham, who lives in Beersheba, the meaning of the name Beersheba as the "well of seven" and "the well of the oath" becomes clear only after they conclude their treaty. Similarly, the city of Bethel was already called that in the time of Abraham (12:8), but only after the story of Jacob (28:18) we will learn why this place is named "the House of God." This process of reinterpreting place names shows that a lofty potential was originally laid on this place, which can only be later realized, through the actions of the Patriarchs.

**Offer him there as a burnt offering.** The expression *le-ha'alot olah*, "to bring as a burnt offering" is also ambiguous. God's command to Abraham, translated very literally, means, "take him up there in ascension." In the end, this ascension was in fact realized – not in the sense of a sacrifice or burnt offering, however, but only in the senses of ascending the mountain and personal advancement. The true meaning of God's words was revealed only after the fact, after Abraham undertook to act according to his initial (and at that moment quite correct!) understanding of these words as a command to sacrifice Isaac as a burnt offering. Initially, Abraham could not possibly have understood God's words otherwise, for their true meaning emerged only later, when Abraham was already in the process of carrying out the necessary actions as he initially understood them.

It is important to note that not only in antiquity (Abraham lived ca. the 20th century BCE), but even many centuries later, sacrificing one's children was by no means a rare event among the nations of the world. Among the ancient populations of Canaan and Phoenicia in particular, this practice was in fact quite common.

The Torah, however, categorically prohibits any human sacrifice, which is also one of the lessons of the *Akedat Yitzchak*. Even if "ideally" – that is, from the Divine point of view – a person must be sacrificed, in reality that is totally unacceptable. A man must not become a lamb; rather, he must be replaced by a lamb.

## 26.6. Three Potential Heirs (22:3)

ג וַיַּשְׁכֵּם אַבְרָהָם בַּבֹּקֶר וַיַּחֲבשׁ אֶת־חֲמֹרוֹ וַיִּקַּח אֶת־
שְׁנֵי נְעָרָיו אִתּוֹ וְאֵת יִצְחָק בְּנוֹ וַיְבַקַּע עֲצֵי עֹלָה וַיָּקָם
וַיֵּלֶךְ אֶל־הַמָּקוֹם אֲשֶׁר־אָמַר־לוֹ הָאֱלֹהִים:

*[3] So early next morning, Abraham saddled his
ass and took with him two of his servants and
his son Isaac. He split the wood for the burnt
offering, and he set out for the place of which
God had told him.*

**[3] So early next morning.** This is the time of *hesed*, when
God is ready to render additional mercy to the world that
has just awakened. Abraham hopes for Divine *hesed* – and
sets off to find out who will be his heir.

**And took with him two of his servants and his son Isaac.**
The Hebrew is *ne'arav*, "his youths." Since the Torah specifically indicates that Abraham took with him two "youths,"
they cannot be considered mere servants. There is an indication here of something more substantial. The Midrash argues
that these two youths were Ishmael and Eliezer, because the
matter of who would become Abraham's rightful heir had
now once again been called entirely into question. Note
that the term *na'ar*, "youth," can also mean a "subordinate,"
and is not necessarily related to age. It is therefore possible
that "his youths" refers to Eliezer and Ishmael.

And so, we have three people walking along the road with
Abraham: Isaac, Ishmael and Eliezer. All three are adherents
of monotheism, "sons of the Covenant" (meaning the commandment of circumcision), and all three are Abraham's
disciples and his potential heirs. Isaac is about to be sacrificed. But what will happen beyond that is unclear, with all
options equally viable.

Should Abraham's heir be his son Isaac, in whom the
realization of Abraham's teachings will happen through a
nation? Or will that heir be Abraham's disciple Eliezer, who

represents "teachings having no nationalist component"? Or will it perhaps be Ishmael, in whom there is a nationalist element, except that it is integrated with Egypt? On they go to Mount Moriah, to unravel this riddle.

## 26.7. Three Days on the Road: Abraham's Awareness of His Actions (22:4)

ד בַּיּוֹם הַשְּׁלִישִׁי וַיִּשָּׂא אַבְרָהָם אֶת־עֵינָיו וַיַּרְא אֶת־הַמָּקוֹם מֵרָחֹק:

*[4] On the third day Abraham looked up and saw the place from afar.*

**[4] On the third day.** For three days Abraham proceeds with the knowledge that he must sacrifice his son. Abraham is given these three days in order to ponder the situation and to rethink his entire life.

It is difficult for Abraham to sacrifice his son Isaac, not because the sacrifice of children was something unthinkable (for as we have already noted, it was then quite common), but because he himself had grappled precisely with that issue all his life. He taught the world *chesed* – that people must be shown mercy, and surely not be deprived of their lives by our own hands. For Abraham to sacrifice his son was a violation of every one of his teachings and aims.

Abraham was not being asked to carry out God's order in a frenzy of religious ecstasy, without having time to give it the least thought. Because sacrificing a child is not a decision that anyone can make lightly, when children were sacrificed in ancient cults, their parents were often made to ingest a potion specially designed to induce a trance. But Abraham, on the contrary, had to do nothing but walk for three consecutive days, in order to eliminate any possible trace whatsoever of religious ecstasy. This waiting period forced him to contend with the full depth of the crisis in the matter of his posterity.

**Abraham looked up and saw the place from afar.** Only after three days of careful deliberation, and after consciously confirming in his own mind that he was ready to follow God's command, could Abraham see Mount Moriah from afar. It was a signal to him that the time had come to make his final decision.

When under the pressure of a conflict situation our stress intensifies to a sufficiently high degree, only then do we begin to see also the "place" where the conflict will be resolved.

### 26.8. Abraham Chooses Isaac (22:5)

ה וַיֹּאמֶר אַבְרָהָם אֶל־נְעָרָיו שְׁבוּ־לָכֶם פֹּה עִם־הַחֲמוֹר
וַאֲנִי וְהַנַּעַר נֵלְכָה עַד־כֹּה וְנִשְׁתַּחֲוֶה וְנָשׁוּבָה אֲלֵיכֶם׃

*[5] Then Abraham said to his servants, "You stay here with the ass. The boy and I will go up there; we will worship and we will return to you."*

**[5] Stay here with the ass.** Nothing prevented Abraham from proceeding to the mountaintop in the company of all of his companions. But having "seen the place from afar" and now feeling the need to come to a decision, Abraham performs an action of utmost importance: he chooses Isaac and separates him from Ishmael and Eliezer.

**The boy and I will go up there.** Until now, Isaac had been forced upon Abraham as his heir. But now that God has again made the problem of posterity an open question, Abraham, after giving it his full concentration during three days of travel, is already making his own independent choice.

When Abraham himself, with no immediate direction from God, singles out Isaac and understands that he must proceed with him, leaving the others in place, this is a critical personal advancement for Abraham. Only after making this independent decision can his dialogue with Isaac begin. The Torah does not tell us of any earlier conversations between Abraham and Isaac, while they lived together in Beersheba. Apparently, there had been no serious dialogue between them during all that time, because Abraham was not ready for it. Dialogue between them becomes possible only after Abraham, on his own, singles out Isaac for sacrifice.

Abraham also instructs Ishmael and Eliezer to "stay here with the ass." The word *hamor*, "donkey," has a common root with *homer*, "materiality." (Similarly, the meaning of the well-known concept of "the Messiah riding a white donkey" is that spirituality, which the Messiah symbolizes, is advancing on a foundation of materiality. But, moreover, it is white, that is, purified – materiality that is not something alien to spirituality and interfering with it, but materiality that serves as a basis for spirituality.) Ishmael and Eliezer are equated to an ass not in any "animal" sense, but in the fact that they remain entirely in this purely material world.

The Midrash tells how Abraham, after "seeing the place from afar," asked his companions what they saw on the mountain. Only Isaac answered that he (like Abraham himself) saw the image of the Temple there. Ishmael and Eliezer saw nothing, and Abraham therefore left them "with the ass" – at the level of materiality.

With his instruction to sacrifice Isaac, God removed Isaac from the status of Abraham's posterity, "sawing" the connection between them. And now when Abraham separates Isaac from the others, not under pressure but by his own choice, he connects with Isaac "face to face," replacing their former "back-to-back" connection. He realizes that he has no option for the sacrifice except Isaac. From that moment, Abraham proceeds with Isaac not by force of circumstances but freely and deliberately – although he still does not know what will happen next.

**We will worship and we will return to you.** Abraham tells the youths, "we will worship and we will return," both in the plural – that is, he has hopes for a positive outcome, even if he does not know exactly how that will happen. In any event, Ishmael and Eliezer are no longer his fellow travelers, and he understands that to continue God's teachings, he and Isaac must be together.

### 26.9. "We Will Worship and We Will Return to You"

The words "we will worship and we will return to you" also express a non-trivial and essential concept in Judaism concerning the connection between mystical experience and its surrounding reality.

Actually, "we will worship" is expressed in the original Hebrew as *nishtachave*, "we will bow." Grammatically this is a very problematic word. It is difficult to understand it as a reflexive verbal form of *binyan hishtaf'el*, in which the letter *shin* is auxiliary and not part of the root. (This rare *binyan* is not among the seven *binyanim* common in modern Hebrew. Other examples of words in such *binyanim*: *shichtuv*, "rewriting;" *shichzur*, "renovation;" *shichpul*, "excavation;" *shidrug*, "leveling"). In this case, the root of the word *nishtachave* is *chet-vav-hey*, recalling the name of Chavah (Eve), "the mother of all living things" (3:20). Thus, *nishtachave*, "we shall worship," means "let us return to the source of all life."

Note that what is meant is not bowing in the modern sense of the word, but submission by prostrating oneself. This form of greeting was adopted with respect to God and also to flesh-and-blood kings; it expresses self-deprecation and complete self-denial. As it relates to the *sefirot*, such submission is "dissolution in Divinity;" when a person ceases to be himself and becomes "naught," thereby achieving unity with Divinity.

Here we see the difference between Jewish mysticism and the mysticism of other nations. Among non-Jewish mystics, the idea is widespread that the goal of man is to merge completely with God, to cease being a separate entity, and to dissolve in Divinity. But the Jewish mystical ideal is different: the feeling of dissolution in Divinity is vitally important, but following that one must come back to himself. The main feature of this process is not even the dissolution, but the return to one's original self afterwards.

Nonetheless, one must not return empty-handed, but must bring a particle of the mystical experience back to this world.

In saying "we will worship and we will return to you," Abraham expresses the idea that after worship and total dissolution in the Divine, it is possible to return to earthly life. This is a highly unconventional religious outlook.

Judaism is a religion of life in this world, not a religion of death that is realized in the afterlife. The Torah says: "I have put before you life and death ... choose life" (Deut. 30:19). The *Akedah* is telling us that death did not happen, and life was renewed.

We find an expression of this same idea later, during the Temple period, when on Yom Kippur the High Priest would enter the Holy of Holies with a rope tied around his leg. The usual explanation is that this rope was a precaution: Since no one but the High Priest is allowed to enter the Holy of Holies, in the event that the High Priest should suddenly die there, the rope could be used to pull him back out. But as this was highly unlikely to happen, the custom has a simpler and more natural explanation.

Rather, the purpose of the rope was to remind the High Priest that he had to exit the Holy of Holies after completing his task there; otherwise he might have been tempted to stay there forever. The Holy of Holies is a place so sublime, and affords such a pure feeling of unity with God, that it is conceivable that the High Priest might not have wanted to return from there at all. But remaining in the Holy of Holies would be highly improper behavior on his part, and he therefore needed to be reminded that he had entered the Holy of Holies only as our agent, to bring out something from there back to our ordinary world.

The rope is for "pulling out" the High Priest, as it were – to restrain him from succumbing to the desire to "remain in Heaven" (that is, to escape death). After the exit of the High Priest from the Holy of Holies, that is, at the end of Yom Kippur, the people would arrange a feast on his behalf – to celebrate that he had yet again returned from that other world safe and sound.

Such is Judaism's approach to the world. Since in this ordinary world there is no obvious and direct contact with

God, to accomplish that it is sometimes necessary to enter the so-called "higher realms," which means severing to some extent one's connection with this lower world. But we cannot completely break away from this world; we must return to it eventually. One can enter those "higher realms" only in order to bring something down from there, but not for the sake of the ascent itself.

## 26.10. "And the Two Walked Off Together" (22:6)

וַיִּקַּח אַבְרָהָם אֶת־עֲצֵי הָעֹלָה וַיָּשֶׂם עַל־יִצְחָק בְּנוֹ
וַיִּקַּח בְּיָדוֹ אֶת־הָאֵשׁ וְאֶת־הַמַּאֲכֶלֶת וַיֵּלְכוּ שְׁנֵיהֶם
יַחְדָּו:

*[6] Abraham took the wood for the burnt offering and put it on his son Isaac. He himself took the firestone and the knife; and the two walked off together.*

**[6] And put it on his son Isaac.** Here, for the first time, Abraham views Isaac as "his son."

**And the two walked off together.** Until now they were far from each other. Initially, Abraham had done everything himself: "Abraham saddled his ass, ... he split the wood, ... and he set out for the place of which God had told him" – all in the singular. There was still no dialogue between him and Isaac at that stage. Abraham was in a state of confusion. Not knowing who would succeed him, he therefore did everything himself.

But now Abraham approaches Isaac. He transfers the

wood to him, and leaves the donkey (as a symbol of materiality) below. "The two walked off together" indicates that now, for the first time, there is true unity between Abraham and Isaac. This has come about because Abraham has now made his choice.

### 26.11. Gevurah as Subordinate to Hesed (22:7)

ז וַיֹּאמֶר יִצְחָק אֶל־אַבְרָהָם אָבִיו וַיֹּאמֶר אָבִי וַיֹּאמֶר
הִנֶּנִּי בְנִי׃...

*[7] Then Isaac said to his father Abraham, "Father!" And he answered, "Yes, my son." ...*

When Abraham and Isaac come together by choice, when they are joined face to face, a dialogue begins between them. This is the most important moment of the *Akedah*.

**[7] Isaac said to his father Abraham, "Father!."** Isaac is not merely addressing Abraham to get his attention. The Torah would have no need to inform us of that. Rather, it means that Isaac is now aware of Abraham as his father, and is acknowledging that.

*Gevurah*, the attribute of Isaac, now addresses *chesed*, the attribute of Abraham, and says that he is aware of *chesed* as his "father" and its foundation. *Gevurah* tells *chesed* that it does not absolutize itself, that it is only secondary, and that it is only a product of *chesed*. The goal is not to realize justice, nor the attribute of the court and the law, for these do not per se constitute value. On the contrary, the goal is kindness and grace. Justice and the law are only auxiliary (albeit necessary) tools for a more complete realization of *chesed*.

Isaac recognizes that all his qualities come from Abraham, and he therefore subordinates himself to his father's aspirations. This correction of *gevurah* is a most important aspect of the *Akeidah* story.

*Chesed* is a complete, semantic attribute with the well-defined goal of bestowing kindness on all, so long as it remains possible and so long as there is no conflict with other counteracting *sefirot*. In all events, *chesed* always remains the principal consideration.

The situation with *gevurah*, however, is different. *Gevurah* is a compelling desire for equity and correctness. But if *gevurah* decides that this desire outweighs all other considerations, then the result is universal collapse. To make achieving justice one's only goal, to the exclusion of all else, is a huge mistake.

Moreover, according to the Kabbalah, evil is born precisely from the absolutization of the attribute of *gevurah*. Separating *gevurah* from *chesed* is a source of evil, because evil takes root in the world as the result of a desire for excessively harsh application of law, judgment, and order. Everything in the world is imperfect, and therefore, when the attribute of judgment is excessively applied, the entire universe will be blamed and found guilty, and cannot continue to exist. Therefore, *gevurah* must be a subordinate attribute, not an all-compelling one.

**And he answered, "Yes, my son."** The Hebrew is, *hineni beni*, "Here I am, my son." Seeing that Isaac (*gevurah*) has realized his subordination, Abraham (*chesed*) says to him: *Hineni*, "Here I am." (It is the second *hineni* in this story.) Abraham is addressing these words not only to Isaac, but also to God. Abraham acknowledges that Isaac is his son. Until now, only the Torah itself speaks of Isaac as Abraham's son. Abraham had referred only to Ishmael, but not to Isaac, as "my son."

*Chesed*, too, admits that it is not absolute, that it needs *gevurah* for proper self-actualization. This means establishing contact, a face-to-face connection, when each has come to an understanding that he needs the other, and also feels a desire to engage in dialogue with him. Each of the two ideals alone represents only one side of life; for full realization the two ideals must be united.

### 26.12. "God Will See" (22:7-8)

ח :וַיֹּאמֶר הִנֵּה הָאֵשׁ וְהָעֵצִים וְאַיֵּה הַשֶּׂה לְעֹלָה...
וַיֹּאמֶר אַבְרָהָם אֱלֹהִים יִרְאֶה־לּוֹ הַשֶּׂה לְעֹלָה בְּנִי
:וַיֵּלְכוּ שְׁנֵיהֶם יַחְדָּו

*[7] ... And he said, "Here are the firestone and the wood; but where is the sheep for the burnt offering?"*
*[8] And Abraham said, "God will see to the sheep for His burnt offering, my son." And the two of them walked on together.*

**[7] Where is the sheep for the burnt offering?.** Isaac, the attribute of *gevurah*, strives to ensure that everything is just right. Seeing fire and firewood, he therefore asks where the lamb is, and wants to hear in response how the problem can be corrected.

**God will see.** Abraham (*chesed*) tells Isaac (*gevurah*) that to this question – which is completely legitimate from the point of view of logic – there is no real answer. By saying, "God will see," Abraham wants to convey to Isaac that *gevurah* should not demand absolute correctness from the world. In life, the most important things are revealed unexpectedly and illogically, because life is immeasurably more complex than any mere correctness, and does not fit into a formal scheme. Thus, Abraham's choice of words is intended not to appease Isaac, but to change his worldview.

**And the two of them walked on together.** Isaac's g*evurah* is already less severe. He is ready to accept the world as it is, even if it still seems to him illogical and wrong.

**God will see.** The Midrash connects the word *yir'eh*, "will see," with *yir'ah*, "fear" or "awe," from which the name of Mount Moriah is derived. God will provide – that is, He will find a way out of the contradiction. In a situation where we have conflicting aspirations of *chesed* and *gevurah*, we must strive to let both be realized simultaneously. And since we are unable to reconcile them on our own, we hope for Divine support – that God will see, that is, "discern" and will find a way to make reconciliation possible. This is exactly why Abraham and Isaac are finally united here, on the way to Mount Moriah.

But besides discernment, Moriah contains the idea of trepidation, *yir'ah*. It is not the fear of suffering injury, but the desire to comply with one's assigned task and Divine mission. It is this striving and sense of responsibility that helps to us to achieve the harmonization of *chesed* and *gevurah*.

The essence of trepidation is awareness of distance, a sense of distance from God. Here is manifest the connection between "vision" and "trembling." In order to see, you have to move back some distance. Similarly, trembling also requires remoteness – awareness of one's finiteness and smallness compared with Divinity's infinitude. Once you see things in this light, you begin to understand that your attribute is only one of many, and is therefore in itself incomplete. On this basis it is now possible to unite it with other attributes.

Thus, Moriah is both a "mountain of discretion" and a "mountain of trepidation." Uniting *chesed* and *gevurah* is possible only if there is awe in relation to God, and at the same time, only when it happens by the Almighty's discretion.

The integration of seemingly incompatible attributes is possible only as part of a larger effort to solve the Divine task that God "sees" for us – because only in the course of making this decision do you truly understand that you need your fellow man, and that he complements you just as you complement him. The unification of *chesed* and *gevurah* then happens not by diminishing one attribute at the expense of another, but through compromise, and through awareness of the need for both in the face of the Divine task.

**And the two of them walked on together.** This phrase appears twice here, in close succession. First, Abraham and Isaac walk together in a mostly physical sense – separating themselves from Ishmael and Eliezer, and understanding that only they are the Jewish nation. But now they also "walk on together" spiritually, having come to understand that they complement each other and can only achieve completion through a genuine union.

### 26.13. The Akedah, the Binding of Isaac (22:9)

ט וַיָּבֹאוּ אֶל־הַמָּקוֹם אֲשֶׁר אָמַר־לוֹ הָאֱלֹהִים וַיִּבֶן שָׁם

אַבְרָהָם אֶת־הַמִּזְבֵּחַ וַיַּעֲרֹךְ אֶת־הָעֵצִים וַיַּעֲקֹד אֶת־
יִצְחָק בְּנוֹ וַיָּשֶׂם אֹתוֹ עַל־הַמִּזְבֵּחַ מִמַּעַל לָעֵצִים:

*[9] They arrived at the place of which God had told him. Abraham built an altar there; he laid out the wood; he bound his son Isaac; he laid him on the altar, on top of the wood.*

**[9] He bound his son Isaac.** *Akeidah,* "binding," is what *gevurah,* the attribute of judgment, requires. *Gevurah* should be bound, made dependent on and subjected to *chesed.* It should not be completely eliminated, however. In no way should *gevurah* ever be destroyed. Isaac must therefore be bound, but not sacrificed.

## 26.14. Abraham's Double Name: "Abraham! Abraham!" (22:10-11)

י וַיִּשְׁלַח אַבְרָהָם אֶת־יָדוֹ וַיִּקַּח אֶת־הַמַּאֲכֶלֶת לִשְׁחֹט
אֶת־בְּנוֹ: יא וַיִּקְרָא אֵלָיו מַלְאַךְ יי מִן־הַשָּׁמַיִם וַיֹּאמֶר
אַבְרָהָם | אַבְרָהָם וַיֹּאמֶר הִנֵּנִי:

*[10] And Abraham picked up the knife to slay his son.*
*[11] Then an angel of the Lord called to him from heaven: "Abraham! Abraham!" And he answered, "Here I am."*

**[10] Abraham! Abraham!.** With this special form of address at this moment, Abraham receives a new, doubled name. He now has three names: "Abram," "Abraham," and

"Abraham-Abraham," which means that he has risen to new heights.

Only seven times in all of Tanach do we find the duplication of a name. But in three of those instances the duplication is merely "mechanical" – the same name appears at the end of one phrase and also at the beginning of the next, thus creating an apparent duplication of the given name. Noah's name is so repeated: "This is the line of Noah – Noah was a righteous man" (6:9), as is Shem's (11:10) and Terah's (11:27).

Each of these instances only "hints" at a double name; there is no true name duplication in these. The Kabbalah views these three cases of "mechanical name doubling" as preparation for the emergence of the true double names that Abraham and then Jacob (46:2), Moses (Exodus 3:4) and Shmuel (I Sam. 3:10) will have. That is, Noah, Shem and Terah are in some sense a preparation for the birth of Abraham, Jacob, Moses, and Samuel.

The doubling of a person's name indicates unity of *nefesh* and *neshamah*. These two terms are both most often translated as "soul," but they are not identical. The *nefesh* is the lower, "outer" side of the soul, what a person is today, while *neshamah* is a person's inner essence, what he aspires to be and the level he is capable of reaching. Thus, one's *neshamah* is his future level, his vector of development. Addressing a person in double suggests equivalence of his *nefesh* and his *neshamah* – the person has completed his assigned task, for which he was created. In other words, the doubled name symbolizes potential completely realized.

It should be noted that among the three Patriarchs, only Isaac is never addressed in double. This is because Isaac's *nefesh* was completely "annulled" after the events of the *Akedah*, leaving him with only a *neshamah*. Isaac in his lifetime thus became, in a certain sense, "a man of the World to Come," exceeding and transcending, as it were, the level of a doubled name, as achieved by Abraham and Jacob. The doubled name of the other Patriarchs indicates full completion of their assigned tasks. Although they did not achieve perfection, they completely realized the tasks assigned to them by God.

But there is yet another aspect to this. Abraham, Jacob, and Samuel all have a separator between the first and second instances of their doubled names, which in printed Torah texts appears as a simple vertical line, known as *pesik* or *pasek*: "Abraham | Abraham..." The effect is that although the two name instances are joined by a conjunctive cantillation mark, which according to standard cantillation rules would normally make them a single continuous unit, the separator renders them more disconnected than connected.

(A clearer example of this principle can be seen in the word *ba-esh* at Deut. 9:21. The pronunciation of that word would normally have been softened to *va-esh* because of the conjunctive accent on the preceding word, *oto*, and because *oto* ends with a vowel. But in this case the *pesik* before *ba-esh* negates the conjunctive, softening effect of that preceding accent. Such examples of this effect in Tanach are in fact quite rare.)

Only in the case of Moses' doubled name no such separator appears, with the effect that the two consecutive instances of his name, following their conjunctive cantillation symbols, are truly one continuous and unbroken unit.

Moses, as it were, "united himself with his own goal." He so fully realized the unity of his *nefesh* and *neshamah* that any question of their separation could never even arise. But as concerns Abraham, Jacob, and Samuel on the other hand, although they too achieved unity, their *nefesh* and *neshamah* nonetheless remained two distinct components with actual distance between them.

**"Here I am."** Just as he did at the very beginning of the *Akeidah*, when God first called upon him to sacrifice Isaac, here again Abraham answers, *hineni*, "Here I am," but this time to Isaac himself.

This is the third *hineni* of the *Akeidah*. In order to arrive at his new level of communion with God, Abraham, when addressed by Isaac near the middle of the narrative, again had to answer, "here I am." The lesson is that one can advance in fellowship with God only by also advancing in his fellowship with fellow human beings.

When God addresses a person by name, He is addressing Himself to that person's true essence – to his life's goal. (We have noted previously that in Hebrew one's name expresses his goal in life.) When Abraham, in response to just such an appeal, responds to God, "Here I am," he is remedying Adam's sin, as it were. Abraham's "Here I am" is the belated reply to God's question to Adam in the Garden of Eden, "Where are you?" (3:9). Adam, who could not bring himself to answer that question, hid himself instead. More than two thousand years would elapse before Abraham could at length finally answer the question God had posed at the beginning of Creation to all mankind.

There is an important parallel in the Kabbalah between Abraham and Adam. They are both located on the right line of the *sefirot*. Adam is *chochmah* (wisdom), and Abraham is *chesed*, directly beneath it. Each of them is the birth of something new. Adam is the birth of humanity, and Abraham is the birth of the Jewish people. In view of this parallelism, Abraham had to correct Adam's mistake – in particular, by answering and not avoiding God's question, and by teaching the Jewish people and all of humankind how to adopt that samc mindset.

## 26.15. Binding, but Not Sacrifice (22:12)

יב וַיֹּאמֶר אַל־תִּשְׁלַח יָדְךָ אֶל־הַנַּעַר וְאַל־תַּעַשׂ לוֹ
מְאוּמָה כִּי | עַתָּה יָדַעְתִּי כִּי־יְרֵא אֱלֹהִים אַתָּה וְלֹא
חָשַׂכְתָּ אֶת־בִּנְךָ אֶת־יְחִידְךָ מִמֶּנִּי׃

*[12] And he said, "Do not raise your hand against the boy, or do anything to him. ...*

God tells Abraham that the binding is itself sufficient – the sacrifice has been averted, and there is no need to destroy *gevurah*. The binding of Isaac is therefore not just a physical action or mere ancillary preparation for the sacrifice. Rather, it is a form of dialogue, of contact and mutual enlightenment.

Although Abraham was of course extremely fond of Isaac, he might have tacitly entertained the thought that perhaps *gevurah* had to be destroyed for the sake of "higher correctness" – so that *chesed* alone would remain in the world. Perhaps it is with that objective (albeit by God's command!) that Abraham binds his son to the altar, grasps the knife, and stretches his hand toward his son. But at that very moment God stays Abraham's hand – because Abraham can no longer stop himself. God also commands him: "Do not raise your hand against the boy, or do anything to him!" That is, do no damage to *gevurah*.

Abraham and Isaac in the course of the *Akedah* together tread a path of personal development. Isaac agrees to be tied up, which means that *gevurah* is agreeing to limit itself. This is Isaac's advancement. And *chesed* stops short in the face of bound and helpless *gevurah*. This is Abraham's advancement.

The *kavanot* (Kabbalistic lessons on the meaning of the prayers) note that when a person reads the story of *Akeidat Yitzchak* each morning, he should envision himself tying up, as it were, the attribute of *din* (strict law, an alternate name of the *gevurah* attribute), which represents the "accusers of Israel." We must not ask God to destroy them, but only that He not allow them any freedom of action.

### 26.16. "On the Mount of the Lord There is Vision" (22:12-14)

...כִּי | עַתָּה יָדַעְתִּי כִּי־יְרֵא אֱלֹהִים אַתָּה וְלֹא חָשַׂכְתָּ אֶת־
בִּנְךָ אֶת־יְחִידְךָ מִמֶּנִּי: יג וַיִּשָּׂא אַבְרָהָם אֶת־עֵינָיו וַיַּרְא
וְהִנֵּה־אַיִל אַחַר נֶאֱחַז בַּסְּבַךְ בְּקַרְנָיו וַיֵּלֶךְ אַבְרָהָם וַיִּקַּח
אֶת־הָאַיִל וַיַּעֲלֵהוּ לְעֹלָה תַּחַת בְּנוֹ: יד וַיִּקְרָא אַבְרָהָם שֵׁם־
הַמָּקוֹם הַהוּא יי | יִרְאֶה אֲשֶׁר יֵאָמֵר הַיּוֹם בְּהַר יי יֵרָאֶה:

*[12] ... For now I know that you fear God, since you have not withheld your son, your favored one, from Me."*
*[13] When Abraham looked up, his eye fell upon a ram, caught in the thicket by its horns. So Abraham went and took the ram and offered it up as a burnt offering in place of his son.*
*[14] And Abraham named that site Adonai-yireh, whence the present saying, "On the mount of the Lord there is vision."*

**[12] That you fear God.** It is not "fear," but "trembling," *yir'ah*," that is here associated with *yir'eh*": "the Lord will see."

**On the mount of the Lord there is vision.** Such trust in divine discretion is true reverence. It is not a feeling of fear, but of complete reliance on God in a situation that by all appearances can have no logical resolution. When Abraham reaches this stage, Isaac is replaced by a ram. Having succeeded at learning to fully rely on God's support, Abraham earns a doubled name for himself.

**A ram, caught in the thicket by its horns.** The Hebrew includes the word *achar*, after "ram," which, although not always translated here, means "behind" (i.e., "A ram, behind, caught in the thicket by its horns"). Not only in terms of its physical location relative to Abraham, but also in time, this ram "came from behind," meaning that it had been "prepared from the very beginning" – from the Six Days of Creation. We shall soon explain this in further detail.

**[13] When Abraham looked up.** It would seem that Abraham had arrived at the pinnacle. First he saw this place from a distance, then he climbed the mountain. But then it turned out that he could climb even higher. The words "When Abraham looked up" in this verse are clearly a continuation of verse 4: "On the third day Abraham looked up and saw the place from afar." When Abraham reaches this even greater height, he learns that there is indeed a way out of his hopeless situation, and a ram appears.

The Midrash says that this ram was created at the end of the Sixth Day of Creation, in the twilight just before *shabbat* – that is, at the very end of the process of Creation, when God added certain supernatural "items of special designation" to the world that was otherwise already complete. Since that time, the ram had been waiting for Abraham's arrival on Mount Moriah, so that it could be sacrificed.

Previously, however, Abraham did not see the ram; only now does he acquire the ability to see the solution that had been prepared for him so very long ago.

Thus, God added these "items of special designation" to the world as pressure valves that afford relief from "hopeless" situations. But they always remain invisible until we become capable of perceiving them.

**[14] And Abraham named that site Adonai-yireh.** These words mean "The Lord will see." Abraham uses the same words that he had previously spoken to Isaac, "God will see to the sheep for His burnt offering." Understanding that "the Lord will see" is an expression of hope for synthesis even in the face of all the contradictions that remain, for in the Divine light it is possible to unite even things that to human eyes seem irreconcilable. By giving the place this name, Abraham wishes to convey to all people the new understanding that has now been revealed to him.

**Whence the present saying, "On the mount of the Lord there is vision."** The temple must stand only on Mount Moriah, the Temple Mount, which highlights our awareness that God will find a solution to problems that seem unsolvable to us, through our complementary relationship with others who internally strive for the same goals, even if outwardly they seem very different from us.

### 26.17. A Blessing to the Nations (22:15-18)

טו וַיִּקְרָא מַלְאַךְ יי אֶל־אַבְרָהָם שֵׁנִית מִן־הַשָּׁמָיִם: טז וַיֹּאמֶר בִּי נִשְׁבַּעְתִּי נְאֻם־יי כִּי יַעַן אֲשֶׁר עָשִׂיתָ אֶת־ הַדָּבָר הַזֶּה וְלֹא חָשַׂכְתָּ אֶת־בִּנְךָ אֶת־יְחִידֶךָ: יז כִּי־

בָּרֵךְ אֲבָרֶכְךָ וְהַרְבָּה אַרְבֶּה אֶת־זַרְעֲךָ כְּכוֹכְבֵי הַשָּׁמַיִם
וְכַחוֹל אֲשֶׁר עַל־שְׂפַת הַיָּם וְיִרַשׁ זַרְעֲךָ אֵת שַׁעַר אֹיְבָיו: ** יח וְהִתְבָּרֲכוּ בְזַרְעֲךָ כֹּל גּוֹיֵי הָאָרֶץ עֵקֶב אֲשֶׁר שָׁמַעְתָּ
בְּקֹלִי:

*[15] The angel of the Lord called to Abraham a
second time from heaven,
[16] and said, "By Myself I swear, the Lord
declares: Because you have done this and have
not withheld your son, your favored one,
[17] I will bestow My blessing upon you and make
your descendants as numerous as the stars of
heaven and the sands on the seashore; and your
descendants shall seize the gates of their foes.
[18] All the nations of the earth shall bless
themselves by your descendants, because you
have obeyed My command."*

[15] **The angel of the Lord called to Abraham a second time from heaven.** Abraham's enhanced understanding, expressed in the name that he gives to this mountain, "The Lord Will See," brings with it a commensurate increase in his reward. The angel of God calls to Abraham a second time and proclaims that all mankind will be blessed through him.

[18] **All the nations of the earth shall bless themselves by your descendants.** This is a confirmation of the promise made at the beginning of the *Lech Lecha* portion: "And all the families of the earth shall bless themselves by you" (12:3).

**All the nations of the earth shall bless themselves by your descendants, because you have obeyed My command.**

The peoples of the earth will be blessed through Abraham's posterity because of his achievements. For Abraham, this repetition of the blessing signifies that although the future path lies through Isaac, through the national element, the universal component will also remain.

**Because you have obeyed My command.** The Hebrew word *ekev*, which means "due to the fact that," has the same root as the name "Jacob." In other words, the fact that the *Akedah* has taken place, and the connection between Abraham's *chesed* and Isaac's *gevurah* has now been established, makes possible the birth of Isaac's son Jacob, who would add his own attribute to theirs - *tiferet* (adornment). Thus, the Torah will later call Jacob "a mild man who stayed in camp" (25:27); literally, "who dwelled in tents." Note that "tents" is in the plural. These are, simultaneously, the tents of both Abraham and Isaac.

### 26.18. Abraham's Return (22:19)

יט וַיָּשָׁב אַבְרָהָם אֶל־נְעָרָיו וַיָּקֻמוּ וַיֵּלְכוּ יַחְדָּו אֶל־
בְּאֵר שָׁבַע וַיֵּשֶׁב אַבְרָהָם בִּבְאֵר שָׁבַע:

*[19] Abraham then returned to his servants, and they departed together for Beer-Sheba; and Abraham stayed in Beer-Sheba.*

**[19] Abraham then returned.** The verb is in the singular. Physically, both Abraham and Isaac returned, but mentally - only Abraham. Because Isaac, having attained the level of self-sacrifice, remained at that height all the days of his life.
    Everything that Isaac will ever do from here onward - eat,

drink, practice agriculture, live with his wife, and anything whatsoever – will be a life lived always from the perspective of Mount Moriah. Isaac is a very vigorous person, because holiness, in the Jewish conception, means participation in the fullness of life (and not disengagement from the world). But even so, Isaac never went back to being "one of the boys." ("Abraham then returned to his servants" is more literally translated as "Abraham then returned to his boys." Abraham did so, but Isaac never did.)

Thus, the "Sacrifice of Isaac" did in fact occur – in the metaphysical sense. It could never have happened as a physical reality, because then it would have lost all its meaning. The whole point of the *Akedah* was to make contact with Heaven, in order that all of life thereafter would continue bringing Heavenly radiance down to this earth.

**And Abraham stayed in Beer-Sheba.** These words seem to contradict what very soon follows: "Sarah died in Kiriath-Arba – now Hebron." We will deal with this discrepancy below.

# Chapter 27

# The Birth of Rebekah

## 27.1. The Birth of Rebekah (22:20-24)

כ וַיְהִי אַחֲרֵי הַדְּבָרִים הָאֵלֶּה וַיֻּגַּד לְאַבְרָהָם לֵאמֹר הִנֵּה
יָלְדָה מִלְכָּה גַם־הִוא בָּנִים לְנָחוֹר אָחִיךָ: כא אֶת־עוּץ
בְּכֹרוֹ וְאֶת־בּוּז אָחִיו וְאֶת־קְמוּאֵל אֲבִי אֲרָם: כב וְאֶת־
כֶּשֶׂד וְאֶת־חֲזוֹ וְאֶת־פִּלְדָּשׁ וְאֶת־יִדְלָף וְאֵת בְּתוּאֵל: כג
וּבְתוּאֵל יָלַד אֶת־רִבְקָה שְׁמֹנָה אֵלֶּה יָלְדָה מִלְכָּה לְנָחוֹר
אֲחִי אַבְרָהָם: כד וּפִילַגְשׁוֹ וּשְׁמָהּ רְאוּמָה וַתֵּלֶד גַּם־הִוא
אֶת־טֶבַח וְאֶת־גַּחַם וְאֶת־תַּחַשׁ וְאֶת־מַעֲכָה:

[20] *Some time later, Abraham was told, "Milcah too has borne children to your brother Nahor:*
[21] *Uz the first-born, and Buz his brother, and Kemuel the father of Aram;*
[22] *and Kesed, Hazo, Pildash, Jidlaph, and Bethuel"* –
[23] *Bethuel being the father of Rebekah. These eight Milcah bore to Nahor, Abraham's brother.*
[24] *And his concubine, whose name was Reumah, also bore children: Tebah, Gaham, Tahash, and Maacah.*

**[20] Some time later, Abraham was told, "Milcah too has borne children."** In the story of the *Akeidah*, thanks to the connection that was established between Abraham's *chesed* and Isaac's *gevurah*, an opportunity now arose for the future birth of *tiferet* – Isaac's son Jacob. Therefore, immediately after the *Akeidah*, Abraham is informed of the birth of Rebekah (Isaac's wife and Jacob's mother).

## 27.2. Nahor's Family in Relation to the Family of Abraham

All the marriages of the Patriarchs as related in the book of Genesis were contracted with members of Terah's family line, who had remained *ivrim*, and which consisted of two main branches: the branch of Abraham and the branch of Nahor.

We noted earlier (11:29) that Milcah, Nahor's wife, was the daughter of Haran and also Sarah's sister; that is, Nahor and Abraham both married their nieces, who were descended from Terah's other wife.

We have noted as well based on the Midrash that the relationship of the Terah family's branches can be summarized as follows. After the events in Ur Kasdim (Ur of the Chaldees, the "Chaldean furnace"), when it became clear that the Hebrews of Babylon were being persecuted (Abraham was cast into the furnace and lived, but Haran died), the question arose as to how the members of Terah's family were to behave in the given situation.

Terah, a purveyor of idols, although not an active supporter of Ever's religious system, sought to return to Canaan (11:31), to the Land of the Hebrews (40:15) – apparently motivated by nationalist considerations. (In this sense we can consider him to a prototype of "non-religious Zionism.") But he made it only as far as Haran, and settled there.

His sons, Abraham and Nahor, who survived the disaster of Ur Kasdim, differ on the question of what direction to choose for the family. Nahor (who in a sense can be considered a prototype of cosmopolitan Jewry) prefers to integrate into the Aramaean culture, the dominant culture of the time. However, he does not manage to survive as a Hebrew: his family very quickly assimilates, and his children are already called Aramaeans: "Betuel the Aramean ... Laban the Aramean" (25:20).

Nahor, a cosmopolitan universalist, considers it proper to influence the culture of the peoples of the world from within. It is interesting to note that such a point of view, *galut lishmah*, "exile with a religious purpose," is still alive and well among the Jewish people. Rabbi Samson Raphael Hirsch, for example, who lived in Germany in the middle of the 19th century, argued that it is the calling of the Jewish people to live among other enlightened nations – Germany, for example – and to influence them from within.

Abraham, on the other hand, represents the concept of "advancing toward the universal through the national." He goes to the Land of Israel not to return to nature and to the earth (as did Terah), but as a means of rehabilitating the entire world, when "all the families of the earth shall bless themselves by you" (12:3). In contemporary terms, this is the approach of the religious-Zionist movement.

However, to withdraw into oneself on a nationalist plane alone, even one with a universalistic orientation, would be improper. The men of Abraham's family (Isaac, Jacob) therefore married daughters of Nahor's family (Rebekah, Rachel and Leah), in order to impart a spirit of universality to the national Jewish worldview.

## 27.3. Twelve Sons and a Daughter

As we read the Torah, we often neglect the genealogy lists – the descendants of Nahor in this chapter, for example. However, apart from the concrete factual importance of genealogical links, they include also one more essential piece of information.

In the Torah's genealogies there is usually a main line in which there are only a few children, and then a side branch in which, on the contrary, there are many children. This corresponds to the idea that the privileged, such as the nobility, should have very few heirs "so as not to inflate the elite," while there should always be a multitude of ordinary, lower-class people.

Moreover, we see several times in the Torah that a younger, subordinate member of a family's secondary branch has twelve sons and a daughter (twelve true sons and one "spurious"); in other words, he has "12.5 children" (heirs) succeeding him. The reason for this is that the main and subsidiary lines represent the solar and lunar lines, respectively. Thus, the secondary line must usually consist of exactly 12.5 children, corresponding to the ratio of the lunar and solar cycles (in the sense that approximately 12.5 lunar months are contained in one solar year).

For example, Ham, Noah's son (10:8,15), has a main line, Cush, whose son was Nimrod, and a younger line, Canaan, who had twelve children (in the Torah text eleven sons are enumerated, plus one additional one, the "Canaanite tribes," likewise a separate nation).

Ever too has two sons. Peleg is the eldest, from whom came Terah and the Abrahamitic race, while the supplemental line, Joktan, had 12.5 sons (10:26).

In the Terah family, the eldest line is Abraham's, through

whom runs the primary identification, and Abraham has two primary sons Isaac and Ishmael (Keturah is a side line), while Nahor, as we see here, has twelve sons and a daughter (Rebekah, although she is the daughter of Betuel, is mentioned here not by mere chance). Abraham's main line will go through Isaac, while Ishmael has twelve sons and a daughter (25:13, 28:9).

But this aspect is seen most prominently in Jacob. He, too, has 12.5 sons, which tells us that initially Jacob was meant to be only a side line, and his brother Esau the main line. Jacob, however, managed to achieve the level of progenitor of the Chosen People – by turning his side line into the primary. For a line to become the primary, it is not enough for its founder to be born first. The greatness of Jacob was that although he was the younger he "became" the older (25:33), and so the secondary became primary. Later we shall analyze all this in greater detail.

# Weekly Portion
# Chayei Sarah

# Chapter 28

# Hebron and the Machpelah Cave

## 28.1. Sarah's Life and Her Three Victories

The central figure of the two portions *Chayei Sarah* and *Toledot* is Isaac. The *Chayei Sarah* portion describes his marriage, while in the *Toledot* portion we read about Isaac's life as a self-sufficient family man.

The *Chayei Sarah* portion ("The Life of Sarah") consists of three short narratives, each devoted to a separate topic. The first of these tells of Sarah's death, and her burial by Abraham in the Cave of Machpelah. It further describes how Abraham's "servant" (Eliezer, according to the midrash) goes in search of a wife for Isaac, and brings back Rebekah, who takes Sarah's place as matriarch of the family. The portion ends with Abraham's marriage to Keturah, the birth of their children, and Abraham's death and burial.

Sarah, and her death and burial, are thus mentioned only at the beginning of the portion, but after that almost never again. What, then, is the meaning of this chapter's title *Chayei Sarah* considering that the names of the weekly portions, as we have noted previously, are chosen to reflect the actual meaning of the Torah text, and are not just mechanically extracted from the first words of each of those portions, as it might superficially seem.

The answer is that everything in the *Chayei Sarah* portion is the result of the life that Sarah lived. For it deals with the three most important victories that Sarah won *after* her death, through which she was able to guide her family in the proper direction as she perceived it.

The first of these is that Hebron became a vital Jewish center after Abraham buried Sarah there. (Hebron remained second in importance only to Jerusalem among the major cities of the Land of Israel.) As discussed earlier, Abraham was inclined to live in Beersheba, within the domain of its Philistine king Abimelech. But Sarah, who was focused on creating the future Jewish people, believed that the center of their family life should be Hebron, because living there required an autonomous government position, as we shall explain in more detail below. Through her death in Hebron, Sarah forced Abraham to move the family center to there, and later we will see that Isaac and Jacob did in fact live in Hebron.

Sarah's second victory was Abraham's decision to choose a wife for Isaac from among their *ivrim* (Hebrew) relatives, rather than have him marry a woman from one of the other nations. Abraham, as we have noted, inclined toward universalism, and was therefore perfectly satisfied being married to his Egyptian maidservant Hagar, even to the extent that he considered their son Ishmael a possible successor to his life's work. But Sarah's "nationalist-Jewish" orientation carried the day, and following her lead Abraham ultimately decided to seek a bride for Isaac only from within their kindred family.

And finally, Sarah's third victory is told in the story of Abraham's children from Keturah. On the one hand, it was very proper for Abraham to take another wife for himself after Sarah's death, rather than remain unmarried. But by this time, Abraham already understood unequivocally that only Sarah's son Isaac could be his heir, and he therefore willingly sent all his sons from Keturah "eastward, to the land of the East" (25:6) – giving them gifts, but not making them his heirs.

Thus, we see Sarah's influence on Abraham not only in his obeying her instructions during her lifetime, the imperative that was established with the expulsion of Hagar and Ishmael [21:12]). Even beyond that, Sarah successfully built her relationship with Abraham, enabling him to advance in the aspect of *gevurah*. And now, even after she is gone, her opinion and wishes remain decisive for Abraham.

In light of all of the above, it becomes clear why this entire weekly portion bears the name *Chayei Sarah*, "The Life of Sarah."

## 28.2. Hebron as a National Political Center (23:1-2)

א וַיִּהְיוּ חַיֵּי שָׂרָה מֵאָה שָׁנָה וְעֶשְׂרִים שָׁנָה וְשֶׁבַע שָׁנִים שְׁנֵי חַיֵּי שָׂרָה: ב וַתָּמָת שָׂרָה בְּקִרְיַת אַרְבַּע הִוא חֶבְרוֹן בְּאֶרֶץ כְּנָעַן וַיָּבֹא אַבְרָהָם לִסְפֹּד לְשָׂרָה וְלִבְכֹּתָהּ:

*[1] Sarah's lifetime-the span of Sarah's life-came to one hundred and twenty-seven years.*
*[2] Sarah died in Kiriath-Arba-now Hebron-in the land of Canaan; ...*

## [1] The span of Sarah's life... [2] Sarah died in Kiriath-Arba.

Even Sarah's death is a part of her life – in the sense that even through her death she was able to advance the Jewish nation in its development by shifting the center of her family's activity from Beersheba to Hebron.

**[2] Sarah died in Kiriath-Arba – now Hebron – in the land of Canaan.** The last time we were told where Abraham was living, that place was Beersheba (22:19). But Sarah then moves to Hebron. As already mentioned, Hebron is the center of Judea and the embodiment of the attribute of *malchut*, "kingdom." While Abraham was living in Hebron God gave him an opportunity to create statehood, but Abraham was not ready for that. He had the opportunity to assume the leadership of Sodom and to rehabilitate that wicked city, but he did not wish to do so.

Abraham therefore leaves Hebron after the destruction of Sodom and settles in Philistia, so that in Beersheba, far from the capital and from state politics, he can remain an exclusively spiritual leader. Sarah, however, understands that this approach is wrong, and once again moves Abraham towards Hebron – a place of nationalist-political, and not only spiritual, self-identification.

If Beersheba had become the center of Jewish life and the formation of the Jewish people, that would have made Abraham and his family representatives of spirituality among the Philistines, but it would have meant also that spirituality on the one hand and material concerns and state power on the other would remain two entirely unrelated affairs.

The Philistines were quite satisfied with that arrangement, actually, and agreed to accept Abraham as their most prominent religious leader. Even Abimelech himself, the King of Gerar, came to Abraham, made an alliance with him, and asked for his spiritual patronage.

The Jewish approach, however, rejects the principle of

"separation of church and state", because Judaism insists on treating everything in the world as a single integrated reality, which means that national-political dialogue with God is no less important than individual dialogue. Abraham himself could not attain this level, which would be achieved only later by his grandchildren, Jacob's sons, who would by that time be *Israel*, and not only *ivrim*, Hebrews. Abraham still operates only at an individual level, rather than conducting dialogue with God at the national level. He is therefore quite content with his status as spiritual leader of the Philistine state.

But Sarah, who is not satisfied with that arrangement, moves before her death to Hebron. Hebron is not in Philistia, but in the Land of Canaan, where there is no unified state (each city is its own independent state). Political and state responsibility in Hebron therefore cannot be avoided: life's national-political and spiritual dimensions are there united.

### 28.3. Sarah Redirects Abraham to Hebron (23:2-3)

‎...וַיָּבֹא אַבְרָהָם לִסְפֹּד לְשָׂרָה וְלִבְכֹּתָהּ: וַיָּקָם אַבְרָהָם
‎מֵעַל פְּנֵי מֵתוֹ...

*[2] ... and Abraham proceeded to mourn for Sarah and to bewail her.*
*[3] Then Abraham rose from beside his dead ...*

[2] **Abraham proceeded.** After the *Akeidah*, Abraham returned to Beersheba. But now he moves on to Hebron.

It is quite possible that when Sarah moved to Hebron, Abraham did not follow her immediately. Perhaps he did not completely share her aspirations. But Sarah's death in Hebron prompted Abraham to acknowledge that city's importance and to make it central to the life of the future Jewish people.

**To mourn for Sarah and to bewail her.** Recognizing the force of Sarah's influence on the creation of the Jewish people, Abraham comes, first of all, "to mourn for Sarah," which means he perceived the magnitude of his loss; and then "to bewail her" – which refers to his expressing an emotional reaction.

**[3] Then Abraham rose from beside his dead.** A person must not allow the death of a loved one to enslave him; he must live on. But this verse has a supplementary meaning as well. "Then Abraham rose from beside (that is, under the influence of) his dead" means that Sarah's death is itself an elevating force for Abraham that causes him to rise.

## 28.4. Abraham's Dual Status (23:3-4)

וַיְדַבֵּר אֶל־בְּנֵי־חֵת לֵאמֹר׃ ד גֵּר־וְתוֹשָׁב אָנֹכִי עִמָּכֶם...
תְּנוּ לִי אֲחֻזַּת־קֶבֶר עִמָּכֶם וְאֶקְבְּרָה מֵתִי מִלְּפָנָי׃

*[3] ..., and spoke to the Hittites, saying,*
*[4] "I am a resident alien among you; sell me a*
*burial site among you, that I may remove my*
*dead for burial."*

**[4] I am a resident alien among you.** With these words Abraham emphasizes his paradoxical status. He is an "alien" and a "resident" at the same time. An alien receives nothing except by grace; a resident receives by right. These are opposite concepts, but Abraham's status incorporates them both.

Abraham was originally a stranger and wanderer, because he came from somewhere else. He later settled on this land, and it was here, in Hebron, that he concluded political alliances, and was even victorious in battle. But he failed to leverage his fruits of victory, and went instead to live in the territory of the Philistines, with the result that his status is now indeterminate once again.

**Sell me a burial site among you.** This is an application for a change of status. Purchasing the Machpelah, as well as the lessons that Abraham will learn from his conversations with the Hittites, will enable him to put down roots in Hebron and to create a base for the Jewish people here.

### 28.5. "Bury your dead in the choicest of our burial places" (23:5-6)

ה וַיַּעֲנוּ בְנֵי־חֵת אֶת־אַבְרָהָם לֵאמֹר לוֹ: ו שְׁמָעֵנוּ ׀ אֲדֹנִי
נְשִׂיא אֱלֹהִים אַתָּה בְּתוֹכֵנוּ בְּמִבְחַר קְבָרֵינוּ קְבֹר אֶת־
מֵתֶךָ אִישׁ מִמֶּנּוּ אֶת־קִבְרוֹ לֹא־יִכְלֶה מִמְּךָ מִקְּבֹר מֵתֶךָ:

*[5] And the Hittites replied to Abraham, saying to him,*
*[6] "Hear us, my lord: you are the elect of God among us. Bury your dead in the choicest of our burial places; none of us will withhold his burial place from you for burying your dead."*

**[6] You are the elect of God among us.** The Hittites, it would seem, respond to Abraham's request more than positively.

Their words evidence the reverence they feel toward Abraham in deference to his elevated status as a spiritual personality.

**None of us will withhold his burial place from you for burying your dead.** But that elevated status is not without its dangers as well.

They might tell Abraham: "Since you are so great, you can bury your dead in any tomb, and no one will refuse you. But on the other hand, if you are truly that great, you should not be occupying yourself with such trifles as the purchase of a private burial plot."

But the real truth is that if not for this purchase, Hebron would not have become a future center for the Jewish people.

Abraham internalized the message that Sarah conveyed to him when she left to die in Hebron. He needed not merely to bury his wife, but also to create a foothold for the future nation. He therefore must not bury Sarah in someone else's tomb. He must acquire this land as his legal possession.

Such situations are encountered often in life: we use other people's means to solve our immediate problems, instead of creating our own opportunities and thereby achieving strategic advancement. Clearly, it is usually much easier to use a ready-made solution than to create one's own, but using what belongs to someone else will never give us the real support we need in critical situations. It is of course possible to bury our dead in someone else's plot. But if the goal is to create a spiritual center that will then influence humanity for centuries to come, that solution will simply not work. For that reason, Abraham cannot accept their offer.

## 28.6. The Purchase of the Machpelah Cave (23:7-9)

ז וַיָּקָם אַבְרָהָם וַיִּשְׁתַּחוּ לְעַם־הָאָרֶץ לִבְנֵי־חֵת: ח
וַיְדַבֵּר אִתָּם לֵאמֹר אִם־יֵשׁ אֶת־נַפְשְׁכֶם לִקְבֹּר אֶת־מֵתִי
מִלְּפָנַי שְׁמָעוּנִי וּפִגְעוּ־לִי בְּעֶפְרוֹן בֶּן־צֹחַר: ט וְיִתֶּן־לִי
אֶת־מְעָרַת הַמַּכְפֵּלָה אֲשֶׁר־לוֹ אֲשֶׁר בִּקְצֵה שָׂדֵהוּ בְּכֶסֶף
מָלֵא יִתְּנֶנָּה לִי בְּתוֹכְכֶם לַאֲחֻזַּת־קָבֶר:

*[7] Thereupon Abraham bowed low to the people of the land, the Hittites,*
*[8] and he said to them, "If it is your wish that I remove my dead for burial, you must agree to intercede for me with Ephron son of Zohar.*
*[9] Let him sell me the cave of Machpelah that he owns, which is at the edge of his land. Let him sell it to me, at the full price, for a burial site in your midst."*

**[7] Thereupon Abraham bowed low to the people of the land, the Hittites.** Failing to feel and show gratitude is among the most repulsive of human vices, but by following the Patriarchs' example we can avoid this shortcoming. Abraham does not neglect his duty to bow to the Hittites. When people are prepared to help us, it is our obligation to acknowledge their offer and to express our gratitude, even if what they are offering is not suitable for our needs and the discussion is still ongoing.

**[9] Let him sell me the cave of Machpelah that he owns.** We have previously mentioned the Midrash that tells how already decades earlier, when the three angels visited him, Abraham decided to make this cave located in Hebron the site of a future burial plot for his family, after learning that Adam and Eve were buried there.

Nonetheless, deciding on a plan and actually implementing it are two entirely different things, and great effort is needed to bridge that gap. Moreover, it is possible that after moving to Beersheba, Abraham might even have abandoned his earlier plan concerning the Machpelah cave. But Sarah, by coming to die in Hebron, forced Abraham to realize his long-standing intention. Actualizing the aspect of *gevurah* is Sarah's enduring role in their personal family relations.

## 28.7. A Funerary Cave as a Foothold for the Jewish Nation

We wish to draw attention to two points in Abraham's words. Note first that he wants to pay full price for the cave, and not receive it as a gift. A gift, having no legal force, could later revert to its previous owner, but property transferred through a legal sale can never be taken from the buyer. Secondly, Abraham asks only for the cave, but not for the field. All he needs is a place to bury Sarah.

A burial cave is something that cannot be uprooted; it is like a peg hammered into the ground that will never move. A burial property implies an eternal connection with the place, independent of the ebb and flow of life events surrounding it. Our attitude towards the dead and buried is an essential, not a functional, relation. Thus, the first Jewish acquisition in the Land of Canaan is a burial plot – an eternal possession.

We note in passing that in Middle Eastern culture a person's willingness to abandon the graves of his (presumptive) ancestors is deemed an indisputable indicator that he is not really their descendant. Therefore, those Israelis today who offer to abandon the graves of our ancestors in Hebron, because they believe that by making concessions to the Arabs in such matters we will increase their desire to make peace with us, are sadly and completely mistaken.

However, achieving the objective of possessing the land along with a burial plot has disadvantages as well as advantages. Burial creates a place of memory, where people rarely go, for such a place is only used to remember the dead. People often live and work a considerable distance away. Under pressure from Sarah's wish, Abraham anchors himself in Hebron, but in fact, he plans only to stake a claim there for a memorial, not yet to make it a center of his activity. We will see later, however, how Abraham's attitude will change in the process of making this purchase.

## 28.8. The Machpelah Cave and the Universalism of Jewish Tradition

The name of the cave is Machpelah, meaning "double." There are various explanations for this. The two main ones are that it is a two-story cave and that couples are buried there (Adam and Eve, Abraham and Sarah, Isaac and Rebekah, Jacob and Leah). For four thousand years, from the days of Abraham until our own times, this cave has been among the most important Jewish shrines, and has always been a place of Jewish pilgrimage. Toward the end of the Second Temple period, King Herod built a magnificent edifice above the cave in the same architectural style he used to renovate the Temple in Jerusalem. That building, which is well preserved even today, is the only surviving building of the Herodian period, because the Romans, who destroyed the Temple in Jerusalem, conducted no hostilities in Hebron.

The Arabs who arrived in the seventh century built a mosque over that Herodian building, but Crusaders later turned the building into a Christian church. The Muslims then returned and removed all traces of its church use. Finally, in 1967, the Jews reclaimed their dominion over Hebron and Machpelah. Today it is half synagogue, half mosque.

That building above the Machpelah Cave is probably the oldest building in the world (the Western world, at least). Besides that, it never collapsed even under the ravages of time. The building continues to be alive and active, and is still used for the original purpose for which it was built.

We have also noted that the special significance of the Machpelah Cave includes the fact that it is considered the tomb of Adam and Eve. The Midrash says that the Cave of Machpelah is the gateway to the Garden of Eden, through which Adam was "returned to the ground from which [he] was taken" (3:19).

The meaning of this Midrash is that Jewish tradition, as symbolized by the Cave of Machpelah, starts with Adam. That is, it has not only Jewish national significance, but also universal significance, applicable to all of humanity. Judaism begins not only from Abraham and Sarah, but from Adam and Eve.

For this reason, the tomb in which Adam and Eve are buried is the right choice for Abraham. As he puts down roots in the Land of Israel, Abraham chooses a location that is relevant to all of mankind, thereby declaring that Jewish nationalism has a universal purpose.

### 28.9. Ephron the Son of Zohar: "Ash on Radiance"

The man who owned the Machpelah Cave, and from

whom Abraham wanted to buy it, was Ephron the son of Zohar the Hittite. This cannot have happened by mere happenstance. The venerable Machpelah Cave would not have randomly come to be owned by just anyone.

Nor is it by chance that the Torah tells us the name of the cave's owner, which also carries for us important information. The name "Ephron" derives from the Hebrew word *afar*, "dust," which is also phonetically related to *efer*, "ash," or something dark. But his father's name, "Zohar" (Hebrew *Tzochar*), on the contrary, denotes "brightness," "whiteness," or "shining." (Linguistically it is closely related to the words *tzohorayim*, "(after)noon," and *zohar*, "shining.")

Thus, the name "Ephron son of Zohar" means "ash upon radiance" or "darkness, child of light." It describes a person coming from some remarkable lineage, who had a brilliant beginning, and who, no doubt, became the owner of the Machpelah Cave hardly by accident, for he is the keeper of a vital universal tradition. This "son of radiance" is now already "sullied with ashes," for he has descended to the "dust." Yet, he still has all the hidden potential of light, although he might himself not even be aware of it. Abraham, besides purchasing the Machpelah Cave from Ephron, must also assume this potential from him.

Ephron sees no special virtues in the Machpelah Cave. Were he aware of them, he would not be selling that Cave to Abraham. Although he still has reverence for the wise, he no longer has his own wisdom and understanding, for he is now just one of the simple folk. Such people are weak in knowledge, but they still have natural human understanding and candor. We will soon see how Ephron is able to actualize these characteristics.

## 28.10. Purchasing the Field, and Abraham's Status (23:10-11)

י וְעֶפְרוֹן יֹשֵׁב בְּתוֹךְ בְּנֵי־חֵת וַיַּעַן עֶפְרוֹן הַחִתִּי אֶת־
אַבְרָהָם בְּאָזְנֵי בְנֵי־חֵת לְכֹל בָּאֵי שַׁעַר־עִירוֹ לֵאמֹר: יא
לֹא־אֲדֹנִי שְׁמָעֵנִי הַשָּׂדֶה נָתַתִּי לָךְ וְהַמְּעָרָה אֲשֶׁר־בּוֹ לְךָ
נְתַתִּיהָ לְעֵינֵי בְנֵי־עַמִּי נְתַתִּיהָ לָּךְ קְבֹר מֵתֶךָ:

*[10] Ephron was present among the Hittites; so Ephron the Hittite answered Abraham in the hearing of the Hittites, all who entered the gate of his town, saying,*
*[11] "No, my lord, hear me: I give you the field and I give you the cave that is in it; I give it to you in the presence of my people. Bury your dead."*

**[11] "No, my lord, hear me: I give you the field and I give you the cave that is in it.** Ephron now obligates Abraham to yet other conditions for the purchase: the cave is not for sale without its field.

Stressing his people's legal conventions, Ephron says: "According to standard regulations as we practice them here, one may not purchase a burial site in isolation. We cannot allow the cave to pass to aliens who will use it exclusively for graves. However, the land *can* be sold on such terms that the buyer will live on it, and then he can also bury his dead on the same land if he so chooses. Therefore, if you please, purchase not only the cave, but the field as well."

Thus, Ephron's demand that Abraham purchase not only the cave but also its surrounding land is a demand for Abraham to intensify his connection with the place and to raise his status in Hebron. Ephron persuades Abraham: "If you want us to fully recognize your right to bury your dead on our land, then you must not treat it as only a memorial site, without your having any real connection to the land itself. Acquire the field and work it, plant on it and harvest its yield. It is not even necessary that you fully relocate yourself to here. But a part of your life and your work – at least one of the fields that you own – should be here."

Abraham was originally a cattle herder and shepherd – nomadic occupations. But gradually the Jewish people must give up shepherding and become farmers. Buying a field near Hebron was the first step in that direction.

## 28.11. Abraham Bows Twice to the Hittites (23:12)

יב וַיִּשְׁתַּחוּ אַבְרָהָם לִפְנֵי עַם הָאָרֶץ:

*[12] Then Abraham bowed low before the people of the land,*

Abraham bows again to the Hittites. If Abraham's earlier bow can be explained as a matter of simple etiquette, this second bow is clearly of a different character. Moreover, if it were just a sign of politeness, it is unlikely that the Torah would specifically tell us about it. The Torah does not tell of every action, but only those of some value for all generations. Of what significance, then, are these bowings of Abraham?

In Hebron, Abraham had planned to buy only a cave, as a memorial site for the dead. However, now he is also buying a field, a place that supports life. Ephron has taught him that memory alone is insufficient; that without life in Hebron there will be no real memory either. Abraham bows to the Hittites in gratitude to them for having taught him this valuable lesson.

Abraham, "the elect of God" among the Hittites as they have called him (verse 6), is neither too proud nor ashamed to actively acknowledge that he has learned an important lesson from Ephron and the Hittites.

Prior to this conversation Abraham had been planning to return to Beersheba after Sarah's funeral, such that only the gravesite would remain in Hebron. But a center of Jewish life has now just been created in Hebron. Abraham will live there henceforth, as will both Isaac and Jacob after him.

Judaism would never claim that the Jews know everything there is to know, that they have nothing to learn from others. Even Abraham, the greatest of the Jewish Patriarchs, has something to learn from the Canaanites, and feels no reason to be ashamed of that. Our chosenness for transmitting the Divine light to the nations of the world in no way contradicts the reality that we can and must learn from others. Moreover, we must express to them our gratitude for those lessons.

## 28.12. Drawing Up the Contract (23:13-16)

יג וַיְדַבֵּר אֶל־עֶפְרוֹן בְּאָזְנֵי עַם־הָאָרֶץ לֵאמֹר אַךְ אִם־ אַתָּה לוּ שְׁמָעֵנִי נָתַתִּי כֶּסֶף הַשָּׂדֶה קַח מִמֶּנִּי וְאֶקְבְּרָה אֶת־מֵתִי שָׁמָּה: יד וַיַּעַן עֶפְרוֹן אֶת־אַבְרָהָם לֵאמֹר לוֹ: טו אֲדֹנִי שְׁמָעֵנִי אֶרֶץ אַרְבַּע מֵאֹת שֶׁקֶל־כֶּסֶף בֵּינִי וּבֵינְךָ מַה־הִוא וְאֶת־מֵתְךָ קְבֹר: טז וַיִּשְׁמַע אַבְרָהָם אֶל־עֶפְרוֹן וַיִּשְׁקֹל אַבְרָהָם לְעֶפְרֹן אֶת־הַכֶּסֶף אֲשֶׁר דִּבֶּר בְּאָזְנֵי בְנֵי־חֵת אַרְבַּע מֵאוֹת שֶׁקֶל כֶּסֶף עֹבֵר לַסֹּחֵר:

*[13] and spoke to Ephron in the hearing of the people of the land, saying, "If only you would*

*hear me out! Let me pay the price of the land; accept it from me, that I may bury my dead there."*

*[14] And Ephron replied to Abraham, saying to him,*

*[15] "My lord, do hear me! A piece of land worth four hundred shekels of silver–what is that between you and me? Go and bury your dead."*

*[16] Abraham accepted Ephron's terms. Abraham paid out to Ephron the money that he had named in the hearing of the Hittites–four hundred shekels of silver at the going merchants' rate.*

**[13] In the hearing of the people of the land.** A purchase transaction of this kind is deemed legitimate only when made with public consent, "in the hearing of the people of the land."

**Let me pay the price of the land; accept it from me.** Abraham consents to Ephron's proposal, and is prepared to buy the field, which will also include rights of burial.

**[15] A piece of land worth four hundred shekels of silver – what is that between you and me?.** Four hundred silver shekels were then an enormous sum. But in this case the Torah calls it insignificant, because burying Sarah in the Machpelah Cave will mean a new stage in the formation of the Jewish nation.

**[16] At the going merchants' rate.** It was silver of the highest grade, negotiable currency.

The Talmud has the following to say about the Machpelah story: "This is one of three places concerning which the peoples of the world cannot possibly tell Israel that they have wrongly appropriated foreign property." And that is because the Machpelah sale was not just a run-of-the-mill, everyday transaction, but a major event in world history. Since the entire Western world recognizes the biblical text as sacred, the Torah's account of this purchase is a legal document testifying to the universal recognition of our ownership of the Machpelah territory.

## 28.13. "The field with its cave ... passed to Abraham as his possession" (23:17-20)

**יז** וַיָּקָם ׀ שְׂדֵה עֶפְרוֹן אֲשֶׁר בַּמַּכְפֵּלָה אֲשֶׁר לִפְנֵי מַמְרֵא הַשָּׂדֶה וְהַמְּעָרָה אֲשֶׁר־בּוֹ וְכָל־הָעֵץ אֲשֶׁר בַּשָּׂדֶה אֲשֶׁר בְּכָל־גְּבֻלוֹ סָבִיב: **יח** לְאַבְרָהָם לְמִקְנָה לְעֵינֵי בְנֵי־חֵת בְּכֹל בָּאֵי שַׁעַר־עִירוֹ: **יט** וְאַחֲרֵי־כֵן קָבַר אַבְרָהָם אֶת־שָׂרָה אִשְׁתּוֹ אֶל־מְעָרַת שְׂדֵה הַמַּכְפֵּלָה עַל־פְּנֵי מַמְרֵא הִוא חֶבְרוֹן בְּאֶרֶץ כְּנָעַן: **כ** וַיָּקָם הַשָּׂדֶה וְהַמְּעָרָה אֲשֶׁר־בּוֹ לְאַבְרָהָם לַאֲחֻזַּת־קָבֶר מֵאֵת בְּנֵי־חֵת:

*[17] So Ephron's land in Machpelah, near Mamre-the field with its cave and all the trees anywhere within the confines of that field-passed*
*[18] to Abraham as his possession, in the presence of the Hittites, of all who entered the gate of his town.*
*[19] And then Abraham buried his wife Sarah in the cave of the field of Machpelah, facing Mamre-now Hebron-in the land of Canaan.*

*[20] Thus the field with its cave passed from the Hittites to Abraham, as a burial site.*

**[17] And all the trees anywhere within the confines of that field.** It is now the agricultural aspect of Abraham's acquisition that is emphasized. A field and its trees require active care and cultivation. They cannot be abandoned to their own fate, with the proprietor arriving to tend to them only very occasionally. They are the essence of life itself, not just a memorial to the once-living.

**[19] Facing Mamre - now Hebron - in the land of Canaan.** Mamre was one of Abraham's political allies (14:13). Thus, this purchase restores Abraham not only to Hebron, but also to the point of his political responsibility, his political activity in the "Land of Canaan." Later (24:3) we see that Abraham did indeed live in the land of Canaan, and not in the land of the Philistines.

**[20] Thus the field with its cave passed.** Literally, "Thus the field and its cave rose." When the Jews take possession of the Land, it is elevated, and it illuminates the world. But without the Jews, the Holy Land has no light to bestow on humanity.

# Chapter 29

# The Marriage of Isaac and Rebekah

## 29.1. The Command to Marry Isaac to Kindred Family (24:1-4)

א וְאַבְרָהָם זָקֵן בָּא בַּיָּמִים וַיי בֵּרַךְ אֶת־אַבְרָהָם בַּכֹּל:
ב וַיֹּאמֶר אַבְרָהָם אֶל־עַבְדּוֹ זְקַן בֵּיתוֹ הַמֹּשֵׁל בְּכָל־
אֲשֶׁר־לוֹ שִׂים־נָא יָדְךָ תַּחַת יְרֵכִי: ג וְאַשְׁבִּיעֲךָ בַּיי
אֱלֹהֵי הַשָּׁמַיִם וֵאלֹהֵי הָאָרֶץ אֲשֶׁר לֹא־תִקַּח אִשָּׁה לִבְנִי
מִבְּנוֹת הַכְּנַעֲנִי אֲשֶׁר אָנֹכִי יוֹשֵׁב בְּקִרְבּוֹ: ד כִּי אֶל־אַרְצִי
וְאֶל־מוֹלַדְתִּי תֵּלֵךְ וְלָקַחְתָּ אִשָּׁה לִבְנִי לְיִצְחָק:

*[1] Abraham was now old, advanced in years,
and the Lord had blessed Abraham in all things.
[2] And Abraham said to the senior servant of his
household, who had charge of all that he owned,
"Put your hand under my thigh
[3] and I will make you swear by the Lord, the God
of heaven and the God of the earth, that you will
not take a wife for my son from the daughters of
the Canaanites among whom I dwell,*

*[4] but will go to the land of my birth and get a*
*wife for my son Isaac."*

**[1] Abraham was now old.** That is, his activity had now ceased. Abraham had received from God all that he could, and his era was about to end. The last two stories about Abraham that now follow speak of his actions toward his children. First Abraham finds a suitable wife for Isaac, and then he sends the sons of Keturah "eastward toward the east." The fact that Abraham's slave, having been charged by Abraham with the task of finding a wife for Isaac, gives an account upon his return not to Abraham, but directly to Isaac, testifies to Abraham's retirement from affairs.

**[2] And Abraham said to the senior servant.** Like everywhere else in the entire Torah, a "slave/servant" refers to a patriarchal form of "servitude," in which the slave or servant is actually nothing less than a subordinate, junior member of the family.

**The senior servant of his household.** The Midrash identifies this servant with Eliezer, whom the Torah introduced earlier using the same words (15:2).

**Put your hand under my thigh.** Although Abraham under normal conditions fully trusts Eliezer, here he exacts from him an oath associated with God's Covenant of circumcision.
In that era circumcision was the only tangible "sacred object." No other act of holiness in the time of the Patriarchs left its lasting mark on matter. In later times, however, the situation changed. For example, after Solomon built the Temple on Mount Moriah, that mountain became holy forever, and remained so even after the destruction of the

Temple, because its holiness had been "imprinted" there in the physical material. The same applies, to cite another more familiar example, to a Torah scroll. Even if it becomes damaged or corrupted and therefore unfit for reading, it nevertheless remains sacred, and must not be discarded. Rather, it must be put into a *genizah*.

However, this form of holiness came into existence only after the Exodus from Egypt and the giving of the Torah. In the days of the Patriarchs it did not yet exist, for holiness made no physical imprint on matter. For example, the story of the *Akeidah* did not turn Mount Moriah into a "holy mountain." It remained an ordinary place to be treated in the usual way – to be plowed, sown, and the like. (Thus we see that before David undertook the building of the Temple, there was a barn with a threshing floor on the Temple Mount. This was quite normal then, but in later periods it would have been impossible.)

Until the creation of the Jewish nation at Mount Sinai, holiness would just come and go, leaving no permanent imprint on anything material. Thus, the only object on which tangible holiness remained in the days of the Patriarchs was circumcision, the sign of God's Covenant that was associated with bearing children. The essential mission of the Patriarchs, however great they may have been, was to create posterity to tread the path they had laid. The Covenant of the Patriarchs is the covenant of posterity. The oath that Abraham imposes on Eliezer relates specifically to this aspect.

**[3] That you will not take a wife for my son from the daughters of the Canaanites among whom I dwell.** We can infer from these words that by the end of his life Abraham had left Beersheba, a region of Philistia, and returned to Canaan, to Hebron. The Midrash adds that the "Canaanites" referred to here are Aner, Eshkol and Mamre, Abraham's allies (14:3) – very respectable people with whom one could enjoy friendship, maintain common business dealings, go together into battle (15:24), and even learn from them important spiritual lessons (23:12). And yet, it is unacceptable for Isaac to marry one of their daughters. Although they are good people, a nation cannot be built through them.

**[4] But will go to the land of my birth and get a wife for my son Isaac.** In modern Hebrew, *moladti* means "my homeland", but here it means not so much a homeland as a kindred family. Abraham sends his servant to Aram, the country he had left (although he continues to call it "my homeland," or, literally, "my land"). They are to go to the city of Haran, where his relatives live, in order to find a wife for Isaac among them. This is a victory of Sarah, who believed that the roots of the Chosen People were necessarily to maintain in the *ivrim* (Hebrews) ethnic community exclusively.

## 29.2. The Importance of Living in the Holy Land (24:5-9)

ה וַיֹּאמֶר אֵלָיו הָעֶבֶד אוּלַי לֹא־תֹאבֶה הָאִשָּׁה לָלֶכֶת אַחֲרַי אֶל־הָאָרֶץ הַזֹּאת הֶהָשֵׁב אָשִׁיב אֶת־בִּנְךָ אֶל־הָאָרֶץ אֲשֶׁר־יָצָאתָ מִשָּׁם: ו וַיֹּאמֶר אֵלָיו אַבְרָהָם הִשָּׁמֶר לְךָ פֶּן־תָּשִׁיב אֶת־בְּנִי שָׁמָּה: ז יי ׀ אֱלֹהֵי הַשָּׁמַיִם אֲשֶׁר לְקָחַנִי מִבֵּית אָבִי וּמֵאֶרֶץ מוֹלַדְתִּי וַאֲשֶׁר דִּבֶּר־לִי וַאֲשֶׁר נִשְׁבַּע־לִי לֵאמֹר לְזַרְעֲךָ אֶתֵּן אֶת־הָאָרֶץ הַזֹּאת הוּא יִשְׁלַח מַלְאָכוֹ לְפָנֶיךָ וְלָקַחְתָּ אִשָּׁה לִבְנִי מִשָּׁם: ח וְאִם־לֹא תֹאבֶה הָאִשָּׁה לָלֶכֶת אַחֲרֶיךָ וְנִקִּיתָ מִשְּׁבֻעָתִי זֹאת רַק אֶת־בְּנִי לֹא תָשֵׁב שָׁמָּה: ט וַיָּשֶׂם הָעֶבֶד אֶת־יָדוֹ תַּחַת יֶרֶךְ אַבְרָהָם אֲדֹנָיו וַיִּשָּׁבַע לוֹ עַל־הַדָּבָר הַזֶּה:

*[5] And the servant said to him, "What if the woman does not consent to follow me to this land, shall I then take your son back to the land from which you came?"*

*[6] Abraham answered him, "On no account must you take my son back there!*

*[7] The Lord, the God of heaven, who took me from my father's house and from my native land, who promised me on oath, saying, 'I will assign this land to your offspring'-He will send His angel before you, and you will get a wife for my son from there.*

*[8] And if the woman does not consent to follow you, you shall then be clear of this oath to me; but do not take my son back there."*

*[9] So the servant put his hand under the thigh of his master Abraham and swore to him as bidden.*

**[5] What if the woman does not consent.** The manner in which Eliezer responds to Abraham is perturbing. The word *ulai*, "what if" or "perhaps," is usually used in a positive sense, to indicate a desired condition, rather than an undesired one. The Midrash therefore believes that subconsciously Eliezer was actually hoping that the lady would *not* consent and that his mission would fail, because Eliezer had plans of his own for the marriage of Isaac.

**[6] On no account must you take my son back there!** (Literally, "Beware, lest you take my son back there!") Should any conflict arise between finding a suitable marriage partner and living in the Land of Israel, Abraham gives priority to living in the Holy Land. As Abraham's departure to the land of Canaan was a new stage in the religious development of all mankind, there was no turning back.

**[8] But do not take my son back there.** The Hebrew here uses the word *rak*, an intensified form of "only." Thus, we can translate Abraham's words as, "Whatever you do, you must not take my son back there!" The argument of returning for the sake of marriage is a temptation from which one must be on guard. And so Abraham adds, "Beware!" And then he further adds, "You must not take my son back there."

We have noted earlier that the two branches of the Terah family had different views on the proper path of development for the Jewish people. Should that path be nationalistic or cosmopolitan? Marriage to a representative of the "cosmopolitan branch" would increase the element of universalism in the family – something very positive. But at the same time the cosmopolitan line must not become the dominant one.

Abraham's son must therefore not move to Haran, even if a completely "Jewish" environment exists there where monotheism is professed. As good as living conditions abroad might be, proper development is possible only in the Land of Israel.

**[7] The Lord, the God of heaven.** When the Almighty sent Abraham to Canaan, He was still only "the God of Heaven." But (above, verse 24:3) as Abraham was exacting an oath from Eliezer, he referred to "the Lord, the God of Heaven and the God of the earth." Only as the result of Abraham's activity and subsequently that of the Jewish people, does "the God of Heaven" also becomes "the God of the earth."

It is relatively easy for a person to acknowledge that there is "God in Heaven" who is in charge of spiritual matters, and that He defines "salvation of the soul in the afterlife" and the like. But admitting God into one's earthly life is much more difficult. This is the task of Judaism.

For the Jewish people, this point is reflected also in the differences between life in the Land of Israel and life in the Diaspora. In the Diaspora, the Lord is the God of Heaven, while on the earth an entirely different set of principles is operative. One who lives there seeks to know God by committing to exclusively spiritual pursuits that belong to the heavens."

But in the Land of Israel everything is different. It is impossible to approach God there without knowing Him as "God on earth." This is why the ideological conflict in Judaism today between "diaspora spirituality" (which describes the contemporary *haredim* – the "ultra-orthodox" trend in Judaism) and "the spirituality of the Land of Israel" (religious Zionism) is so acutely felt.

## 29.3. The Well as a Place of Matchmaking (24:10-11)

י וַיִּקַּח הָעֶבֶד עֲשָׂרָה גְמַלִּים מִגְּמַלֵּי אֲדֹנָיו וַיֵּלֶךְ וְכָל־
טוּב אֲדֹנָיו בְּיָדוֹ וַיָּקָם וַיֵּלֶךְ אֶל־אֲרַם נַהֲרַיִם אֶל־עִיר
נָחוֹר: יא וַיַּבְרֵךְ הַגְּמַלִּים מִחוּץ לָעִיר אֶל־בְּאֵר הַמָּיִם
לְעֵת עֶרֶב לְעֵת צֵאת הַשֹּׁאֲבֹת:

*[10] Then the servant took ten of his master's camels and set out, taking with him all the bounty of his master; and he made his way to Aram-naharaim, to the city of Nahor.*
*[11] He made the camels kneel down by the well outside the city, at evening time, the time when women come out to draw water.*

**[11] By the well.** We repeatedly find in the Torah stories of first meetings and matchmaking at the well. It was typically the young girls who went out to fetch water, and this practice created one of the few public situations where it was possible to meet them.

**At evening time.** Eliezer finds himself at the well in the afternoon, which is the time of Isaac, the man of *gevurah*. He is going to verify (verification is an action connected with *gevurah*) the girl's spiritual qualities, asking her to show him exceptional kindness, which will require of her a considerable expenditure of time and effort. Had this happened in the morning, when people are full of energy, it would have been less difficult for the girl to fulfill his request. But in the evening when the day is ending, what he was asking of her was considerably more difficult, and the assistance she would provide for Eliezer would be commensurately much more noteworthy.

### 29.4. Everyday Stories about the Patriarchs' Slaves

The story of choosing a wife for Isaac is told in the Torah in great detail. Four times it is told and retold – at first glance, the same thing over and over again. First how Eliezer envisioned Isaac's future bride, then how Rebekah actually conducted herself, then Eliezer's retelling to the girl's relatives about what he had envisioned, and finally, yet again, his recounting to them how Rebekah conducted herself.

We imagine it would have been possible instead to tell of Eliezer's plans just once, and then to refer back to them: "And so did it happen," or, "He told it all just that way", or something similar (just as in verse 66, for example: "The servant told Isaac all the things that he had done"). The fourfold telling and retelling is especially puzzling when we consider that many of the fundamental laws of the Torah are written only as extremely terse instructions, often nothing more than an allusion. Thus, there is a clear disproportionality here. But since these stories have been given such a prominent place in the Torah, we understand that their analysis and comparison must be very important.

The Talmud addresses this question directly, with the comment: "The mundane stories of the Patriarchs' servants are more precious to God than even the details of the commandments given to their descendants."

The legislative Torah is at the level of Moses, and indeed, Moses was the greatest of all Prophets. But the level of the Patriarchs was incomparably higher. At the level of Moses, there are commandments – obligations in which the Divine light is concentrated. In the lives of the Patriarchs, however, there were no specific commandments, and yet their entire lives consisted of Revelation and the realization of Divinity. The Book of *Bereshit* (Genesis), the Book of the Patriarchs, is therefore the first and most fundamental book of the Torah, because it is the book of God's teachings.

Not only the conversations of the Patriarchs themselves, but even those of their servants, carry that light to us.

## 29.5. Above-Normal Hesed (24:12-14)

**יב** וַיֹּאמַר ׀ יי אֱלֹהֵי אֲדֹנִי אַבְרָהָם הַקְרֵה־נָא לְפָנַי הַיּוֹם וַעֲשֵׂה־חֶסֶד עִם אֲדֹנִי אַבְרָהָם: **יג** הִנֵּה אָנֹכִי נִצָּב עַל־עֵין הַמָּיִם וּבְנוֹת אַנְשֵׁי הָעִיר יֹצְאֹת לִשְׁאֹב מָיִם: **יד** וְהָיָה הַנַּעֲרָ אֲשֶׁר אֹמַר אֵלֶיהָ הַטִּי־נָא כַדֵּךְ וְאֶשְׁתֶּה וְאָמְרָה שְׁתֵה וְגַם־גְּמַלֶּיךָ אַשְׁקֶה אֹתָהּ הֹכַחְתָּ לְעַבְדְּךָ לְיִצְחָק וּבָהּ אֵדַע כִּי־עָשִׂיתָ חֶסֶד עִם־אֲדֹנִי:

*[12] And he said, "O Lord, God of my master Abraham, grant me good fortune this day, and deal graciously with my master Abraham:*
*[13] Here I stand by the spring as the daughters of the townsmen come out to draw water;*
*[14] let the maiden to whom I say, 'Please, lower your jar that I may drink,' and who replies, 'Drink, and I will also water your camels'–let her be the one whom You have decreed for Your servant Isaac. Thereby shall I know that You have dealt graciously with my master."*

**[12] And he said.** Eliezer had arrived at the "city of Nahor." But instead of asking directly where Nahor lives, he stakes a highly unusual venture.

**[14] Let the maiden to whom I say, 'Please, lower your jar that I may drink,' and who replies, 'Drink, and I will also water your camels'.** He wants to find a girl having a remarkably exceptional standard of kindness, *chesed* – such that when he asks her for water to drink, she will offer to water his camels as well.

Since Isaac is *gevurah*, his wife should be *chesed*, because all the wives of the Patriarchs were their "opposites" in personal qualities, as if counterbalancing them. (Sarah is *gevurah* to Abraham's *chesed*; Rebekah is *chesed* to Isaac's *gevurah*.) A wife should be a man's *ezer kenegdo* – "a counterweight of assistance" (2:18). *Chesed* is therefore precisely that criterion that guides Eliezer here. If a girl is prepared, even without being asked, to water a dozen camels, then her level of *chesed* is so great that she can become a suitable wife for Isaac.

Even if the girl, in response to Eliezer's request, will give water only to him, she will thereby have already manifested *chesed*. She will surely be in a hurry, because it is now evening, and it is reasonable that she would say, "The well is right in front of you – help yourself, why are you asking me?" (Moreover, as we will note below [verse 32] Eliezer was not alone. The girl could simply have suggested that he ask his servants to assist.)

But if her thinking runs something like this: "When a person standing directly in front of a well asks others to give him water to drink, we must assume that he is unable to draw water even for himself, let alone for his camels. Thus, his camels, too, are almost certainly not watered; I should really water them as well" – then such thinking will absolutely demonstrate an abundance of *chesed* on her part, way above the norm.

## 29.6. Rebekah's Conduct at the Well (24:15-20)

**טו** וַיְהִי־הוּא טֶרֶם כִּלָּה לְדַבֵּר וְהִנֵּה רִבְקָה יֹצֵאת אֲשֶׁר יֻלְּדָה לִבְתוּאֵל בֶּן־מִלְכָּה אֵשֶׁת נָחוֹר אֲחִי אַבְרָהָם וְכַדָּהּ עַל־שִׁכְמָהּ: **טז** וְהַנַּעֲרָ טֹבַת מַרְאֶה מְאֹד בְּתוּלָה וְאִישׁ לֹא יְדָעָהּ וַתֵּרֶד הָעַיְנָה וַתְּמַלֵּא כַדָּהּ וַתָּעַל: **יז** וַיָּרָץ הָעֶבֶד לִקְרָאתָהּ וַיֹּאמֶר הַגְמִיאִינִי נָא מְעַט־מַיִם מִכַּדֵּךְ: **יח** וַתֹּאמֶר שְׁתֵה אֲדֹנִי וַתְּמַהֵר וַתֹּרֶד כַּדָּהּ עַל־יָדָהּ וַתַּשְׁקֵהוּ: **יט** וַתְּכַל לְהַשְׁקֹתוֹ וַתֹּאמֶר גַּם לִגְמַלֶּיךָ אֶשְׁאָב עַד אִם־כִּלּוּ לִשְׁתֹּת: **כ** וַתְּמַהֵר וַתְּעַר כַּדָּהּ אֶל־הַשֹּׁקֶת וַתָּרָץ עוֹד אֶל־הַבְּאֵר לִשְׁאֹב וַתִּשְׁאַב לְכָל־גְּמַלָּיו:

*[15] He had scarcely finished speaking, when Rebekah, who was born to Bethuel, the son of Milcah the wife of Abraham's brother Nahor, came out with her jar on her shoulder.*

*[16] The maiden was very beautiful, a virgin whom no man had known. She went down to the spring, filled her jar, and came up.*

*[17] The servant ran toward her and said, "Please, let me sip a little water from your jar."*

*[18] "Drink, my lord", she said, and she quickly lowered her jar upon her hand and let him drink.*

*[19] When she had let him drink his fill, she said, "I will also draw for your camels, until they finish drinking."*

*[20] Quickly emptying her jar into the trough, she ran back to the well to draw, and she drew for all his camels.*

**[15] He had scarcely finished speaking, when Rebekah ... came out.** A question properly posed is already half answered. Because Eliezer has expressed the problem so well, the solution is close at hand.

**"Drink, my lord."** Rebekah's words alone do not coincide with Eliezer's original conception of what was to happen (24:14), but when taken together with her actions, her words do in fact correspond to what he expected. Once again this is meant to underscore that Eliezer's plan was not some kind of magical test requiring precise, literal fulfillment, but only a check of Rebekah's *chesed*. However, in Eliezer's later retelling of the same events to Rebekah's relatives (verses 43-46), he describes the events as if the girl had repeated his words exactly. Thus, Eliezer creates for the relatives the impression of a "magical coincidence" as a basis for seeking their consent to the marriage.

**[16] She went down ... and came up. [17] The servant ran toward her and said.** Eliezer does not ask Rebekah for water immediately, but waits for her to move away from the well somewhat, and only then runs up to her. Thus, he makes his test of her *chesed* that much more decisive.

**[18] She quickly lowered her jar ... [19] When she had let him drink his fill, she said, "I will also draw for your camels."** Rebekah is herself in a hurry, but she does not rush Eliezer. She does not tell him from the outset, "Drink, and then I will also draw for your camels," which would have forced him to drink quickly. Rather, she waits until he has completely finished drinking, and only then mentions watering the animals. Thus, Rebekah goes even beyond what Eliezer had envisioned.

If a person standing at a well asks to be given water, when by all appearances he can just take it himself, it is not unreasonable to conclude that he must be engaging in some form of mockery. But no such thought occurs to Rebekah. Rather, she reasons that he most probably has some actual problem and needs her help. Such a level of *chesed* is rarely encountered in real life.

## 29.7. Rebekah and the Hospitality of the Nahor Family (24:21-27)

כא וְהָאִישׁ מִשְׁתָּאֵה לָהּ מַחֲרִישׁ לָדַעַת הַהִצְלִיחַ יי
דַּרְכּוֹ אִם־לֹא: כב וַיְהִי כַּאֲשֶׁר כִּלּוּ הַגְּמַלִּים לִשְׁתּוֹת
וַיִּקַּח הָאִישׁ נֶזֶם זָהָב בֶּקַע מִשְׁקָלוֹ וּשְׁנֵי צְמִידִים עַל־
יָדֶיהָ עֲשָׂרָה זָהָב מִשְׁקָלָם: כג וַיֹּאמֶר בַּת־מִי אַתְּ הַגִּידִי
נָא לִי הֲיֵשׁ בֵּית־אָבִיךְ מָקוֹם לָנוּ לָלִין: כד וַתֹּאמֶר אֵלָיו
בַּת־בְּתוּאֵל אָנֹכִי בֶּן־מִלְכָּה אֲשֶׁר יָלְדָה לְנָחוֹר: כה

וַתֹּאמֶר אֵלָיו גַּם־תֶּבֶן גַּם־מִסְפּוֹא רַב עִמָּנוּ גַּם־מָקוֹם
לָלוּן: **כו** וַיִּקֹּד הָאִישׁ וַיִּשְׁתַּחוּ לַיָי: **כז** וַיֹּאמֶר בָּרוּךְ יָי
אֱלֹהֵי אֲדֹנִי אַבְרָהָם אֲשֶׁר לֹא־עָזַב חַסְדּוֹ וַאֲמִתּוֹ מֵעִם
אֲדֹנִי אָנֹכִי בַּדֶּרֶךְ נָחַנִי יָי בֵּית אֲחֵי אֲדֹנִי:

*[21] The man, meanwhile, stood gazing at her,
silently wondering whether the Lord had made
his errand successful or not.*
*[22] When the camels had finished drinking,
the man took a gold nose-ring weighing a half-
shekel, and two gold bands for her arms, ten
shekels in weight.*
*[23] "Pray tell me," he said, "whose daughter are
you? Is there room in your father's house for us
to spend the night?"*
*[24] She replied, "I am the daughter of Bethuel
the son of Milcah, whom she bore to Nahor."*
*[25] And she went on, "There is plenty of straw
and feed at home, and also room to spend the
night."*
*[26] The man bowed low in homage to the Lord*
*[27] and said, "Blessed be the Lord, the God of
my master Abraham, who has not withheld His
steadfast faithfulness from my master. For I have
been guided on my errand by the Lord, to the
house of my master's kinsmen."*

**[21] The man, meanwhile, stood gazing at her, silently
wondering whether the Lord had made his errand successful or not.** While Rebekah waters the camels, Abraham's
servant stands astonished at the goings on, but still remains
silent. For although the girl's behavior is remarkable, he

knows he has given Abraham his sworn oath to find a wife for Isaac only from Abraham's relatives.

**[22] When the camels had finished drinking, the man took a gold nose-ring.** After the camels had finished drinking, although the girl did not ask for any compensation or reward, Eliezer gives her gifts. Although this of course goes beyond the norms of ordinary day-to-day communication, there is also no formal matchmaking happening here yet.

When, later, Eliezer retells this story to Rebekah's relatives, he changes events in places – as if he first asked her about the relationship, and only then gave her gifts – because otherwise, Rebekah's relatives would not have made sense of his actions. They are not interested in any degree of *chesed*. But they are very impressed by the coincidences.

**[23] Whose daughter are you? Is there room in your father's house for us to spend the night?** By asking whose daughter she is, and whether they can spend the night, Eliezer is trying to determine whether these are Abraham's relatives, and how hospitable the girl's family is. That is, have they preserved Abraham's traditions of hospitality, which for him, as a manifestation of love for one's fellow humans, are a core religious principle?

**[25] "There is plenty of straw and feed at home, and also room to spend the night." [26] The man bowed low in homage to the Lord.** Upon learning that Rebekah's family has ample place for lodging, and that they are always prepared to receive travelers (it is the accepted custom of the family, and their house has been specially adapted for this), Eliezer bows to the Lord in gratitude.

## 29.8. Eliezer Meets Rebekah's Family (24:28-33)

כח וַתָּרָץ הַנַּעֲרָ וַתַּגֵּד לְבֵית אִמָּהּ כַּדְּבָרִים הָאֵלֶּה: כט
וּלְרִבְקָה אָח וּשְׁמוֹ לָבָן וַיָּרָץ לָבָן אֶל־הָאִישׁ הַחוּצָה אֶל־
הָעָיִן: ל וַיְהִי ׀ כִּרְאֹת אֶת־הַנֶּזֶם וְאֶת־הַצְּמִדִים עַל־יְדֵי
אֲחֹתוֹ וּכְשָׁמְעוֹ אֶת־דִּבְרֵי רִבְקָה אֲחֹתוֹ לֵאמֹר כֹּה־דִּבֶּר
אֵלַי הָאִישׁ וַיָּבֹא אֶל־הָאִישׁ וְהִנֵּה עֹמֵד עַל־הַגְּמַלִּים עַל־
הָעָיִן: לא וַיֹּאמֶר בּוֹא בְּרוּךְ יי לָמָּה תַעֲמֹד בַּחוּץ וְאָנֹכִי
פִּנִּיתִי הַבַּיִת וּמָקוֹם לַגְּמַלִּים: לב וַיָּבֹא הָאִישׁ הַבַּיְתָה
וַיְפַתַּח הַגְּמַלִּים וַיִּתֵּן תֶּבֶן וּמִסְפּוֹא לַגְּמַלִּים וּמַיִם לִרְחֹץ
רַגְלָיו וְרַגְלֵי הָאֲנָשִׁים אֲשֶׁר אִתּוֹ: לג ויישם (וַיּוּשַׂם) לְפָנָיו
לֶאֱכֹל וַיֹּאמֶר לֹא אֹכַל עַד אִם־דִּבַּרְתִּי דְּבָרָי וַיֹּאמֶר דַּבֵּר:

[28] The maiden ran and told all this to her
mother's household.
[29] Now Rebekah had a brother whose name
was Laban. Laban ran out to the man at the
spring—
[30] when he saw the nose-ring and the bands
on his sister's arms, and when he heard his sister
Rebekah say, "Thus the man spoke to me." He
went up to the man, who was still standing
beside the camels at the spring.
[31] "Come in, O blessed of the Lord," he said,
"why do you remain outside, when I have made
ready the house and a place for the camels?"
[32] So the man entered the house, and the
camels were unloaded. The camels were given
straw and feed, and water was brought to bathe
his feet and the feet of the men with him.
[33] But when food was set before him, he said,
"I will not eat until I have told my tale." He said,
"Speak, then."

**[30] When he saw the nose-ring and the bands on his sister's arms.** Here the Torah contrasts the selflessness of Rebekah's actions with the self-interest (by all appearances, at least) of Laban's motives. Nonetheless, the hospitality practiced by the entire Nahor family is also emphasized.

**[33] I will not eat until I have told my tale.** Now that Eliezer has completed the first part of his assignment – finding a suitable woman for Isaac – he must also carry out the next part, ensuring that her relatives will give her hand in marriage. We will soon see how he accomplishes that, by dramatizing his retelling of the events and altering the emphasis in his story.

But in addition to negotiations with the family of the bride, the Torah here includes also a parallel subplot – the development of Eliezer himself. The text alternately refers to him as "the slave," "the man," and (here) "blessed of the Lord," but these variations are not accidental. Earlier we mentioned that in Eliezer's words to Abraham at the beginning of the story, "What if the girl does not consent to follow me ..." there was an indication that Eliezer actually had his own views on whom Isaac should marry. Here he must surmount those previous attitudes.

## 29.9. Changes of Emphasis in Eliezer's Retelling of His Assigned Task (24:34-38)

**לד** וַיֹּאמַר עֶבֶד אַבְרָהָם אָנֹכִי: **לה** וַיי בֵּרַךְ אֶת־אֲדֹנִי מְאֹד וַיִּגְדָּל וַיִּתֶּן־לוֹ צֹאן וּבָקָר וְכֶסֶף וְזָהָב וַעֲבָדִם וּשְׁפָחֹת וּגְמַלִּים וַחֲמֹרִים: **לו** וַתֵּלֶד שָׂרָה אֵשֶׁת אֲדֹנִי בֵן לַאדֹנִי אַחֲרֵי זִקְנָתָהּ וַיִּתֶּן־לוֹ אֶת־כָּל־אֲשֶׁר־לוֹ: **לז** וַיַּשְׁבִּעֵנִי אֲדֹנִי לֵאמֹר לֹא־תִקַּח אִשָּׁה לִבְנִי מִבְּנוֹת

הַכְּנַעֲנִי אֲשֶׁר אָנֹכִי יֹשֵׁב בְּאַרְצוֹ: **לח** אִם־לֹא אֶל־בֵּית־
אָבִי תֵּלֵךְ וְאֶל־מִשְׁפַּחְתִּי וְלָקַחְתָּ אִשָּׁה לִבְנִי:

*[34] "I am Abraham's servant," he began.*

*[35] "The Lord has greatly blessed my master, and he has become rich: He has given him sheep and cattle, silver and gold, male and female slaves, camels and asses.*

*[36] And Sarah, my master's wife, bore my master a son in her old age, and he has assigned to him everything he owns.*

*[37] Now my master made me swear, saying, 'You shall not get a wife for my son from the daughters of the Canaanites in whose land I dwell;*

*[38] but you shall go to my father's house, to my kindred, and get a wife for my son.'"*

The events as Eliezer retells them are somewhat different from how they actually happened. Starting off with Abraham's prominence and wealth, and emphasizing that all of that will pass to Isaac, Eliezer further shifts the emphases in his description of the task he was charged to perform.

**[38] But you shall go to my father's house, to my kindred, and get a wife for my son.** Abraham had instructed Eliezer to find a wife for Isaac from Abraham's kin. But when retelling the events, Eliezer says that he was ordered to look for a girl from Abraham's "father's house." "Kin" is a broad concept, whereas "father's house" is much more specific. Eliezer intentionally narrows the task set by Abraham, representing the situation as even more of a miracle than it actually was.

And Rebekah's relatives are indeed duly impressed.

## 29.10. Eliezer's Personal Issues with Finding a Wife for Isaac (24:39)

לט וָאֹמַר אֶל־אֲדֹנִי אֻלַי לֹא־תֵלֵךְ הָאִשָּׁה אַחֲרָי:

*[39] And I said to my master, 'What if the woman does not follow me?'*

**[39] What if the woman does not follow me?** We have already mentioned that Eliezer's use of the word *ulai*, "what if," here and also above (verse 5), seems strange, because that word usually indicates a condition that the speaker actually does want to occur. Was Eliezer actually hoping that his mission would fail? The Midrash believes that that was indeed the case, as we shall very soon explain.

At the same time, the Midrash notes that here the word *ulai* is written with the letter *vav* omitted. This is also unusual, but has the effect that the word can also be read as *elai*, "to me." (In Eliezer's original conversation with Abraham above (verse 5), the word is written the usual way, in full, including the letter *vav*.)

So, what is this all about? It seems that Eliezer himself had a daughter, and he had therefore for a long time been hoping that Isaac would marry her. The "what if" that escaped from Eliezer's mouth was a (possibly only subconscious) expression of his hope that his current mission would fail, in order that his daughter could marry Isaac. In the process of completing the mission Eliezer had to overcome his misguided hope. And he does in fact change his approach, as indicated by his replacing the original, conventional "what if" with the unusual "what if" that he uses here.

## 29.11. Eliezer's "Cursedness"

Here is how the Midrash describes the situation. Having received the assignment to go to Haran, Eliezer remarks candidly to Abraham: "Well, you know, I myself have a daughter. Why not have Isaac marry *her*?" Abraham answers Eliezer with what seems at first glance a highly incomprehensible statement: "No, it is not possible for Isaac to marry your daughter. Because my son is blessed, and you are cursed."

Doesn't Abraham's reply to Eliezer seem far too harsh? After all, Eliezer is a righteous individual who "had charge of all that Abraham owned" (24:2), which the Midrash understands to refer not only to Abraham's property, but also to Eliezer's responsibility for instructing Abraham's servant-disciples. The Midrash adds that Eliezer was Abraham's best student, "drawing living waters" from his master Abraham, and using them to water yet other disciples. Eliezer had even been considered a potential heir to Abraham (15:2-3). How, then, could Abraham utter such harsh words to such a beloved disciple?

We must take into account, however, that these words are not those of the Torah text itself, but of the Midrash, and thus should be understood not literally, but only as the expression of an important idea that the authors of the Midrash wish to convey.

The concept of *berachah*, "blessing," means increasing, expanding, and advancing. The classic Jewish formula for reciting blessings to God, which begins, "Blessed are You, o Lord, our God," means that through our efforts, Divine holiness increases and spreads throughout the world. Accordingly, a "curse" (the antithesis of blessing) means the cessation and impossibility of self-advancement, the mere mechanical repetition of something heard earlier. If you can only repeat after your teacher, but do not generate anything new, that is a curse. But one who is truly blessed can reveal in the world something new that was not previously recognized.

Eliezer is a wonderful person, full of love of God and of Abraham, but he is "cursed" in the sense that he can only repeat after his teacher. And so Abraham says to him: "My son must advance further, by discovering new phenomena in the world. Your daughter would provide no opportunity for such advancement."

Eliezer's daughter is not appropriate for Isaac, not because she is bad as a person, but because she cannot help him advance. She will listen to him with admiration and repeat his words, but she cannot be his "counterweight," because although her father is a disciple of Abraham, she herself is unable to advance. She can comprehend what she has heard, and perhaps even "take charge over the house," by educating younger students in the essentials of Divine teachings. But she lacks the potential for independent development. Such is Eliezer's daughter.

In order for a wife to be a "counterweight helper" (2:18) to her husband, she must be at his level, and in some ways even surpass him. Abraham therefore wants Isaac to marry a woman who is capable of being spiritually independent, and who can bring him blessings and advancement.

## 29.12. Eliezer's Correction

And so the Midrash puts into Abraham's mouth the statement that Eliezer is cursed. But at the same time, as we've just noted (verse 31), Laban calls Eliezer "blessed of the Lord," which is, of course, not by mere happenstance.

In the course of fulfilling his mission, Eliezer changed. He performed not only what Abraham had instructed him; rather, he began to formulate on his own methods of choosing a bride and of persuading her relatives. Having received a harsh refusal from Abraham, Eliezer was able to part with his cherished dream of marrying his daughter to Isaac. But at the same time he also became more resourceful in accomplishing his mission. He puts his own understanding into the mission, revealing his desire for it to succeed. Thus, he enhances his assignment with that new understanding, and through this he acquires blessings and sheds the "curse."

Every human being has been created in the image and likeness of God (1:26-27). Becoming like the Creator by acquiring His characteristics is the most important element of our advancement. Since God is first and foremost the Creator – "In the beginning God created the heaven and the earth" (1:1) – independent creativity is the most important aspect of human likeness to God. By demonstrating a creative attitude toward his mission, Eliezer has found his blessing.

Throughout the story the Torah refers to Eliezer alternately as *eved*, "servant" (or "slave"), and as *ish*, "man," which denotes a significant, autonomous individual. This variation in how the Torah refers to Eliezer is meant to tell us that at times Eliezer behaves as only an implementer of Abraham's instructions, but at other times he acts as an autonomous individual in his own right.

## 29.13. Eliezer's Methods of Persuading Rebekah's Family (24:40-61)

מ וַיֹּאמֶר אֵלָי יי אֲשֶׁר־הִתְהַלַּכְתִּי לְפָנָיו יִשְׁלַח מַלְאָכוֹ אִתָּךְ וְהִצְלִיחַ דַּרְכֶּךָ וְלָקַחְתָּ אִשָּׁה לִבְנִי מִמִּשְׁפַּחְתִּי וּמִבֵּית אָבִי: **מא** אָז תִּנָּקֶה מֵאָלָתִי כִּי תָבוֹא אֶל־מִשְׁפַּחְתִּי וְאִם־לֹא יִתְּנוּ לָךְ וְהָיִיתָ נָקִי מֵאָלָתִי: **מב** וָאָבֹא הַיּוֹם אֶל־הָעָיִן וָאֹמַר יי אֱלֹהֵי אֲדֹנִי אַבְרָהָם אִם־יֶשְׁךָ־נָּא מַצְלִיחַ דַּרְכִּי אֲשֶׁר אָנֹכִי הֹלֵךְ עָלֶיהָ: **מג** הִנֵּה אָנֹכִי נִצָּב עַל־עֵין הַמָּיִם וְהָיָה הָעַלְמָה הַיֹּצֵאת לִשְׁאֹב וְאָמַרְתִּי אֵלֶיהָ הַשְׁקִינִי־נָא מְעַט־מַיִם מִכַּדֵּךְ: **מד** וְאָמְרָה אֵלַי גַּם־אַתָּה שְׁתֵה וְגַם לִגְמַלֶּיךָ אֶשְׁאָב הִוא הָאִשָּׁה אֲשֶׁר־הֹכִיחַ יי לְבֶן־אֲדֹנִי: **מה** אֲנִי טֶרֶם אֲכַלֶּה לְדַבֵּר אֶל־לִבִּי וְהִנֵּה רִבְקָה יֹצֵאת וְכַדָּהּ עַל־שִׁכְמָהּ וַתֵּרֶד הָעַיְנָה וַתִּשְׁאָב וָאֹמַר אֵלֶיהָ הַשְׁקִינִי נָא: **מו** וַתְּמַהֵר וַתּוֹרֶד כַּדָּהּ מֵעָלֶיהָ וַתֹּאמֶר שְׁתֵה וְגַם־גְּמַלֶּיךָ אַשְׁקֶה וָאֵשְׁתְּ וְגַם הַגְּמַלִּים הִשְׁקָתָה: **מז** וָאֶשְׁאַל אֹתָהּ וָאֹמַר בַּת־מִי אַתְּ וַתֹּאמֶר בַּת־בְּתוּאֵל בֶּן־נָחוֹר אֲשֶׁר יָלְדָה־לּוֹ מִלְכָּה וָאָשִׂם הַנֶּזֶם עַל־אַפָּהּ וְהַצְּמִידִים עַל־יָדֶיהָ: **מח** וָאֶקֹּד וָאֶשְׁתַּחֲוֶה לַיי וָאֲבָרֵךְ אֶת־יי אֱלֹהֵי אֲדֹנִי אַבְרָהָם אֲשֶׁר הִנְחַנִי בְּדֶרֶךְ אֱמֶת לָקַחַת אֶת־בַּת־אֲחִי אֲדֹנִי לִבְנוֹ: **מט** וְעַתָּה אִם־יֶשְׁכֶם עֹשִׂים חֶסֶד וֶאֱמֶת אֶת־אֲדֹנִי הַגִּידוּ לִי וְאִם־לֹא הַגִּידוּ לִי וְאֶפְנֶה עַל־יָמִין אוֹ עַל־שְׂמֹאל: **נ** וַיַּעַן לָבָן וּבְתוּאֵל וַיֹּאמְרוּ מֵיי יָצָא הַדָּבָר לֹא נוּכַל דַּבֵּר אֵלֶיךָ רַע אוֹ־טוֹב: **נא** הִנֵּה־רִבְקָה לְפָנֶיךָ קַח וָלֵךְ וּתְהִי אִשָּׁה לְבֶן־אֲדֹנֶיךָ כַּאֲשֶׁר דִּבֶּר יי: **נב** וַיְהִי כַּאֲשֶׁר שָׁמַע עֶבֶד אַבְרָהָם אֶת־דִּבְרֵיהֶם וַיִּשְׁתַּחוּ אַרְצָה לַיי: **נג** וַיּוֹצֵא הָעֶבֶד כְּלֵי־כֶסֶף וּכְלֵי זָהָב וּבְגָדִים וַיִּתֵּן לְרִבְקָה וּמִגְדָּנֹת נָתַן לְאָחִיהָ וּלְאִמָּהּ: **נד** וַיֹּאכְלוּ וַיִּשְׁתּוּ הוּא וְהָאֲנָשִׁים אֲשֶׁר־עִמּוֹ וַיָּלִינוּ וַיָּקוּמוּ בַבֹּקֶר וַיֹּאמֶר שַׁלְּחֻנִי לַאדֹנִי: **נה** וַיֹּאמֶר אָחִיהָ וְאִמָּהּ תֵּשֵׁב הַנַּעֲרָ אִתָּנוּ יָמִים אוֹ עָשׂוֹר אַחַר תֵּלֵךְ: **נו** וַיֹּאמֶר אֲלֵהֶם אַל־תְּאַחֲרוּ אֹתִי וַיי הִצְלִיחַ

דַּרְכִּי שַׁלְחוּנִי וְאֵלְכָה לַאדֹנִי: **נז** וַיֹּאמְרוּ נִקְרָא לַנַּעֲרָ
וְנִשְׁאֲלָה אֶת־פִּיהָ: **נח** וַיִּקְרְאוּ לְרִבְקָה וַיֹּאמְרוּ אֵלֶיהָ
הֲתֵלְכִי עִם־הָאִישׁ הַזֶּה וַתֹּאמֶר אֵלֵךְ: **נט** וַיְשַׁלְּחוּ אֶת־
רִבְקָה אֲחֹתָם וְאֶת־מֵנִקְתָּהּ וְאֶת־עֶבֶד אַבְרָהָם וְאֶת־
אֲנָשָׁיו: **ס** וַיְבָרְכוּ אֶת־רִבְקָה וַיֹּאמְרוּ לָהּ אֲחֹתֵנוּ אַתְּ
הֲיִי לְאַלְפֵי רְבָבָה וְיִירַשׁ זַרְעֵךְ אֵת שַׁעַר שֹׂנְאָיו: **סא**
וַתָּקָם רִבְקָה וְנַעֲרֹתֶיהָ וַתִּרְכַּבְנָה עַל־הַגְּמַלִּים וַתֵּלַכְנָה
אַחֲרֵי הָאִישׁ וַיִּקַּח הָעֶבֶד אֶת־רִבְקָה וַיֵּלַךְ:

[40] He replied to me, 'The Lord, whose ways I have
followed, will send His angel with you and make
your errand successful; and you will get a wife for
my son from my kindred, from my father's house.
[41] Thus only shall you be freed from adjuration:
if, when you come to my kindred, they refuse
you – only then shall you be freed from my
adjuration.'
[42] "I came today to the spring, and I said: O
Lord, God of my master Abraham, if You would
indeed grant success to the errand on which I
am engaged!
[43] As I stand by the spring of water, let the
young woman who comes out to draw and to
whom I say, 'Please, let me drink a little water
from your jar,'
[44] and who answers, 'You may drink, and I will
also draw for your camels'—let her be the wife
whom the Lord has decreed for my master's son.'
[45] I had scarcely finished praying in my heart,
when Rebekah came out with her jar on her
shoulder, and went down to the spring and drew.
And I said to her, 'Please give me a drink.'
[46] She quickly lowered her jar and said, 'Drink,

and I will also water your camels.' So I drank, and she also watered the camels.

[47] I inquired of her, 'Whose daughter are you?' And she said, 'The daughter of Bethuel, son of Nahor, whom Milcah bore to him.' And I put the ring on her nose and the bands on her arms.

[48] Then I bowed low in homage to the Lord and blessed the Lord, the God of my master Abraham, who led me on the right way to get the daughter of my master's brother for his son.

[49] And now, if you mean to treat my master with true kindness, tell me; and if not, tell me also, that I may turn right or left."

[50] Then Laban and Bethuel answered, "The matter was decreed by the Lord; we cannot speak to you bad or good.

[51] Here is Rebekah before you; take her and go, and let her be a wife to your master's son, as the Lord has spoken."

[52] When Abraham's servant heard their words, he bowed low to the ground before the Lord.

[53] The servant brought out objects of silver and gold, and garments, and gave them to Rebekah; and he gave presents to her brother and her mother.

[54] Then he and the men with him ate and drank, and they spent the night. When they arose next morning, he said, "Give me leave to go to my master."

[55] But her brother and her mother said, "Let the maiden remain with us some ten days; then you may go."

[56] He said to them, "Do not delay me, now that

*the Lord has made my errand successful. Give*
*me leave that I may go to my master."*
*[57] And they said, "Let us call the girl and ask*
*for her reply."*
*[58] They called Rebekah and said to her, "Will*
*you go with this man?" And she said, "I will."*
*[59] So they sent off their sister Rebekah and*
*her nurse along with Abraham's servant and*
*his men.*
*[60] And they blessed Rebekah and said to her,*
*"O sister!*
*May you grow*
*Into thousands of myriads;*
*May your offspring seize*
*The gates of their foes."*
*[61] Then Rebekah and her maids arose, mounted*
*the camels, and followed the man. So the servant*
*took Rebekah and went his way.*

**[40] The Lord, whose ways I have followed, will send His angel with you.** Eliezer mentions the angel, and also his own possible release from the oath, in terms somewhat different from those that Abraham had actually used. Abraham merely said, "you will get a wife for my son from there" (24:7), but Eliezer adds that the angel will lead him specifically to Abraham's family.

**[41] If ... they refuse you – only then shall you be freed from my adjuration.** Abraham expressed it differently: "And if the woman does not consent to follow you, you shall then be clear of this oath to me" (24:8). By changing the wording, Eliezer shifts the responsibility for the decision to Rebekah's family – her father and her brother.

**[43] As I stand by the spring of water, let the young woman who comes out to draw ... [45] I had scarcely finished praying in my heart, when Rebekah came out.** Eliezer presents the story as an act of magic, as if to say, "I simply stated what I wished to happen, and it literally happened exactly that way, which obviously means that a Higher Power has interceded on my behalf. So you'd better not even *think* of interfering with the Divine will."

**[47] And she said, 'The daughter of Bethuel, son of Nahor, whom Milcah bore to him.' And I put the ring on her nose.** By changing the order of events in his retelling (saying that he first asked Rebekah whose daughter she was, and only then gave her presents), Eliezer creates the impression that her family is exactly what he was looking for, and the accuracy with which the girl fulfilled his plans demonstrates Divine predestination. Rebekah's display of *chesed* is deemphasized in his telling of the story.

**[49] And if not, tell me also, that I may turn right or left.** For success in the negotiations, it is important for Eliezer to mention that other options also exist.

**Right or left.** That is, to other relatives of Abraham. Once Eliezer puts it this way, Laban and Bethuel agree to give Rebekah in marriage.

We note several other points in which the retelling by Eliezer differs from the task that Abraham originally assigned to him.

In his conversation with Bethuel and Laban, Eliezer always emphasizes the universal element, avoiding any mention of the Land of Israel, and omitting Abraham's words, "I will assign this land to your offspring" (24:7). Such an orientation to the Holy Land would only be alien to them.

Abraham said to Eliezer: "The Lord, the God of Heaven, who took me from my father's house" (24:7). But Eliezer conveys Abraham's words to Bethuel and Laban differently: "The Lord, whose ways I have followed, will send His angel with you and make your errand successful" (24:40). Here the idea of chosenness is elided. Having a relationship with God is presented as a reward for good behavior: Because Abraham behaved properly, God sent an angel to help choose a wife for his son. This level of thinking is accessible and comprehensible to Bethuel and Laban, who are Hebrews by origin, but deeply assimilated. The ideas of chosenness and mission are alien to them.

**[51] And let her be a wife to your master's son, as the Lord has spoken.** Eliezer had now achieved his goal. Rebekah's relatives recognized that a miracle sent from Above had occurred, and that this was not their choice to make.

**[55] But her brother and her mother said, "Let the maiden remain with us some ten days; then you may go."** The family's consent had just been received – or so it seemed – but first thing the next morning, there is already a problem. With yesterday's enthusiasm now quickly dissipating, Rebekah's relatives begin to have misgivings about whether or not to let their daughter go.

**[56] Do not delay me, now that the Lord has made my errand successful.** Eliezer understands that postponing a decision is the first step to its reversal, and that in dealing with such people it is of utmost importance to strike while the iron is hot. Once again he emphasizes the Divine will and insists on immediate execution of the agreements already concluded. Rebekah's family has no way out but to summon and ask Rebekah herself, and once they have heard her consent to depart, they must come to terms with it.

**[58] They called Rebekah and said to her, "Will you go with this man?" And she said, "I will."** It turns out that Rebekah is not only a person of *chesed*; she possesses *gevurah* as well, and can insist that decisions already made must be carried out. Later, too, as Isaac's wife, she realizes the very same synthesis: "*Hesed* within *gevurah*."

### 29.14. The Prohibition of Parents Using Coercion in the Matter of a Child's Marriage

Jewish tradition also concludes from this story that it is forbidden to marry off one's children without their consent. Regardless of the opinions of her relatives, only Rebekah's wishes were decisive.

Respecting one's parents and their wishes is of course a principle of the highest importance in Judaism, but in matters of marriage it takes on only secondary importance at best. If the children in a proposed marriage do not themselves agree with their parents' opinions about the appropriateness of the match, they have full rights under Jewish religious law to insist on their point of view, and the parents have no right to force them.

There are situations in modern literature where a father forces his daughter to marry a stranger. Although she implores her father for relief, it is to no avail, and the marriage must proceed. But in Jewish society this could never happen.

A classic example is the Talmudic story of Rabbi Akiva. Akiva in his youth was an ignorant shepherd, working for one of the wealthiest inhabitants of Jerusalem, whose daughter, Rachel, he wanted to marry. Although Rachel's wealthy and influential father, being categorically against such a marriage, deprived his daughter of her inheritance, the girl did not need to beg him for mercy to allow her to marry Akiva – she simply left home and married him without further ado. Such behavior is explicitly sanctioned by Jewish religious law.

(The Talmud then goes on to relate how Rachel, after selling her luxurious hair to a wigmaker in order to have funds to live on, sends her husband away to study. In a few short years the simple "Akiva the shepherd" becomes *Rabbi Akiva*, arguably the greatest of all Talmudic sages. But that is a story for another time.)

### 29.15. Isaac in God's Field (24:62-63)

סב וְיִצְחָק בָּא מִבּוֹא בְּאֵר לַחַי רֹאִי וְהוּא יוֹשֵׁב בְּאֶרֶץ הַנֶּגֶב: סג וַיֵּצֵא יִצְחָק לָשׂוּחַ בַּשָּׂדֶה לִפְנוֹת עָרֶב וַיִּשָּׂא עֵינָיו וַיַּרְא וְהִנֵּה גְמַלִּים בָּאִים:

*[62] Isaac had just come back from the vicinity of Beer-lahai-roi, for he was settled in the region of the Negeb.*
*[63] And Isaac went out walking in the field toward evening and, looking up, he saw camels approaching.*

**[62] Isaac had just come back from the vicinity of Beer-lahai-roi.** This is the place to which Hagar fled after Abraham sent her and Ishmael away at Sarah's insistence (16:14). It is on the edge of the desert, and Isaac is now returning from there. The harshness of the desert corresponds to Isaac's soul.

**For he was settled in the region of the Negeb.** Isaac, although not yet married, lives apart from Abraham. Perhaps a certain estrangement occurred in their relationship after Sarah's death.

**[63] And Isaac went out walking in the field.** The field was for Isaac a place of work, both material and spiritual, and a meeting place with God ("And Isaac sowed in that land, and that year received a hundredfold: the Lord blessed him" (26:12)).

**Toward evening.** This is the time of *gevurah*.

Abraham, Isaac and Jacob each have a different approach to the place for communing with God. Abraham meets God on the mountain ("On the mount of the Lord there is vision" (22:14)). For Isaac, the meeting place, as we see here, is just a field. And Jacob defines the place of meeting with God as a "house" (Bethel, "The House of God," 28:17-19) .

Abraham is a mountain towering over the world. Jacob, through his dialogue with God, will build the House of Israel. But Isaac maintains a consistently low profile. Any kind of prominence is alien to him, and he downplays his own virtues. The symbol of his communion with God is therefore just a field. It should be noted as well that Isaac is the only one of the Patriarchs who pursued farming and agriculture. (Abraham and Jacob were engaged only in cattle breeding and shepherding.)

## 29.16. Rebekah Meets Isaac (24:64-67)

סד וַתִּשָּׂא רִבְקָה אֶת־עֵינֶיהָ וַתֵּרֶא אֶת־יִצְחָק וַתִּפֹּל
מֵעַל הַגָּמָל: סה וַתֹּאמֶר אֶל־הָעֶבֶד מִי־הָאִישׁ הַלָּזֶה
הַהֹלֵךְ בַּשָּׂדֶה לִקְרָאתֵנוּ וַיֹּאמֶר הָעֶבֶד הוּא אֲדֹנִי וַתִּקַּח
הַצָּעִיף וַתִּתְכָּס: סו וַיְסַפֵּר הָעֶבֶד לְיִצְחָק אֵת כָּל־
הַדְּבָרִים אֲשֶׁר עָשָׂה: סז וַיְבִאֶהָ יִצְחָק הָאֹהֱלָה שָׂרָה
אִמּוֹ וַיִּקַּח אֶת־רִבְקָה וַתְּהִי־לוֹ לְאִשָּׁה וַיֶּאֱהָבֶהָ וַיִּנָּחֵם
יִצְחָק אַחֲרֵי אִמּוֹ:

[64] *Raising her eyes, Rebekah saw Isaac. She
alighted from the camel*
[65] *and said to the servant, "Who is that man
walking in the field toward us?" And the servant
said, "That is my master." So she took her veil
and covered herself.*
[66] *The servant told Isaac all the things that
he had done.*
[67] *Isaac then brought her into the tent of his
mother Sarah, and he took Rebekah as his wife.
Isaac loved her, and thus found comfort after
his mother's death.*

**[64] Raising her eyes, Rebekah saw Isaac. She alighted from
the camel:** Rebekah's behavior can be understood as simple
modesty. But literally translated the text means, "She fell off
the camel." The sense is not simply that she dismounted, but
that she was stunned, or disappeared from view.

We have already mentioned that after the story of the
*Akeidah*, Isaac lacked a soul at the *nefesh* level, that is, a
soul at the level of an ordinary person (or animal). Isaac pos-
sessed only the highest level of soul, *neshamah*, because
Isaac had already attained the level of belonging to the
World to Come.

Although all this did not prevent Isaac from becoming a successful farmer, everyday communication with him was nonetheless quite difficult. Rebekah, upon seeing Isaac for the first time, was stunned that she was about to marry an angel, and she therefore "fell off the camel."

A significant problem in the relationship of Isaac and Rebekah was the absence of contact – that is, communication – between them, unlike, for example, Abraham's relationship with Sarah, or Jacob's with Rachel and Leah. There are many conversations in the Torah between Abraham and Sarah, and between Jacob and his wives, but there are almost no conversations between Isaac and Rebekah. As just one example, perhaps it was for this reason that Rebekah could not convey her thoughts to Isaac concerning which of their two sons Jacob and Esau should receive Isaac's final blessing. Rebekah was therefore forced to resort to deception, which only caused further conflict in the family.

### [67] Isaac then brought her into the tent of his mother Sarah ... and Isaac found comfort after his mother's death.

By very briefly alluding to Isaac's mental crisis after Sarah's death, this verse connects the present story with the beginning of the *Chayei Sarah* portion, where the Torah had nothing at all to say about that crisis. Isaac's parental home was Sarah's home, not Abraham's. Sarah (*gevurah*), was much closer to Isaac than Abraham (*chesed*) was. Thus, only by marrying Rebekah, "Isaac found comfort after his mother's death."

It is even possible that Abraham intentionally commissioned his servant Eliezer to conduct the search for a wife for Isaac, because he felt that that search would be better executed by his agent, rather than conducting that search himself.

Therefore, upon Eliezer's return with Isaac's bride after executing that mission, he goes not to Abraham, but directly to Isaac. Moreover, that fact is an indication that there has been a transition of command from one generation to the next. The Torah informs us that Abraham gave birth to Isaac at the age of one hundred (21:5), that Isaac married Rebekah at the age of forty (25:20), and that Abraham died at the age of one hundred seventy-five (25:7). Thus, after Isaac's marriage Abraham continued to live another thirty-five years – a long time, relatively speaking. But from the moment of Isaac's marriage, the leadership passes to him.

### 29.17. Isaac's "Lack of Initiative" as the Attribute of Gevurah

The fact that Abraham is *chesed* and Isaac is *gevurah* is also the reason that Abraham has been a leader all his life, while Isaac has been led. Abraham is proactive. He takes initiative to build the world around him. But Isaac is a reactive – he waits until he has observed in which direction a situation will develop, and only then he reacts to it.

*Chesed* seeks to spread out and it therefore actively advances – it is proactive, while *gevurah* wants to maintain the status quo, and only reacts to what already exists – it is reactive. Abraham all his life has taken the initiative to move to new places, but Isaac constantly retreats, moving only when compelled by external circumstances. He does not even marry on his own – his father and his father's servant choose his wife for him. Later he retreats from the Philistines; his wife imposes on him her view of which of their sons he is to bless; and so on.

This quality of Isaac – "submission to life's circumstances" – is the most important property of *gevurah*. *Gevurah* can only react to what has already happened (judgment, the attribute of the court, can only operate in this mode), whereas *chesed*, mercy, takes initiative to remake the world.

Chapter 30

# Abraham's Other Children

### 30.1. Keturah and Her Children (25:1-4)

א וַיֹּסֶף אַבְרָהָם וַיִּקַּח אִשָּׁה וּשְׁמָהּ קְטוּרָה: ב וַתֵּלֶד לוֹ
אֶת־זִמְרָן וְאֶת־יָקְשָׁן וְאֶת־מְדָן וְאֶת־מִדְיָן וְאֶת־יִשְׁבָּק
וְאֶת־שׁוּחַ: ג וְיָקְשָׁן יָלַד אֶת־שְׁבָא וְאֶת־דְּדָן וּבְנֵי דְדָן
הָיוּ אַשּׁוּרִם וּלְטוּשִׁם וּלְאֻמִּים: ד וּבְנֵי מִדְיָן עֵיפָה וָעֵפֶר
וַחֲנֹךְ וַאֲבִידָע וְאֶלְדָּעָה כָּל־אֵלֶּה בְּנֵי קְטוּרָה:

*[1] Abraham took another wife, whose name was Keturah.*
*[2] She bore him Zimran, Jokshan, Medan, Midian, Ishbak, and Shuah.*
*[3] Jokshan begot Sheba and Dedan. The descendants of Dedan were the Asshurim, the Letushim, and the Leummim.*
*[4] The descendants of Midian were Ephah, Epher, Enoch, Abida, and Eldaah. All these were descendants of Keturah.*

## [1] Abraham took another wife, whose name was Keturah.

After the story of Isaac's marriage, when it seems that Abraham's life is nearing its end, suddenly we read that Abraham is taking a new wife named Keturah, who will bear him many more children.

Jewish tradition states as a general principle that "there is no earlier or later in the Torah" –the order of events as presented in the Torah cannot be assumed to correspond to the chronological sequence of those events as they actually occurred. We therefore cannot discount the real possibility that Abraham's marriage to Keturah occurred before, not after, the events of Isaac's marriage. If such is the case, then the reason that the Torah mentions Abraham's marriage to Keturah only now is that, the story of Keturah logically relates to the conclusion of Abraham's life.

The Midrash believes that Keturah is Hagar, who, after being expelled from Abraham's house remained unmarried while she waited for Abraham to call her back. And eventually Abraham did exactly that. But why, after all the problems and unpleasantness Abraham had experienced with Hagar, did he marry her again? The answer is that a change of name indicates a change in one's essence. Since Hagar is now called Keturah, she is no longer Hagar, as she was before.

The Midrash derives the name "Keturah" from *ketoret*, "incense," which has a unique ability to soar, rise, and cleanse. After Hagar had experienced such ennobling advances in her character, Abraham could marry her again.

Of course, Hagar cannot catch up with Sarah even after this correction, nor do Abraham's children from Keturah inherit with Isaac. However, she is a worthy and especially close and important person for Abraham.

Hagar's return in the form of Keturah means that even after she had left Abraham, she nonetheless resolved not to abandon his heritage. Thus, she remained faithful to Abraham not only in the physical sense (which, we note in passing, was also essential in this case, since a woman who marries another man after divorce may no longer return to her previous husband), but, above all, by remaining loyal to Abraham's teachings. Hagar demonstrated that those teachings were meaningful and precious to her in a personal way, irrespective of marriage. And as Ishmael's roots are in Hagar, her return also made Ishmael's repentance possible, as we shall see below.

We note too that Midian, the son of Abraham and Keturah, will later appear in the book of Exodus (2:15 ff.), when Moses flees Egypt for Midian and marries Zipporah, daughter of Jethro, the priest of Midian. Jethro himself also plays a significant role in the development of the Jewish people (Exod. 18; Num. 10). This shows that some elements of spirituality in Abraham's other descendants were likewise important for the further development of the Jewish people.

### 30.2 Passing on the Heritage to Isaac (25: 5-6)

ה וַיִּתֵּן אַבְרָהָם אֶת־כָּל־אֲשֶׁר־לוֹ לְיִצְחָק: ו וְלִבְנֵי הַפִּילַגְשִׁים אֲשֶׁר לְאַבְרָהָם נָתַן אַבְרָהָם מַתָּנֹת וַיְשַׁלְּחֵם מֵעַל יִצְחָק בְּנוֹ בְּעוֹדֶנּוּ חַי קֵדְמָה אֶל־אֶרֶץ קֶדֶם:

*[5] Abraham willed all that he owned to Isaac;*
*[6] but to Abraham's sons by concubines*
*Abraham gave gifts while he was still living, and*
*he sent them away from his son Isaac eastward,*
*to the land of the East.*

**[5] Abraham willed all that he owned to Isaac.** This refers primarily to the rights to the Land of Israel, which was "all that he owned," because without it the realization of Abraham's mission would have been impossible.

**[6] But to Abraham's sons by concubines.** "Concubines" are mentioned here in the plural. According to the simple meaning of the text, Keturah and Hagar are actually two distinct persons (which of course does not negate the validity of the Midrash we cited above). In any case, this is not about Ishmael, who did not go to the East (see verse 9), but only about the children of Keturah enumerated in this passage.

**Abraham gave gifts.** According to the Midrash, these "gifts" were methods for communicating with spirits. For Jews, this is "unclean knowledge" (which is therefore prohibited to them), but no such ban applies to non-Jews.

**And he sent them away from his son Isaac eastward, to the land of the East.** Abraham understood that only Isaac was his true heir, and that all his other sons had to be sent away, receiving no share in his inheritance. Once again this is Sarah's spiritual strength at work. Jewish tradition has emphasized this point by naming this entire weekly portion *Chayei Sarah*.

### 30.3. The Fullness of the Realization of Abraham

The fact that Keturah bore more children to Abraham in his old age is significant, because it means that, in addition to the Jewish heritage that he created, Abraham also had a great deal of other spiritual content that he accumulated in his lifetime. Abraham bequeathed to Isaac the most essential things: the Covenant with God, and the Land of Israel. But Abraham had something else too: mystical knowledge – the ability to communicate with spirits (oriental meditative practices).

Such knowledge is of no use to Jews, and it may even interfere with their fulfillment of the Jewish mission to transfer monotheism to humanity. It is therefore in many respects prohibited. But other nations are not restricted this way, and for them the ability to communicate with "spirits" can be positive. Abraham does not want to see this spiritual knowledge lost. He wants to bequeath it to humanity, and he therefore transfers that knowledge to the sons of Keturah. (Perhaps it was for this very purpose that he decided to have children from Keturah.) Abraham then sends Keturah's sons to the East.

In other words, the totality of Abraham's self-realization is much broader than which he has accomplished through Isaac. God charged Abraham with the creation of the Jewish people, because without that rigid framework, Abraham's central purpose could not have been realized. But it was important that Abraham, as a person of great versatility, would realize not only his primary potential, but his secondary aspects as well. He is therefore the spiritual father of all mankind, and not only the Patriarch of the Jewish people. The children that Abraham bore from Keturah, as they spread eastward, remain Abraham's descendants, and carry with them important elements of his heritage.

It is possible that just this completeness of goal realization is what is referred to immediately below (verse 8) when the Torah says of Abraham that he died "old and contented." In other words, besides realizing the tasks that God had required of him, Abraham realized also what he himself wanted to accomplish.

## 30.4. Abraham's Death and Burial (25:7-11)

ז וְאֵלֶּה יְמֵי שְׁנֵי־חַיֵּי אַבְרָהָם אֲשֶׁר־חָי מְאַת שָׁנָה
וְשִׁבְעִים שָׁנָה וְחָמֵשׁ שָׁנִים: ח וַיִּגְוַע וַיָּמָת אַבְרָהָם
בְּשֵׂיבָה טוֹבָה זָקֵן וְשָׂבֵעַ וַיֵּאָסֶף אֶל־עַמָּיו: ט וַיִּקְבְּרוּ
אֹתוֹ יִצְחָק וְיִשְׁמָעֵאל בָּנָיו אֶל־מְעָרַת הַמַּכְפֵּלָה אֶל־
שְׂדֵה עֶפְרֹן בֶּן־צֹחַר הַחִתִּי אֲשֶׁר עַל־פְּנֵי מַמְרֵא: י
הַשָּׂדֶה אֲשֶׁר־קָנָה אַבְרָהָם מֵאֵת בְּנֵי־חֵת שָׁמָּה קֻבַּר
אַבְרָהָם וְשָׂרָה אִשְׁתּוֹ: יא וַיְהִי אַחֲרֵי מוֹת אַבְרָהָם
וַיְבָרֶךְ אֱלֹהִים אֶת־יִצְחָק בְּנוֹ וַיֵּשֶׁב יִצְחָק עִם־בְּאֵר לַחַי
רֹאִי:

*[7] This was the total span of Abraham's life: one hundred and seventy-five years.*
*[8] And Abraham breathed his last, dying at a good ripe age, old and contented; and he was gathered to his kin.*
*[9] His sons Isaac and Ishmael buried him in the cave of Machpelah, in the field of Ephron son of Zohar the Hittite, facing Mamre,*
*[10] the field that Abraham had bought from the Hittites; there Abraham was buried, and Sarah his wife.*
*[11] After the death of Abraham, God blessed his son Isaac . And Isaac settled near Beer-lahai-roi.*

**[8] Old and contented.** With a sense of having completely realized his mission.

**[9] His sons Isaac and Ishmael buried him.** The order of Abraham's sons' participation in his burial shows that Ishmael understood that he was subordinate to Isaac. Having acknowledged the correct family hierarchy, he can now take up his worthy position within it.

**Isaac settled near Beer-lahai-roi.** Since the Torah closely associates Beer-lahai-roi with Hagar and Ishmael (16:14), the Midrash believes that Isaac, having decided that Abraham should not be alone after Sarah's death, tried to return Hagar to him. Isaac had followed her to Beer-lahai-roi, and was therefore returning from there when he was met by Eliezer with Rebekah (24:63).

Isaac, being *gevurah*, justice, gives no thought to his mother's earlier conflicts with Hagar, nor to his own past conflicts with Ishmael. He believes that it would be proper for Abraham to marry, and he therefore leads Hagar back to his father. Perhaps it was this act that served to improve Isaac's relationship with Ishmael, and led to Ishmael's recognition of his primacy.

**[7] This was the total span of Abraham's life: one hundred and seventy-five years. [8] And Abraham breathed his last, dying at a good ripe age.** The Midrash emphasizes the influence that Abraham's death had even on his grandchildren, Isaac's sons Jacob and Esau. When Isaac was born, Abraham was one-hundred years old, and when Jacob and Esau were born, Isaac was sixty years old. Thus, by the time Abraham died, Jacob and Esau were already fifteen years old (175 – 100 – 60 = 15). In other words, Abraham lived long enough to influence even his grandsons Jacob and Esau, but only in their early youth.

When the Torah says that Abraham died "at a good ripe age, old and contented," the Midrash understands these words to mean that Esau became corrupted only at fifteen years of age, after the death of Abraham, who therefore did not witness it. Moreover, the Midrash believes that it was

Abraham's death itself that caused Esau to veer from the proper path, because Esau lost faith in the justice of a world in which such great saints die. Faith that is too naive, when confronted with every aspect of life, and is still unable to find answers to life's most complex questions, can lead a person to nonbelief. We must therefore never glorify or admire naive faith.

**[11] After the death of Abraham, God blessed his son Isaac.** The fullness of Abraham's life is realized only when Isaac continues his father's work of creating the Jewish people.

### 30.5. Ishmael's Descendants (25:12-18)

יב וְאֵלֶּה תֹּלְדֹת יִשְׁמָעֵאל בֶּן־אַבְרָהָם אֲשֶׁר יָלְדָה הָגָר הַמִּצְרִית שִׁפְחַת שָׂרָה לְאַבְרָהָם: יג וְאֵלֶּה שְׁמוֹת בְּנֵי יִשְׁמָעֵאל בִּשְׁמֹתָם לְתוֹלְדֹתָם בְּכֹר יִשְׁמָעֵאל נְבָיֹת וְקֵדָר וְאַדְבְּאֵל וּמִבְשָׂם: יד וּמִשְׁמָע וְדוּמָה וּמַשָּׂא: טו חֲדַד וְתֵימָא יְטוּר נָפִישׁ וָקֵדְמָה: טז אֵלֶּה הֵם בְּנֵי יִשְׁמָעֵאל וְאֵלֶּה שְׁמֹתָם בְּחַצְרֵיהֶם וּבְטִירֹתָם שְׁנֵים־ עָשָׂר נְשִׂיאִם לְאֻמֹּתָם: יז וְאֵלֶּה שְׁנֵי חַיֵּי יִשְׁמָעֵאל מְאַת שָׁנָה וּשְׁלֹשִׁים שָׁנָה וְשֶׁבַע שָׁנִים וַיִּגְוַע וַיָּמָת וַיֵּאָסֶף אֶל־עַמָּיו: יח וַיִּשְׁכְּנוּ מֵחֲוִילָה עַד־שׁוּר אֲשֶׁר עַל־פְּנֵי מִצְרַיִם בֹּאֲכָה אַשּׁוּרָה עַל־פְּנֵי כָל־אֶחָיו נָפָל:

*[12] This is the line of Ishmael, Abraham's son, whom Hagar the Egyptian, Sarah's slave, bore to Abraham.*
*[13] These are the names of the sons of Ishmael, by their names, in the order of their birth: Nebaioth, the first-born of Ishmael, Kedar, Adbeel, Mibsam,*

*[14] Mishma, Dumah, Massa,*
*[15] Hadad, Tema, Jetur, Naphish, and Kedmah.*
*[16] These are the sons of Ishmael and these are their*
*names by their villages and by their encampments:*
*twelve chieftains of as many tribes.–*
*[17] These were the years of the life of Ishmael:*
*one hundred and thirty-seven years; then he*
*breathed his last Abraham's son, whom Hagar*
*the Egyptian, Sarah's slave, bore to Abraham.*
*and died, and was gathered to his kin.–*
*[18] They dwelt from Havilah, by Shur, which*
*is close to Egypt, all the way to Asshur; they*
*camped alongside all their kinsmen.*

**[12] This is the line of Ishmael.** Before going on to the detailed account of Isaac's family, the Torah briefly enumerates the lineage of Ishmael's descendants. The Torah often adopts this scheme – before moving on to the main line, the side line is briefly discussed; first a brief coverage of Ishmael, followed by much detail about Isaac, or first briefly about the descendants of Esau, and then in detail about Jacob.

**Abraham's son, whom Hagar the Egyptian, Sarah's slave, bore to Abraham.** Once again, the hierarchy of relationships is emphasized. In the end, Ishmael too is Abraham's son, and he carries his father's potential.

**[16] These are the sons of Ishmael and these are their names by their villages and by their encampments. twelve chieftains of as many tribes.** That is, they are not just a nomadic tribe, but an organized system, carriers of a particular culture.

**[17] These were the years of the life of Ishmael.** one hundred and thirty-seven years; then he breathed his last ... **and was gathered to his kin:** The Midrash notes that the words describing Ishmael's death are very similar to the Torah's description a little earlier of Abraham's death. The Midrash understands from this that Ishmael died a righteous man.

**[18] They dwelt from Havilah, by Shur, which is close to Egypt, all the way to Asshur; they camped alongside all their kinsmen.** The Divine promise that the descendants of Ishmael would become a very numerous people came true. Because of Abraham's care and concern for Hagar's son, the blessing of innumerable descendants went to Ishmael rather than to Isaac.